Waterford Institute of Tech

FrontPage® 98
Web Pages

DAVE RASMUSSEN
RICHARD CRAVENS

PRIMA PUBLISHING

Publisher: Matthew H. Carleson
Managing Editor: Dan J. Foster
Acquisitions Editor: Jenny Watson
Project Editor: Kevin W. Ferns
Technical Reviewer: Ben Thompson
Copy Editor: Barton Reed
Interior Layout: Marian Hartsough
Cover Design: Prima Design Team
Indexer: Katherine Stimson

ISBN: 0-7615-1348-5
Library of Congress Catalog Card Number: 97-76505
Printed in the United States of America

98 99 AA 10 9 8 7 6 5 4 3 2

Special thanks to my wife, friends, and family, who endured my roller coaster of emotions throughout this project. It's finally done.

Now, about that list of things I was supposed to do when the book was finished . . .

—Dave Rasmussen

To Daver, who paid the ultimate price in Korea.

—Richard Cravens

CONTENTS AT A GLANCE

CONTENTS

SATURDAY EVENING
Live and Hyperlinked 129

ACKNOWLEDGMENTS

Writing a book like this was both fun and frustrating. Early betas, bugs, and elastic software deadlines are enough to take years off any author or editor's life. And yet somehow it came to be, due in no small part to the staff of great people at Prima Publishing.

I'd like to personally thank Kevin Ferns, Ben Thompson, Bart Reed, Jenny Watson, Dan Foster, and their staff of professionals, most of whom I've never had the pleasure of meeting.

—Dave Rasmussen

Thanks to Jenny Watson, Dan Foster, Kevin Ferns, Deb Abshier, and Matt Carleson. A great big warm fuzzy thanks to Nancy Almond, Jesse Fisk Cravens, Richard Mansur, and Norma Fisk.

—Richard Cravens

ABOUT THE AUTHORS

DAVE RASMUSSEN has been active in many areas of the communications software industry since 1990, and he has experience in technical support, program design, product management, and business development. He has written extensively on serial communications and pyrotechnics, and has been a technical editor on a variety of Windows applications for major trade publishers. He and his wife, Cherie, live in Columbia, Missouri, where they enjoy family life and the fireworks, fishing, cycling, mushroom hunting, and wood cutting that goes along with it.

RICHARD CRAVENS currently operates his Web development and marketing firm, Osage Digital Communications, Inc. (**www.osagedigital.com**), from Columbia, Missouri. Cravens has worked in multimedia and advertising production since 1979. Since entering the software industry in 1991, he has helped design, develop, and market general communications software and Web client/server applications such as PROCOMM PLUS for Windows and Spyglass Enhanced Mosaic. He is the author of Prima Publishing's *The Essential Windows NT 4 Book* and *ACT! 3.0 Fast & Easy*.

INTRODUCTION

Welcome to the exciting new world of Microsoft FrontPage 98. You don't need for me to hype the Internet here, since it's definitely over-hyped as it is, and you didn't pick up this book if you were unaware of the role an Internet Web site can play in letting you interact with the world.

Who Should Read This Book?

Will you really be able to create a Web site in a weekend? Yes, you will, but it helps if you are prepared. A bottle of your favorite extra-strength headache reliever shouldn't be necessary, but a supply of chocolate chip cookies and a comfortable, quiet place to create might help. The most important preparation, however, is for you to think about the message you want your Web site to project, and what you want to learn from those who visit your site.

This book walks you through the process of creating a professional, attractive, and useful Web site in one weekend. You will find that Front-Page lets you incorporate just about any feature you wish to include in your Web site—colored backgrounds, sounds, video, images, and attractive fonts. Most of these features appear in Figure I.1.

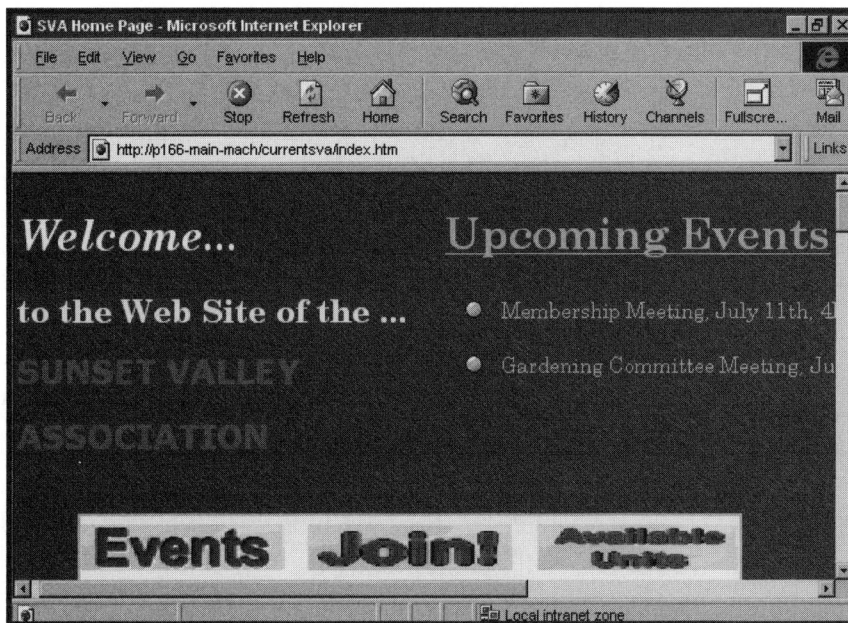

Figure I.1

A FrontPage Web site with frames, colors, and fonts.

In order to create a site for the Internet that can be viewed by folks surfing the Web, the site must be created in Hypertext Markup Language, or HTML. Until recently, if you wanted to create your own Web site, you were required to become an expert at using HTML. To create anything but a primitive, one-page site, you also needed to be a guru of Web site interaction and a student of cryptic, coded programming modules called Common Gateway Interface (CGI) scripts (pocket protectors were optional).

FrontPage allows people without those particular skills to create polished, attractive, smoothly meshed Web sites. Even if you have done some HTML coding or have picked up a few pre-fab CGI scripts off the Net, FrontPage gives you a great deal of freedom to create sophisticated Web sites. In fact, the really useful and fun sites are much more than HTML Web pages. What may appear to a visitor as a single Web page may be a collection of objects that lets the visitor see pictures, find out when the site was last updated, and search through the site for just what he or she is looking for. With the inclusion of input forms, visitors can interact with a Web site, leave information, and even contribute to it.

What Does This Book Cover?

In this book, as in real life, the weekend begins on Friday evening. This weekend is broken up into seven sessions; each session should take you three or four hours at most to complete. Unless you are very familiar with Web design and HTML, the sessions should be followed in order. But don't be afraid to skip around if there is a topic you're particularly interested in learning.

Here's a whirlwind tour of what you'll accomplish this weekend:

Friday Evening: Creating a Web Site in One Night In this session, you'll learn the basics of creating a Web page in FrontPage, including how to start a new site, edit a page, and insert graphics. You'll learn about Front-Page Explorer, FrontPage Editor, and the HTML that lurks under your Web site's covers.

Saturday Morning: Making Your Site Look Good. After a good night's rest, you'll learn about the components used in a Web page, such as heading styles, character attributes, and special styles. You'll understand how to use bullets, line numbering, and indentations. Finally, you'll learn about tables and their uses.

Saturday Afternoon: Designing Graphics with Image Composer. After a satisfying lunch, you'll dive into the basics of Image Composer and learn how easy it is to warp, rotate, and size text and graphics to add special visual effects. You'll be introduced to GIF and JPEG graphics and learn how to create and modify them. Finally, you'll learn how to import your graphics into FrontPage and your Web site.

Saturday Night: Live and Hyperlinked. As darkness falls, you'll learn about the mechanics of a Web page, including bookmarks and hyperlinks. You'll also create both textual and graphical hyperlinks. Before you go to bed, you'll learn how to follow and understand your hyperlinks in the FrontPage Explorer.

Sunday Morning: Letting Visitors Plug In With Forms. This session introduces you to forms and their properties, including checkboxes, radio buttons, text edit boxes, and drop-down menus. You'll experiment using FrontPage to process your form information. Before the mid-morning break, you'll learn how to create a public bulletin board using forms.

Sunday Afternoon: Activating FrontPage's Handy Components. This session teaches you about FrontPage's cool built-in controls, called FrontPage Components. Among the controls you'll master are Comment Text, the To Do List, Headers and Footers, Scheduling Images, and Page Insertions. Finally, you'll use Page Substitution and Timestamping, and you'll create a dynamic Table of Contents.

Sunday Evening: Publishing Your Site on the World Wide Web. The final session teaches you the ins and outs of how to get your awesome site on the Web. Topics include shopping for an Internet service provider and Web site provider, domain names, and publishing your site. Final topics explain maintaining your Web site and attracting visitors to it.

Appendix A, Installing FrontPage, lists everything you need to know to get FrontPage up and running on your computer, if you haven't already done so. I recommend that you have everything installed before Friday evening to make the most of your time. You should also have access to Microsoft Internet Explorer 4.0 or Netscape Navigator 4.0. The appendix also offers important Web browser information if you are a first-time user or you wish to upgrade your current browser.

Special Elements to Look For

As you read through this book, you'll notice some special features that will help you get the most from each session:

NOTE Notes provide additional information or enhance a discussion in the text by emphasizing a particular point.

TIP Tips offer helpful hints, suggestions, or alternate methods for a procedure.

CAUTION Cautions warn you about mistakes and pitfalls that inexperienced users often fall into.

FIND IT ON ▶
THE WEB This graphic appears next to paragraphs that contain a Web address that may be helpful to the discussion.

Are You Ready?

So you think you're ready to build a Web site? As long as you stay within the parameters set in this book, your path to online bliss should be a relatively quick and painless one. But you need to make sure you do your part as well, so stock the fridge with your drink of choice, let your spouse deal with the rugrats, and prepare to have a little fun this weekend.

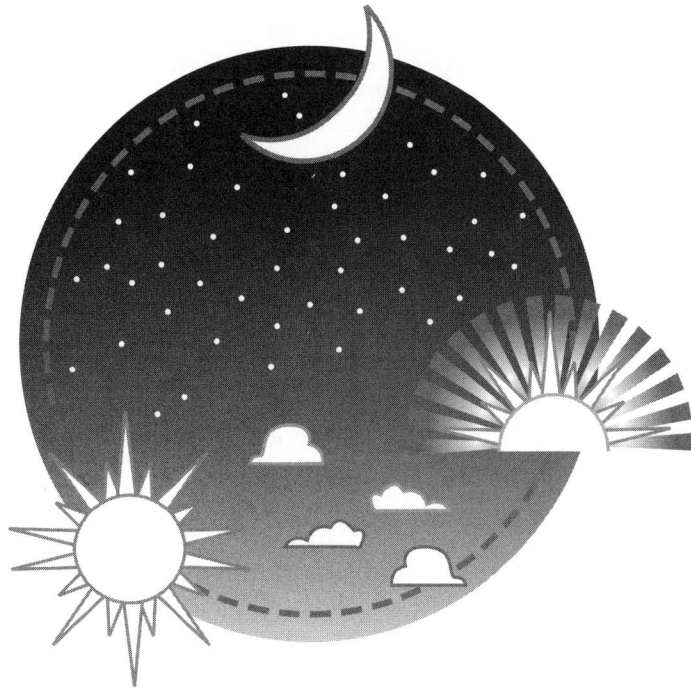

FRIDAY EVENING

Creating a Web Site in One Night

- ✪ Starting a New Site with FrontPage Explorer
- ✪ Editing a Page with FrontPage Editor
- ✪ Inserting a Graphic in a Web Page
- ✪ Previewing Your Work in a Browser
- ✪ Testing Your Site with the Personal Server

C reate a Web site in one night? Sounds daunting, doesn't it? Well, you've already installed FrontPage 98 and played around with it just enough to get excited. You've got some ideas for a Web site, but you want to find out how to implement them correctly. If you're like most folks diving into this process, the whole thing is a little mind-boggling. The Editor? The Explorer? When do you get to create a Web site? How about right now? You'll start off by creating and testing a real-life Web site. Tonight.

Getting the TCP/IP Test out of the Way

For the most part, the TCP/IP test, the Personal Web Server, and the Server Administrator function in the background while you create your Web site with FrontPage Explorer and FrontPage Editor. TCP/IP stands for Transmission Control Protocol/Internet Protocol. Internet Protocol is the set of rules that programmers follow so that your computer can exchange data with others. Transmission Control Protocol is an additional layer of rules that programmers use to specifically ensure that data gets transported correctly. TCP/IP enables all kinds of computers to speak to each other over the Web—Macintoshes, Windows 95 systems, and so on.

One of the handy things about FrontPage is that it checks and, if necessary, installs TCP/IP connectivity. Passing the test doesn't mean that your system is directly connected to the Internet, but that your computer should be able to connect to the Internet. If you're working on a stand-alone system or on a network and are planning to copy your Web site to a server, the TCP/IP protocol on your system simulates connecting with the Internet and lets you work as if you were on the Web. To run the TCP/IP test, follow these steps:

1. Select Start, Run, from the Windows 95 Taskbar.

2. Click on browse to navigate to the FrontPage folder. Open the dialog box and double-click on the tcptest.exe icon (see Figure 1.1). Click on OK in the Run dialog box.

3. In the FrontPage TCP/IP Test dialog box, click on the Start Test button, as shown in Figure 1.2.

4. When the test acknowledges that your machine is compatible with the TCP/IP protocol, the results look something like what is shown in Figure 1.3.

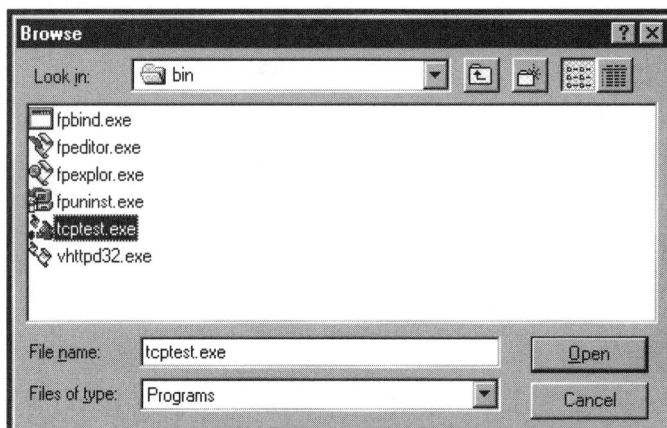

Figure 1.1

Locating the TCP/IP test.

Figure 1.2

Starting the TCP/IP test.

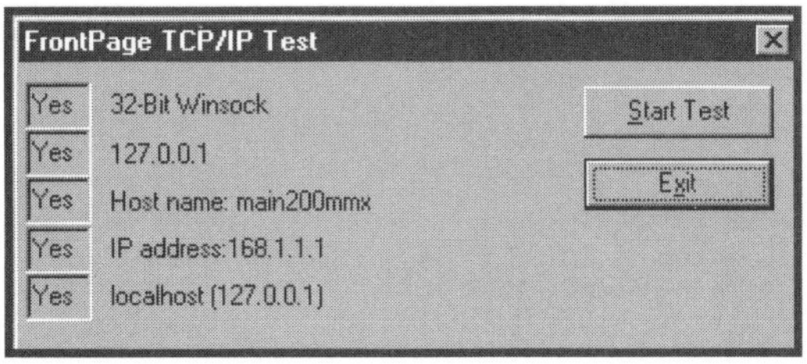

Figure 1.3

TCP/IP results: You passed!

If your system is not TCP/IP enabled, don't panic. If your computer does not yet have TCP/IP capability, here's the routine:

1. You'll be prompted to install TCP/IP using the Network tool in the Control Panel. You need to install new files from your Windows 95 CD-ROM during this process, so have it handy. The Network dialog box is shown in Figure 1.4.

2. In the Network dialog box, click on the Configuration tab. When Windows presents you with the Network dialog box, you should select TCP/IP from the Configuration tab and then click on OK to install TCP/IP on your system.

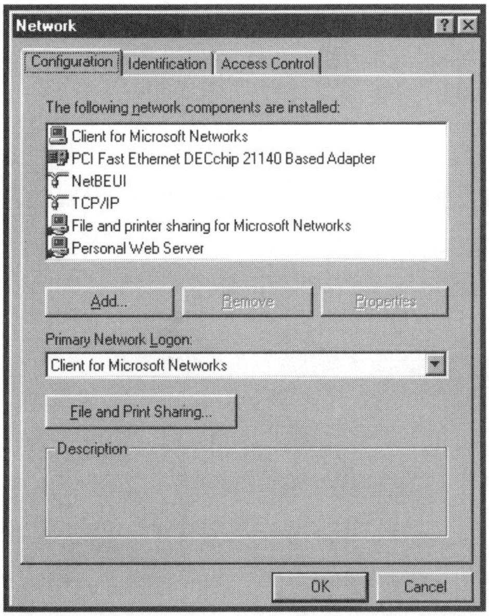

Figure 1.4

Installing TCP/IP.

3. Select the Add… button.

4. Select Protocol in the Select Network Component and click on the Add button.

5. On the left side of the Select Network Protocol dialog box, select Microsoft as the Manufacturer and TCP/IP as the Network Protocol.

6. Click on OK to exit the Select Network Protocol dialog box.

7. Select OK to exit the Network dialog box.

After rebooting, you can have fun creating your Web site.

Starting a New Site with FrontPage Explorer

FrontPage Explorer is what makes FrontPage the powerful program it is. By the time this weekend is over, you'll have generated Web sites with dozens of files that are linked together like a spider's web. Click on a picture and zoom, you're off to a section of text. Click on another hotspot and you're off to another Web site. FrontPage Explorer keeps all these connections straight. When the time comes to upload your Web site to a site provider, FrontPage Explorer makes sure all your files get to their final locations safely. To use FrontPage Explorer to create a new Web site, follow these steps:

1. Click on the Start menu from the Windows 95 Taskbar and select Programs, and then click on the Microsoft FrontPage icon.

2. Click on the Create a New FrontPage Web button in the Getting Started dialog box and then click on OK, as shown in Figure 1.5.

TIP

You now must select what type of web you would like to build. Here you must fight temptation by avoiding Microsoft's built-in templates. You will have plenty of time to use these templates later. I firmly believe you must crawl before you learn to walk. By learning the fundamentals of FrontPage and starting at the beginning, you'll be able to conquer the Web more quickly.

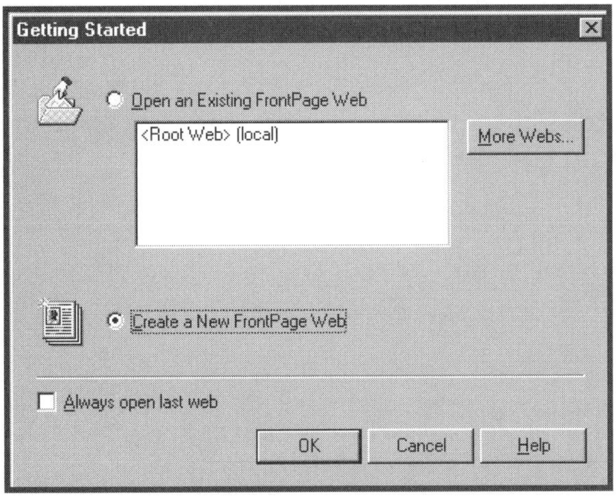

Figure 1.5

Starting a new
FrontPage web.

3. In the New FrontPage Web dialog box, select the Empty Web list item and enter a name for your Web site, as shown in Figure 1.6. Even though a filename can be 256 characters long under Windows 95, you may be working with programs that transfer these files to other systems. It's best, therefore, to limit all filenames to eight

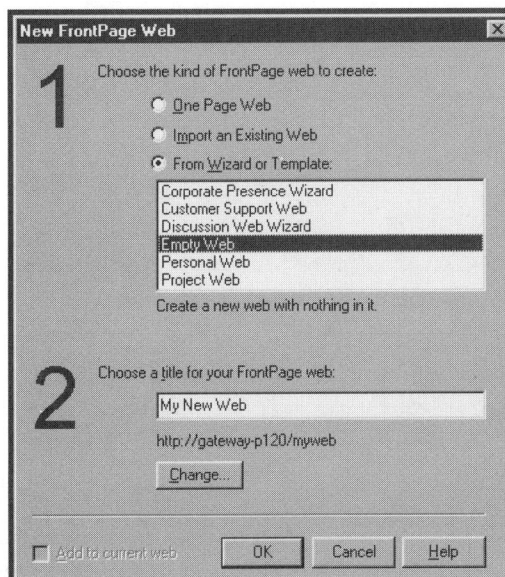

Figure 1.6

Name your new
FrontPage site.

characters and follow the old-fashioned DOS file naming rules—
no spaces, periods, or commas.

4. Enter your name and password and then click on OK in the Name
and Password Required dialog box, as shown in Figure 1.7.

After entering your name and password, you'll see the Navigation view of
the Web site you just created, as shown in Figure 1.8. Because you haven't
added any pages yet, the view is quite bare.

Figure 1.7

Enter your name
and select a
password.

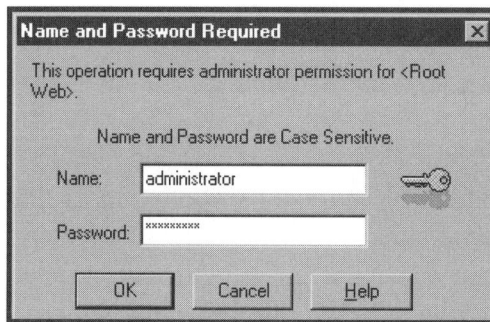

Figure 1.8

The Navigation
view of your new
FrontPage web.

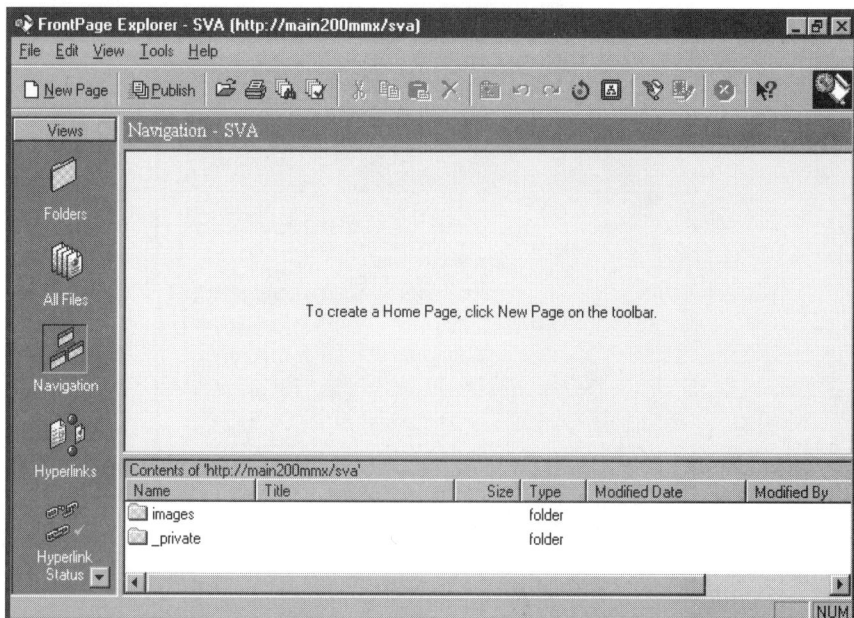

To create a Home Page, click New Page on the toolbar.

Understanding FrontPage Views

FrontPage offers a variety of ways to look at your Web site. Notice the Views column on the left side of the screen. You'll see a view of your site by Folders, All Files, Navigation, Hyperlinks, Hyperlink Status, Themes, and Tasks.

Take a quick look at the different views by clicking on each of the buttons in the Views column. You'll notice that the Folders view gives you a Windows Explorer-like display of the folder structure of your site, whereas the All Files view shows a list of every file in your site. To use FrontPage Explorer to examine your Web site, follow these steps:

1. Switch to the Folder view by clicking on it, as shown in Figure 1.9. Your embryonic Web site already has two folders. FrontPage creates these folders for you and stores necessary files as you construct your Web site. You're not required to keep track of these files because FrontPage Explorer does it for you.

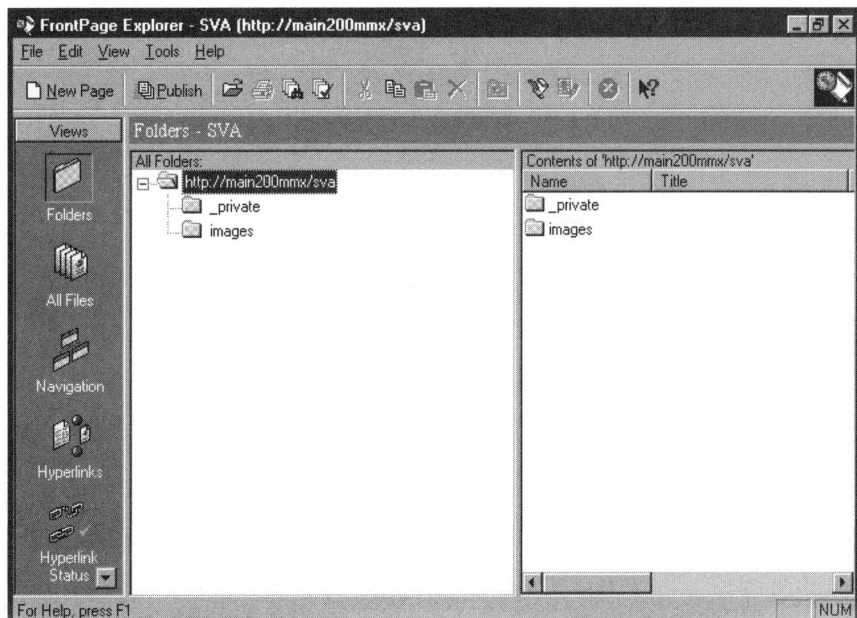

Figure 1.9

Your Web site in Folders view.

2. You can drag the split bar between the left and middle sides of the FrontPage Explorer window to the left or the right. You can also drag the split bar between the middle and right columns of the FrontPage Explorer window in exactly the same manner. Experiment with making minor changes in the sizing of the Folders view, as shown in Figure 1.10. Changing the size of the FrontPage Explorer windows comes in handy when you want to see all the columns in the Folders view, or when you want to see many Web hyperlinks. You don't have many hyperlinks yet, but as your site grows like a spider's web, you will.

TIP

You can adjust the Folders view by clicking on and dragging the split bars between columns. For example, in Figure 1.11, you're able to see the Modified column by narrowing the Title column.

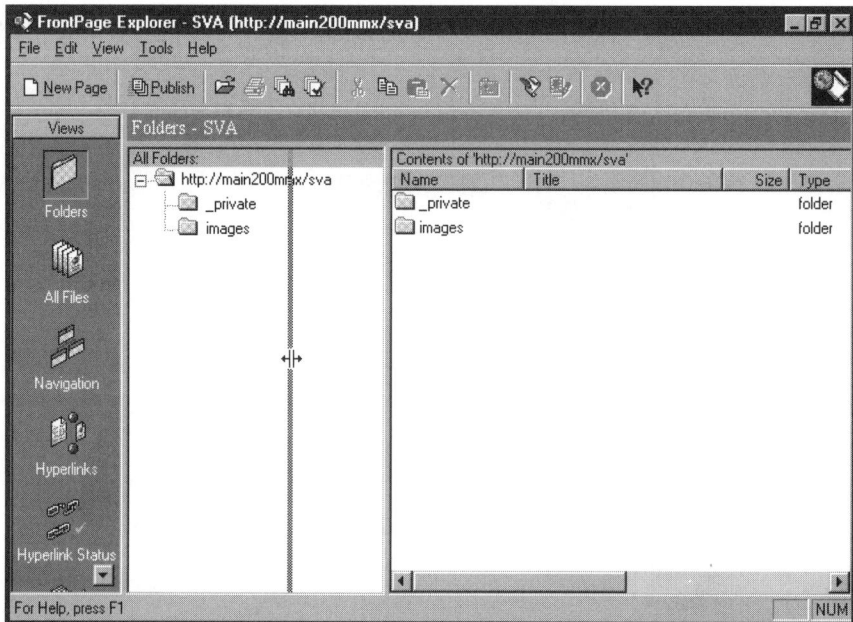

Figure 1.10

Getting more information on your files.

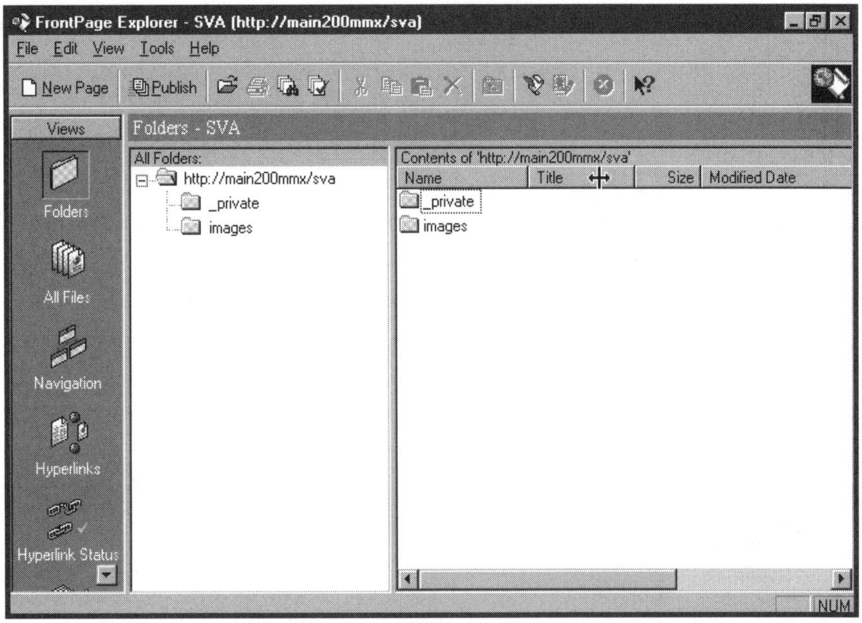

Figure 1.11

Making some space
for folder names.

3. Click on the Hyperlinks button in the FrontPage Explorer Views column, as shown in Figure 1.12. This view shows the links between pages in your Web site, but so far, you don't have any. When you do, you'll note the change they make in the Hyperlinks view.

So far, FrontPage Explorer hasn't been all that exciting. Fortunately, it's not supposed to be. It's there, in the background, like the basketball player who sets the pick or the offensive lineman who protects the quarterback. You get the picture. It's the unsung hero of FrontPage.

What exactly does it do? FrontPage Explorer makes sure that all the components of your Web site are organized and in place. Your Web site's components should function in harmony so that your visitors are greeted by a well-ordered Web site.

What does FrontPage Explorer ask of you in return? It requires you to open the Web site first in FrontPage Explorer when you work on a Web

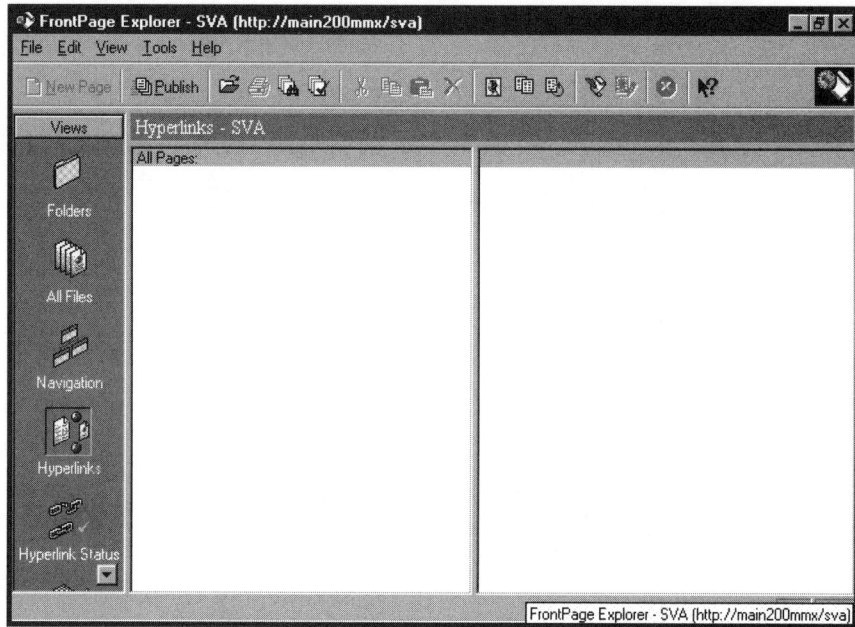

Figure 1.12

The Hyperlinks view.

page. Therefore, you can forget about FrontPage Explorer when you start creating your first Web page.

To create your first Web page, you should change back to the Navigation view of FrontPage by clicking on the Navigation button in the Views column. Remember, keeping FrontPage Explorer open at all times ensures the integrity of your Web site. To create your home page from FrontPage Explorer, follow these steps:

1. Switch back to Navigation view, if you haven't done so already.

2. As the Navigation window suggests, you can create a new page by clicking on the New Page icon to the far left of the icon bar. Doing so will create the page. Double-click on the Home Page icon, as shown in Figure 1.13. This launches the FrontPage Editor, where your home page will come to life.

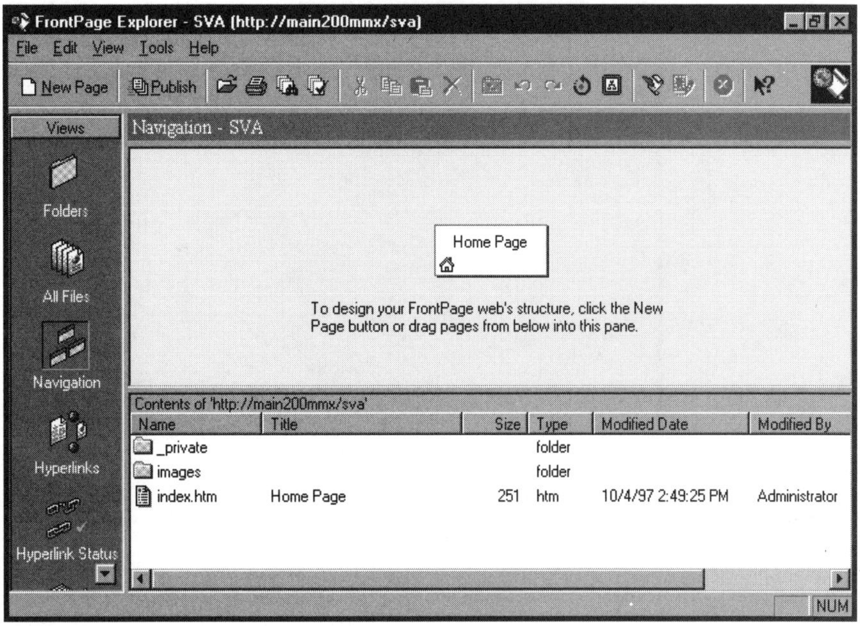

Figure 1.13

FrontPage has created your home page!

Editing a Page with FrontPage Editor

Your word processing skills will come in handy now. Most common word processing conventions apply; for example, the up and down arrows move your cursor around the text you create. Ctrl+Home moves you to the top of the page, and Ctrl+End moves you to the bottom. The Home key moves you to the left edge of the text, and the End key moves you to the end of the line of text.

Because Web browsers operate in all kinds of environments, only standardized text formats can be reliably viewed by everyone who visits your site. Rather than selecting from a wide variety of fonts and text sizes and styles, you are constricted to defined HTML styles. To enter heading text, for example, follow these steps:

1. Type a heading. Figure 1.14 shows my heading, "Welcome to the SVA Web Site."

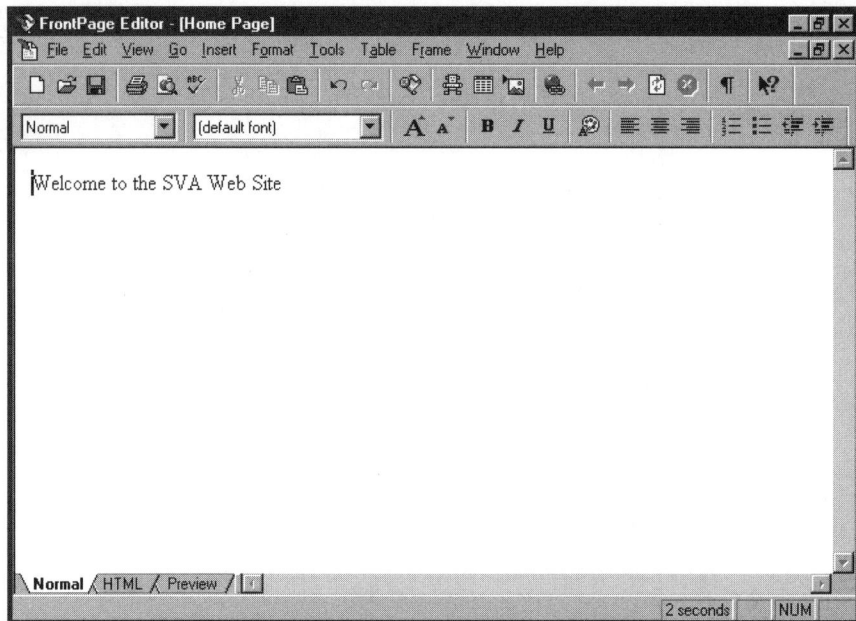

Figure 1.14

Creating a heading
on a Web page.

2. Click anywhere in the text you've typed with the FrontPage Editor insertion bar. Pull down the Change Style list (the one that currently reads "Normal") from the Format toolbar in FrontPage Editor and select Heading 1 (see Figure 1.15).

To change styles, follow these steps:

1. Click in the paragraph to which you are assigning a new style.
2. Scroll down the list of formats in the Change Style list and select a different format style for the selected paragraph, as shown in Figure 1.16.

To edit text, follow these steps:

1. Place the insertion point where you want to delete the text.
2. To delete the character after the insertion point, press the Delete key. To delete the character before the insertion point, press the left

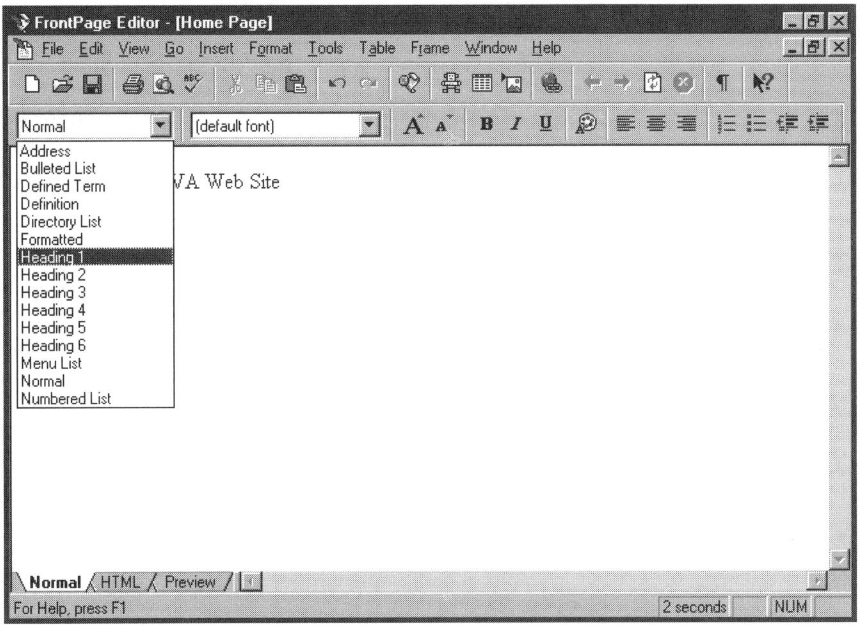

Figure 1.15

Assigning a
Heading 1 style.

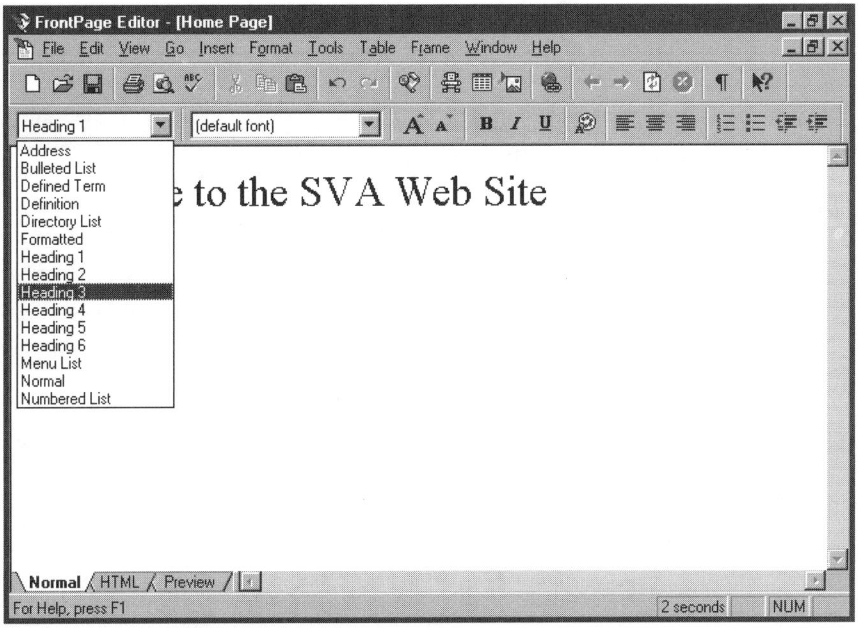

Figure 1.16

Changing styles.

arrow key. You can also select the text you want to delete, and then press the Delete key; the block of text is deleted.

3. To insert new text, make certain that the cursor is where you want the new text to begin and type the text you want to insert, as shown in Figure 1.17.

TIP If you want to insert new text before or after text you've already typed, try using the Home, End, Ctrl+Home and Ctrl+End key combinations to move to the beginning or end of the text quickly.

To cut text, follow these steps:

1. Left-click and drag the mouse over the text you wish to cut.

2. Right click on the highlighted area. Select Cut from the pop-up

Figure 1.17

Getting your message on your Web page.

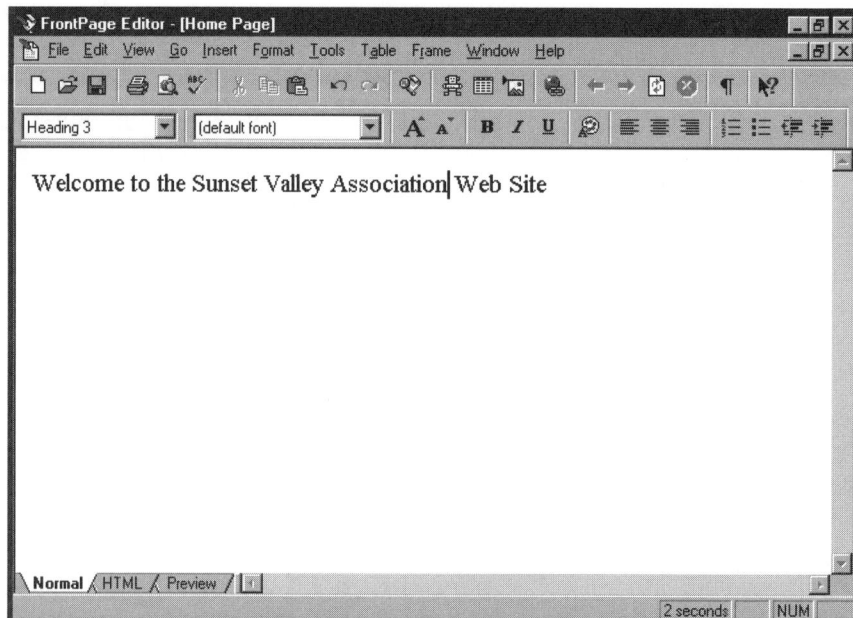

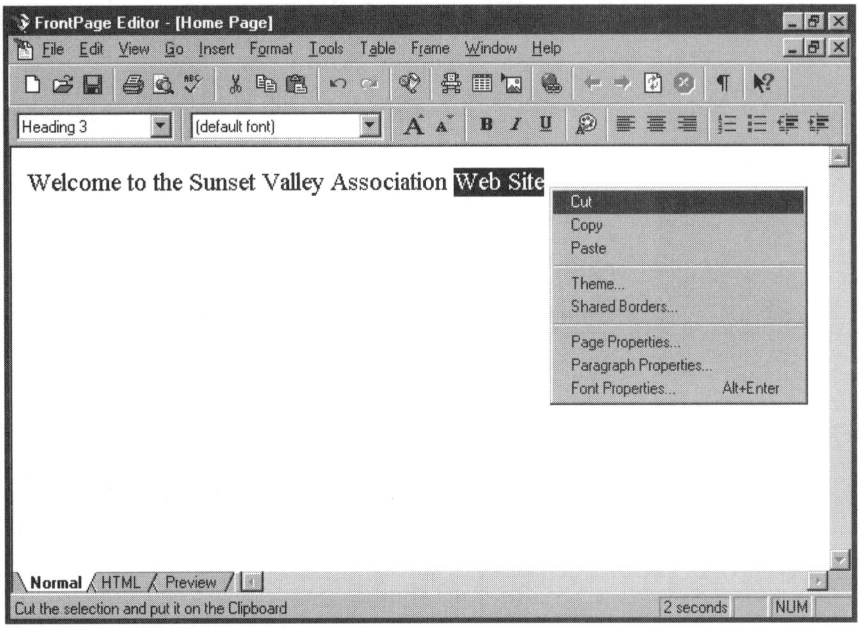

FrontPage Editor - [Home Page]

File Edit View Go Insert Format Tools Table Frame Window Help

Heading 3   (default font)

Welcome to the Sunset Valley Association Web Site

| Cut |
| Copy |
| Paste |
| Theme... |
| Shared Borders... |
| Page Properties... |
| Paragraph Properties... |
| Font Properties...   Alt+Enter |

Normal / HTML / Preview /

Cut the selection and put it on the Clipboard   2 seconds   NUM

Figure 1.18

Slicing and dicing text.

menu, as shown in Figure 1.18. The text is deleted from the page and placed onto the Windows Clipboard. If you want to insert the text elsewhere, continue to step 3.

3. Place your insertion point where you want to paste text. (You can also insert an image this way.)

4. Right-click and then select Paste from the shortcut menu.

5. Take some time to practice cutting and pasting (or copying) text. An example of where copying (and a little editing) helps create a page quickly is shown in Figure 1.19. Here, the text "4 PM Meeting Room" was copied after it was typed on the first line and then pasted on each subsequent line (instead of retyping). Copying works exactly like cutting, except that it does not delete the text you highlight.

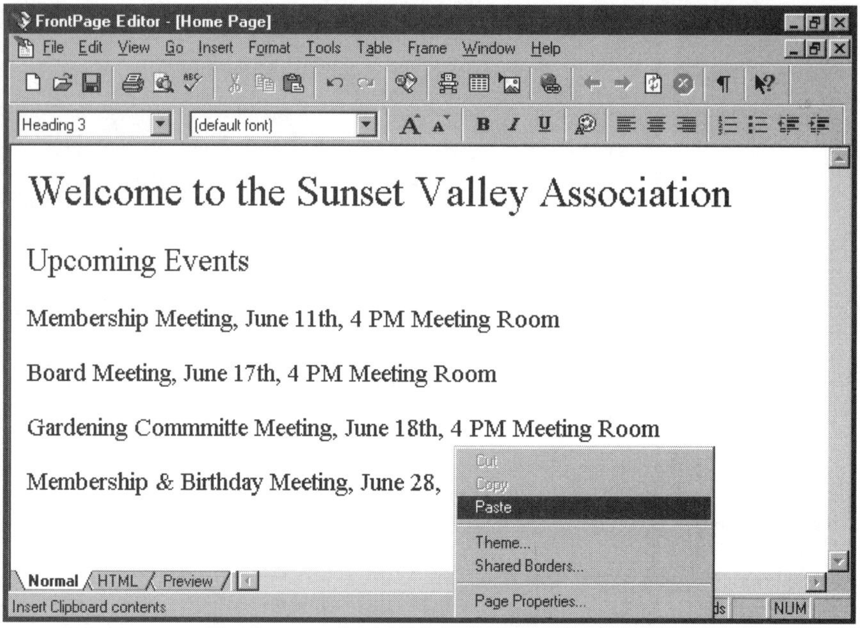

Figure 1.19

Why type when
you can copy
and paste?

Inserting a Graphic in a Web Page

You can insert images in FrontPage Editor by copying them through the Windows 95 Clipboard, just as you would copy an image into any Microsoft Office application. You can also insert images from a Web site or from a file. To insert a graphic from the Web site, follow these steps:

1. Place your cursor where you want the image to appear on your page and then select Insert, Image.

2. Click on the Clip Art tab in the Image dialog box.

3. Choose the Shapes Category and select a graphic. I selected the multi-colored circle of arrows, as shown in Figure 1.20.

TIP   You'll learn to create your own images in the Saturday Afternoon session. For now, you'll borrow from FrontPage's clip art collection.

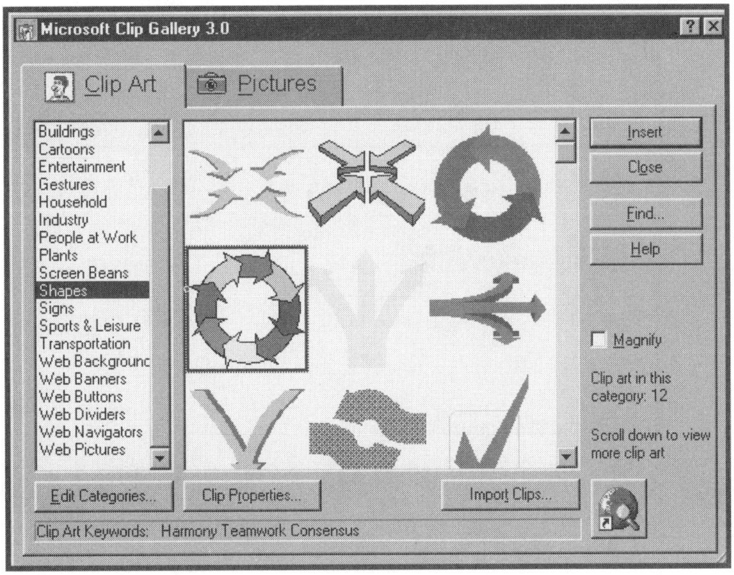

Figure 1.20

They're called icons, but they are actually cute little pictures.

4. Double-click on a clip art selection that fits your page. The selected image is placed on your Web page, as shown in Figure 1.21.

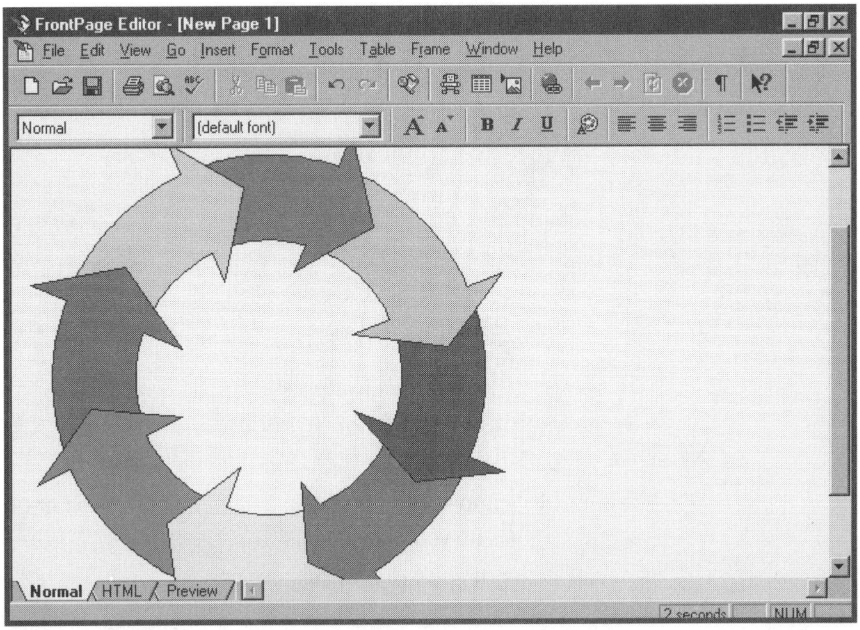

Figure 1.21

A graphic image on your page.

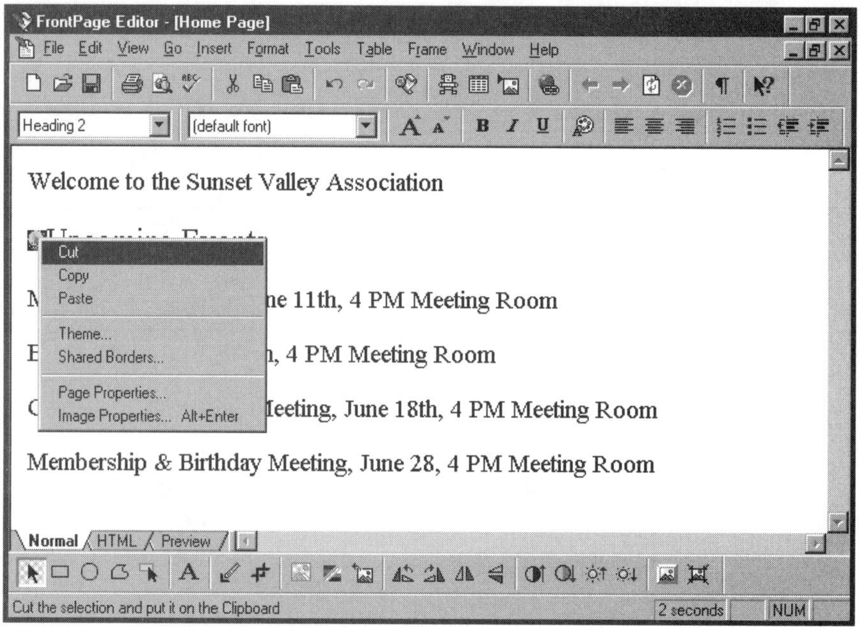

Figure 1.22

Cut and Paste
works for
images, too!

To cut and paste text or graphic images, follow these steps:

1. Right-click on the text or graphic.
2. Select Cut or Copy from the pop-up menu, as shown in Figure 1.22.
3. Place your insertion point at the place on the page where you want to copy the image or text.
4. Right-click and select Paste from the shortcut menu.

Take some time to practice cutting, copying, and pasting text and graphic images.

TIP

If you're comfortable with the click-and-drag method of cutting and pasting from other Microsoft Office applications, feel free to click and drag text or graphics in FrontPage as well. Holding down the Ctrl key when you click and drag selected text or images copies the selected object, as shown in Figure 1.23.

FrontPage Editor - [Home Page]

File Edit View Go Insert Format Tools Table Frame Window Help

Heading 3   (default font)

Welcome to the Sunset Valley Association

Upcoming Events

● Membership Meeting, June 11th, 4 PM Meeting Room

● Board Meeting, June 17th, 4 PM Meeting Room

Gardening Commmitte Meeting, June 18th, 4 PM Meeting Room

Membership & Birthday Meeting, June 28, 4 PM Meeting Room

Normal / HTML / Preview /

2 seconds   NUM

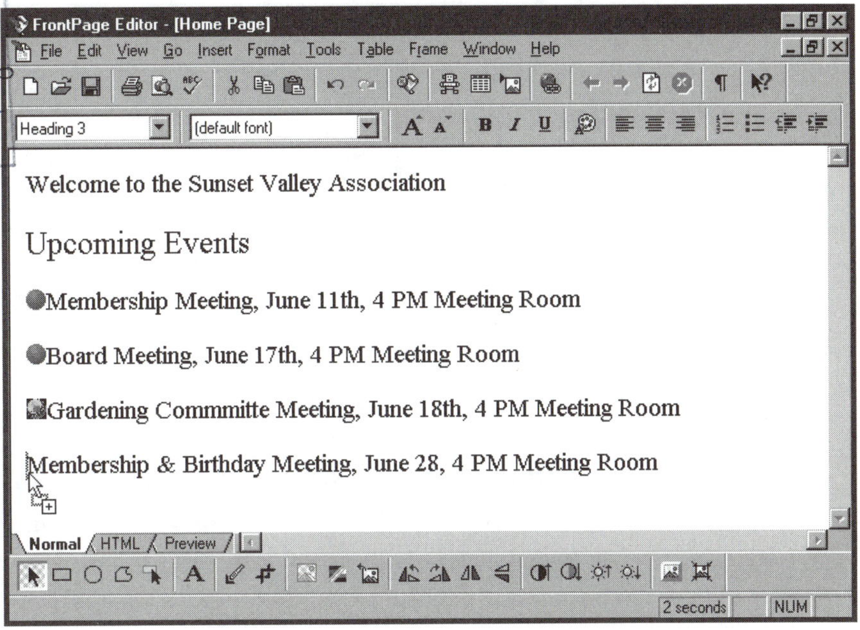

Figure 1.23

Click and drag to
copy images.

Touching Up the Page with Spell-Checking

Before you post your page, you should check the spelling. Nothing is
more annoying to a visitor or embarrassing to a site host than spelling
errors jumping off the page. This is the World Wide Web equivalent of
having a big blob of ketchup on your nose when you meet an important
client. First impressions are everything on Web sites.

Fortunately, FrontPage comes with a built-in spell-checker that can catch
your spelling mistakes before they display. To check spelling, follow these
steps:

1. Click on the Check Spelling button in the FrontPage Editor
   toolbar, which brings up the Spelling dialog box, as shown in
   Figure 1.24.

2. When the Spelling dialog box detects a word not in the FrontPage
   dictionary, it prompts you to change the spelling. If the word
   is spelled correctly, click on Ignore All. If the word is spelled

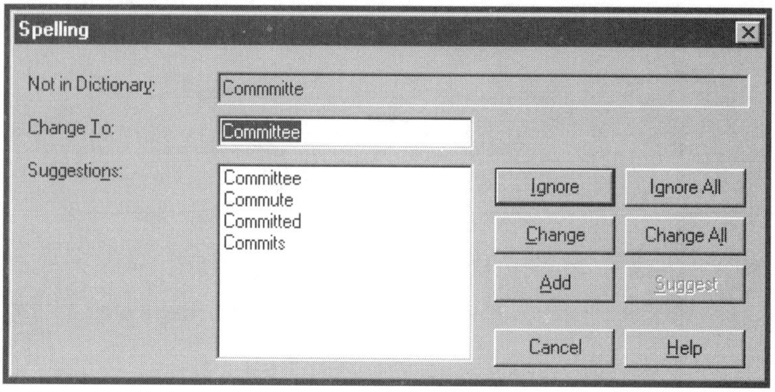

Figure 1.24

Spell-checking avoids silly typos.

incorrectly, click on Change if you want to change the spelling of only that occurrence of the word, or Change All if you want to change the spelling of that word throughout the entire page.

3. When the spelling check is complete, click on OK in the FrontPage dialog box.

In my example, the spell-checker identified the misspelled word "commmitte" and correctly suggested changing it to "committee."

Taking a Peek at HTML

The FrontPage Editor translates the text you create into HTML code. For many people, the nice thing about this is that they don't even know it's happening. Still, you should take a quick peek at the code and see what you've accomplished. To view or copy HTML code in FrontPage Editor, follow these steps:

1. Click on the HTML tab at the bottom of the screen, as shown in Figure 1.25. From the menu line, you could also select View, HTML, to view the HTML window.

2. Use the vertical scroll bar to move up and down to view the Hypertext Markup Language. Notice that your text is surrounded by HTML markings such as <body> and </body> or <h1> and </h1>.

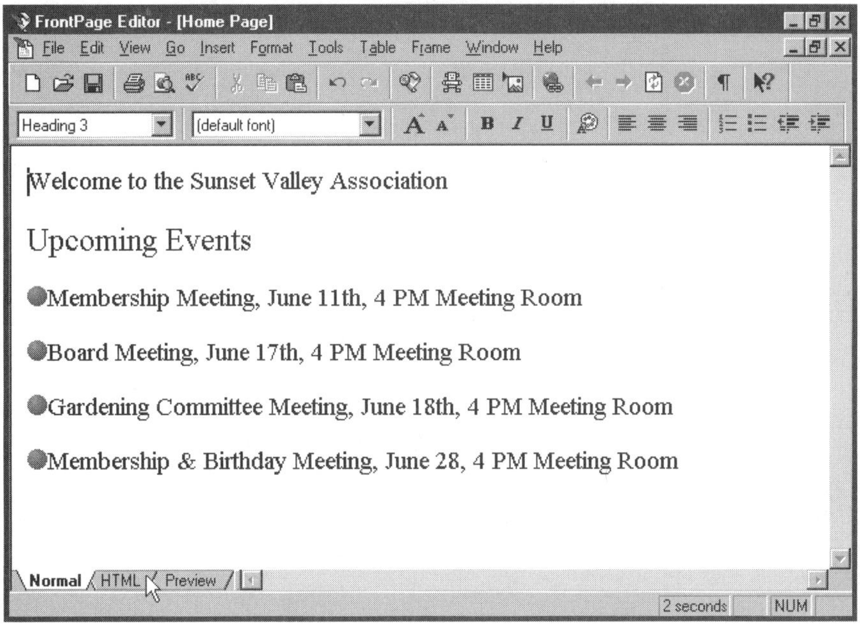

Figure 1.25

The tab bar:
Normal, HTML,
and Preview.

NOTE The code for Heading 1 is h1. Now you can figure out what h2 is on your own.

3. If you want to copy HTML code, you can use your mouse to select the HTML, right-click, and select Copy. You can also do some editing in the HTML window if you want. The Cut, Paste, and Copy operations, as well as drag and drop, work the same way in the Editor window, as shown in Figure 1.26.

4. To return to the Normal view, simply click on the Normal tab.

5. Any changes you make in the HTML window will be reflected in the Normal window view. For example, if you change the h4 tags to h1 and switch back to the Normal view, you'll see that all your events are as big as the Welcome heading. To undo this action, select the Edit, Undo menu item.

```
<h1>Sunset Valley Association </h1>

<h2>Upcoming Events</h2>

<h4><img src="WB00882_.gif" width="15" height="15" alt="WB00882_.GIF (263 bytes)">Member
Meeting, June 11th, 4 PM Meeting Room </h4>

<h4><img src="WB00882_.gif" width="15" height="15" alt="WB00882_.GIF (263 bytes)">Board
Meeting, June 17th, 4 PM Meeting Room </h4>

<h4><img src="WB00882_.gif" width="15" height="15" alt="WB00882_.GIF (263 bytes)">Garden
Committee Meeting, June 18th, 4 PM Meeting Room </h4>

<h4><img src="WB00882_.gif" width="15" height="15" alt="WB00882_.GIF (263 bytes)">Member
&amp; Birthday Meeting, June 28, 4 PM Meeting Room </h4>
</body>
</html>
```

Figure 1.26

The HTML window: The DNA of your Web page.

TIP

For all of you hardcore coders, you can edit HTML code to your heart's delight in the View or Edit HTML window.

Previewing Your Work in a Browser

Working inside the FrontPage Editor is nice, with both its WYSIWYG (What-You-See-Is-What-You-Get) view and its HTML view. However, WYSIWYG is often a misnomer—the real acid test is to try your page in a browser. FrontPage incorporates Microsoft's Page Viewing engine, so previewing your page is now a breeze. To preview your Web page, follow these steps:

1. Click on the Preview tab (next to the HTML tab), as shown in Figure 1.27.

2. To return to the Normal view, simply click on the Normal tab.

Figure 1.27

Preview: How a
real browser
displays your page.

NOTE In the Preview view, you cannot make changes to your Web page. It's a view-only mode, just like a real browser.

Saving Your Work

You've made some significant changes to your page! It was blank when you opened it from the FrontPage Explorer, and now you've added text and graphics. You've assigned styles to text and even checked the spelling. It's now time to save your work.

Titles, Filenames, and the Index.htm File

FrontPage Web pages are saved with both a filename and a title. The filename is how the page is identified in the Web site URL (Uniform Resource Locator). The URL is the address visitors use to find your site on the World Wide Web. When someone types in your Web address, the filename is the last part of that address.

Every page in a Web site needs a unique filename, but one filename is special. The file named index.htm is the page that visitors to your Web site go to by default, just by typing your Web site address. A specific page name is optional because the index.htm file is automatically opened.

The index.htm file is your Web site home page. It's the page people go to first. After you add new pages to your Web site, this will mean something. For now, index.htm will be your one and only file. It's the first (and for now, only) page visitors will see when they go to your Web site.

Web pages also have titles. Titles can be longer and more descriptive than page filenames. Filenames are no longer constricted to eight characters; however, because your page may end up on Unix or other non-Windows machines, it's best to stick to the old DOS file naming rules. When you name a new page (and so far, you're just saving an existing one), you are prompted to enter a page title and a page name. Enter the title first, and FrontPage helps you out by coming up with the closest possible filename for you. To save a page in FrontPage Editor, follow these steps:

1. Click on the Save button in the toolbar. You're not prompted to enter a filename or title for your page because the filename (index.htm) was assigned in FrontPage Explorer, where you opened the file. The title, "home page," was also generated for you.

2. When you place an image on a page that's not yet part of the Web site, FrontPage prompts you to save that file as part of the site. This is all part of FrontPage Explorer doing its thing quietly in the background. Click on OK when prompted to save image files.

Viewing Your Site Using FrontPage Explorer

When you last looked at your site in FrontPage Explorer, it had two files and no links. Now look at the changes you've made. To view links in FrontPage Explorer, follow these steps:

1. Switch to FrontPage Explorer by clicking on the FrontPage Explorer button in the Editor toolbar, as shown in Figure 1.28.

2. Click on the Hyperlinks button in the FrontPage Explorer Views toolbar. Hyperlinks View shows your home page, but you don't immediately see any links to other pages or graphics. No other pages exist (yet).

3. To see links to individual graphics, click on the Hyperlinks to Images button, as shown in Figure 1.29.

4. To see all links to all graphics files, click on the Repeated Hyperlinks button, as shown in Figure 1.30. Your display should look similar.

TIP

When your Web site gets large (and it will), you can get the graphic images out of the FrontPage Explorer views by turning off the Hyperlinks to Images button.

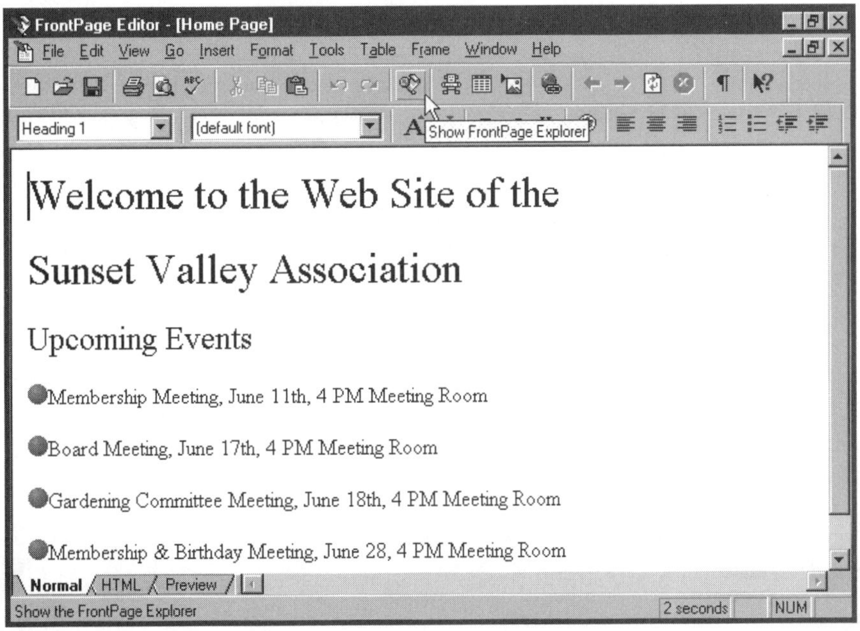

Figure 1.28

Switching to FrontPage Explorer from inside FrontPage Editor.

FrontPage Editor - [Home Page]

File Edit View Go Insert Format Tools Table Frame Window Help

Heading 1   (default font)   Show FrontPage Explorer

Welcome to the Web Site of the

Sunset Valley Association

Upcoming Events

Membership Meeting, June 11th, 4 PM Meeting Room

Board Meeting, June 17th, 4 PM Meeting Room

Gardening Committee Meeting, June 18th, 4 PM Meeting Room

Membership & Birthday Meeting, June 28, 4 PM Meeting Room

Normal / HTML / Preview /

Show the FrontPage Explorer   2 seconds   NUM

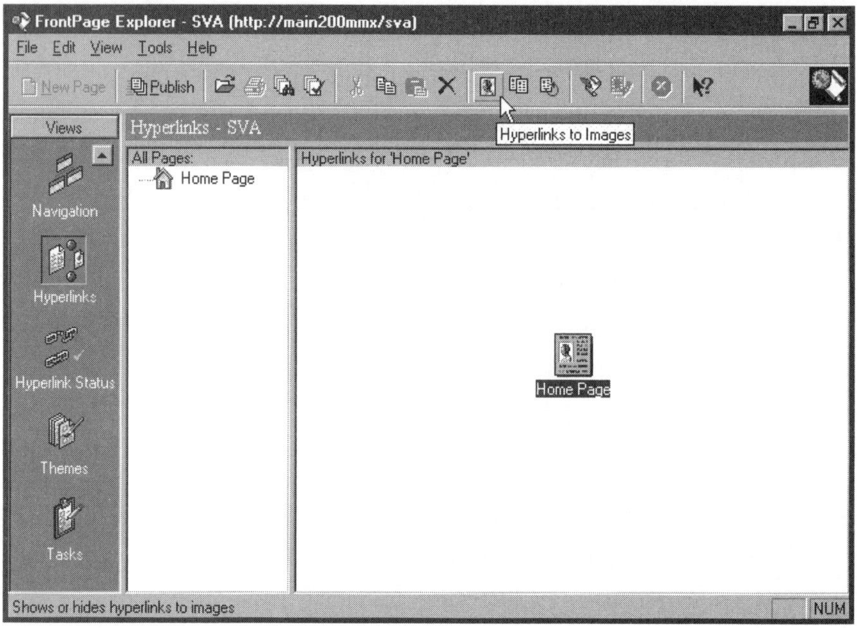

Figure 1.29

Displaying the
Hyperlinks to
Images.

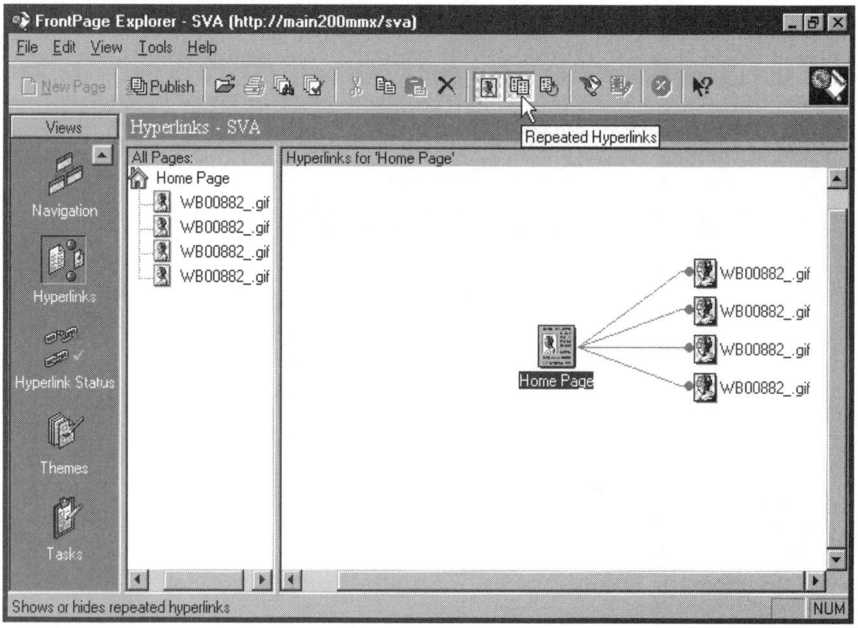

Figure 1.30

The Repeated
Hyperlinks button.

Testing Your Site with the Personal Server

The Preview in Browser menu item in the FrontPage Editor File menu launches the Web browser you have installed (Internet Explorer, Netscape Navigator, or another one) and then opens your Web site using that browser. How handy!

What will your Web site actually look like when someone visits it? It may look a little different than it did in the FrontPage Editor's Preview window, which is why you should use the Preview in Browser menu item.

Some browsers show Web pages somewhat differently. For example, text format, images, and other elements of your page will look different when viewed through other browsers. For this reason, some Web sites have messages that say "Best Viewed with Microsoft Internet Explorer 3.0 or higher" or "Best Viewed using Netscape Navigator 3.0 or higher."

At this stage (that's another way of saying you haven't done all that much yet), the Web sites don't look that different. However, even with what you've created so far, the display of backgrounds and word and line spacing could look different to AOL visitors than they do to visitors using Internet Explorer.

For our purposes this weekend, I'll use Microsoft Internet Explorer to illustrate previewing your Web site. Not surprisingly, Microsoft's browser meshes smoothly with FrontPage-created Web sites.

NOTE Throughout these sessions, you'll keep Microsoft Internet Explorer open quite a bit. I'll keep referring to it by its full name so that you don't confuse it with the Microsoft Front-Page Explorer (not to mention the Windows 95 Explorer). It's like having three kids named William Gates. I'll always use full names so that you don't get confused.

You can "visit" your Web site without even logging on to the Net because FrontPage includes its own server: the Personal Web Server. The Personal

Web Server isn't adequate to run a Web site off your own computer, but it's fine to simulate placing your Web site on the Net.

The Personal Web Server has actually been running the whole time you've had FrontPage Explorer open. You might have noticed it on the Taskbar—just sitting there quietly, doing its job of allowing the links you define in FrontPage Explorer to function.

You can maximize the Personal Web Server by pointing and clicking on the Web Server Idle button in the Windows 95 Taskbar. If you're not viewing the Taskbar, you can press Alt+Tab until the Personal Web Server is selected.

There's really not a lot to see. The Personal Web Server allows you to use a browser and test your Web site. It doesn't have any menus, options, and so on—it just runs.

As you'll see, however, being able to test a Web site before posting it is an important job. As you develop your site over the weekend by adding more complex links and forms that allow for visitor input, you'll appreciate the ability to test all this without consuming days of access time loading and unloading files to your real Internet site provider. To preview a Web site in your browser, follow these steps:

1. Before you preview your site, save your page! Only saved changes appear when you visit your site with a browser.

2. Select the Preview in Browser menu item in the FrontPage Editor file menu, as shown in Figure 1.31.

3. View your Web site as a visitor would. Scroll down, if necessary, to see all the text, as shown in Figure 1.32.

As you enhance your Web site, you can refresh the connection between Internet Explorer and the Web. To refresh your Web site in Internet Explorer, follow these steps:

1. Switch back to FrontPage Editor using the Windows 95 Taskbar or Alt+Tab.

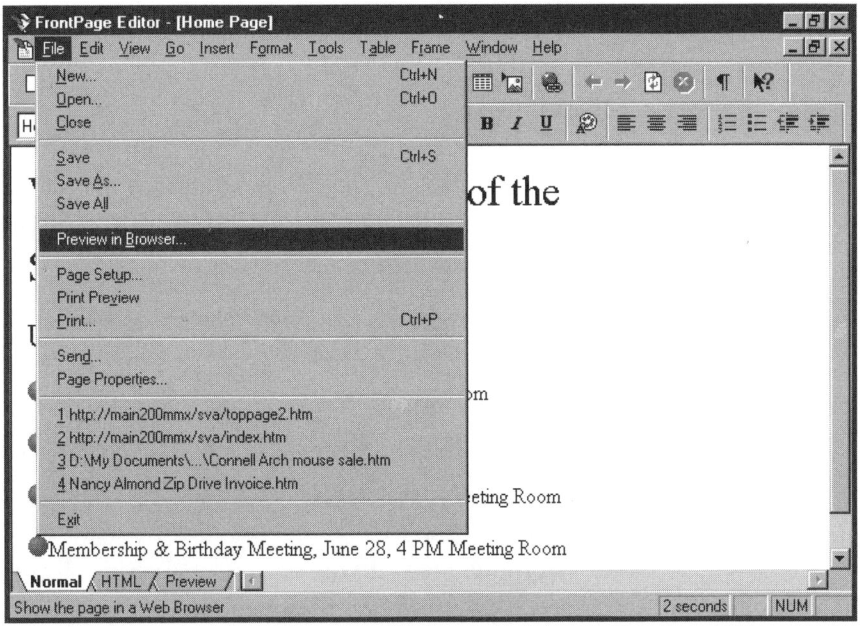

Figure 1.31

The Preview in Browser menu item.

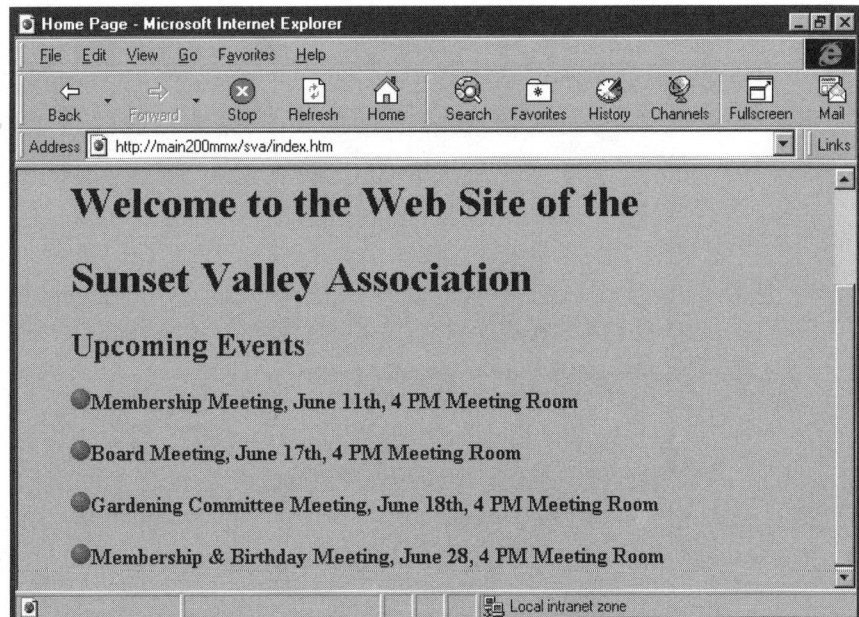

Figure 1.32

Scrolling through your Web site.

2. Make an editing change to the page that you'll be sure to notice when you view it. I'm editing text and adding some new clip art—the little "Microsoft FrontPage" logo, included in the clip art collection as shown in Figure 1.33.

3. Save changes to the file by clicking on the Save button in the toolbar. If you've added image files, click on OK when FrontPage prompts you to save them as part of your Web site.

4. Switch back to your Web browser and note that, so far, the changes are not reflected on the Web.

5. Click the Refresh button on your Web browser's toolbar.

6. Take a fresh look at your Web site. The changes to the file have been uploaded to the Web site. The Microsoft FrontPage Explorer (the one you haven't been to for a while) tracked the changes to the file and integrated them into the Web site. All this appears just as it will on the Internet in Microsoft Internet Explorer, using the Personal Web Server.

Figure 1.33

Show you're powered by Microsoft FrontPage.

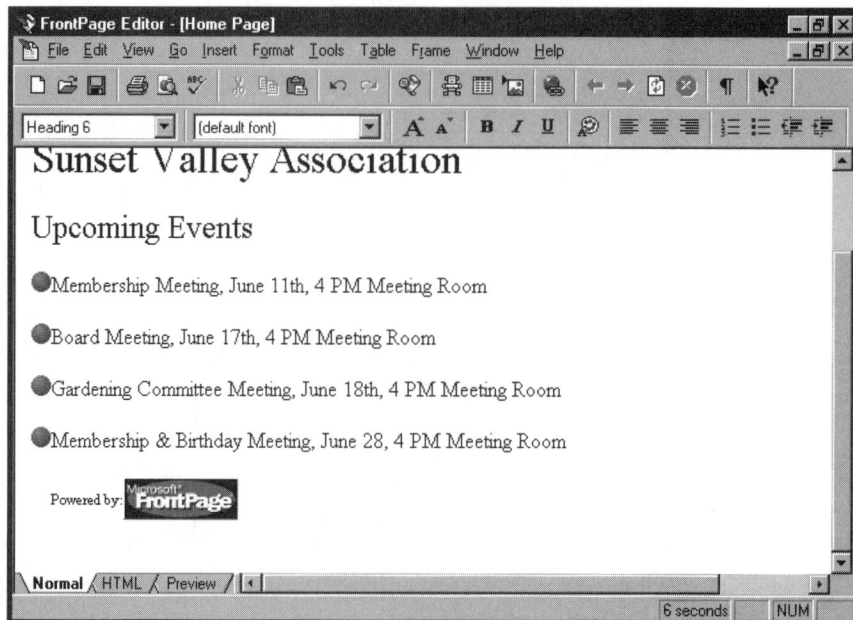

7. Save the changes. Notice the change in the Hyperlinks view in FrontPage Explorer.

8. When you've finished experimenting with the concepts and features I've covered this evening, save the changes to your page in Front-Page Editor and then exit the Editor and FrontPage Explorer.

You've accomplished quite a bit in one evening. You created a real, live Web site, added and deleted a graphic image, cut and pasted text, and formatted a heading. What's more, you tested your site by using a real Web server, changed it, and then tested it again on the server.

Take a Break!

Of course, you've only scratched the surface. Tomorrow you'll explore a variety of ways to format and place your information on a page, including using tables, lists, and graphics (besides that "Under Construction" thing). On Sunday, you'll explore the power of interactive forms that allow you to collect input from visitors to your site. So relax, take a walk if the weather's nice, and get a good night's sleep. You've taken your first big steps, and tomorrow you'll cover many miles.

Making Your Site Look Good

- Changing Heading Styles
- Changing the Formatting of Characters
- Creating Bulleted and Numbered Lists
- Indenting, Outdenting, and Those Other Lists
- Coloring a Web Page

our yourself some coffee and butter your bagel, because you'll be
diving into this morning's activities with energy and enthusiasm.
Now, what was it you did last night? Well, you created a Web site,
added text to a Web page, formatted and edited the text, and even added
a graphic image or two. You then checked out the site using a Web
browser, and if you saw what you expected, you dreamt sweet dreams of
uninhibited hyperlinking and angelic winged windows last night.

Getting a Fresh Start

I have one note of caution to share before you start working. As you work
through this morning's session, you'll add quite a bit to your Web site.
You'll add and link graphic files to the Web site, and before the day is
over, you'll create links within a page, between pages, and even with other
Web sites. FrontPage keeps track of all this for you, allowing you to focus
on the creative aspects of designing your Web site. All you have to do is
cooperate by adhering to a few basic procedures:

- Always open FrontPage Explorer before opening pages in FrontPage
  Editor.

- Open existing Web pages from the Explorer by double-clicking on
  them in the Hyperlinks View or Folder View.

- Save changes to pages in FrontPage Editor to update all links.

To open an existing Web site, follow these steps:

1. Start FrontPage from the Taskbar.

2. In the Getting Started dialog box, you can select the Web site you worked on last night. This dialog box can be bypassed by checking the Always Open Last Web check box. Once you've done that, upon starting FrontPage, the last site you worked on will automatically be loaded for you. If you often work on multiple sites, you might want to leave this check box unchecked.

Changing Heading Styles

On Friday evening, you created a nice Web site that included not only text, but also a heading. Before you experiment more with headings, you should understand how they work.

Defining type font, size, attributes, spacing, and alignment is done differently in FrontPage than in word processing programs. Unlike a word processing document in which you can define the exact appearance of headings as they appear on a printed page (or even onscreen), HTML documents are restricted to one of six types of headings: Heading 1, 2, 3, 4, 5, or 6. Although some Web browsers interpret these headings differently, they do have similar characteristics, regardless of which browser is displaying them. Table 2.1 summarizes the characteristics of the six heading types (see Figure 2.1).

Figure 2.2 shows a page with the top line of text assigned a Heading 1 style, the second line a Heading 2 style, the third line a Heading 3 style, the fourth line a Heading 4 style, and the list of events formatted with a Heading 5 style.

When the cursor is placed in a paragraph, the Change Style list box displays the heading style for that paragraph, as shown in Figure 2.2.

Does the limitation of six predefined headings mean you have no control over how your headings appear when someone visits your page? In part,

Figure 2.1

Six heading sizes.

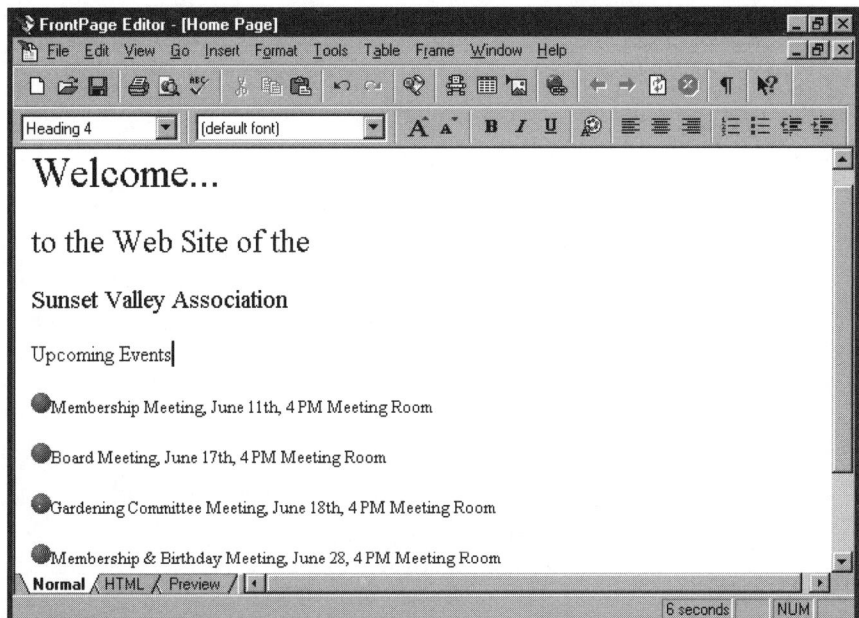

Figure 2.2

Five heading
sizes onscreen.

Types	Characteristics
TABLE 2.1 HTML HEADINGS	
Heading 1	This heading is the largest and is used for major statements. It's normally left-aligned, 24-point boldface type with one line of spacing before and after the paragraph.
Heading 2	No rule states that you can't start a page with a Heading 2 paragraph. It's normally left-aligned, 18-point boldface type with one line of spacing before and after the paragraph.
Heading 3	This heading is normally used for subheadings within a page. It's usually left-aligned, 14-point boldface type with one line of spacing before and after the paragraph.
Heading 4	This heading is normally used for subheadings within a page. It's usually left-aligned, 12-point boldface type with one line of spacing before and after the paragraph.
Heading 5	This heading is actually smaller than normal text and is used for effect. It's usually left-aligned, 10-point boldface type with one line of spacing before and after the paragraph.
Heading 6	This heading is the smallest one. It's often used for footers and fine print in general. It's usually left-aligned, 8-point boldface type with one line of spacing before the paragraph.

the answer to this depends on which browser a visitor to your site is using. Visitors who are armed with the latest from Netscape or Microsoft can see the exact fonts you assign to the text. You'll explore formatting text font a little later in this chapter, but you should be aware that older browsers do not interpret all the fonts you can assign in FrontPage.

What do visitors see when they visit your site with an older browser? Some Web browsers center Heading 1 paragraphs. If the various browsers interpret Heading 1 paragraphs differently, how are you supposed to know what your visitors will view? The rules for this are becoming standardized, but for now, the basic rule to remember is that in any browser, Heading 1 paragraphs are more prominent than Heading 2 paragraphs, and so on down to Heading 6, which is actually smaller than normal text. All browsers display Heading 1 in a large, boldface font, with some spacing above and below the paragraph. To change heading styles, follow these steps:

1. Select the paragraph(s) you want to redefine.

2. Click on the down arrow beside the Change Styles list and select a new style to apply, as shown in Figure 2.3.

The Paragraph Properties dialog box allows you to assign a style to a selected paragraph (or paragraphs). This dialog box also enables you to select paragraph alignment. Paragraph alignment can be default, left, center, or right, which aligns the paragraph to the left, center, or right of the Web page (or table cell, but you'll explore that later in this chapter). The default setting basically leaves the paragraph the way it is. To change heading styles using the Paragraph Properties dialog box, follow these steps:

1. Select Format, Paragraph.

2. Select the style you want to use from the Paragraph Properties dialog box.

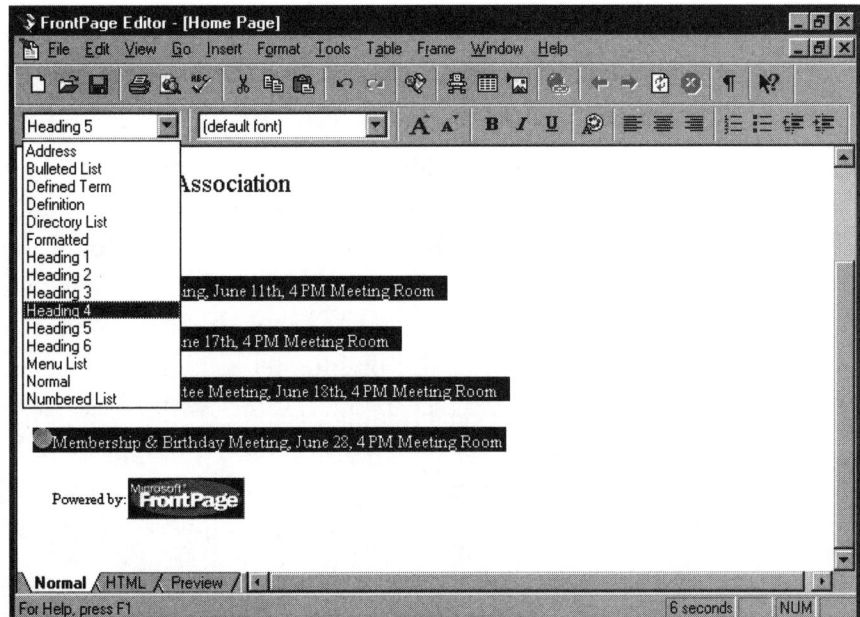

Figure 2.3

Changing the heading style using the Change Styles list.

Figure 2.4

Changing the heading style using the Paragraph Properties dialog box.

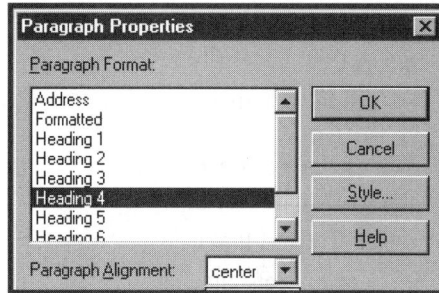

3. Pull down the list of paragraph alignments and select one, as shown in Figure 2.4.

4. Click on OK in the Format Paragraph dialog box.

Changing the Formatting of Characters

How can you customize your headings? You can apply font characteristics such as boldface, italics, and underlining to heading styles, depending on inherent characteristics of the style. For example, you can apply underlining or italics to a Heading 1 style, but you cannot remove the boldface. Figure 2.5 shows a Heading 1 style with italics applied.

You can also select from a large variety of font styles. Just keep in mind that visitors using older browsers do not see them. A good idea is to assign different font styles (such as Arial, Courier, and so on) to the text in your Web site. Be aware that if you have extra fonts, such as Garamond, installed on your machine, visitors will not be able to see that font unless they also have it installed on their computer. Visitors who come to your site via Navigator 3.0 or Internet Explorer 3.0 or higher will see your fonts as you assigned them. Visitors with older browsers miss out, but they'll still be able to read your text—it appears in Times Roman font instead of the one you selected. Heading styles (such as Heading 1, Heading 2, and so on) will be interpreted by every browser.

Font styles, however, make letters larger or smaller. A line that just barely fits on a page using Arial Narrow font becomes two lines when a browser interprets it as Times Roman. This might disrupt the careful symmetry and aesthetic ambiance you so carefully cultivated for your Web site, but that's the price you pay when you use different font styles.

NOTE For the most part, you don't need to be very concerned with the Web audience viewing your pages with older browsers. The fact that these people are on the Web at all means they accept updated software and understand that browsers change quickly. As long as your page looks fine under Navigator 3.0 or higher and Internet Explorer 3.0 or higher, you won't encounter many problems of this sort.

Along with defining character fonts, you can assign boldface, underlining, and/or italics to text. You can change type size (choosing from a list of seven sizes), and you can assign colors to fonts. All this gives you tremendous control over the look of your Web page.

Character styles override the default heading styles. They stay with the text, even if you assign a different heading style. Removing heading formatting can get confusing, especially if you assign character attributes that do not go away. To change a heading to a default heading style, you need to remove all character formatting from the heading, as shown in Figure 2.5.

To enhance characters, follow these steps:

1. Select all the text to which you want to assign special formatting attributes.
2. Select Format, Font.
3. Select a font style from the Font list.
4. Select boldface and/or italics from the Font Style list.
5. Select one of the available text sizes from the Size list.
6. Choose underline, strikethrough, or typewriter-style font display by clicking on the respective check boxes in the Effects area of the dialog box.
7. Choose a color for your text from the Color list.

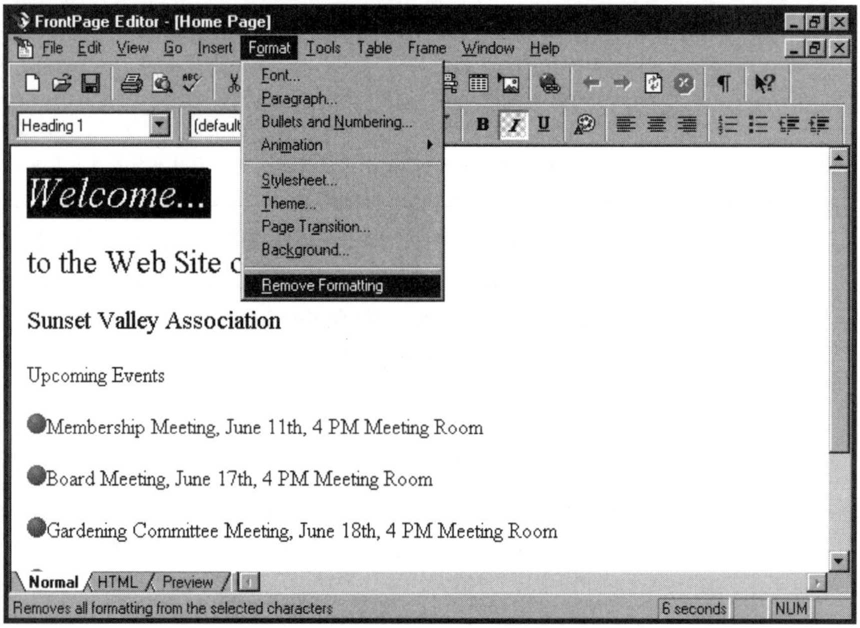

Figure 2.5

Removing character
formatting.

8. Check out the text in the Sample area of the dialog box. You can try different text attributes to see how they look.

9. When everything looks fine, click on OK in the Font dialog box (see Figure 2.6).

About Special Style Attributes

You may have noticed that the Font dialog box has a Special Styles tab. These special style attributes are mainly a holdover from the days when Web browsers couldn't interpret the variety of font styles that most of them now read. Because the Font tab in the Fonts dialog box gives you much more control over font display, there's not that much you need from the Special Styles tab.

The Special Styles tab does have a few interesting font features, however. For instance, you can make text blink—which makes it flash on and off when viewed in a browser. Text formatted to blink won't blink in the FrontPage Editor, but most browsers display the text as blinking. Besides

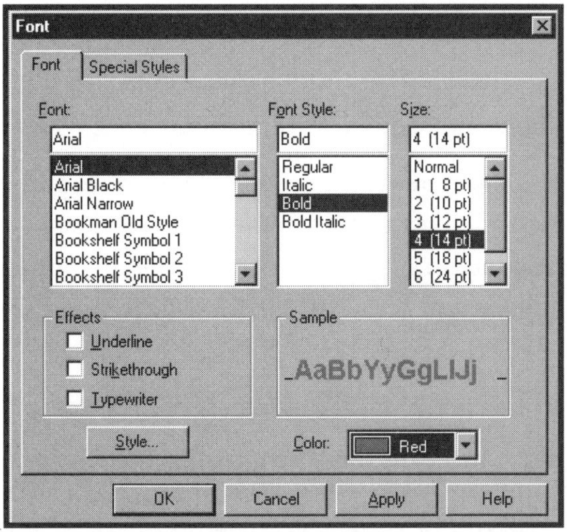

Figure 2.6

Applying font formatting.

being able to add blinking to your text, you can also make text superscript (raised) or subscript (lowered).

Make selections from the Special Styles tab by first selecting the text to which you want to apply the special style. Then, open the Font dialog box, choose the Special Styles tab, and select features by using the check boxes, as shown in Figure 2.7.

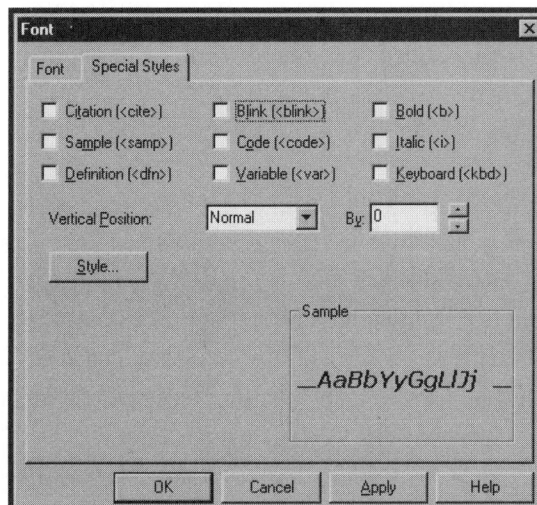

Figure 2.7

Selecting special text features.

To remove formatting, follow these steps:

1. Select all the text from which you want to remove formatting.

2. Select Format, Remove Formatting.

All additional character formatting is stripped from the text, leaving only the format characteristics that come with the assigned heading style. To change text for a selected paragraph back to normal, pull down the Change Style list and select Normal.

Having Fun with Fonts and Colors

I get a lot of feedback on the Web sites I create, and one of the things people seem to like the most is a variety of fonts and colors. Of course, you can overdo any good thing, but in general, folks are pleasantly surprised to find a Web site that uses plenty of color and font styles.

One thing you should avoid is using blue or purple for text colors. These colors are reserved for hyperlink text—something you'll explore in the Saturday Afternoon session.

You need to test your fonts using the Preview tab and the Preview in Browser File menu item in FrontPage Editor. Some fonts don't look the same in the Editor and in a browser. Stay away from the Food font unless you want strange blurry lines to cryptically disguise your text. Again, the basic rule is to have fun, but check your page using your browser before finalizing your font selection. Figure 2.8 shows some font variety to spice up a Web page.

NOTE When you make a number of font changes to your page, the display in FrontPage Editor sometimes goes a little haywire. You can fix this by selecting View, Refresh. You can change the text font by using the Change Font list in the Formatting toolbar. You can also make text larger or smaller, boldfaced, italicized, underlined, and change the color by using the buttons in the Formatting toolbar. In Figure 2.9, I use the Change Text Color button to assign a new color to selected text.

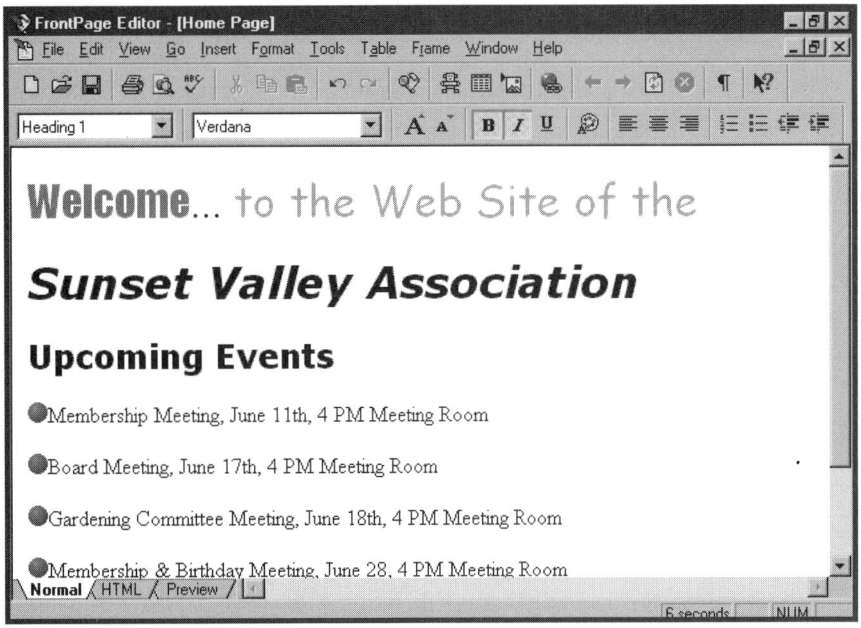

Figure 2.8

Fun with fonts!

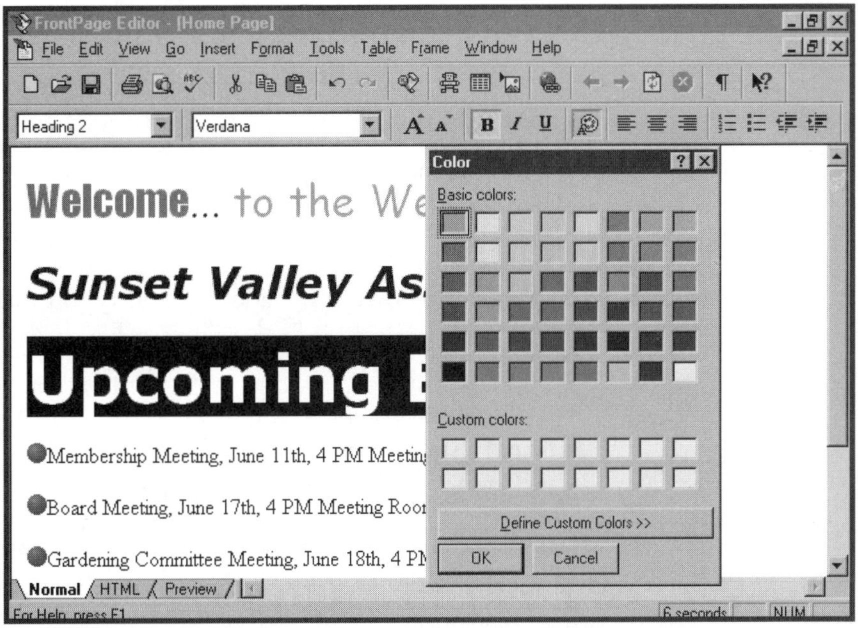

Figure 2.9

Selecting colors from the Color palette.

Creating Bulleted and Numbered Lists

Long lists can get boring, but bullets can help each list item stand out. Bullets add emphasis to each point and help the visitor scan the list and pick out points of interest. Bulleted lists create hanging indent paragraphs with bullets, as shown in Figure 2.10.

Numbers can also help visitors get more out of lists. For one thing, they can quickly tell how many items are in a list. Numbered lists create hanging indent paragraphs also, but with automatically assigned numbers instead of bullets, as shown in Figure 2.11. When you cut and copy paragraphs within a numbered list, the paragraphs are automatically renumbered.

In the Saturday Afternoon session, when you add hyperlinks to your site, you can use numbered or bulleted lists to serve as a table of contents for your Web site. Bullets and numbering are assigned from the Format toolbar in FrontPage Editor.

To create a bulleted list, follow these steps:

1. Place your insertion point in the page where you want to start the bulleted list and type the first item.
2. Press Enter at the end of the first item and then type more items.
3. Select all the paragraphs to which you want to assign bullets and click on the Bulleted List button in the Formatting toolbar, as shown in Figure 2.12.
4. Press Enter twice when you are finished typing the list.

To create a numbered list, follow these steps:

1. Place your insertion point in the page where you want to start the numbered list, and type the first item.
2. Press Enter at the end of the first item and then type more items.
3. Select all the paragraphs to which you want to assign numbers and click on the Numbered List button in the Formatting toolbar, as shown in Figure 2.13.
4. Press Enter twice when you're finished with the list.

Figure 2.10

A bulleted list.

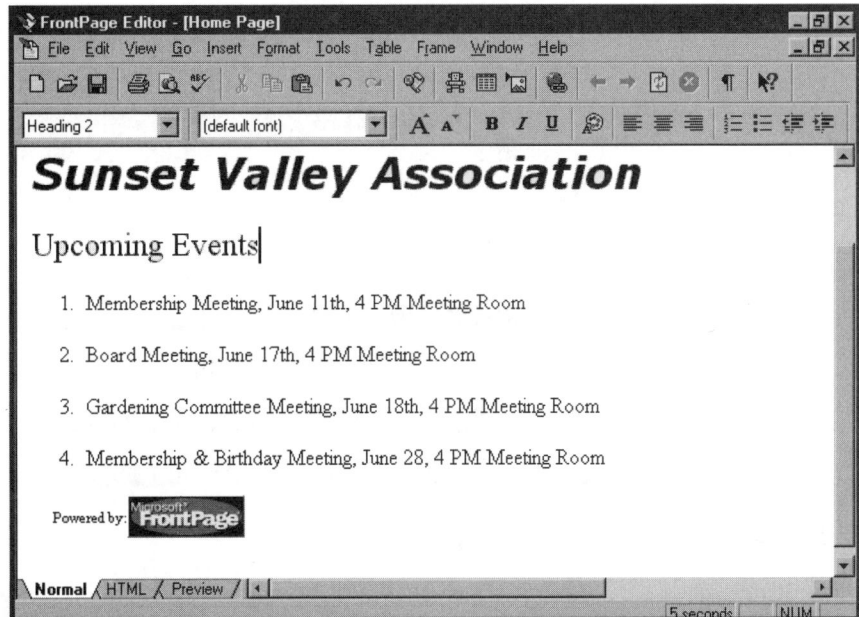

Figure 2.11

A Numbered list.

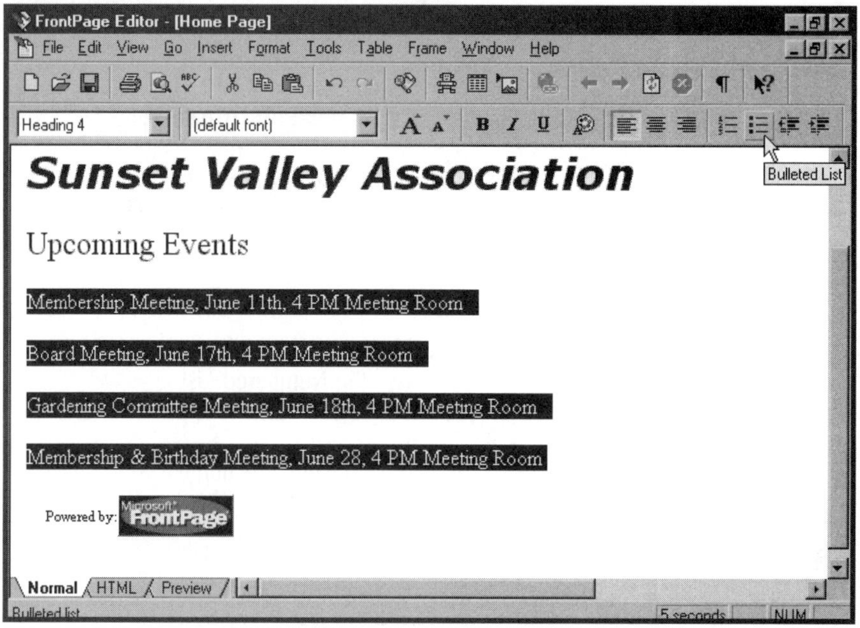

Figure 2.12

The Bulleted List button.

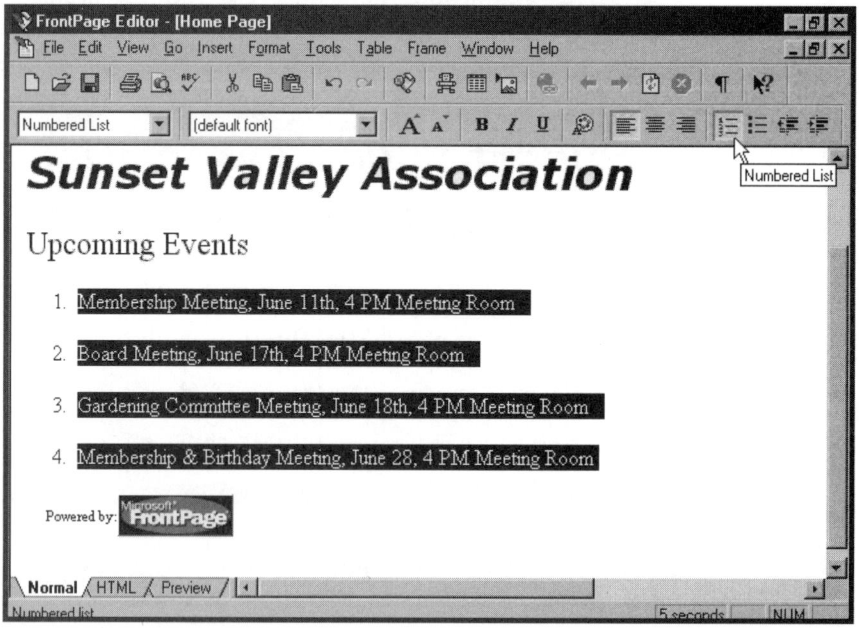

Figure 2.13

The Numbered List button.

To reorder a list, use the cut, copy, and paste techniques you learned in the Friday Evening session, as shown in Figure 2.14.

When you cut, copy, and paste within a numbered list, the numbering is automatically revised to keep the list items in order. When you use the Enter key to create new lines, they are automatically assigned sequential numbers.

TIP

■■■

You can select an *existing* list of paragraphs and assign bullets or numbers. Just select the paragraphs and click on the Numbered List or Bulleted List button on the Formatting toolbar.

When you place your cursor at the end of a numbered or bulleted list item and press enter, FrontPage automatically assigns the list formatting to the next paragraph. This is a nice feature if you're continuing a list. However, sometimes it can seem like you're trapped in a list. It's annoying if you're finished with the list and you can't seem to get back to normal type. The trick to escaping the automatic formatting is to press enter twice.

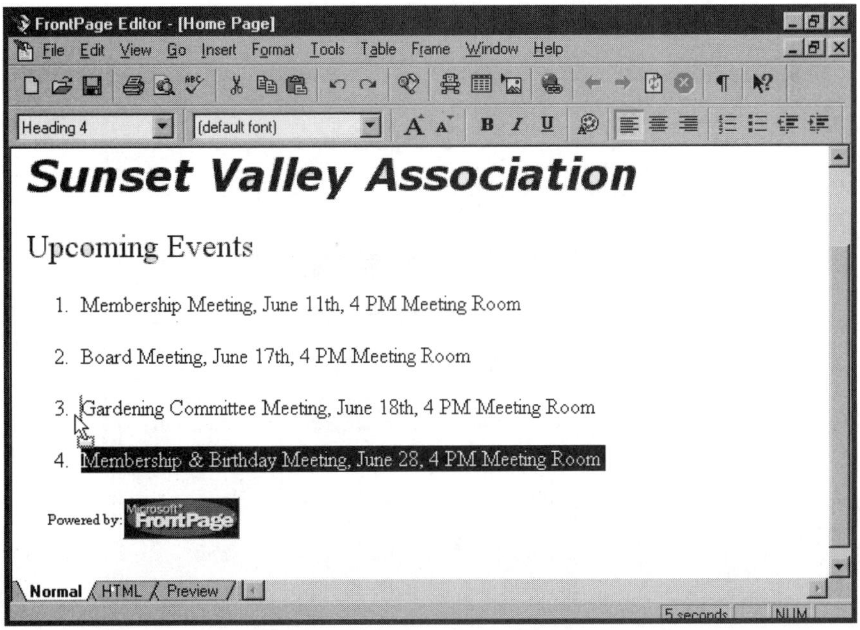

■■■

Figure 2.14

Reordering a list with click-and-drag editing.

A small variety of bullet formats is available. To change or remove bullets, follow these steps:

1. Select the bulleted list paragraphs to be reformatted.
2. Choose Format, Bullets and Numbering.
3. From the Plain Bullets tab in the List Properties dialog box, select a different bullet format (or select the upper-left square to remove the bullets), as shown in Figure 2.15.
4. Click on OK in the List Properties dialog box.

You can also choose from a variety of numbering formats, including roman numerals and letters, and you can reset the starting number so that the first item is not number 1. If you interrupt a list (for example, with a subheading), you may want to start the continued list with a number other than 1 to make it sequential with the preceding list (see the example in Figure 2.16).

To change or remove numbering, follow these steps:

1. Select the numbered list paragraphs to be changed.

Figure 2.15

Loading your page with bullets.

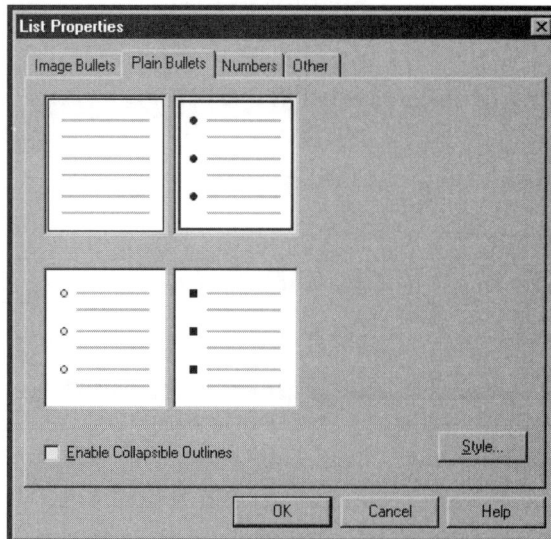

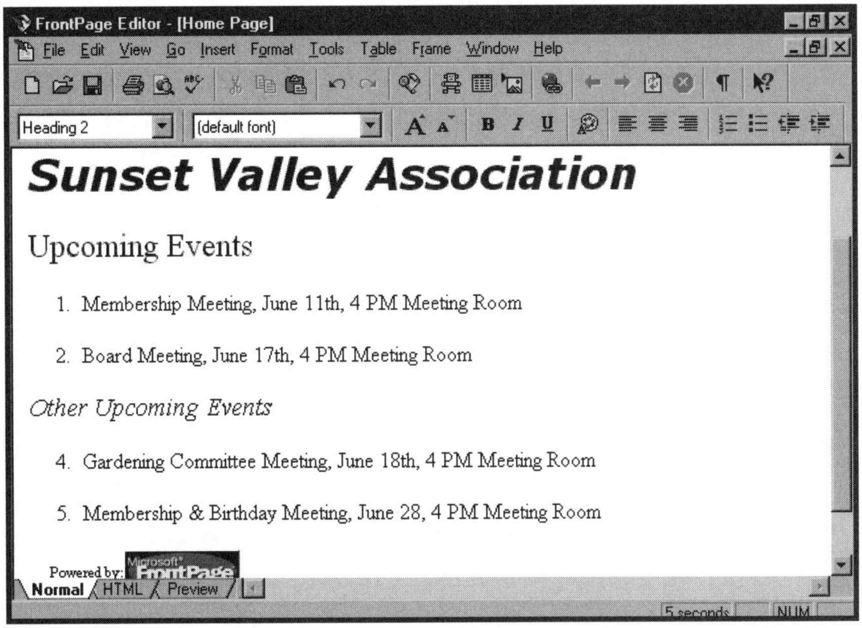

Figure 2.16

Starting a
numbered list
with 4.

2. Choose F<u>o</u>rmat, Bullets and <u>N</u>umbering.

3. From the Numbers tab in the List Properties dialog box, select a different number format (or select the upper-left square to remove numbering).

4. You can change the starting number using the Start At spin control, as shown in Figure 2.17.

5. Click on OK in the List Properties dialog box.

Indenting, Outdenting, and Those Other Lists

Indenting paragraphs is often done on Web sites to create lists of defined terms and definitions. You can indent paragraphs in FrontPage using the Increase Indent button in the Formatting toolbar, but not with the Tab key. You can outdent a paragraph—that is, move its left margin farther to the left—with the Decrease Indent button. Using these two buttons, you can create lists with indented definitions, as shown in Figure 2.18.

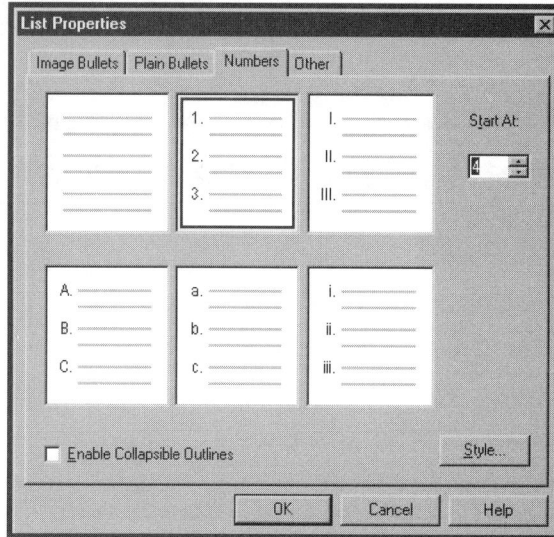

Figure 2.17

Changing the
starting number.

Figure 2.18

Indented
paragraphs.

Indenting Paragraphs

The Increase Indent button moves the left margin for the selected paragraph. You can also use this button to indent a numbered or bulleted list paragraph. FrontPage lets you indent as much as you like—although the practical limit is three or four levels of indenting. To indent a paragraph, follow these steps:

1. Select the paragraph(s) you want to indent.
2. Click on the Increase Indent button in the Formatting toolbar, as shown in Figure 2.19.

To decrease the indentation of a paragraph, follow these steps:

1. Select the paragraph(s) you want to move to the left.
2. Click on the Decrease Indent button in the Formatting toolbar, as shown in Figure 2.20.

Figure 2.19

Indenting a paragraph.

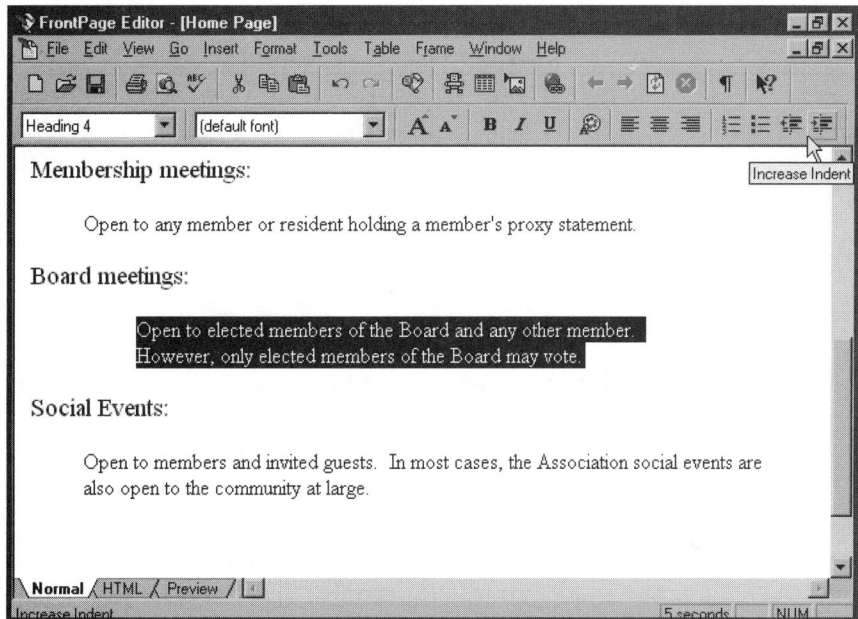

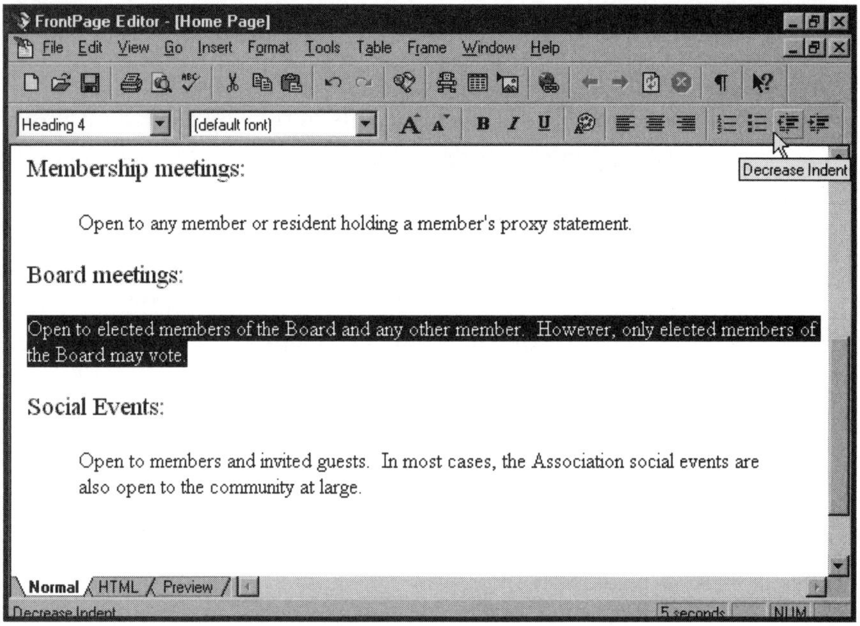

Figure 2.20

"Outdenting" a paragraph.

You can increase the indent on any paragraph, even one that is already indented. Figure 2.21 shows an entire list with defined terms and indented definitions, indented even farther. To indent an indent, follow these steps:

1. Select all the paragraphs to be indented.

2. Click on the Increase Indent button in the Formatting toolbar.

What's with Those Other Lists?

You'll notice other list formats available in the Change Styles list. Directory Lists, Menu Lists, Definitions, and Defined Terms are all styles that incorporate features that are more easily assigned other ways.

The Directory Lists and Menu Lists styles are similar to bulleted lists. Defined Terms and Definition Lists are styles that assign indenting to paragraphs with definitions. These styles reflect the limitations of older browsers and apply list and indenting paragraph attributes that are more easily assigned using numbered lists, bulleted lists, or indenting.

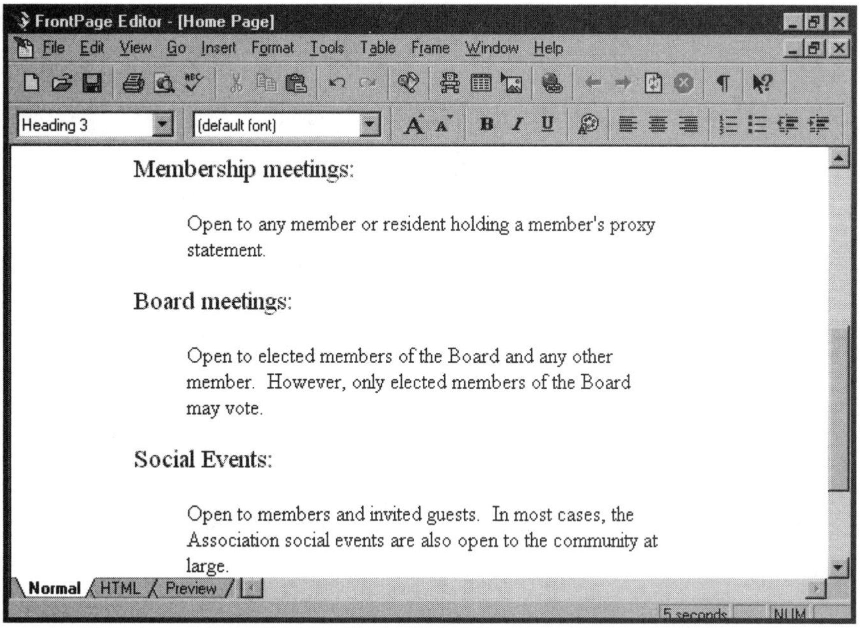

Figure 2.21

Several levels of indenting.

Breaking Up the Page

FrontPage allows you to insert horizontal lines to create aesthetic breaks between the sections of your page. Remember that unlike a sheet of paper, a page attached to your Web site is potentially endless. Horizontal lines can identify breaks between topics or sections of a page. To insert a horizontal line, follow these steps:

1. Place your cursor at the spot where the line is to appear.

2. Select Insert, Horizontal Line, as shown in Figure 2.22: A horizontal line appears.

To remove a horizontal line, follow these steps:

1. Place your cursor to the left of a horizontal line and then click.

2. You can press the delete key on your keyboard, or you can right-click and select Cut from the shortcut menu, as shown in Figure 2.23.

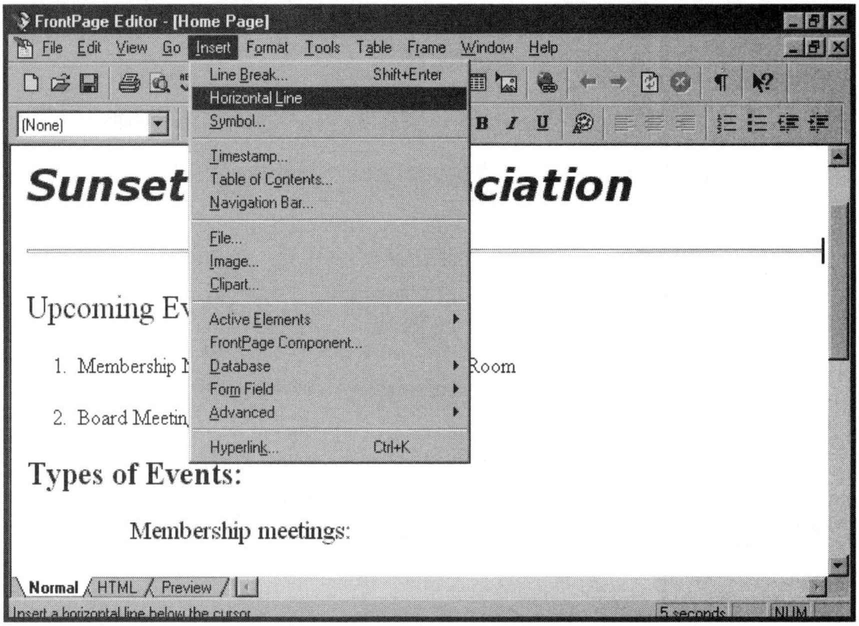

Figure 2.22

Breaking up a page
is easy to do.

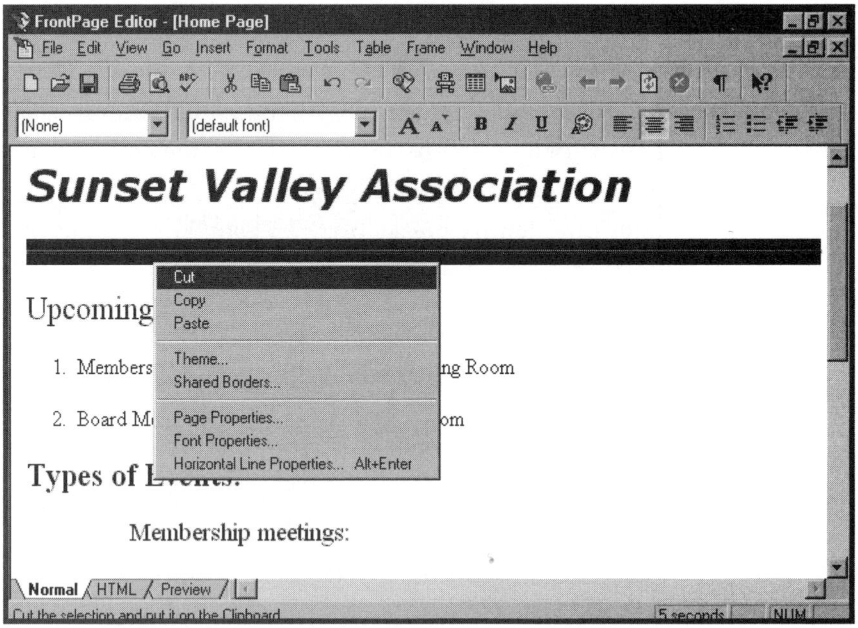

Figure 2.23

Poof! The line
is gone.

Creating Tables Magically

Tables allow you to organize text (and later, graphics) in columns on a page. FrontPage allows you to use tables the same way you use them in word processing programs—to organize information in rows and columns (see Figure 2.24).

You can also use tables to place blocks of text side by side, as shown in Figure 2.25. Placing blocks of text side by side with tables helps you pack more information on a single screen and creates many possibilities for creative layout. No rule states that tables must have visible borders. This way, your page can look like it's arranged in columns.

Let's explore both these ways to use tables. To insert a table, follow these steps:

1. Place your cursor where you want the table to appear.
2. Click on the Insert Table button in the FrontPage Editor toolbar.

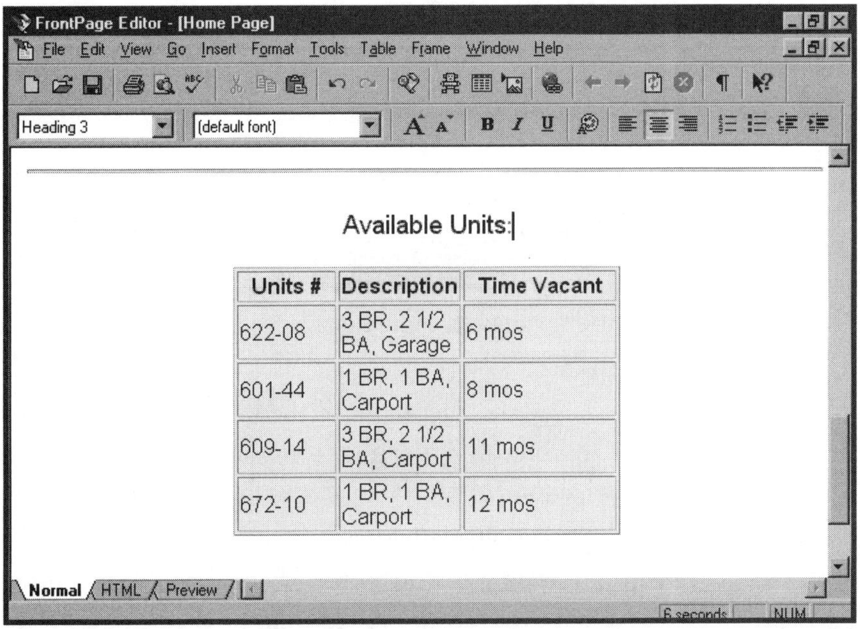

Figure 2.24

Columns and rows of information in a table.

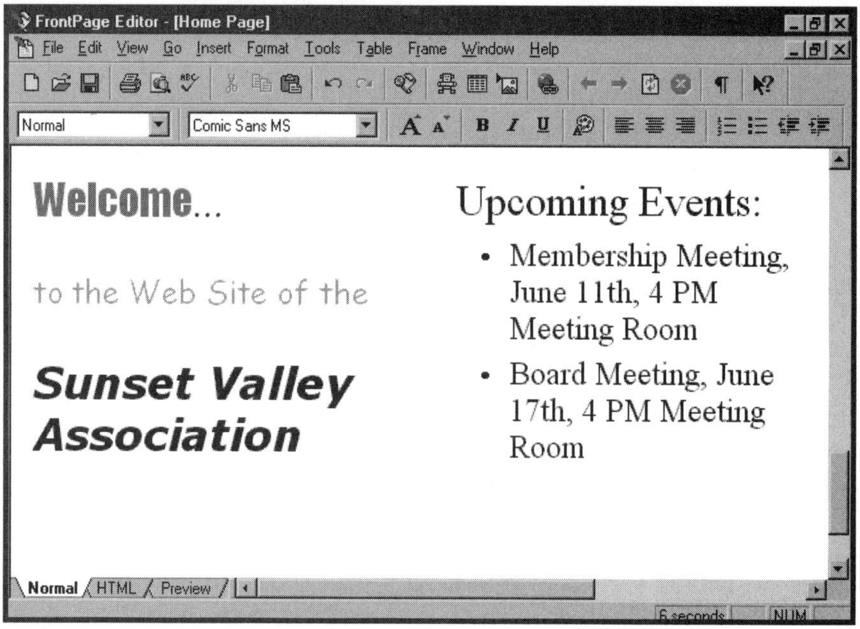

Figure 2.25

Using a table to create page layout columns.

3. Click and drag in the grid to select the number of rows and columns you want in your table, as shown in Figure 2.26.

To change table properties, follow these steps:

1. Right-click anywhere in the table and select Table Properties from the shortcut menu.

2. Change the settings in the dialog box that appears. For example, the settings in Figure 2.27 change the table width to two-thirds of the page (66 percent) and align the table in the center of the page.

3. Choose the alignment of the table in the Alignment drop-down list. You can left align, right align, or center your table. The default selection from this list leaves the table aligned as it was when the table was created.

4. Enter the way you would like text to float around your table in the Float drop-down list. You can have text float to the left of your

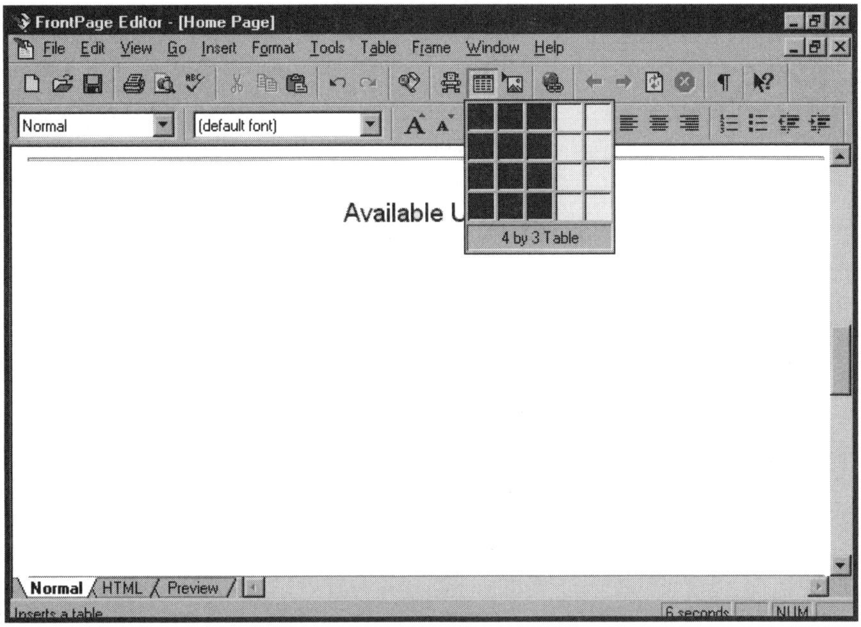

Figure 2.26

Designing your own table.

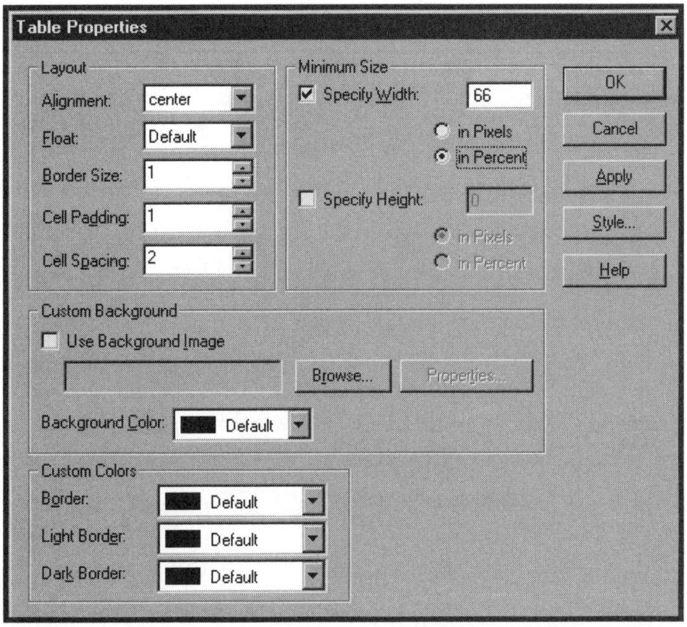

Figure 2.27

Changing table properties.

table, to the right of the table, or not flow around the table at all. The default selection, Default, is not to allow text to flow around the table.

5. Enter the Border Size using the spin box in the Layout area. Unlike page-based layout programs, FrontPage measures border width in screen pixels. If you select 0 in the Border Size area, your table appears without gridlines when your site is visited.

NOTE Don't be fooled by the appearance of gridlines in FrontPage Editor. If you don't assign a border size greater than 0, no gridlines appear when visitors view your site.

6. Assign Cell Padding using the spin box in the Layout area. Like border size, cell padding is measured in pixels. Cell padding applies to all cells in a table. If you're using borders in your table, cell padding keeps your cell contents from smashing up into the cell border.

7. Use the Cell Spacing spin box in the Layout area to control the space between rows in your table. This measurement, too, is in pixels. The default setting of 2 ensures that there are spaces between cells.

8. Click on the In Percent radio button in the Specify Width area of the Table Properties dialog box to determine how much of the screen the table should take up. If you want your table to fill the entire screen, set the width to 100 and select the In Percent option button.

TIP You can define the width of your table in pixels or as a percentage of the screen. Setting the table width to 75 percent causes the table to fill 3/4 of the width of the page.

9. Click on the In Percent radio button in the Specify Height area of the Table Properties dialog box to determine the minimum height

of your table. Without a minimum height, rogue browsers might resize your table, causing unacceptable results. Typically, leaving this value set to 0 is fine.

10. You can set custom colors for the entire table background. You can also set a variety of coloring for cell borders. Light Border color defines the coloring in the upper and left borders of the cell. The Dark Border color defines the coloring for the lower and right borders. You can mix and match border colors to define shadowing effects in the cells. The Border color for the list sets a default color for the cell borders that gets overridden by Light Border or Dark Border colors. However, be aware that these effects will not show up for viewers using Netscape browsers.

11. When you have defined your table, as shown in Figure 2.28, click on OK in the Table Properties dialog box.

12. Take a look at your creation. You defined the alignment, borders, colors, and width of your table. You'll explore adding cells shortly.

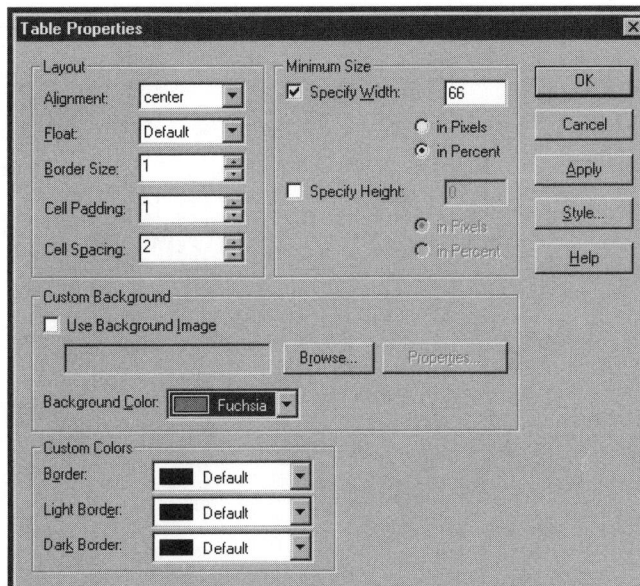

Figure 2.28

Table properties are OK!

To enter text in a table, follow these steps:

1. To enter text in the first cell of the table, just begin typing.

2. To move from cell to cell, use your mouse pointer or press the up-, down-, right- or left-arrow keys. You cannot use the Tab key to move from cell to cell. Are you used to moving from cell to cell in other programs with the Tab key? So am I. It won't work here, though.

The column property you'll most likely want to change is the column width. The logic for doing this is different than when you're working with a spreadsheet, database, or word processing program table. Rather than define columns in terms of inches, it's easier to define column width by percent (unless you want to count pixels). To define relative column widths, follow these steps:

1. Hold your cursor over the top of the column you want to make wider or narrower. The cursor changes to a down arrow, as shown in Figure 2.29. When it does, click to select the row.

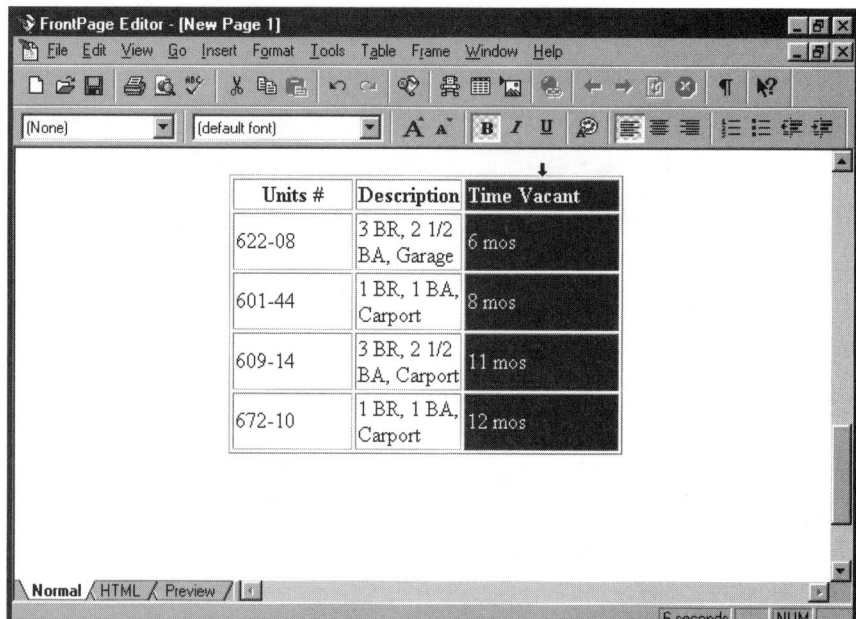

Figure 2.29

Selecting a column with that little down arrow.

2. With the column highlighted, right-click on it and select Cell Properties, as shown in Figure 2.30.

3. Change any cell properties you want. These properties are applied to all selected cells—in this case, the column. For example, you could make a column take up 25 percent of the width of the entire table by using the settings shown in Figure 2.31.

You can format text within a cell by simply using the text formatting techniques you've already explored in this session. Select text and change fonts, text colors, text size, and alignment.

You can also change some of the table properties for a specific cell, such as background and border colors. To change cell format, follow these steps:

1. If you want to format more than one cell, select the cells by clicking and dragging. You can select an entire row or column by moving your cursor to the right of the row or on top of the column

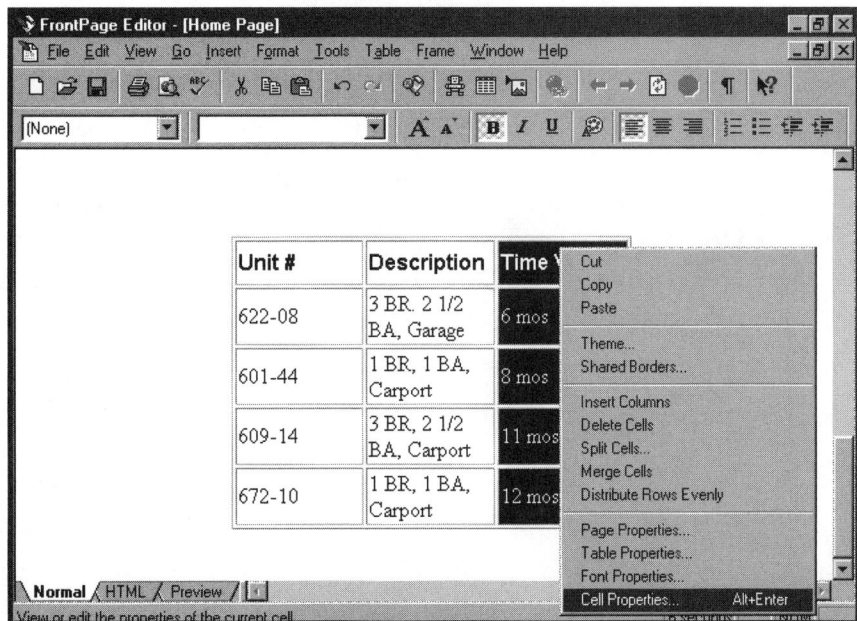

Figure 2.30

Changing
properties for
selected cells.

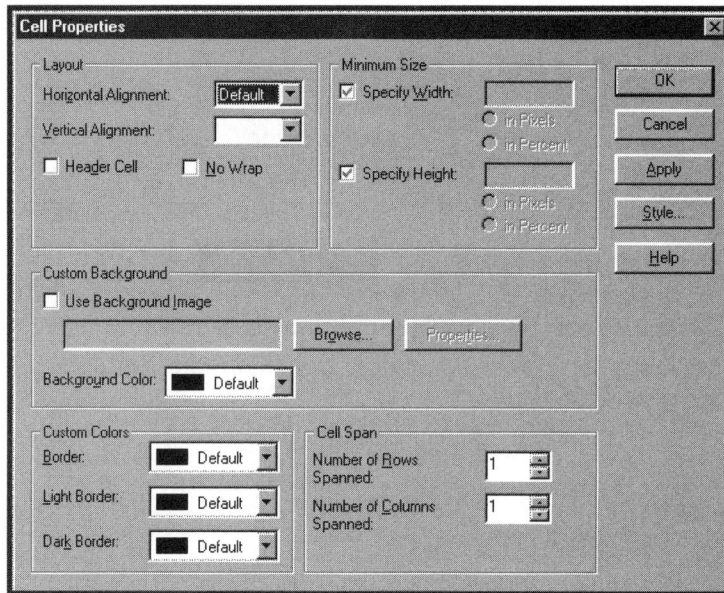

Figure 2.31

Redefining cell
properties.

and then clicking when the cursor becomes an arrow. After you
select the cell(s) you want to format, right-click.

2. Select Cell Properties in the shortcut menu.

3. Change the background or border color, as shown in Figure 2.32.

TIP

You can define some properties for a selected cell; however, row and column properties
take precedence. Don't expect to be able to change the width of a single cell if you've
already defined the width of that cell's column.

To delete a row, column, or an entire table, follow these steps:

1. Select the row, column, or table you want to delete.

2. Press the Delete key.

To insert a row or column, follow this steps:

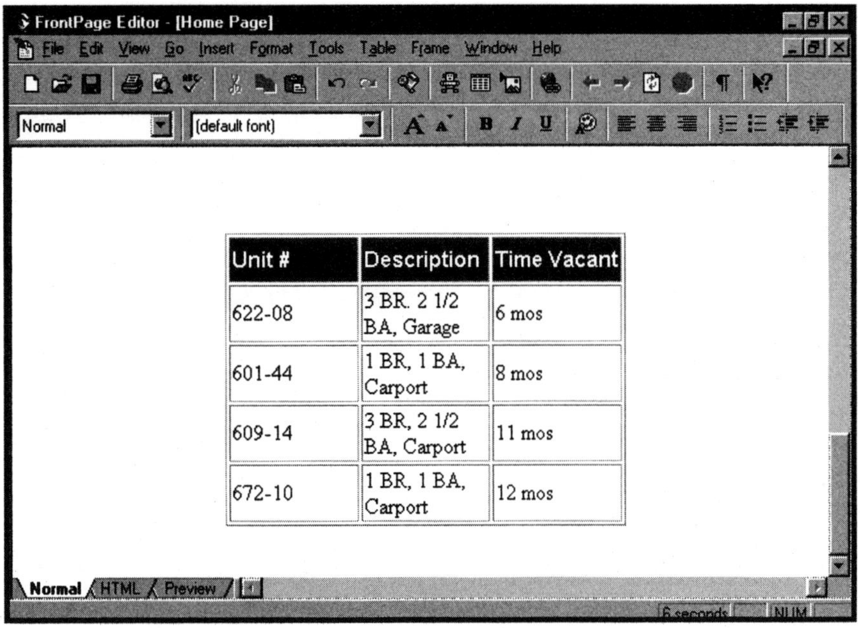

Figure 2.32

Changed cell
background colors.

1. Click (not right-click) in a cell next to where you want to insert the row(s) or column(s).

2. Select Table, Insert Rows or Columns.

3. Click on either the Rows or Columns radio button.

4. Enter the number of new rows or columns in the Number Of spin box.

5. Choose Above selection or Below selection and click on OK in the Insert Rows or Columns dialog box.

Adding Captions to Tables

You can add captions to annotate or provide a title for a table. If you have a line of text you want to associate with a table, captions solve the problem of having to reformat the text each time you reformat the table. Captions stay connected to the table and inherit the alignment properties

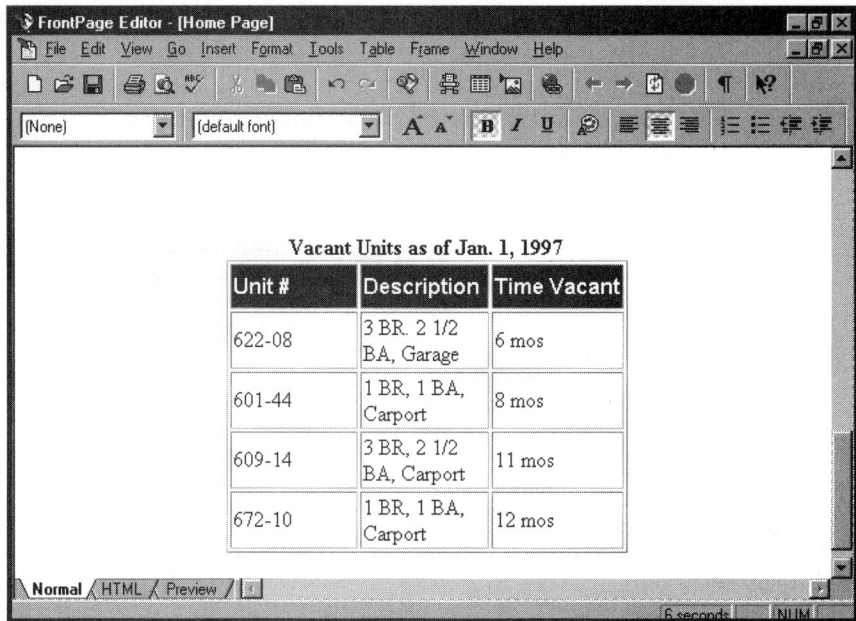

Figure 2.33

A table with
a caption.

assigned to the table. Captions look just like titles, as shown in Figure
2.33. To assign a caption to a table, follow these steps:

1. Click inside the table to which the caption will be attached.

2. Select Table, Insert Caption.

3. Type the caption text.

Coloring a Web Page

You can change the background color for your site, and you can change
the colors of text in your site. Before you go wild redecorating your Web
site, pause to appreciate how effective the clear black text is against the
default beige background. If you're the least bit unhappy with these col-

ors and think you might want to change them, remember the following points:

- ☼ Avoid choosing a background color that makes it difficult to read your text or appreciate your images.

- ☼ When you change background color, you might find that your text colors clash with, or fade into, the background. You can change the text color assigned to any text. Again, just because you can doesn't mean you should. Black text on a light background is easy to read and pleasant to look at. The trick is to experiment, get objective opinions, sleep on it, and make a final decision in the morning. But first, do a lot of experimenting just so you know what's possible.

- ☼ Avoid using blue or purple as text colors. These colors are associated with links, as you'll see in the Saturday Afternoon session. Because we haven't examined links yet, we'll leave this topic alone until you know enough to stay out of trouble.

Now that you appreciate the existing colors and have read the rules, redo your Web page. To change background color, follow these steps:

1. Right-click anywhere on your page in FrontPage Editor and select Page Properties.

2. In the Background tab, select a color from the Background list.

TIP

I strongly advise against changing the hyperlink colors until you have some idea of what a hyperlink is.

3. When you have selected a new background color for your page, click on OK in the Page Properties dialog box.

4. Take a careful look at how the text and graphic images contrast with your new background color. If you hate it, read on.

To remove background color, follow these steps:

1. Right-click on the page and select Page Properties from the short-cut menu.

2. Select a different color from the Background list in the Background tab of the Page Properties dialog box. Click on OK.

FrontPage comes with a nice selection of background images you can use to give your site that classy, professional look. Background images can liven up your page or create the look of a quality sheet of paper. To assign a background image, follow these steps:

1. Right-click anywhere on your page in FrontPage Editor and select Page Properties from the shortcut menu.

2. In the Background tab, click on the Background Image check box, as shown in Figure 2.34.

3. Click on the Browse button.

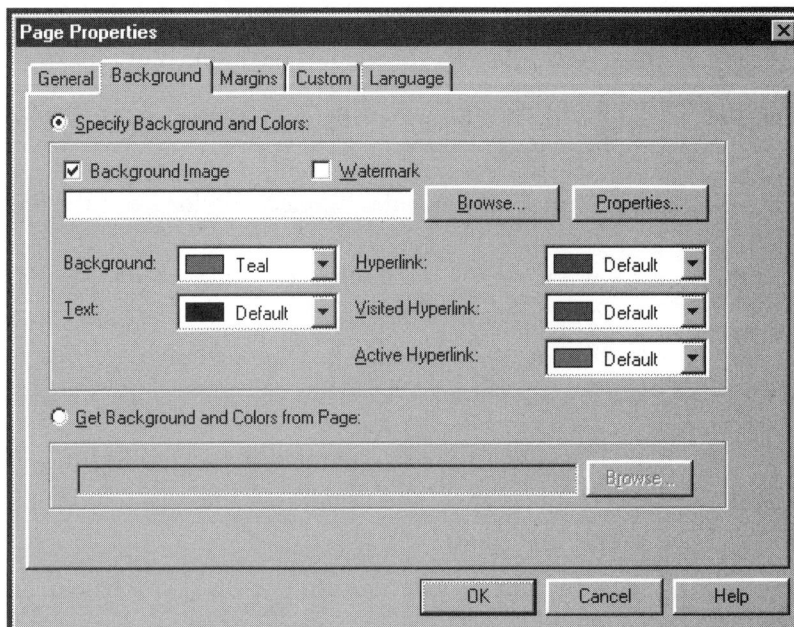

Figure 2.34

Selecting a background image.

4. Click on the Clip Art tab in the Select Background Image dialog box and select Backgrounds from the Category list.

5. Select one of the background patterns and click on OK in the Select Background Image dialog box.

6. Click on OK in the Page Properties dialog box and see how you like the background image. To really see what it will look like, save your page and preview the page in your browser, as shown in Figure 2.35.

7. You can always go back to the Page Properties dialog box, find the Background tab, and uncheck the Background Image check box if you decide you can do without a background image.

TIP The background image is a separate graphic image file that is attached to your Web site when you save the page. Save the image file when you're prompted.

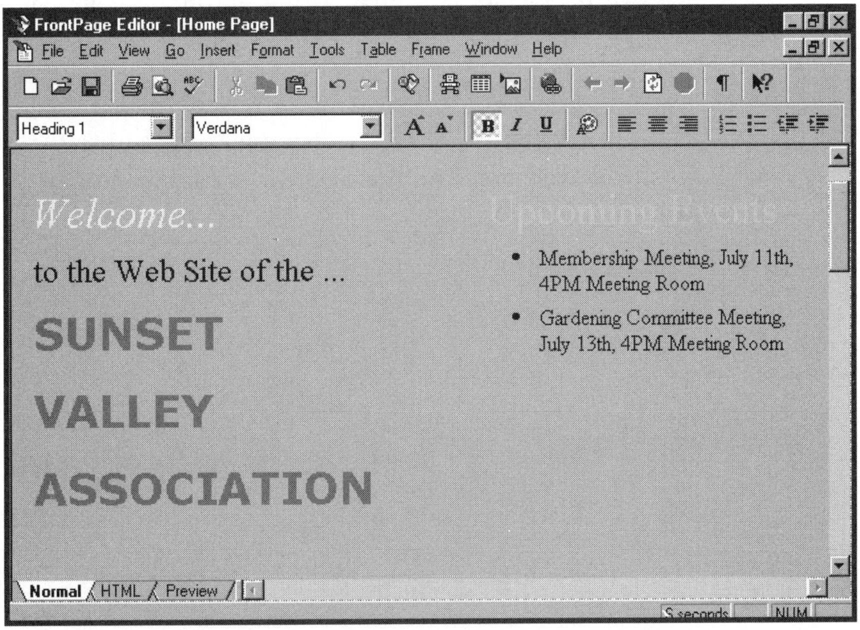

Figure 2.35

Your Web page, with a two-column invisible table, multiple colors, and different fonts.

Lunch Break!

Wow, that was a lot to accomplish before lunch! Before you leave your computer, remember to take the necessary steps to ensure that your files are saved and your hyperlinks are intact:

1. Save your page in FrontPage Editor.
2. Click on OK in the dialog boxes to refresh or create hyperlinks and saved files.

The formatting features you used this morning are all the tools you need to create attractive, easy-to-read Web pages. However, you can do so much more to enhance your site.

The next step in creating a professional page is to create and import customized graphic images. The selection of clip art that comes with FrontPage is OK, but a professional Web site needs unique graphic images.

Later today, you'll create hyperlinks—those zany bits of charged-up text and images that send your visitors off to their destination with a quick click of a mouse. Sunday, you'll automate your page with robots, add interactive forms, and explore the process of copying your Web site to a server. That's quite a bit.

You're well on your way to creating an attractive, useful, fun, and professional Web site. And the weekend's just beginning!

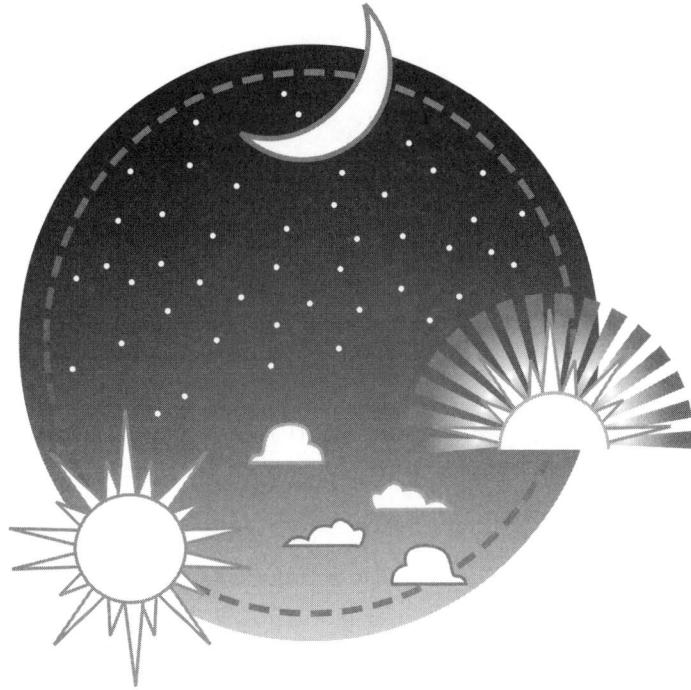

Designing Graphics with Image Composer

- ✿ Welcome to Image Composer
- ✿ Creating Text Sprites with the Image Composer
- ✿ Editing Graphic Images in FrontPage
- ✿ Changing Image File Types in FrontPage Editor
- ✿ Image Hyperlinks in FrontPage Explorer

In the Friday Evening session, you learned how to insert image files into your FrontPage Web site. FrontPage comes with clip art that you can use to liven up your pages without creating original art of your own.

For most Web site designers, that's not quite good enough. Original art can give your Web site a whole new dimension. Unique logos can identify your company and give your site a special look and feel. You can do fun things to stretch, bend, and warp text to make your Web site a real eye-catcher. In Figure 3.1, I combined text with shapes, fills, and shading to create customized buttons to enable visitors to jump to events and see a list of available units. To create graphic images like this, you need a graphic design package.

FrontPage comes bundled with its own first-class graphics package—Microsoft Image Composer. Image Composer allows you to create graphic images with zillions of effects. If you're graphically inclined, you may be inspired to further explore the program on your own, or with a book that only addresses Image Composer. For graphically challenged folks, such as myself, a little knowledge can be a good thing—you, too, can create smooth, sophisticated, and flashy graphic images for your site with Image Composer. If you want to use a different graphics package, skip ahead to this afternoon's session, "Editing Graphic Images in FrontPage."

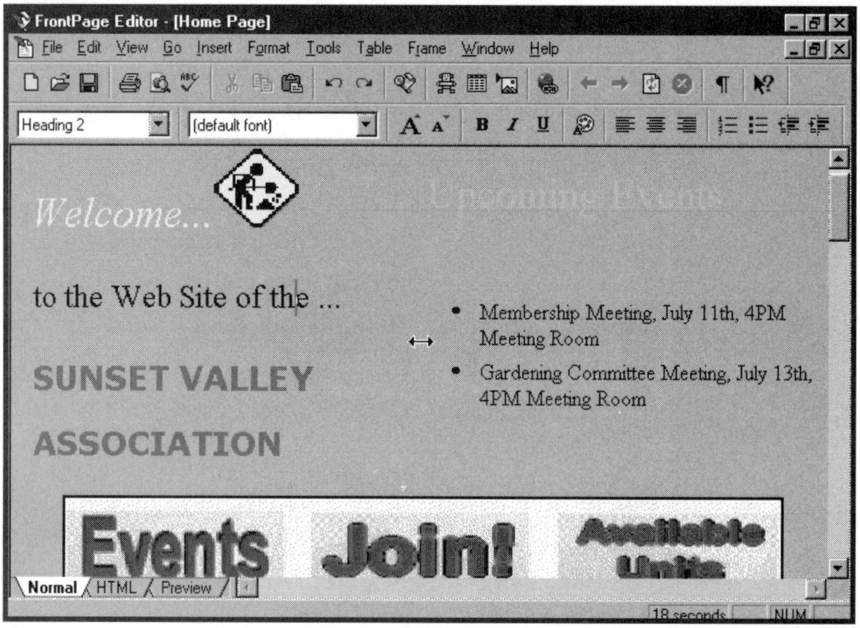

Figure 3.1

Text, shapes, shading, and shadows can be combined to make buttons.

Welcome to Image Composer

Microsoft Image Composer is part of the FrontPage package. It's a handy and helpful graphics package. If you explore all its features, you will be impressed with the collection of tools in Image Composer that modify or enhance scanned photos. Those particular effects, however, are beyond the scope of this book.

You'll concentrate on working with shapes and text in Image Composer. You might be wondering why you should work with graphical text. After all, FrontPage Editor allows you to format text in dozens of fonts with a full palette of colors. You should use graphical text created in Image Composer for three reasons:

✪ Some browsers still can't interpret all the available fonts in FrontPage Editor.

- ○ Using images in standard formats like .gif or .jpg assures you that the Web site will appear almost as it was designed, regardless of being viewed on a Mac or a PC.

- ○ Graphical text can be warped, stretched, filled with sophisticated shading, and combined with shapes to make logos, buttons, signs, and artistic presentations. In short, working with graphical text is a veritable grab bag of artistic confections.

You'll also combine text with shapes. After you become proficient at combining text and graphics, you'll create image maps. Image maps are graphical objects that provide hyperlinks to areas in your Web site or other sites. In the Saturday Evening session, you'll combine hyperlinks with the graphic images you create and put together image maps.

Starting Microsoft Image Composer from FrontPage

If you performed the Typical installation of FrontPage, then Image Composer has been installed for you. If you selected Custom Install and chose not to install Image Composer, you can install it now by running the setup program again and selecting Custom Install and then Image Composer. After Image Composer has been installed, launch it from either FrontPage Editor or FrontPage Explorer. Typically you'll be working in FrontPage Editor when you decide to include a graphic image. Follow these steps to add a graphic image:

1. From FrontPage Editor, select Tools, Show Image Editor, as shown in Figure 3.2.

2. You can also view or open Image Composer from the FrontPage Explorer by double-clicking on the graphic file or by clicking on the Show Image Editor button in the toolbar, as shown in Figure 3.3.

3. If you have installed Image Composer, either of the two preceding steps will launch Image Composer, as shown in Figure 3.4.

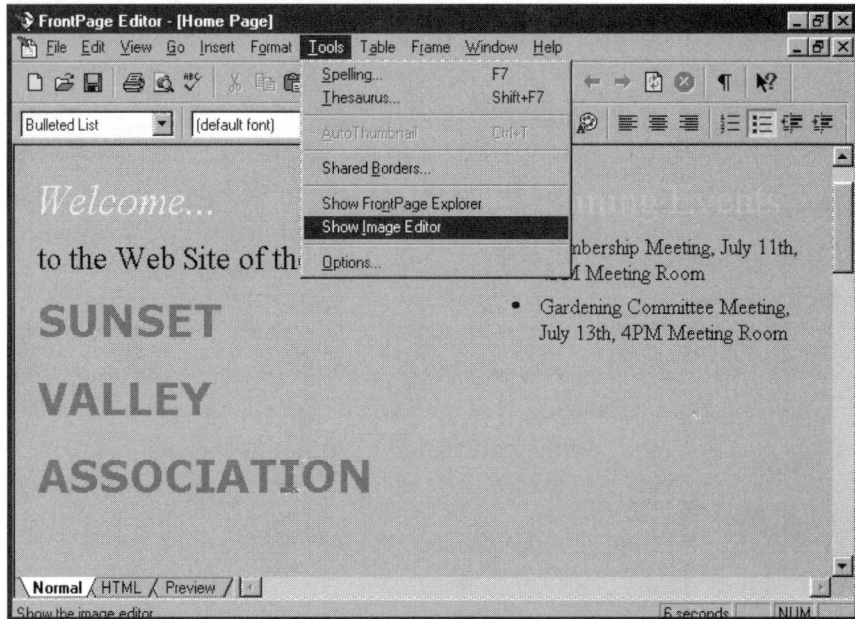

Figure 3.2

Launching Image
Composer from
FrontPage Editor.

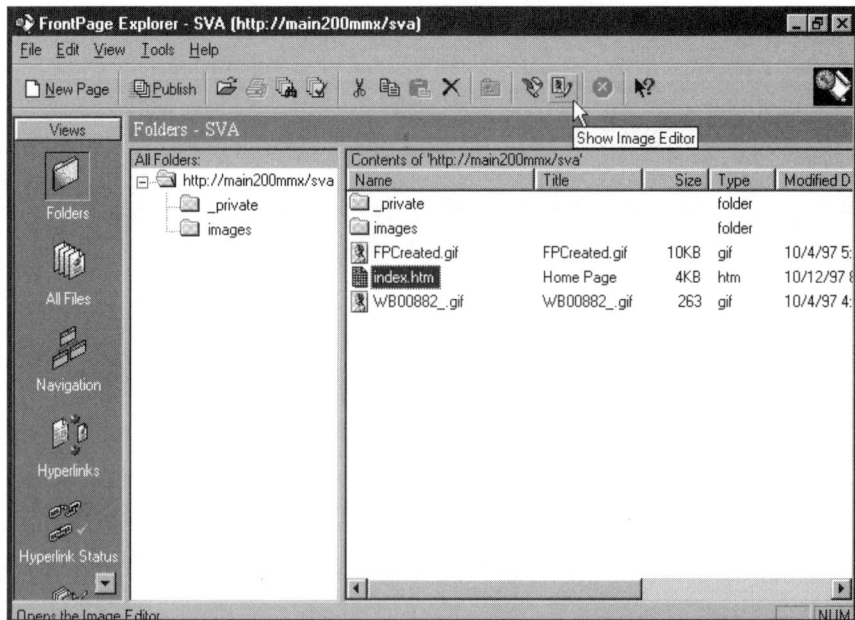

Figure 3.3

Starting Image
Composer from
FrontPage Explorer.

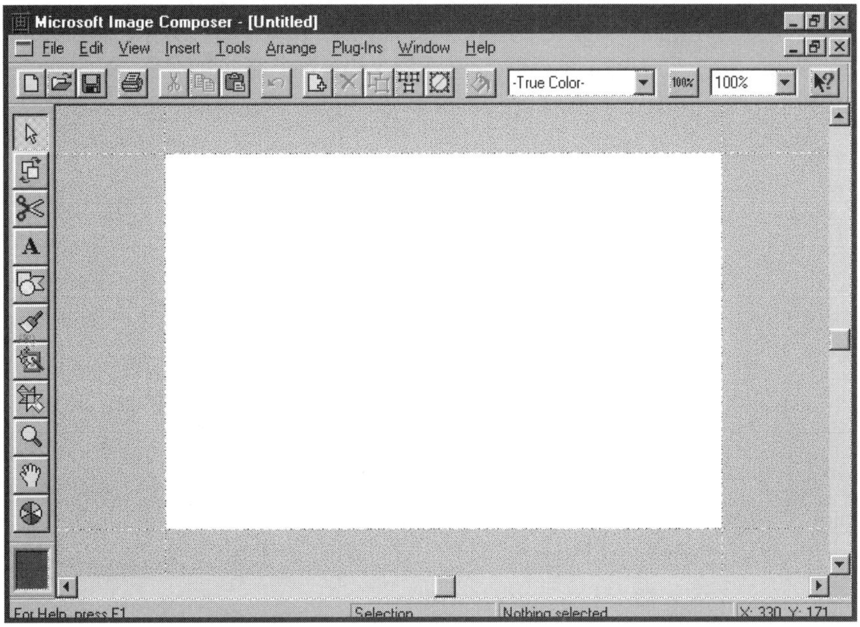

Figure 3.4

Image
Composer—
the digital
canvas awaits.

CAUTION After you launch Image Composer, use the Taskbar to switch back and forth between FrontPage and Image Composer. The two options you just explored for starting Image Composer directly from FrontPage open a new copy of Image Composer each time you use them. If you click four times on the Show Image Editor button in FrontPage Explorer, you end up with four copies of Image Composer running, and that's not a good idea. Microsoft recommends that you don't have more than a couple copies of Image Composer open at a time to save memory. If you have opened Image Composer once, that's enough. After that, use the Taskbar to switch back and forth between FrontPage and Image Composer.

Getting Your Bearings in Image Composer

A *sprite* is the basic element of an Image Composer graphic object. It can be text, a circle, an imported photograph, or a wavy line. A sprite can be created in Image Composer and then edited. Also, sprites can be combined; however, most of the effects available in Image Composer—ranging from color fills to outlines and resizing—are applied to one sprite at a time.

The Image Composer screen isn't very entertaining when you open the program; however, it does have a lot of potential. The Image Composer screen is like a big, empty canvas with many art tools available. You won't work with every tool, but you'll use several of them to get off to a good start. Understanding the Image Composer layout starts with the relationship between the main elements of the screen:

- ✿ The toolbar
- ✿ The toolbox
- ✿ The palette
- ✿ The color swatch
- ✿ The workspace

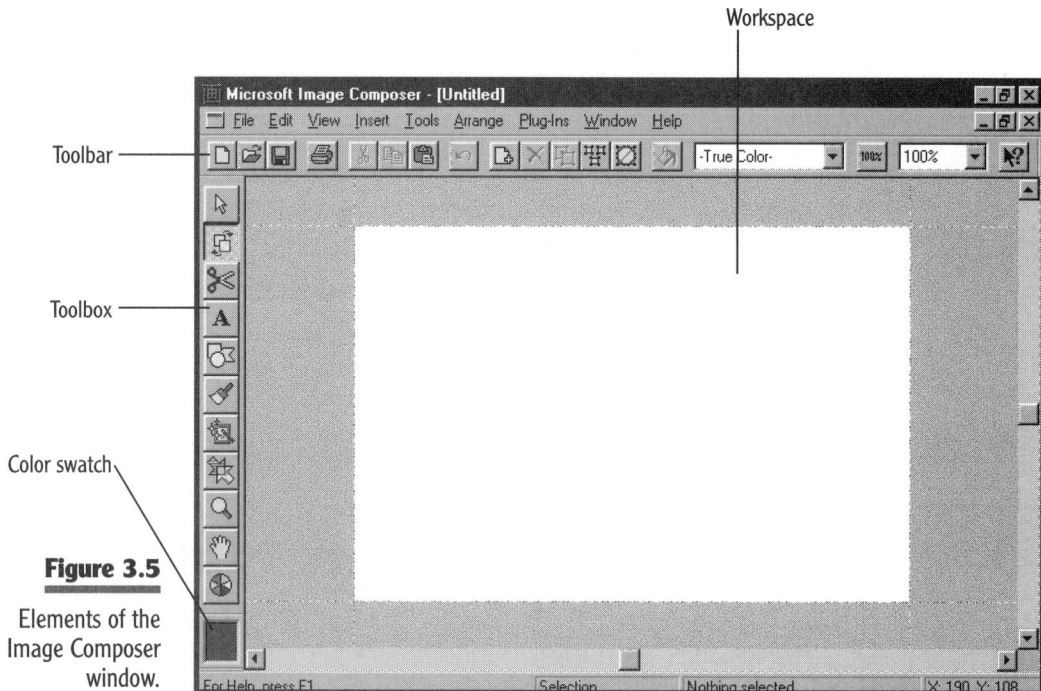

Figure 3.5

Elements of the Image Composer window.

The toolbar shouldn't be too mystifying if you've used other Microsoft Office products. Even your experience with FrontPage should help you recognize the tools for opening, saving, and printing files. The other tools in the toolbar will be identified as needed.

The workspace is where you compose and edit sprites. The color swatch lets you pick a default color to be assigned to the sprites you create.

The heart of working with Image Composer is using the tools in the toolbox. The toolbox is the set of buttons on the left side of the screen. When you point to a button in the toolbox, a helpful tool tip identifies that tool. When you click on a tool in the toolbox, a palette appears at the bottom of the workspace that has features associated with it. You won't use all the tools listed in Table 3.1, but at least you'll get a sense of what they do.

To get familiar with the Image Composer interface, click on different tools in the toolbox and take a peek at the different palettes that appear.

Creating Text Sprites with the Image Composer

The Text tool allows you to enter text, and then transforms it into a graphic image. This enables you to apply the whole range of Image Composer effects to the text. For example, you can give your text a vanishing point (see Figure 3.6).

You can also apply shadows to your text, as shown in Figure 3.7.

After you start working with shapes, graphical text can be combined with shapes to create artistic presentations, like the one shown in Figure 3.8.

To create a text sprite, follow these steps:

1. Click on the Text tool in the Image Composer toolbox, as shown in Figure 3.9.
2. When you select the Text tool, the Text palette appears and your cursor turns into a plus sign. Move the cursor to the point where you want to position the text and then type your text.

TABLE 3.1 IMAGE COMPOSER TOOLS	
Tool Name	**What It Does**
Selection	Selects sprites or other objects.
Arrange	Moves sprites from front to back and aligns them.
Cutout	Cuts out a portion of a sprite for use in other sprites.
Text	Composes lines of text that are transformed into graphic images.
Shapes	Draws rectangles, ovals, polygons, and a variety of lines and shapes that are referred to as *splines*.
Paint	Adds paint-type effects to sprites.
Effects	Transforms your scanned photos into drawings, watercolor paintings, charcoal sketches, or over a dozen other art media.
Texture Transfer	Defines a texture to be used on two or more overlapping sprites.
Zoom	Zooms in to show a close-up of your image. (Click on this button while holding down the Ctrl key to zoom out to see more of the screen.)
Pan	Scrolls the screen when you click and drag.
Color Tuning	Adjusts colors in scanned photos and other images.

3. Click on the Font drop-down list in the Text palette to select a font. You can choose bold and/or italics in the Style drop-down list, if you wish, and a font size in the Size list box. For example, choose 18 point Arial in bold, as shown in Figure 3.10.

4. You can change the script used for your text, but unless your page contains different language characters, you should use Western.

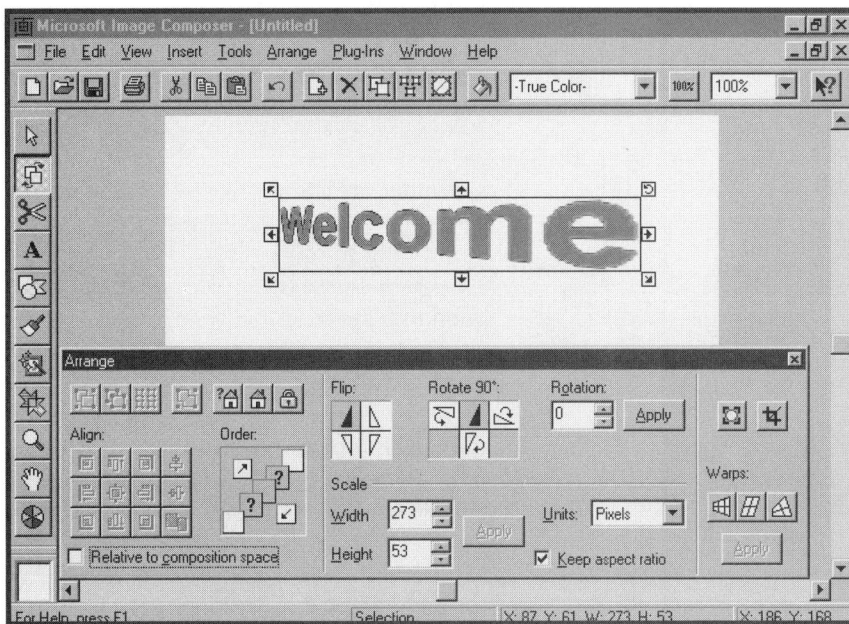

Figure 3.6

Text with a
vanishing point.

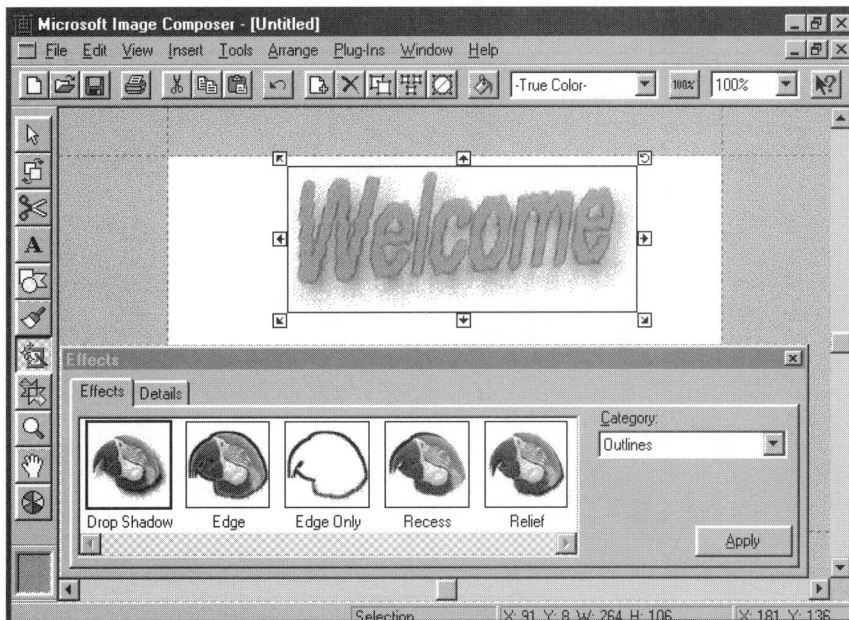

Figure 3.7

Text with a
drop shadow.

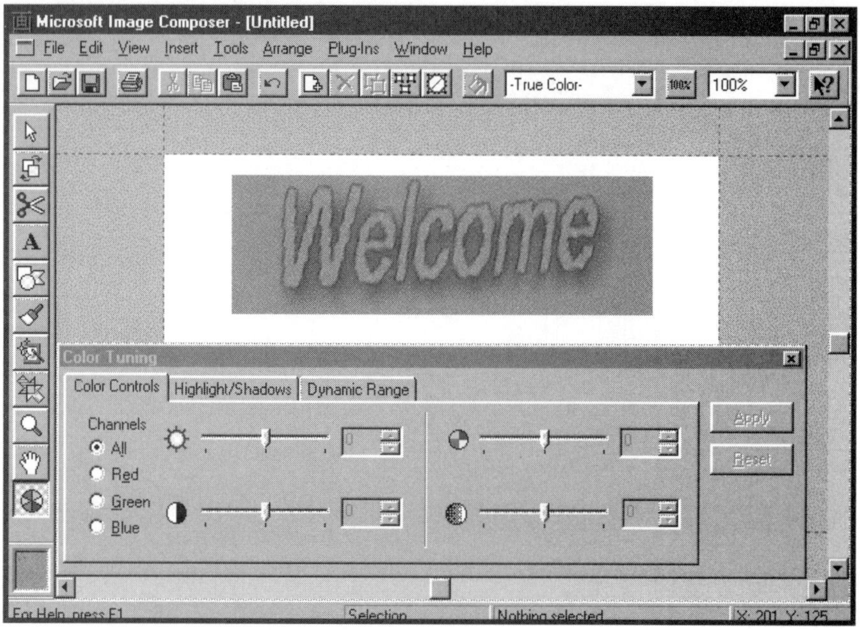

Figure 3.8

Text with a rectangle.

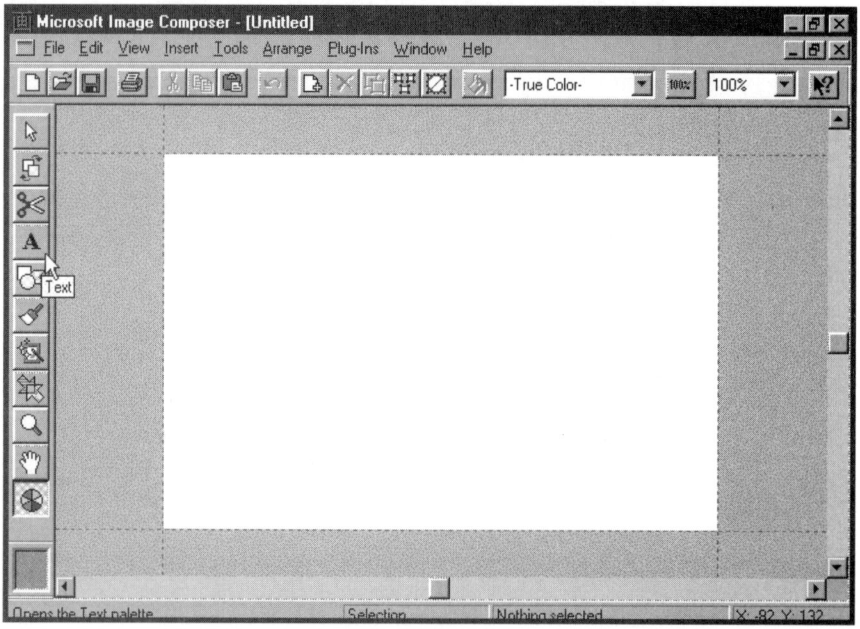

Figure 3.9

The Text tool.

Figure 3.10

Making a large, bold statement in Arial.

5. You can justify your text to the left, center, or right by clicking on the appropriate justification icon.

6. If you want to have your text underlined, check the Underline check box. Likewise, if you prefer to have your text "smoothed out" (that is, anti-aliased), check the Smoothing check box.

7. Once your font looks the way you want it, close the Text palette. An example of a new text sprite is shown in Figure 3.11.

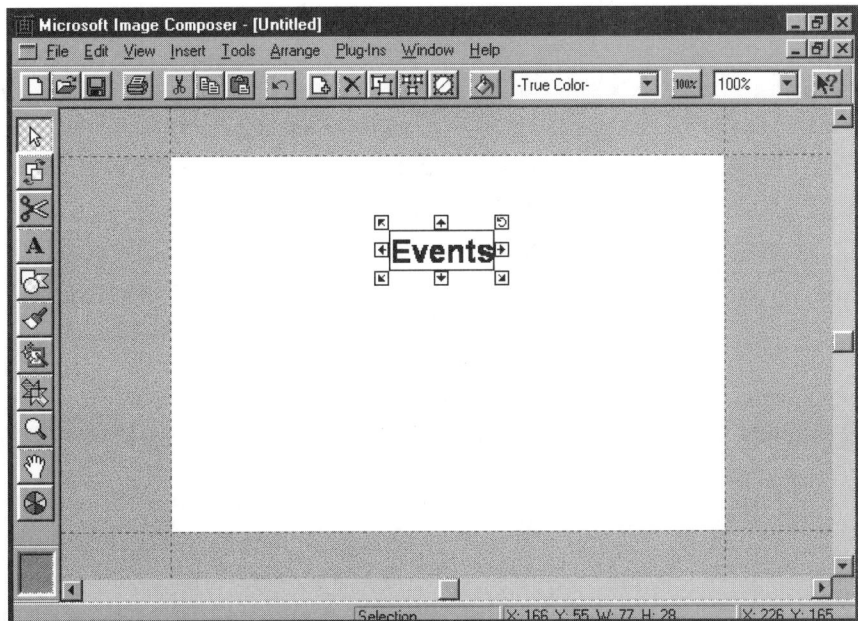

Figure 3.11

Poof! A text sprite appears.

The adjustable slider in the middle of the Text palette is called the Opacity slider. It determines the amount of transparency or opaqueness of your image. Normally, you'll want text to be completely opaque, so leave the slider at 100 percent.

You created a sprite! Note that it's surrounded by sizing handles on the top, bottom, right, and left, as well as on three corners. The upper-right corner handle is the rotation handle, which is used to rotate the sprite. You'll explore sizing later.

Because your text sprite is a graphic image, you cannot edit the text within it. You can, however, change the text in the Text palette and create a new sprite. To edit a text sprite, follow these steps:

1. Highlight the old sprite and delete it by pressing the Delete key.

2. Edit, or completely retype, the text in the Text palette by selecting the sprite, right-clicking, and selecting Edit Text.

3. Close the Text palette when you're finished making changes to the text.

Were you hoping for spell-checking and search-and-replace features? A thesaurus maybe? It's not quite like that. Remember, after you click on the Apply button in the Text palette, your text converts to a graphic image. Don't try editing sprite text. You aren't able to boldface or italicize any more than you are able to edit text chiseled into a stone wall. If you want to edit the text in a sprite, delete it and create a new one.

Moving, Sizing, and Rotating Sprites

So, what *can* you do with text sprites? Tons! After your sprites are generated, you can move, resize, and rotate them. You should do your best to create a sprite in the size you want before you generate it. That means selecting the font before you generate the image with the Apply button.

Rotating text can be visually stunning. Visitors to your Web site will won-der how the text became rotated. Don't overdo it, though—a little rotated text goes a long way.

When you're working with just one sprite, you don't need to move it. When it's time to place your sprite in a Web site, copy it from Image Composer—its location in the workspace doesn't matter. However, soon you'll be working with more than one sprite at a time, so you should prac-tice moving sprites now. To move a sprite, follow these steps:

1. Move your cursor directly over the sprite. The cursor becomes a four-sided arrow, as shown in Figure 3.12.

2. Click and drag to move the cursor to a new location, as shown in Figure 3.13.

3. Release the mouse button when the cursor is where you want to move the selected sprite.

Figure 3.12

Getting ready to move a sprite.

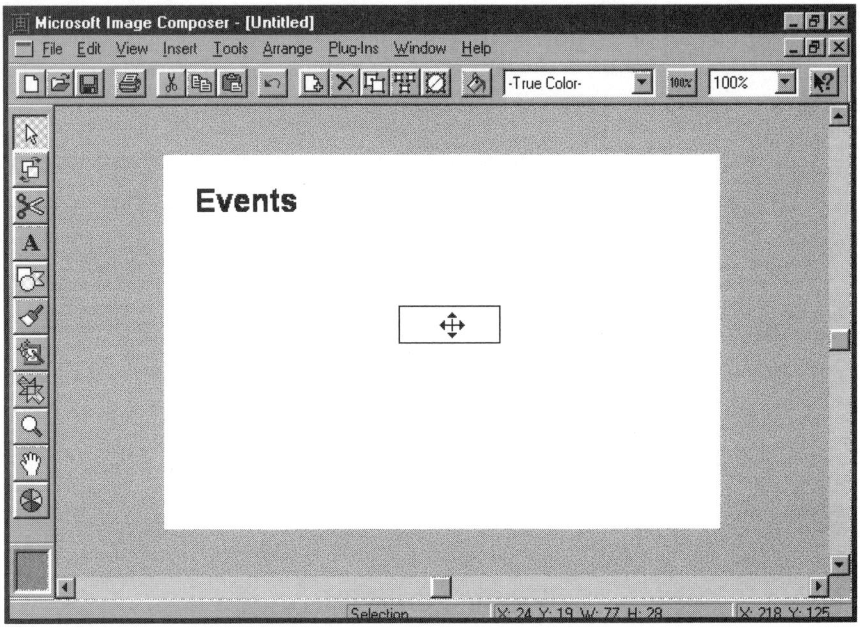

Figure 3.13

A sprite on
the move.

To resize a sprite, follow these steps:

1. Place your cursor over one of the seven arrow cursors.
2. Click and drag the arrow in to shrink the sprite (or out to enlarge the sprite), as shown in Figure 3.14.
3. When you have resized the sprite to your satisfaction, release the mouse button. The sprite is then recomposed in the new size.

TIP

If you try to enlarge a text sprite too much, you'll be warned by Image Composer's quality police that the image quality will suffer. This warning tells you that crisper, sharper-looking text can be created if you select a larger font before you generate the image.

To rotate a sprite, follow these steps:

1. Click on the rotation handle in the upper-right corner of a selected sprite.

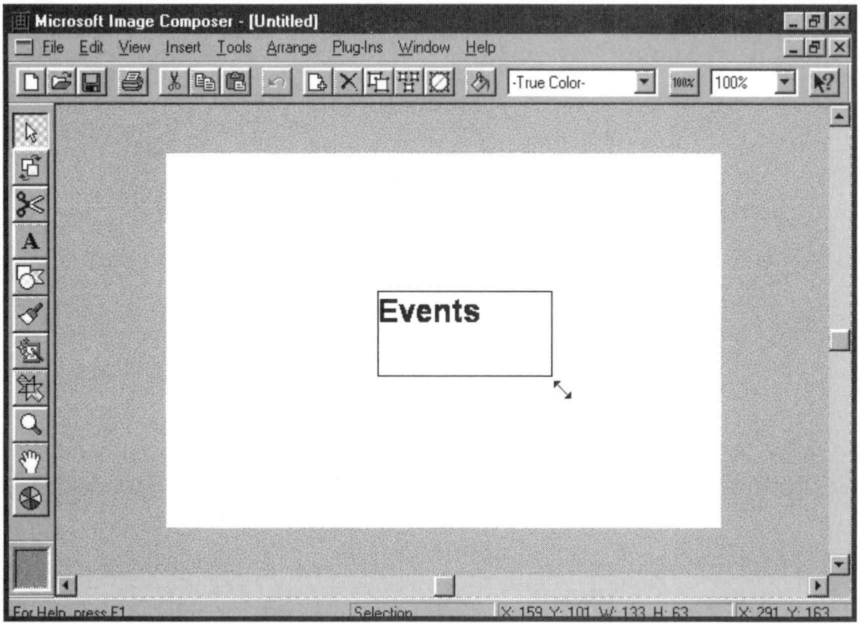

Figure 3.14

Shrinking
the sprite.

2. Drag down and to the right to rotate the sprite clockwise, and up and to the left to rotate the sprite counterclockwise, as shown in Figure 3.15.

3. Release the mouse. The sprite is then recomposed at a tilt, as shown in Figure 3.16.

Special Effect Sprites

The Effects palette is loaded with effects to enhance your text with shadows, outlines, edging, relief, and more. This palette is also stocked with some warp effects that allow you to stretch and reshape your text in many different ways. To outline text, follow these steps:

1. Select the text sprite you want to outline. Then, click on the Effects tool in the toolbox. The Effects palette appears, as shown in Figure 3.17.

Figure 3.15

A tipsy sprite.

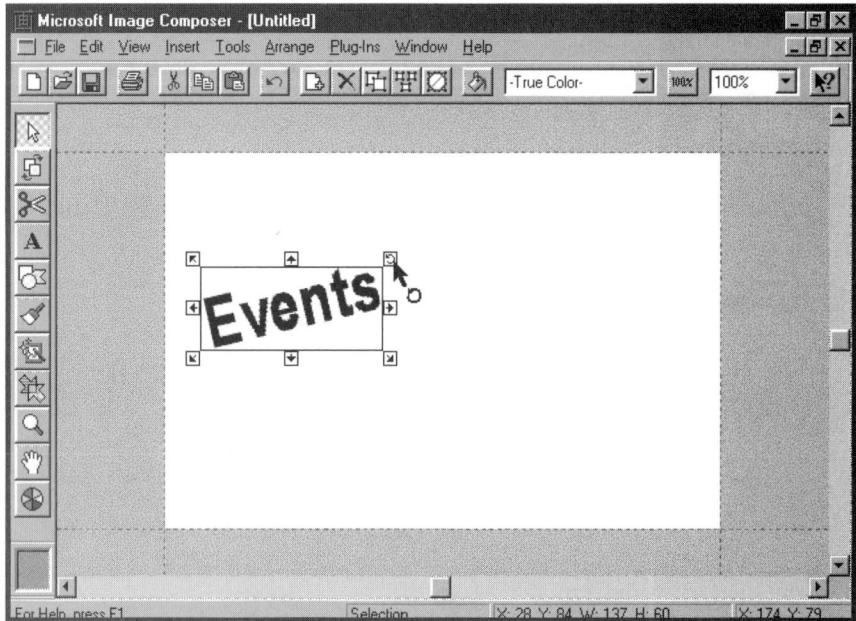

Figure 3.16

A sprite at a tilt.

Figure 3.17

The Effects palette.

2. From the Category drop-down list on the right side of the palette, choose Outlines if that group is not already selected.

3. Click on the Drop Shadow rectangle to select this effect.

4. Click on the Details tab and then click on the Color box to display the Color Picker dialog box.

5. With the True Color tab selected, choose a color to be used for the drop shadow by clicking on it in the Color Matrix box. Experiment by clicking on various colors until you've found the one you like, as shown in Figure 3.18. Click on OK to close the Color Picker.

TIP By holding down the mouse button, scan the Color Matrix list, displaying whatever color is under the cursor. Try it to discover the vibrant color you're after.

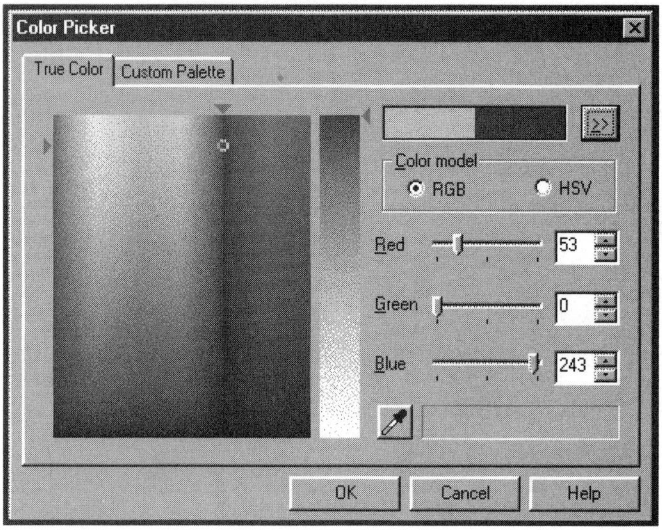

Figure 3.18

Finally finding that elusive special color!

6. Click on the Apply button on the Effects palette to apply your new colorful shadow. Click on X to close the Effects palette.

TIP

If you don't like an effect, use Ctrl+Z or Edit, Undo from the menu. If you apply a second effect, that effect is *added* to the existing effect and does not replace it. You'll get plenty of use out of the Undo command as you experiment with effects. You can use Undo after you have applied an effect.

NOTE

Another color swatch can be found at the bottom of the toolbox. The color swatch inside the palette affects coloring of edges and shadows. You'll explore this other color swatch shortly.

The Opacity slider comes in handy in setting shadows. A 60 percent opaque shadow gives off a shadowy, ethereal vibe, as shown in Figure 3.19.

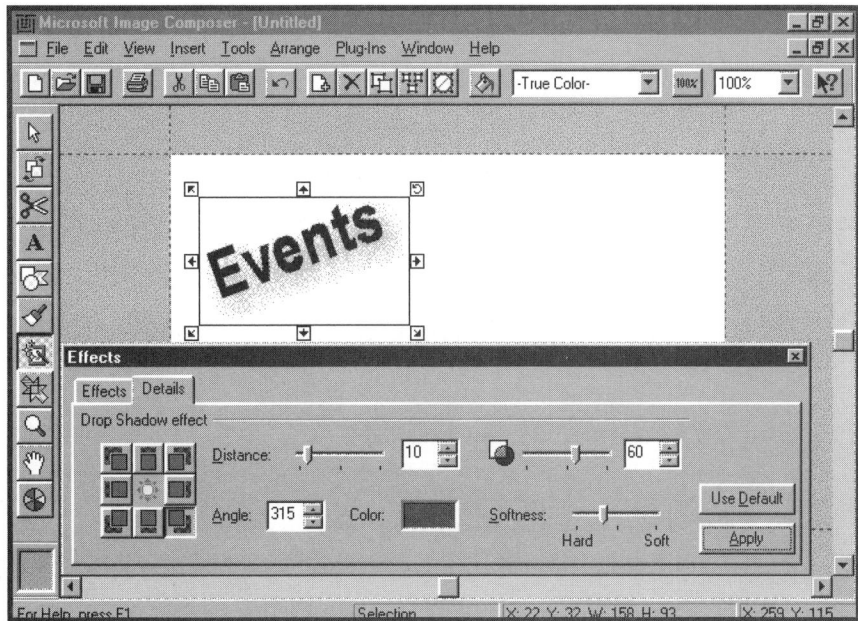

Figure 3.19

A semi-opaque
shadow.

Arranging Your Sprites

Another powerful palette is the Arrange palette. It contains all the tools needed to twist and distort your image. To display the Arrange palette, click on the Arrange tool, as shown in Figure 3.20.

The Arrange palette has four groups: the Align and Order group, the Rotation group, the Scale group, and the Warp group. Each of these groups is discussed in the following sections.

The Align and Order Group

We'll briefly touch on this group, because it's a bit advanced and you won't use it for a little while (at least not this weekend). This group aligns two or more sprites according to the button selected. Tool tips identify the alignment of each button. The Order control allows you to position

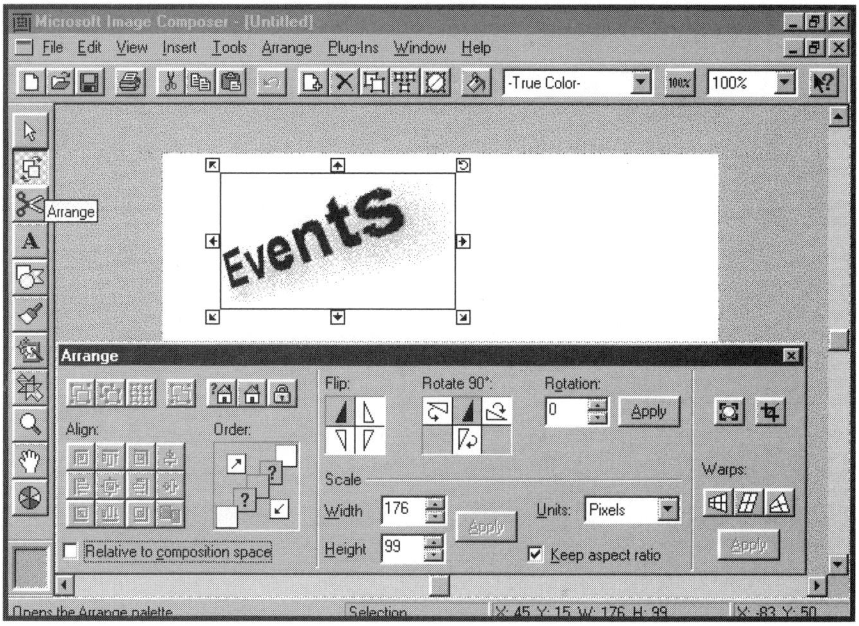

Figure 3.20

The Arrange
palette.

a given sprite relative to another sprite. For example, you probably want
your foreground sprite in front of the background sprite. This control can
set these positions.

The buttons with the cute little houses (located above the Order control)
set and restore the home position of a sprite or group of sprites. For example, you might want to experiment with the placement of a sprite on the
screen. Before doing so, click on the Set Home Position button, which is
shown in Figure 3.21. You can then move the sprite around the screen.
To restore the sprite back to its home position, just click on the Return
to Home Position button.

Figure 3.21

Setting the
home position.

Once satisfied with the position of the sprite, simply click on the Lock button to prevent the sprite from being moved. Should you later discover that the sprite must be moved, click on the Lock button again to unlock the sprite.

The Rotation Group

One group you might use from time to time is the Rotation group. These controls allow you to flip and rotate your sprite image. All you need to do to flip or rotate the image is click on the appropriate flip or rotate button, as shown in Figure 3.22. Remember, you can always select Undo in the Edit menu to erase your flip or rotation.

TIP

Sometimes you might want to rotate an image somewhat, but not a full 90 degrees. If you want to rotate a sprite 30 degrees, for example, type 30 in the Rotation combo box and then click on the Apply button. The sprite will be rotated 30 degrees.

The Scale Group

The Scale group, shown in Figure 3.23, presents the decimal values for the height and width of your sprite. This is just another way to change

Figure 3.22

The Rotation controls.

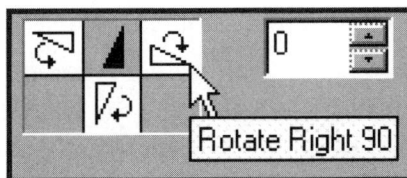

Figure 3.23

The Scale controls.

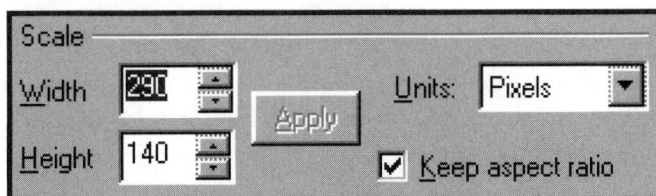

the size of your sprite. However, you'll probably find grabbing a corner of the image and moving it with the mouse much easier.

As with FrontPage tables, you can specify whether the values displayed in the Height and Width spin controls represent pixels or a percentage of the screen. Unless you have reason to do so, leave the Units drop-down list set to Pixels.

The Keep Aspect Ratio check box allows you to massively distort your sprite image. Therefore, if you want to make mild changes to the sprite's appearance, leave this check box checked. On the other hand, if you're looking to wildly distort the image, uncheck the box and keep the Undo menu item handy.

The Warp Group

The Warp group is the most strange and fun of all the groups, but there's not a lot of practical use for it in everyday life. Still, the effects in this group are fun, so try them out and keep the Undo keystrokes (Ctrl+Z) handy. In Figure 3.24, an Escher warp is applied to some text. A time and a place for an intriguing effect like this must exist.

Interactive warps allow you to reshape your text. To apply interactive warps, follow these steps:

1. Select the text sprite to be reshaped.
2. Click on the Arrange tool (if it's not already selected) to display the Arrange palette.
3. Select one of the model warps and read the Help message that appears: "Drag the edges of the bounding box to warp the sprite." Click on OK.
4. Each warp transform model works differently, but they all allow you to reshape your sprite by clicking and dragging with your cursor. In the example shown in Figure 3.24, the second warp transform model is used. The trapezoidal cursor appears and creates a "leavin' ya behind" type of effect.

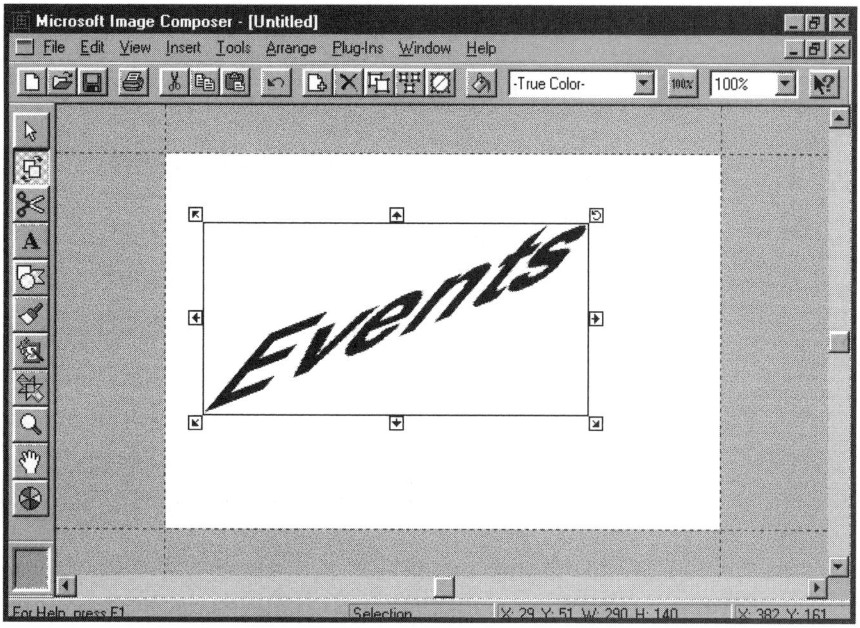

Figure 3.24

Warped events.

5. After you reshape the selected sprite, release the mouse button and use the <u>A</u>pply button in the palette to regenerate your sprite with the selected effect. The regenerated sprite appears in the workspace.

Working with Shape Sprites

Shape sprites are handy for creating buttons and tools for your Web site. Here, you'll create and fill some shapes. In a bit, you'll combine these shapes with text to make buttons. This evening, you'll use those buttons as hyperlinks. To create a rectangular sprite, follow these steps:

1. Click on the Shapes tool in the toolbox. The Shapes palette appears, as shown in Figure 3.25.

2. Select the square icon from the shape tools on the left side of the Shapes palette.

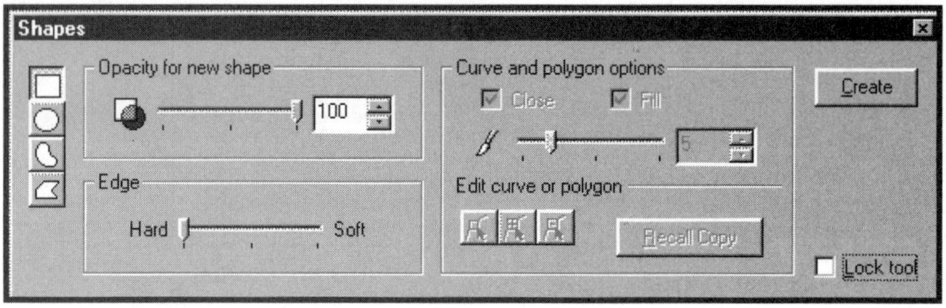

Figure 3.25

The Shapes palette.

TIP

If it's a square you want, hold down the Ctrl key while you draw the rectangle. This keeps the sides equal.

---

3. Click and drag to adjust the lengths of the sides to form a rectangle, as shown in Figure 3.26.

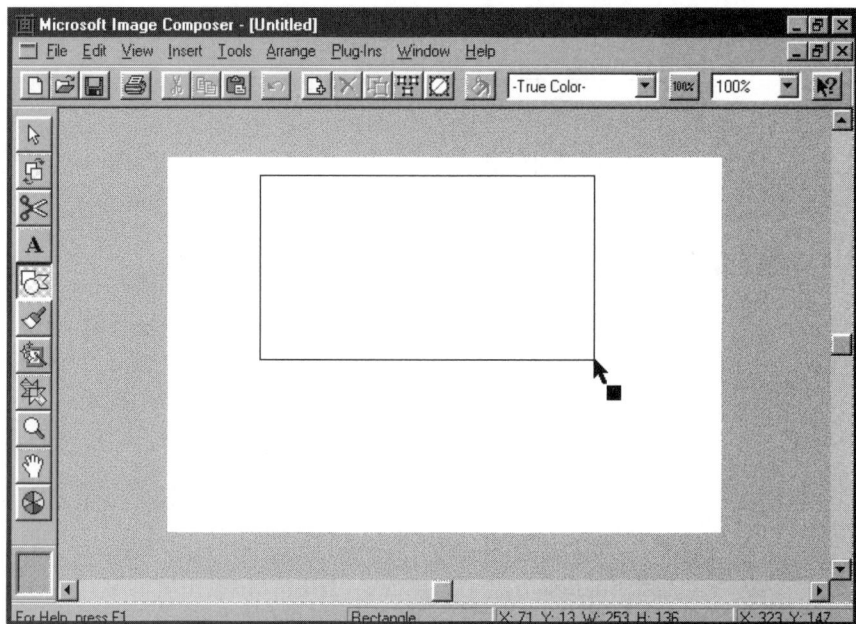

Figure 3.26

Drawing a rectangle.

■ ■

TIP If you need several tries to get your shape right, click on the Lock Tool check box in the lower-right corner of the Shapes palette. This feature keeps your selected shape until you pick a new one.

■ ■

To create an oval sprite, follow these steps:

1. Click on the Shapes tool (if it's not already selected) in the toolbox. The Shapes palette appears.

2. Select the oval icon from the shape tools on the left side of the Shapes palette. Then click and drag to draw your oval in the work-space, as shown in Figure 3.27.

■ ■

TIP To draw a circle, hold down the Ctrl key while you draw the oval.

■ ■

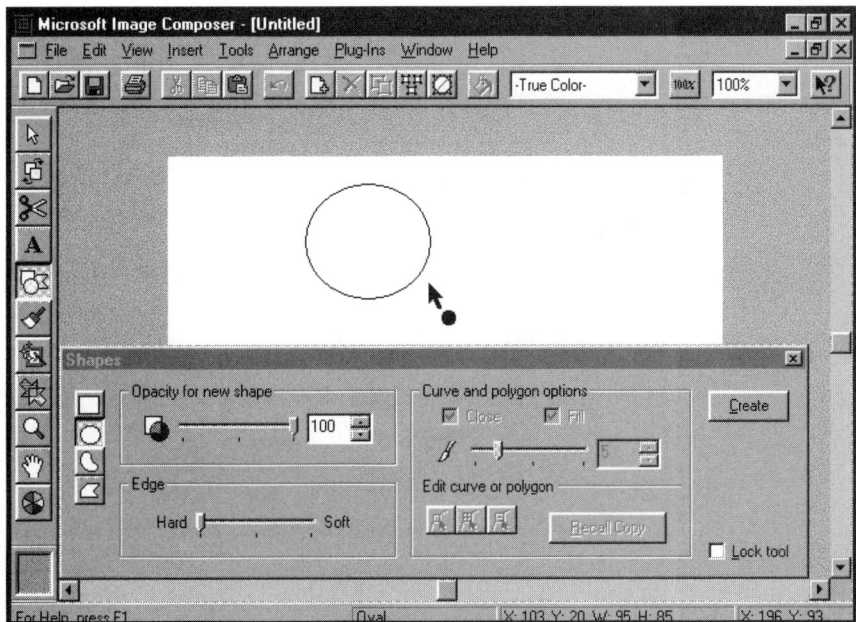

Figure 3.27

Drawing an oval.

Curves and polygons are more flexible and powerful shape tools. Curves are lines with an "S" (for shape). You can use the Curve tool to draw wavy lines, straight lines, shapes, closed shapes, and zigzag lines. Polygons can be any shape.

When you create a curve or polygon, you can select whether the resulting sprite is a closed shape or a line. If you select the Close check box in the Shapes palette with one of these two shape tools, your sprite will be closed, as shown in Figure 3.28. An example of an open curve is shown in Figure 3.29.

To create an open curve, follow these steps:

1. Select the Shapes tool and then click on the Curve tool in the Shapes palette.

2. Deselect both the Close and Fill check boxes in the palette.

NOTE The Close and Fill check boxes are only available for curves and polygons.

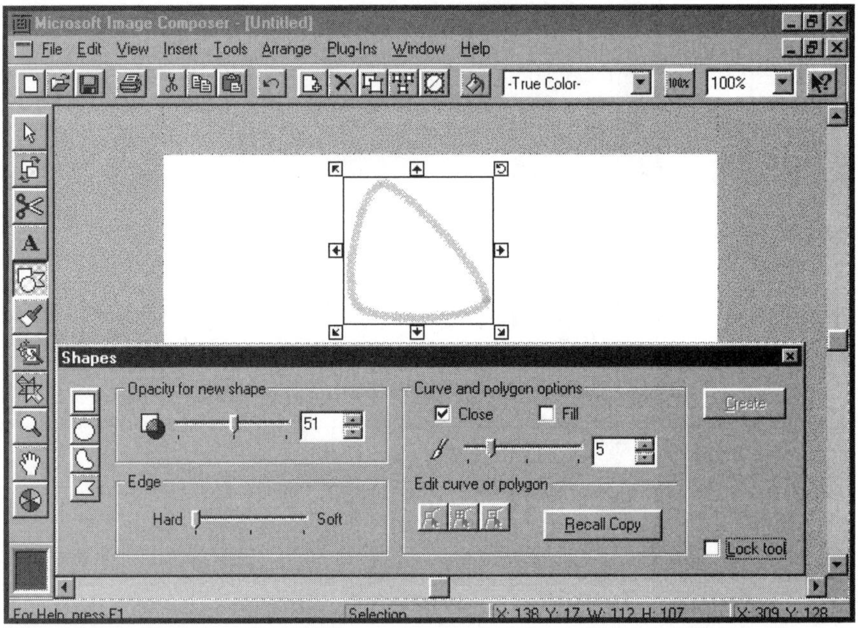

Figure 3.28

A closed curve.

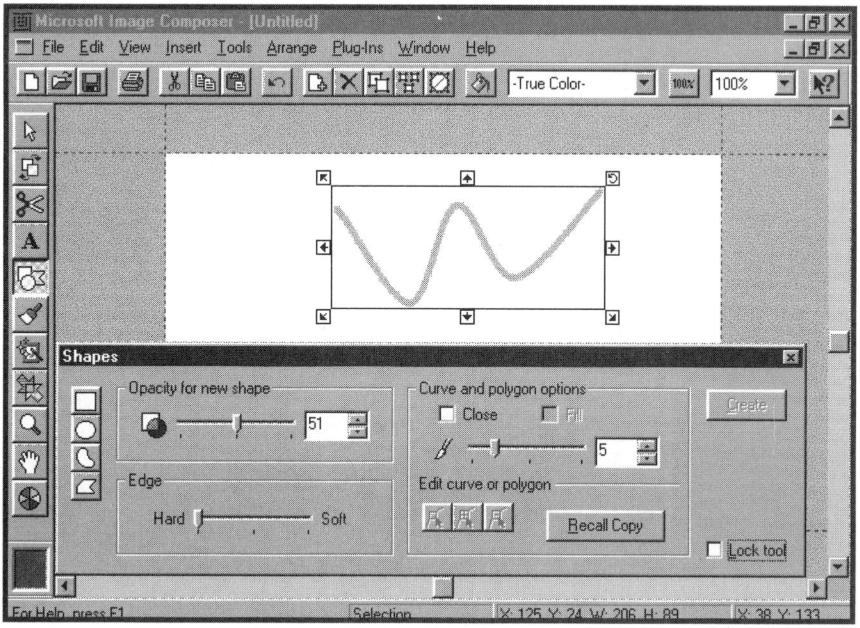

Figure 3.29

An open curve, or
the design for a
roller coaster?

3. With the S-shaped cursor that appears, click in the workspace where you want to start your curve.

4. Continue to click on each nodal point for the curve.

5. When you have traced the shape of your curve, click on the Create button in the Shapes palette. The curve appears in the workspace.

Polygon sprites can be used to create dynamic shapes behind text in buttons. To create a polygon sprite, follow these steps:

1. Select the Shapes tool and then click on the Polygon tool in the Shapes palette.

2. Deselect both the Close and Fill check boxes in the palette if you want to draw an unfilled polygon. Select both check boxes for a filled polygon. Figure 3.30 shows two closed, unfilled polygons.

NOTE A closed polygon can be filled or unfilled. A polygon that isn't closed can't be filled.

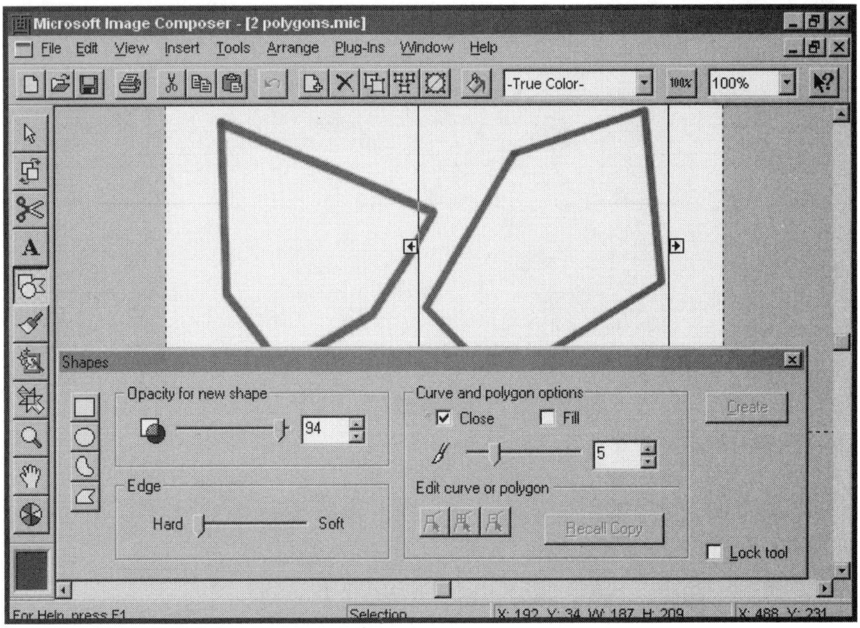

Figure 3.30

Polygon versus
polygon.

3. With the polygonal-shaped cursor that appears, click in the work-space where you want to start your polygon.

4. Continue to click on each nodal point for the polygon.

5. When you have traced the shape of your polygon, click on the Create button in the Shapes palette. The polygon appears in the workspace.

Filling Sprites

Fill colors for sprites can be changed. Image Composer comes with a full supply of colors and hues, shades, and gradient ramps. Image Composer also does a good job of creating color fills in the FrontPage Editor and on your Web site. To change the fill color for a sprite, do the following:

1. Select a sprite by clicking on it.

2. Click on the color swatch in the lower-left corner of the Image Composer window to display the Color Picker dialog box.

3. Click on a color in the True Color palette tab of the Color Picker window (the large palette on the left), as shown in Figure 3.31. Select a hue from the bar to the right of the palette. You can also create a color using the Red, Green, and Blue sliders in the Color Picker dialog box.

TIP
The Eyedropper tool allows you to point to and pick up a color from the workspace. Click on it and try moving it around!

4. When you have selected a fill color, click on OK in the Color Picker dialog box.

5. Select the sprite in the workspace to which you want to apply a color.

6. Select Current Color Fill from the toolbar. The fill color of the selected sprite changes.

Gradients are color fills that blend up to four colors together. You can select separate colors to start in the upper-left, upper-right,

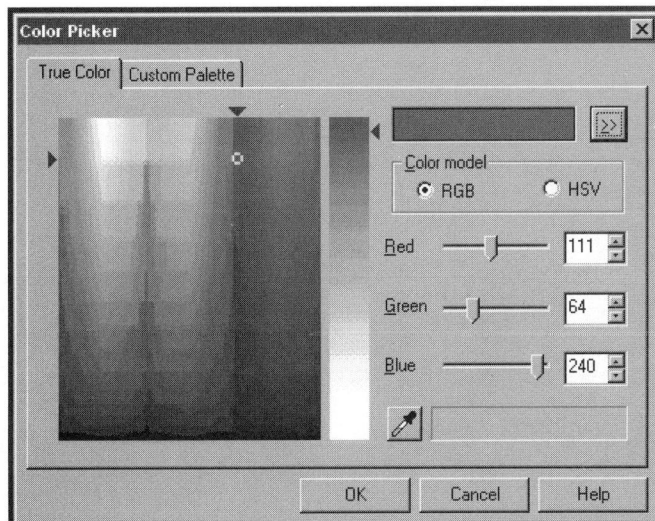

Figure 3.31

Selecting a color in the Color Picker.

lower-left, and lower-right corners. To apply a gradient fill, follow these steps:

1. Select the sprite to which you want to apply the gradient ramp.
2. Click on the Effects tool (if it's not already selected).
3. Select Gradient from the list of effects.
4. Click on the Details tab in the Effects dialog box.
5. Select a color for each corner of the gradient ramp, using the four color swatches that appear. Each color swatch opens the Color Picker window when clicked.

NOTE

You may also select a gradient pattern from one supplied by Microsoft. Click on the Gradient Name list box and experiment to see if you like any of those patterns.

6. After selecting your four colors, click on the Apply button to assign the defined fill to your selected sprite, as shown in Figure 3.32.

Figure 3.32

We elected to use the built-in Red to Blue 45% gradient.

Arranging Sprites

You can move a text sprite onto a shape sprite to create a button. You're already used to clicking on buttons when you use programs. When it comes to designing your Web site, you are the program designer, so you can combine text and shapes to design your own custom buttons. When these graphic images are combined with hyperlinks, they will work as hyperlink buttons for your Web site visitors. Ah, but I'm jumping ahead just a bit. You need to create the button first.

Combining text and graphics to create a customized button requires being able to move the text sprite on top of the shape so that it isn't hidden behind the shape. You can also align sprites so that, for example, the text sprite is centered over the shape sprite. Try this by first creating an image that can be used as a button (see Figure 3.33), and then dragging a text sprite on top of the button image, as shown in Figure 3.34.

To shift a sprite from front to back, move a shape sprite on top of a text sprite, as shown in Figure 3.35. This causes the text to disappear.

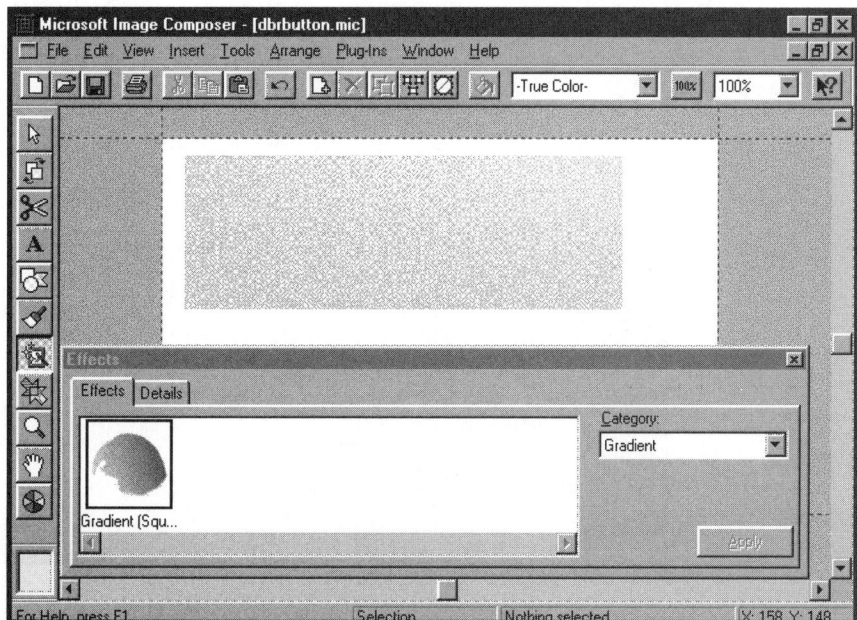

Figure 3.33

Assigning a gradient fill.

Figure 3.34

Some day this will be a button.

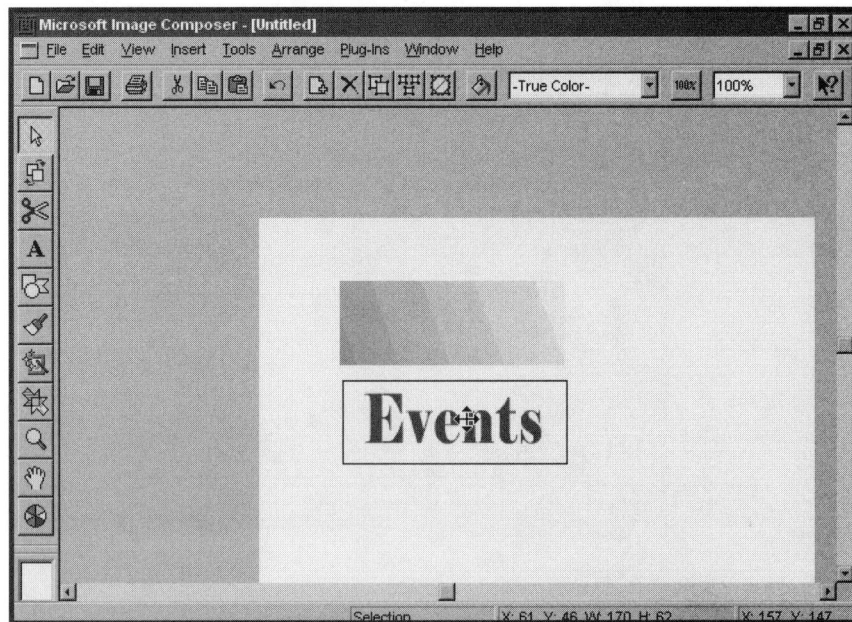

Figure 3.35

Moving a shape on top of text.

To move the shape behind the text (and to make the text visible again), click on the Arrange tool. With the shape selected, click on the Send Backwards button in the Order area of the Arrange palette, as shown in the Arrange palette at the bottom of Figure 3.36.

To align the edges or the centers of two or more selected sprites, follow these steps:

1. With the Arrange tool selected from the toolbox, draw a marquee (border) around all the sprites you want to align.

2. Select one of the alignment options in the Align area of the Arrange palette. In Figure 3.37, a marquee is drawn around a text sprite and a shape, and the Centers Vertically option in the Align area is selected.

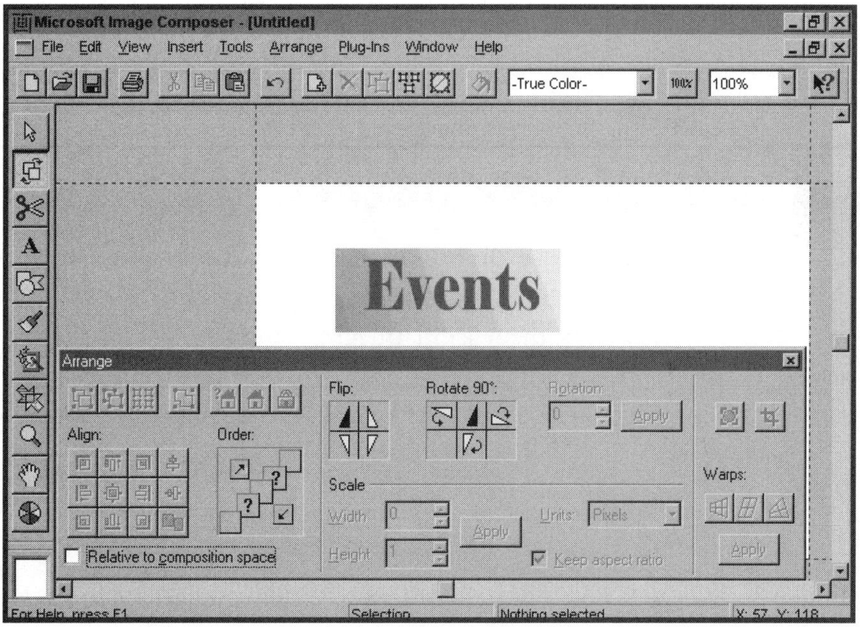

Figure 3.36

The text now reappears.

Figure 3.37

Getting vertically
centered.

Image Composer Files and Web Graphic Images

Suppose you have put together a combination of sprites and now you want to place them in your Web site. The easiest way to do this is to simply copy them from Image Composer to FrontPage Editor. You'll walk through this process and explore other options for sending an Image Composer graphic to FrontPage Editor in the following section.

You can save your sprites in an Image Composer file so that you can use the saved sprites again and again—or you can go back and edit them and bring them back into your FrontPage Web site. Image Composer files, saved in Image Composer format, cannot be imported into a Web site; however, they can be opened in Image Composer and then the sprites can be copied to FrontPage Editor. To save an Image Composer file in Image Composer format, follow these steps:

1. Click on the Save button in the Image Composer toolbar.

2. Use the Save In list to navigate to the folder in which you want to save your file. Make sure Microsoft Image Composer (*.mic) is selected from the Save as type list. Then, enter a filename in the File name area of the Save As dialog box, as shown in Figure 3.38.

3. Click on the Save button to save your file. The next time you want to resave the file, click on the Save button in the toolbar—the file is resaved without opening the Save As dialog box.

Placing Graphic Images in FrontPage

Now that you've created a graphic image, how do you get it into Front-Page? It's simple, and it doesn't matter which program you used to create or edit your graphic image. Microsoft Image Composer is a fine graphics package, but any graphics program can be used to place images in a FrontPage Web site.

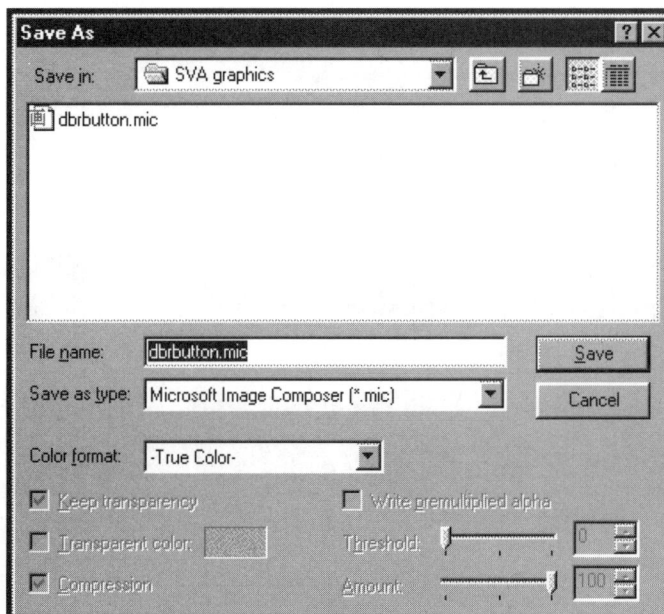

Figure 3.38

Saving an Image Composer file.

The process is as easy as copying the file into FrontPage through the Clipboard—just copy and paste an object within FrontPage or any other Microsoft Office application. To copy a graphic onto your page, follow these steps:

1. Select a graphic image in any graphics program and click on the Copy button in your graphics program, as shown in Figure 3.39.

TIP Ctrl+C copies a selected object to the Clipboard in any Windows application.

2. Switch to FrontPage Editor and place your insertion point where you want the graphic to be inserted.

3. Click on the Paste button in the FrontPage Editor toolbar.

The image appears on your FrontPage Editor Web page, as shown in Figure 3.40.

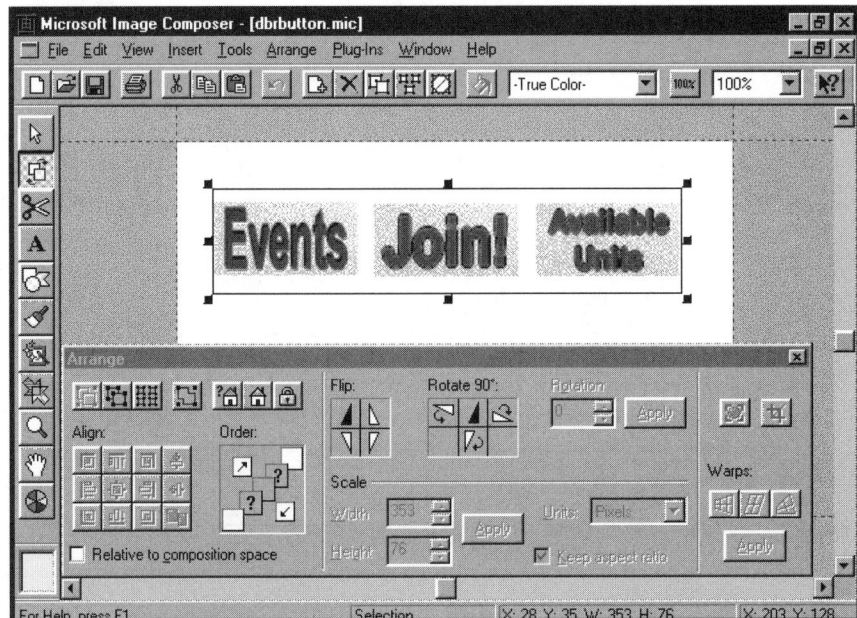

Figure 3.39

Copying an image.

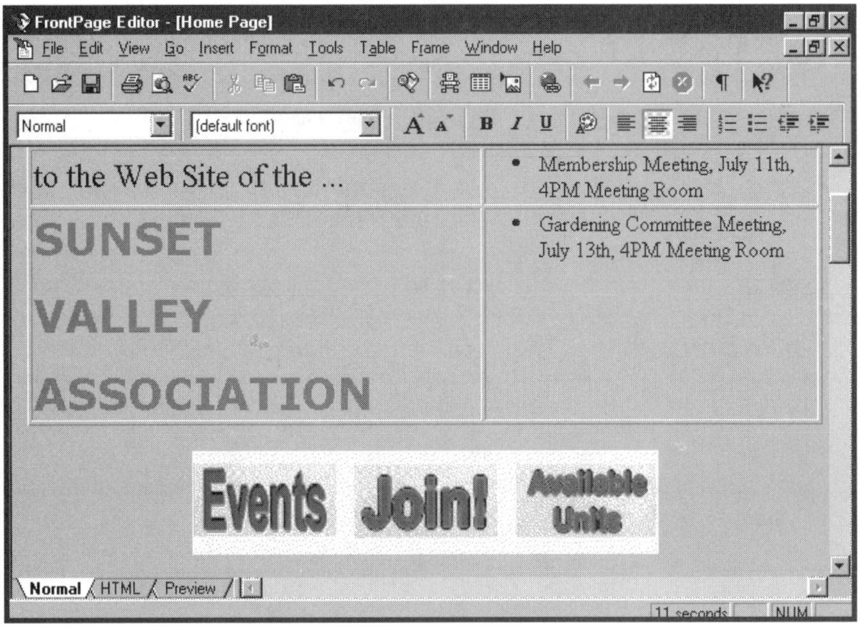

Figure 3.40

An image copied
from Image
Composer to
FrontPage Editor.

GIF and JPEG—Graphic
File Formats for the Web

Computer graphics come in many formats. Image Composer saves graphic image files in its own .mic format. Your scanner might create files using a TIF format. Your paint program might create .pcx files, and the default for CorelDRAW is yet another type of graphics file. Web browsers, however, don't interpret any of the popular graphic formats. Instead, they have their own. Most World Wide Web browsers recognize graphics in either the JPEG (also known as JPG) or GIF format.

The GIF file format was developed by CompuServe. Although images are limited to 256 colors, this graphic format is the most widely recognized on the Web and takes less time to download than other images, such as JPEG.

The JPEG (Joint Photographic Experts Group) format is becoming universally recognized by most Web browsers. JPEG images can display 16.7 million colors.

TABLE 3.2 THE MATCH OF THE CENTURY: GIF VERSUS JPEG	
Format Feature	**Reason to Use**
GIF Transparent color option	You are importing an image with a background you do not want to display.
GIF Interlacing	You want large, slow graphic images to "phase in."
GIF Universally accepted	You want to make sure every visitor can see your image.
JPEG	You want to display more colors for intricate artwork or scanned photos.

Table 3.2 illustrates the differences between GIF and JPEG.

FrontPage can handle any graphic image that can be cut and pasted through the Windows 95 Clipboard. Therefore, all you have to do is open or create your graphic image in your favorite graphics program and then copy it onto your page in FrontPage Editor. Note, however, that you cannot use FrontPage to edit a graphic image.

Saving Image Composer Files as GIF or JPEG Files

You can assign either GIF or JPEG formatting to images after they've been copied into FrontPage Editor.

NOTE You should also know that Image Composer files can be saved as GIF or JPEG files. Both options are available from the Save As Type list in the Save As dialog box. Because you can assign these attributes within FrontPage Editor, this is the easiest way to do it. If you're prepared to tweak the JPEG compression yourself, you'll have more control if you save your image as a JPEG file in Image Composer. For most of us, most of the time, FrontPage Editor works fine as a place to assign GIF or JPEG formatting to an image file.

I think you'll find that copying selected sprites from Image Composer to FrontPage Editor works fine for your weekend session, and it really gives you enough control over your images to do plenty of high-powered image editing.

Editing Graphic Images in FrontPage

After you copy an image into FrontPage Editor, you should save your page right away. Saving the page also prompts you to save any images you've copied onto the page. When you do save those images, they're part of your Web site and can be inserted onto other pages. To save an image as part of a page, follow these steps:

1. Copy the image onto the FrontPage Editor page and click on the Save button in the FrontPage Editor toolbar.

2. FrontPage assigns names to any images on the page that have not yet been saved to the Web site, as shown in Figure 3.41.

3. Click on the OK button to save the image and exit the dialog box.

NOTE You can select the Yes to All button in the Save Image to FrontPage Web dialog box if you are saving multiple images.

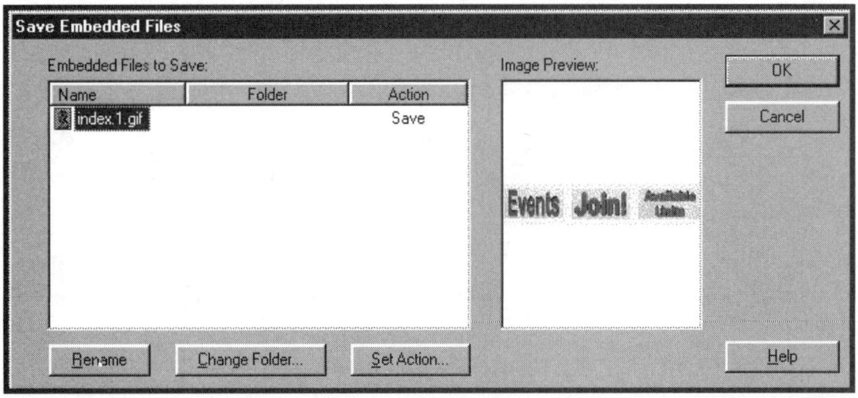

Figure 3.41

Saving linked image files.

Sizing Images

You can't change the content of an image in FrontPage Editor (this is the job of Image Composer or other graphics packages), but you can resize the image. To change the size of an image, follow these steps:

1. Click on the image to select it.

2. Click and drag in to shrink the image or out to expand the image, as shown in Figure 3.42. Compare the image size to that of Figure 3.40.

Making Images Transparent

Some imported images might have backgrounds that you don't want to display. For example, the clip art in Figure 3.43 was copied into FrontPage Editor with a white background that clashes with the gray page background. If

Figure 3.42

Resizing an image in FrontPage Editor.

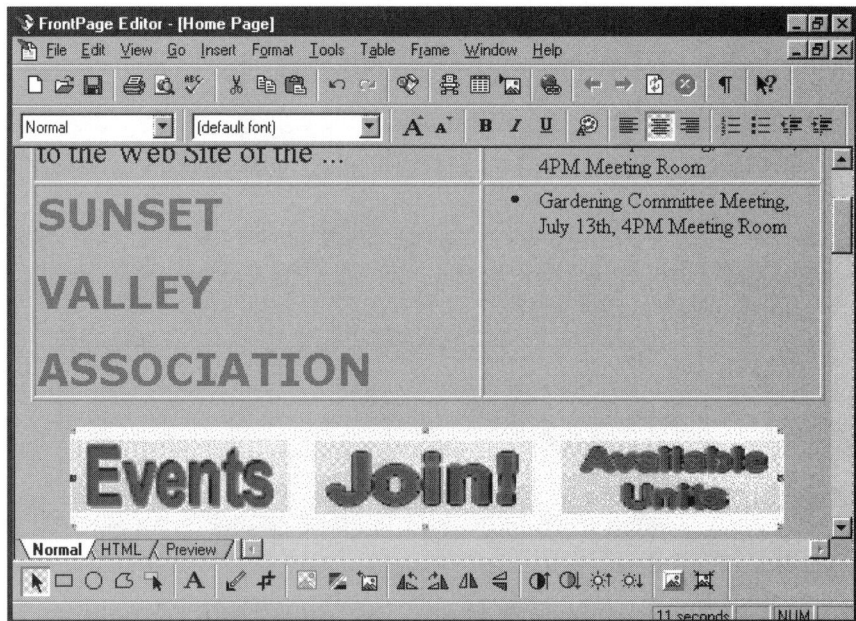

Figure 3.43

The image
background clashes
with the page
background.

the image is in GIF format, you can make one color transparent using the
Make Transparent tool in the Image toolbar. To make a GIF image color
transparent, follow these steps:

1. Select the graphic image in FrontPage Editor. When you select the
   image, the Image toolbar becomes active.

2. Click on the Make Transparent button in the Image toolbar, as
   shown in Figure 3.44.

Figure 3.44

The Make
Transparent tool.

3. Point the eraser-shaped cursor to the color you want to make transparent and click (see Figure 3.45). The selected color becomes transparent.

You can assign one color in an imported image to be transparent. Only GIF files can have a transparent color (one good reason to choose GIF over JPEG format for your graphic). Making a background color transparent helps an image blend into the Web page, as shown in Figure 3.46.

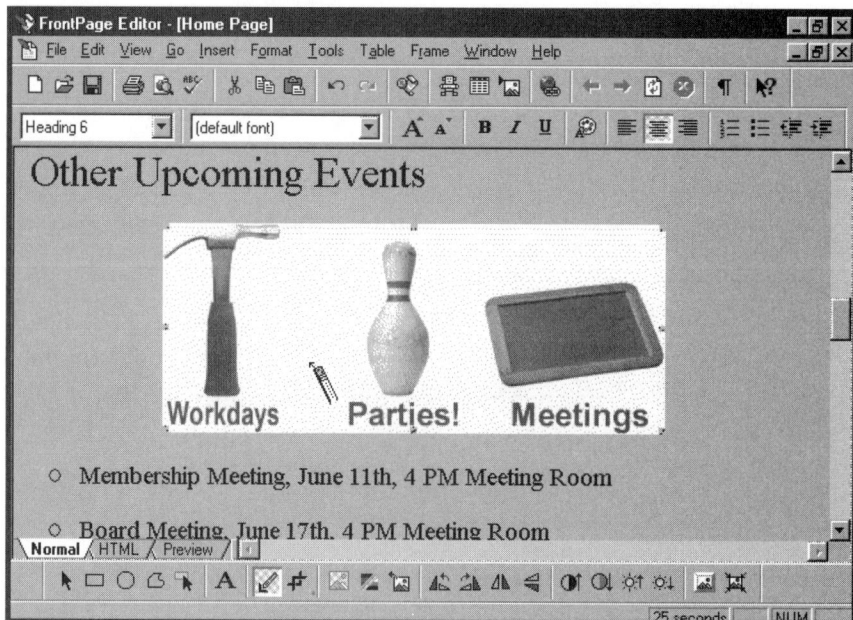

Figure 3.45

Selecting a color to make transparent.

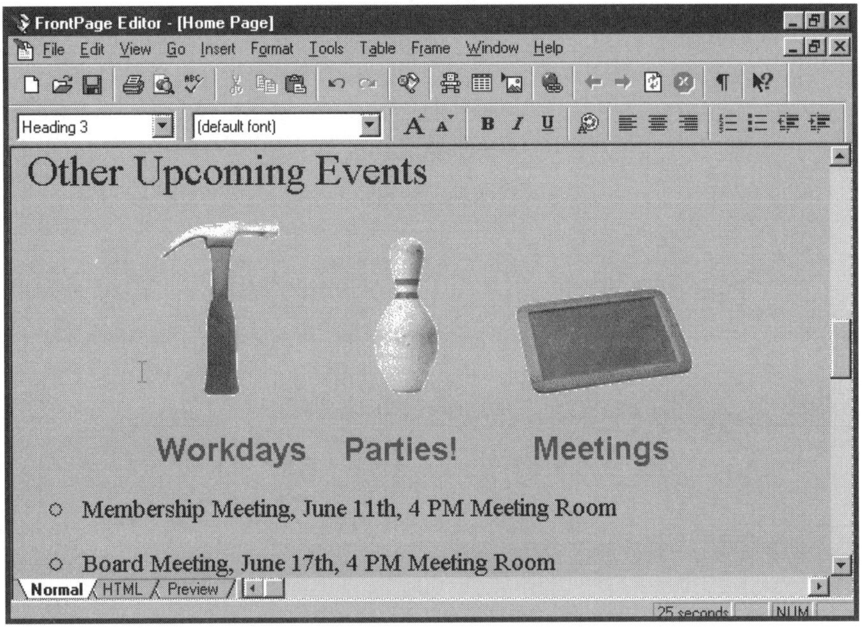

Figure 3.46

Now the images
blend in.

Changing Image File Types
in FrontPage Editor

I've discussed some of the pros and cons of the two image formats.
FrontPage makes your imported image a GIF file by default, and this
usually works well. GIF files can be "phased in" using interlacing, and
they can have one color designated as transparent to help them blend
into a Web page.

Imported photos are sometimes best displayed in JPEG format. Front-
Page lets you change an image file format. To save a graphic as a GIF or
JPEG file, follow these steps:

1. Save the page with the file in FrontPage Editor. If your image hasn't
   been saved to the Web site yet, you'll be prompted to save your
   imported graphic image file, as you discovered earlier.

2. Right-click on the image and select Image Properties from the shortcut menu.

3. Click on the JPEG radio button in the General tab of the Image Properties dialog box (see Figure 3.47). Remember, JPG and JPEG are two ways to refer to the same file format.

TIP

The Quality spin box determines the relationship between the speed with which your image is loaded and the quality of your image. If you select a higher quality number, your image is loaded more slowly, but it will look better. Choose between 1 and 99 (1 being the lowest/worst quality). Normally the default, 75, works well.

4. Select OK to resave the image. You can change the properties of the image file as often as needed.

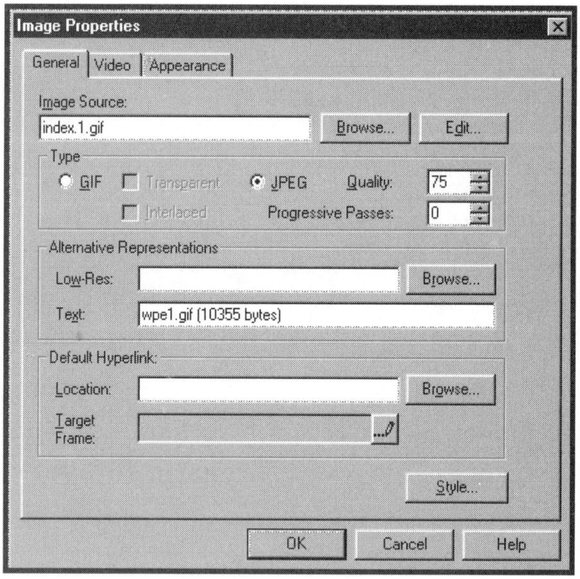

Figure 3.47

Assigning JPEG format.

Remember, your image is actually a separate file that has been linked to the page you're editing in FrontPage Editor.

Watching Your Graphic's Speed

Have you ever waited seconds, minutes, or even hours while a graphic resolves itself on the screen, only to conclude grumpily that it wasn't worth the wait? Think back on that experience and let it guide you when placing graphics on your own site.

FrontPage helps you keep tabs on how long your Web site will take to load in a visitor's browser. On the right side of the status bar, FrontPage Editor displays an estimate of how long your page will take to load if your visitor has a 28.8 Kbps speed modem. As you add graphics, you'll see the number of seconds grow.

Graphics are great, but they do slow down the process of interpreting your page. You can do a few things to mitigate the wait. One is to use smaller graphics. The larger the graphic, the longer it takes to resolve on a visitor's screen. Another option is to interlace the graphic. This option is available for GIF files. Interlaced graphics "fade in" on the page, first displaying as a fuzzy outline, and then filling in.

Interlacing an image file allows your visitors to see the entire image immediately, albeit in a grainy and blurry form. Is that better than having them gnash their teeth while your images flow onto the screen one line at a time from top to bottom? You be the judge. This is hard to test without opening your file with a Web browser—the procedure you experimented with at the end of the Friday Evening session. To make a GIF file interlaced, follow these steps:

1. Right-click on the image and select Properties from the shortcut menu. The Image Properties dialog box appears.

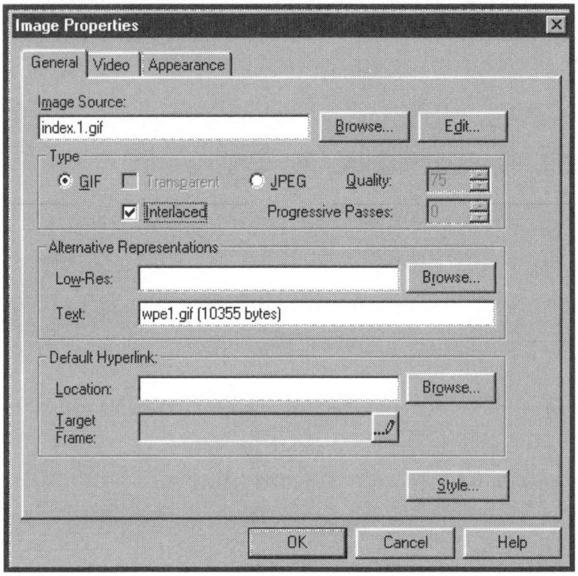

Figure 3.48

Interlacing a
graphic image.

2. To interlace a graphic image, select GIF in the Type area.

3. Click on the Interlaced check box in the Type area, as shown in
   Figure 3.48.

4. Click on OK.

Providing Alternative Text

Alternative text displays when your visitor's browser cannot read your
graphic image. Another benefit to alternative text is that it displays while
the image resolves. This gives your visitors something to read while they
wait for the picture. It also helps your visitors decide whether they want
to wait to see the image or scroll down the page in search of other items.
To assign alternative text, follow these steps:

1. Right-click on the image and select Properties from the shortcut
   menu. The Image Properties dialog box appears.

2. Type some alternative text in the Text field of the Alternative Representations area in the General tab of the Image Properties dialog box, as shown in Figure 3.49.

3. Click on OK.

To place a border around an image so that the alternate text is set off from the text body of the page, follow these steps:

4. Right-click on the image and select Properties from the shortcut menu. The Image Properties dialog box appears.

5. Click on the Appearance tab in the Image Properties dialog box.

6. Use the Border Thickness spin box to assign a border to the selected image, as shown in Figure 3.50. Border thickness is measured in screen pixels.

7. Click on OK. Your image has a border, as shown in Figure 3.51.

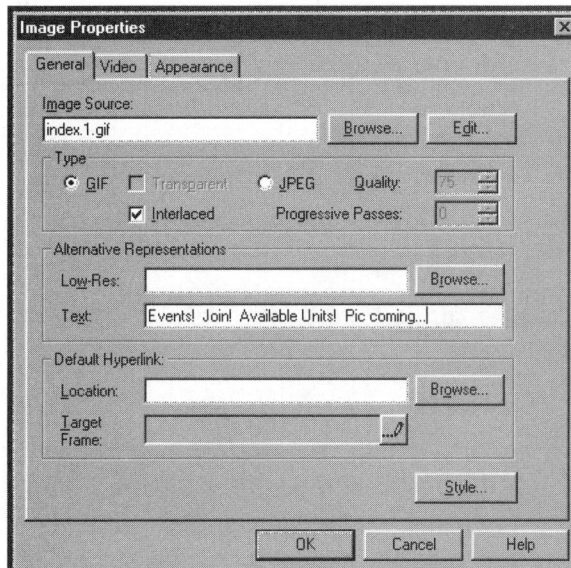

Figure 3.49

Assigning alternative text.

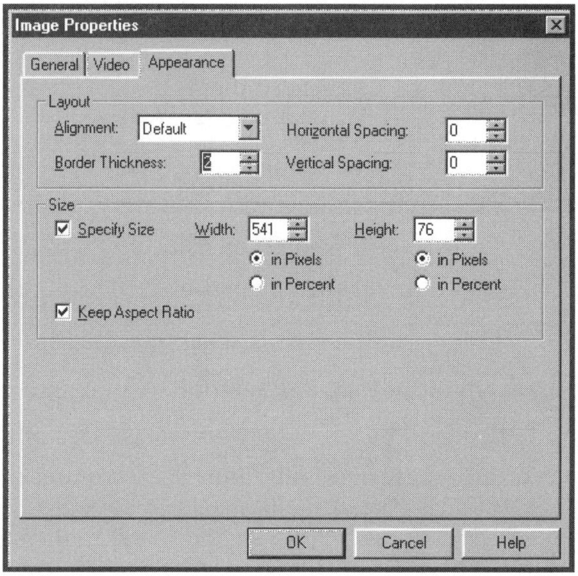

Figure 3.50

Defining border thickness.

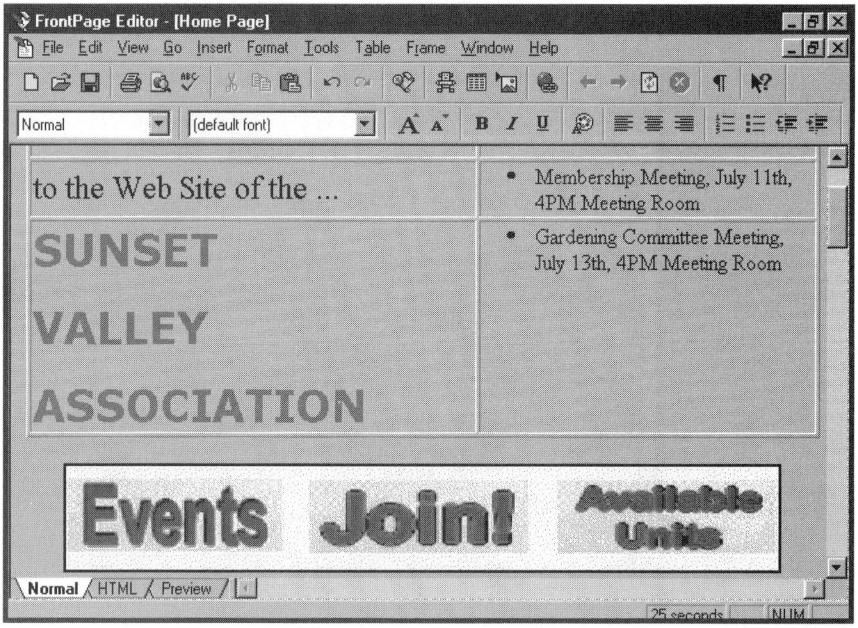

Figure 3.51

A nice border helps the image stand out.

Image Hyperlinks in FrontPage Explorer

You've created graphics and placed them on a page in your Web site. Each image you copy into FrontPage Editor is saved as part of your Web site when you save your page. Remember, you were prompted to save the image file along with your page. What appears to be one "page" is actually an HTML file and linked image files. FrontPage Explorer has kept track of all these files and their hyperlinks. To examine image links, follow these steps:

1. Click on the FrontPage Explorer button in the FrontPage Editor toolbar.

2. Examine the Web in Folders view. Notice that the window shows new image files. FrontPage has assigned the filenames, as shown in Figure 3.52.

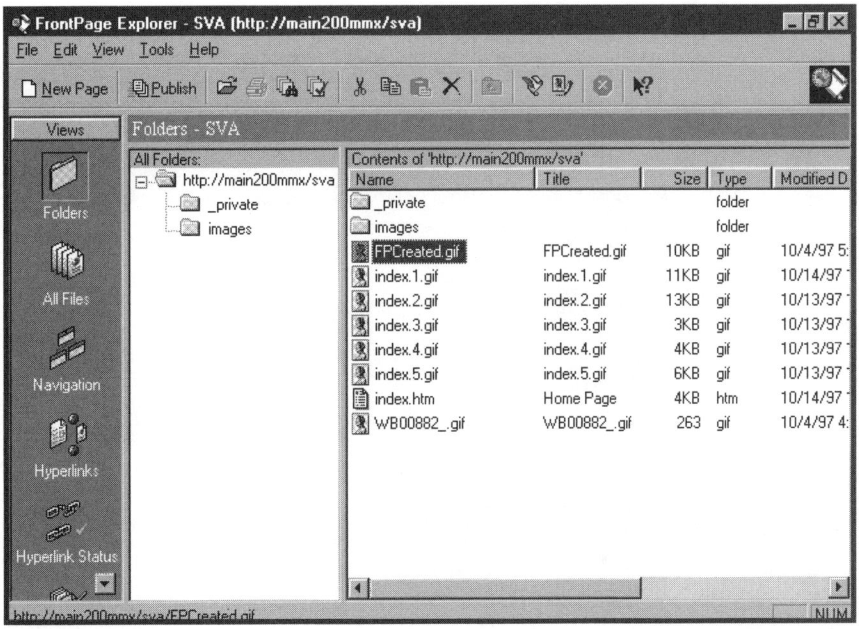

Figure 3.52

Image files in the Folders view.

3. Select Hyperlinks view and press the Hyperlinks to Images button on the toolbar. My site has some additional hyperlinks, but you can see the links to graphic images in Figure 3.53. Notice that the image files are linked to the Home Page.

Optional: Importing Graphic Files

Although cutting and pasting directly into a page in FrontPage Editor is the easiest way to place a graphic image in your Web site, you may not be satisfied with how the image is handled when it is converted automatically. In this case, your option is to convert the graphic file to a GIF or JPEG file using a graphics program. Microsoft Image Composer, for example, provides an export option to both of these formats.

If your graphic image is already in GIF or JPEG format, you can attach it to your Web site through FrontPage Explorer and then link it to any

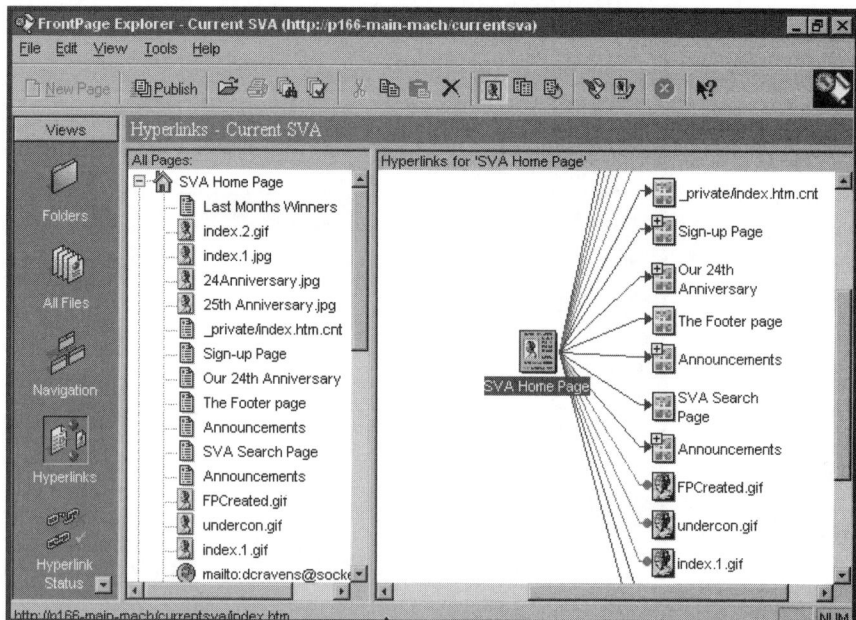

Figure 3.53

Tracking image hyperlinks.

page in the Web site. Here again, by working through the Explorer, you are ensuring that all linked files are organized in the site and that the links are protected by FrontPage. To import a JPEG or GIF file directly into FrontPage Explorer, follow these steps:

1. From the FrontPage Explorer menu, select File, Import.
2. In the Import File to FrontPage Web dialog box, select Add File.
3. From the Add File to Import List dialog box, select image files (.gif, .jpg), as shown in Figure 3.54.
4. Navigate to the folder that contains your saved image file.
5. Double-click on the graphic filename.
6. Click on OK in the Import File to FrontPage Web dialog box.

NOTE

• •

The image file is visible in the Folders view, as shown in Figure 3.55. When you link the image to a page, the link will be visible in Hyperlink view.

• •

If you have a file that's in JPEG or GIF format, it's not necessary to copy and save the file through the Clipboard. After you have added the image to your Web site (which you just practiced), you can insert that image

Figure 3.54

Importing an image file.

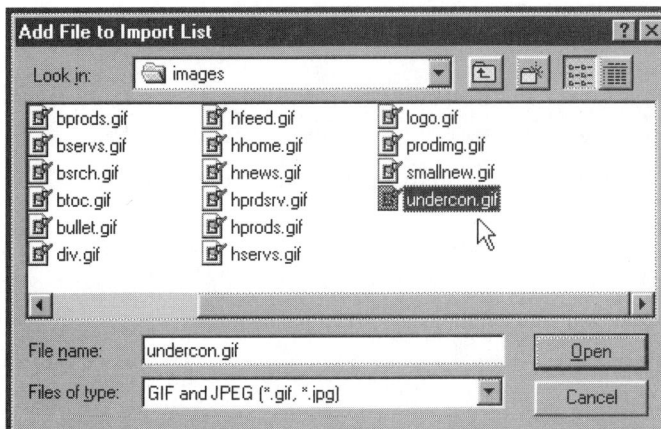

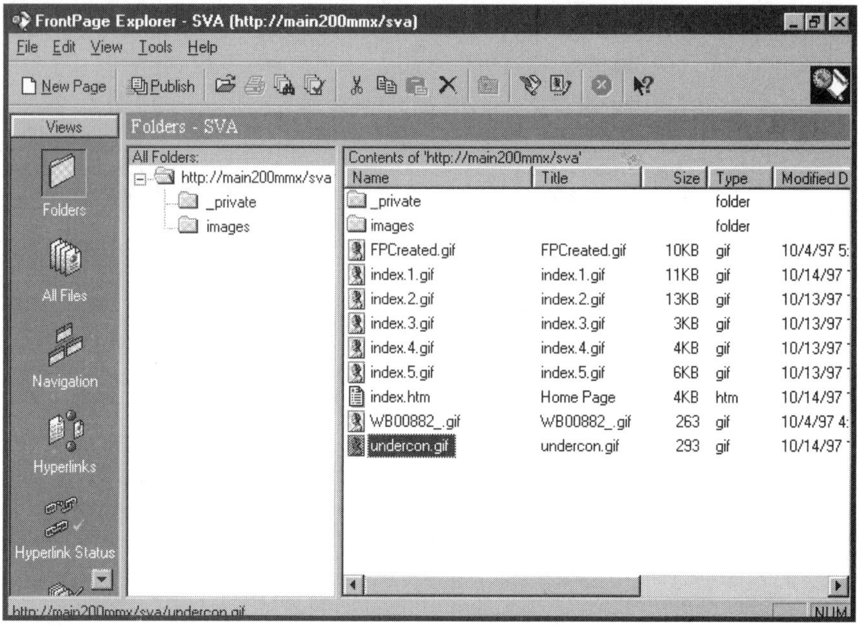

Figure 3.55

Imported image file
in Folder view.

onto any page in the your site. To import a graphic file using FrontPage
Editor, follow these steps:

1. Place your cursor on the page at the location where the image will
   be placed.

2. Select Insert, Image.

3. Select the graphic image you want to use in your current Web page
   and click on OK, as shown in Figure 3.56.

4. Save your page in FrontPage Editor.

NOTE   When you save your page in FrontPage Editor, FrontPage prompts you to confirm
changes in any image files.

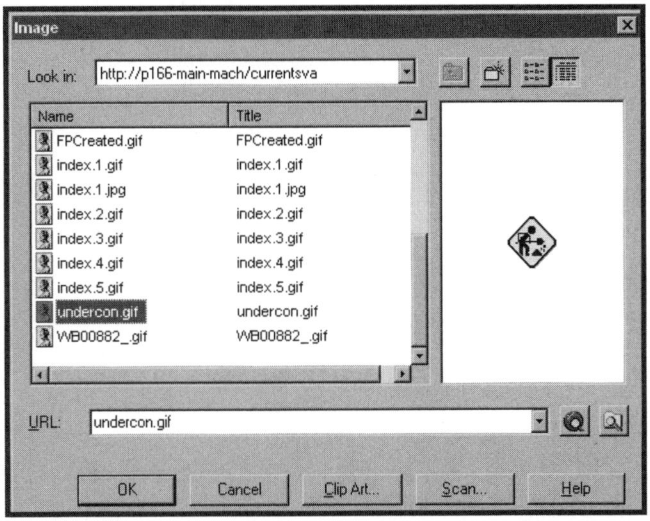

Figure 3.56

Inserting
a previously
imported image in
FrontPage Editor.

Take a Break!

Among font formatting, tables, and images, you've got the tools for creating a fine looking Web site. As you experiment with the tools I've shown you, you'll discover your own tricks for creating unique and entertaining Web sites.

The real magic of Web sites are hyperlinks—special text and graphic objects that, when clicked on, link the visitor to other parts of your Web site or other sites on the World Wide Web.

When you resume your adventure, you'll hyperlink "to the max." So stay tuned—the real excitement is yet to come!

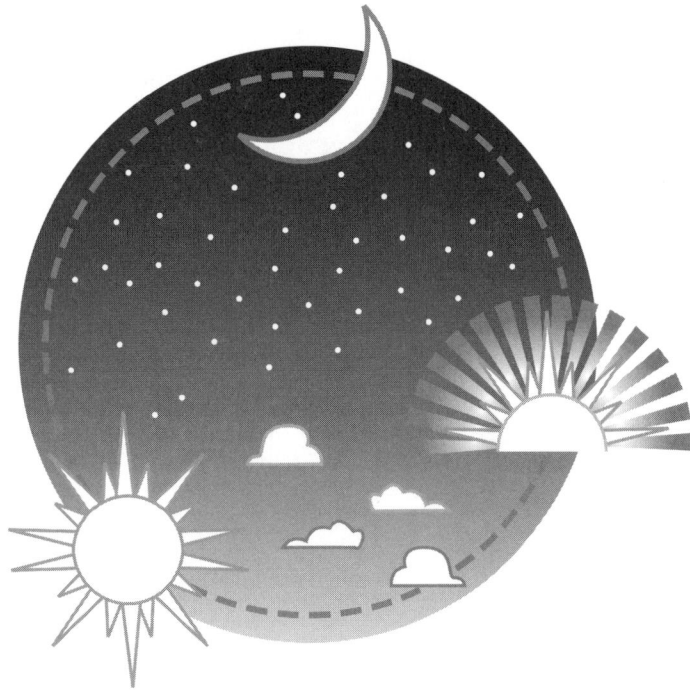

Live and Hyperlinked

- Using Bookmarks
- Creating Hyperlinks to Pages in Your Web Site
- Using Graphics As Hyperlinks
- Creating E-mail Hyperlinks
- Examining Hyperlinks in FrontPage Explorer

Already this weekend you've explored the tools needed to create an attractive Web page with formatted headings, text, and tables. You also got graphical with lines, images, background colors, and patterns for your page.

Now it's time to introduce one of the most powerful features of World Wide Web sites: hyperlinks. Hyperlinks provide you with the capability to click on text or on an image and then zoom to another place. A hyperlink may lead to another spot in the current Web page, to another page in the Web site, or even to another site on the World Wide Web. With hyperlinks, your Web site becomes far more navigable and friendly. Hyperlinks can be thought of as an instant index, allowing your visitors to find exactly what they're looking for with the click of a mouse.

FrontPage makes defining and assigning hyperlinks a breeze. Of course, you need to think about the kinds of hyperlinks that are appropriate for your visitors. What are they looking for? Are they really interested in reading a long introduction to your Web site before they zip off to their area of interest? The trick to designing hyperlinks is to put yourself in the shoes of your visitors; you should make your hyperlinks as helpful and as easy to follow as possible. In this session, you'll explore three basic types of hyperlinks:

- ✪ Hyperlinks within a single Web page. These links are called *bookmarks*.
- ✪ Hyperlinks between pages within your Web site.

✿ Hyperlinks between your site and resources on the World Wide Web.

The basic elements in all hyperlinks are similar: Objects—text (called *hypertext* when it's used with more than one page) or images (called *hotspots*)—that mark the starting points of hyperlinks, and Web sites that mark the destinations of hyperlinks. These destinations can be almost anything with a valid Uniform Resource Locator (URL). The URL can specify another Web page, a Quicktime .AVI file, or a call to a special Web based program called a CGI script. As long as the address is valid, you can reach it by creating a hyperlink.

Building Your Web Site

Up until now, you've had plenty of opportunities to create a Web site of your own. If you've already started, keep at it! After each session, remember your check list:

✿ Always have FrontPage Explorer running when you work on Web pages.

✿ Always open Web pages from FrontPage Explorer (by double-clicking on the file in the Summary or Hyperlinks view).

✿ Save all pages in FrontPage Editor before you exit.

These three steps ensure that your work is saved and that the hyperlinks within your Web site are kept up to date. As you save pages in FrontPage Editor or exit FrontPage Explorer, FrontPage prompts you to import files or save changes to them. That's FrontPage's job.

Using Bookmarks

A bookmark is a form of hyperlink that connects to a place within a Web page. Bookmarks in a Web page permit your visitors to jump right to a selected spot. If your page has more information on it than can be viewed on one screen, bookmarks are especially helpful because they allow your visitors to jump from one area to another on the same page. Creating bookmark hyperlinks involves two steps:

1. Assigning the bookmark
2. Defining the hyperlink

Assigning Bookmarks

The first step in creating bookmark hyperlinks is to assign bookmarks to selected text in your page. You can assign bookmarks to text only—you cannot make a graphic image a bookmark. To assign a bookmark to text, follow these steps:

1. Click and drag to select the text you want to use as a bookmark. This is the target end of a future hyperlink.
2. Select Edit, Bookmark, as shown in Figure 4.1.
3. Enter an easy-to-remember bookmark name in the Bookmark Name area of the Bookmark dialog box, as shown in Figure 4.2. The Other Bookmarks on this Page text box will list the other bookmark targets you've created. Since this is your first target, this should be empty.

TIP You'll find it reduces snags and bugs if you don't include spaces, periods, or colons in your bookmark names.

4. Click on OK in the Bookmark dialog box. A dotted line appears beneath the bookmark text.

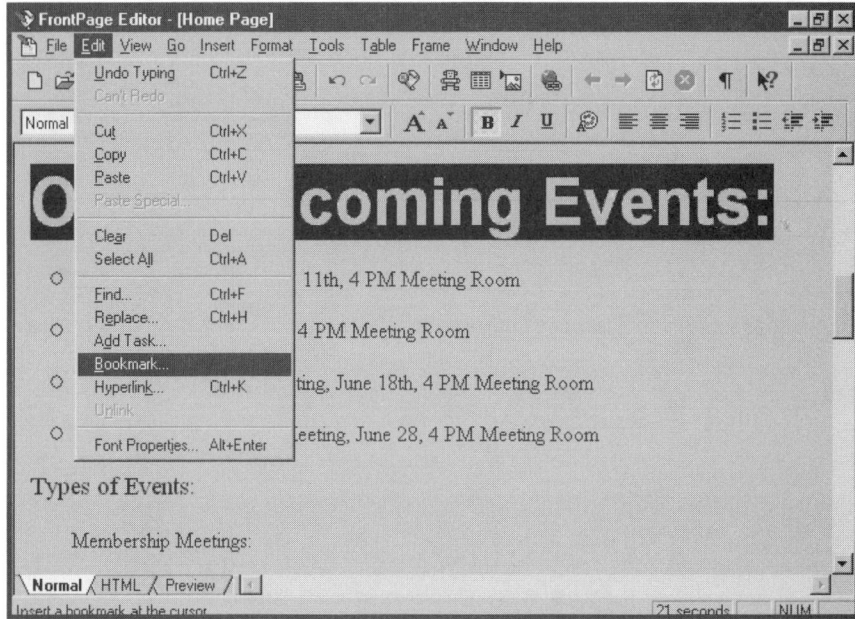

Figure 4.1

Assigning a
bookmark to
selected text.

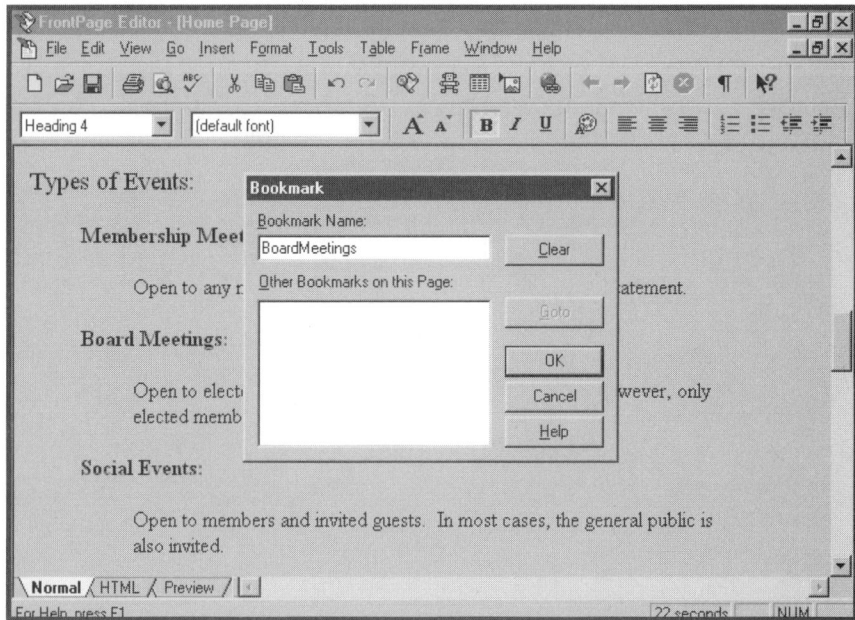

Figure 4.2

Naming your
bookmark.

> **TIP**
>
> Assigning a bookmark to the text at the top of the page lets your visitors jump to the beginning of the page. Try something like the bookmark shown in Figure 4.3.
>
> You can insert a bookmark without selecting text. When you do, a small flag appears in FrontPage Editor to mark the bookmark spot where the cursor was positioned on the page, as shown in Figure 4.4. This flag doesn't show up when visitors see your Web site in their browsers.

To change bookmark properties, follow these steps:

1. Right-click on the bookmark text and select Bookmark Properties from the shortcut menu.

2. Enter a new bookmark name in the Bookmark Name text box, as shown in Figure 4.5.

To clear bookmark properties, follow these steps:

1. Right-click on the bookmark text and select Bookmark Properties from the shortcut menu.

2. Click on the Clear button in the Bookmark dialog box to clear all bookmark connections.

Figure 4.3

This bookmark will let visitors jump back to the top of the page.

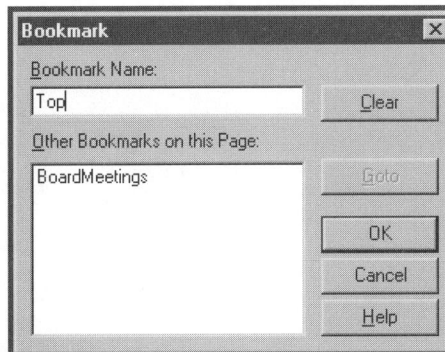

Figure 4.4

A bookmark is indicated by a flag.

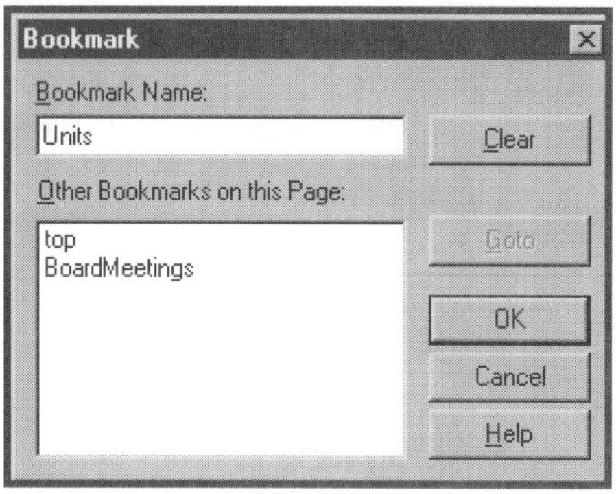

Figure 4.5

Renaming a
bookmark.

Defining Hyperlinks to Bookmarks

After you're satisfied with your assigned bookmarks, you're ready to assign
them hyperlinks. Often, Web sites have a group of hyperlinks—either
hypertext or graphics—at the top of each page so that visitors can jump
to their area of interest. Figure 4.6 shows a page with text at the top, ready
to have hyperlinks assigned to bookmarks.

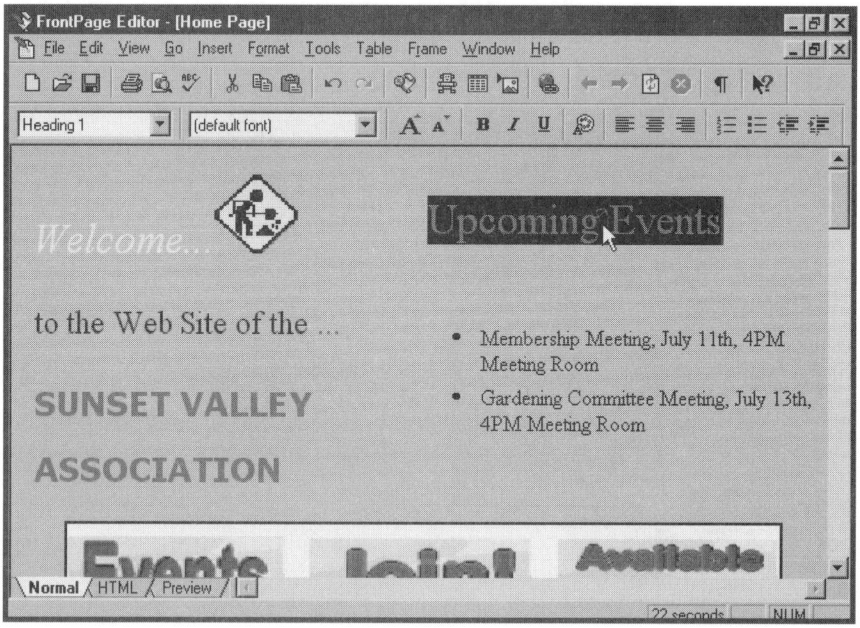

Figure 4.6

Bookmark text—
ready for linking.

Bookmark hyperlinks also can be used to let visitors who have viewed one section of a Web page jump to a related area, or back to the top of a page, as shown in Figure 4.7.

> **TIP**
> Today's modern Web pages don't usually use "Click here" as the text for a hyperlink. Instead, sophisticated and Web-wise visitors know that when they see underlined text in blue, the text is hyperlinked.

To define text hyperlinks to a bookmark, follow these steps:

1. Select the text that will be linked to the bookmark.

2. With the text selected, click on the Create or Edit Hyperlink button in the FrontPage Editor toolbar, as shown in Figure 4.8.

3. In the Create Hyperlink dialog box, pull down the Bookmark list and select the bookmark to which the text will be linked. In this example, the bookmark is top_of_page, as shown in Figure 4.9.

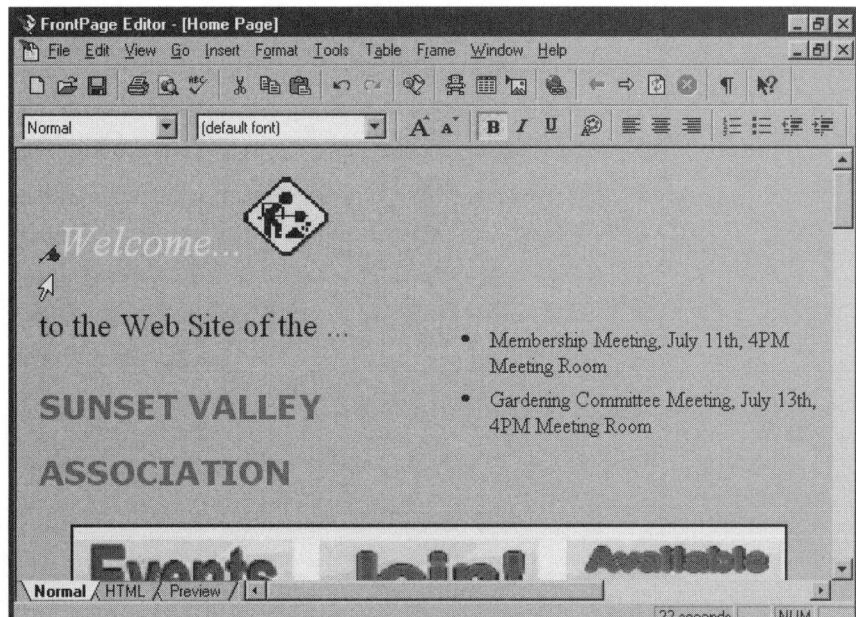

Figure 4.7

A bookmark to take visitors back to the top of the page.

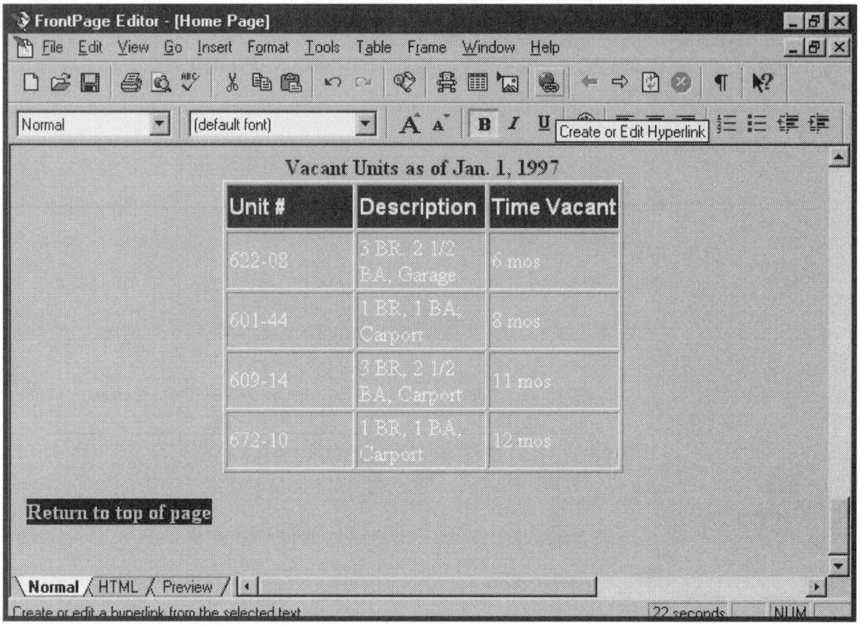

Figure 4.8

Selected text—
ready to hyperlink
to a bookmark.

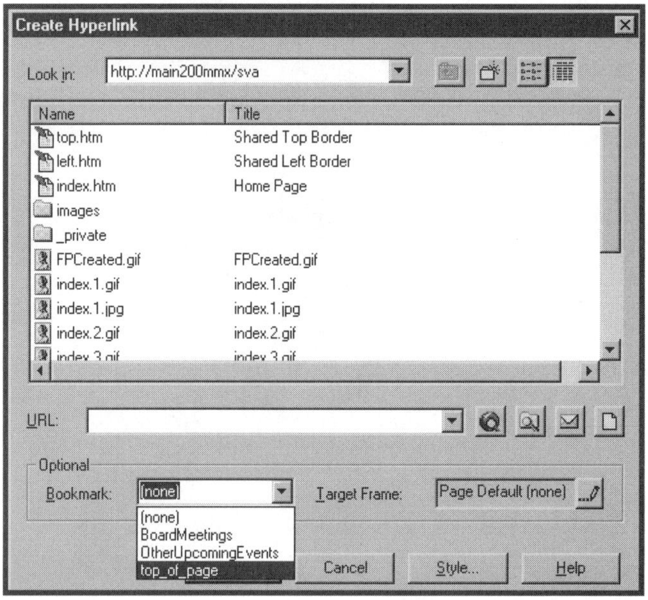

Figure 4.9

Matching a
bookmark to a
hyperlink.

4. Click on OK in the Create Hyperlink dialog box. The text you selected will be blue and underlined, indicating that it's a hyperlink.

To clear bookmark hyperlinks, follow these steps:

1. Click anywhere in the hypertext you have assigned to hyperlink to a bookmark.

2. Pull down the Edit menu and select Unlink, as shown in Figure 4.10.

TIP ■ Hyperlink text can be edited just like regular text. New words can be added to the hypertext, or the entire text can be changed.

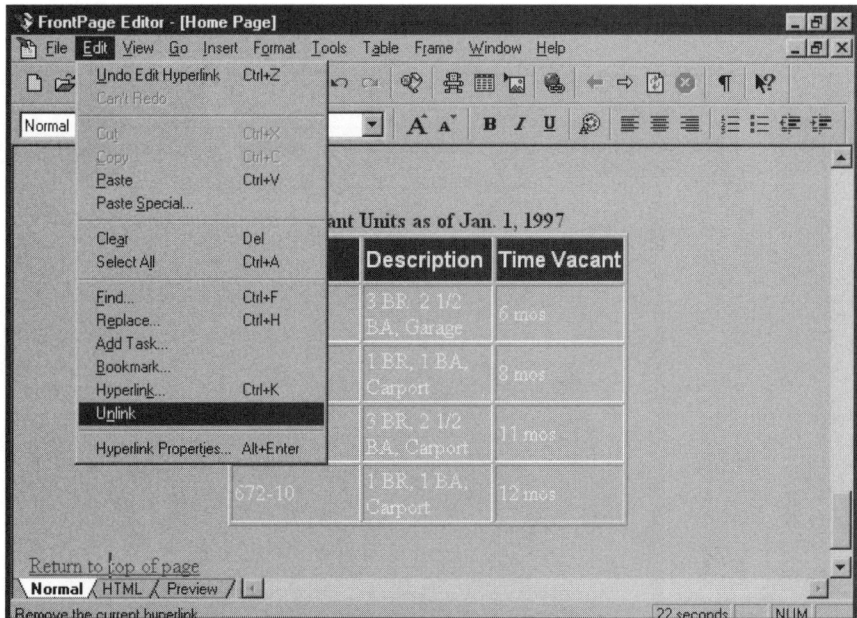

Figure 4.10

Removing a bookmark hyperlink.

Checking Out Your Bookmark Hyperlinks

If your page is longer than one screen, bookmarks help your visitors find what they want. Well-designed Web sites are full of handy bookmarks that anticipate where a visitor wants to go. Put yourself in the shoes of those who come to your Web site looking for information on something, and add bookmarks to help them quickly and easily find what you think they want. You can work through your Web site, testing it in FrontPage Editor. When you move your cursor over a hyperlink, the linked bookmark displays in the status bar (at the bottom of the screen) with a # symbol in front, as shown in Figure 4.11.

Bookmark hyperlinks can be tested in FrontPage Editor without using a browser. To test bookmark hyperlinks, follow these steps:

1. Hold down the Ctrl key on your keyboard while placing your cursor over the hypertext.

2. A hand cursor appears over the linked text (see Figure 4.12), and

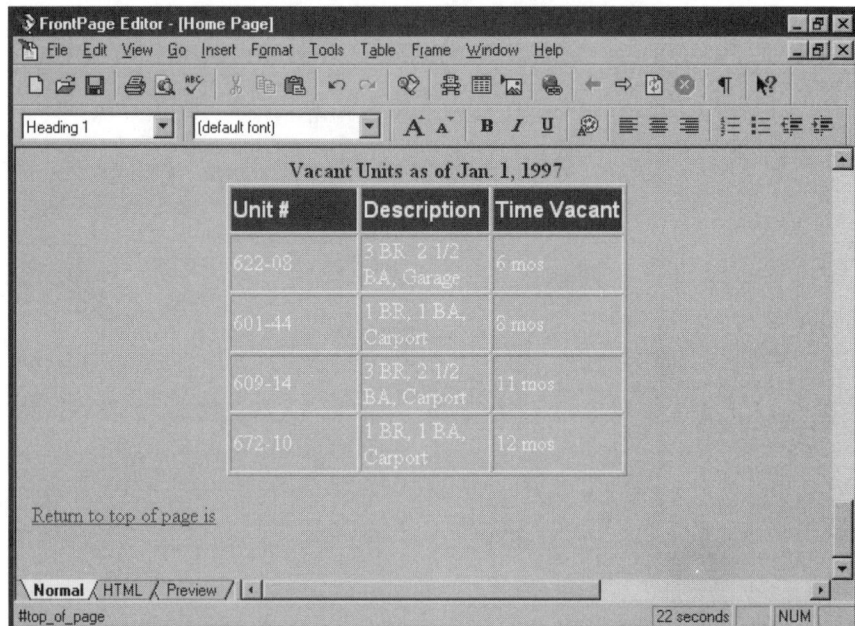

Figure 4.11

Bookmark link indicated in the status bar.

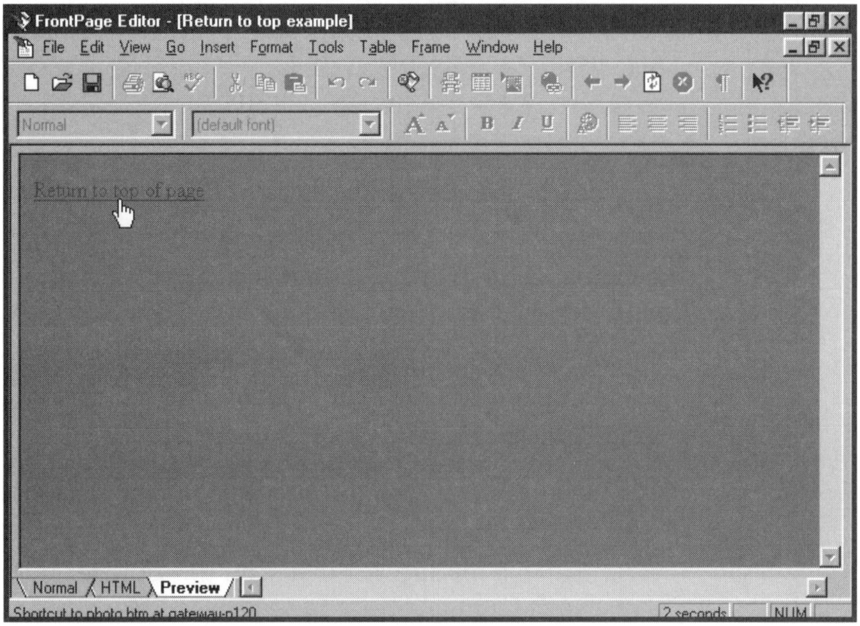

Figure 4.12

Testing a hyperlink
to a bookmark.

the linked bookmark displays with a # sign in front of it in the
FrontPage Editor status bar.

3. With the Ctrl key pressed, click on the hypertext to follow the
hyperlink to the bookmark.

Creating Hyperlinks to Pages in Your Web Site

Up to this point in the book, you've worked with a single page in your Web
site, adding additional files such as graphic images. Now it's time to stretch
and weave your web a bit larger. Because I haven't discussed working with
more than one page in a Web site yet, you'll start there. Usually, pages in
Web sites are hyperlinked so that visitors can jump from one to another.

When creating a Web site, you need to decide which information should
go in a separate Web page. When this happens, you can create that separate Web page "on the fly" as you create a hyperlink to the new page.

After you create a new page and a hyperlink at the same time, you'll also explore the process of creating hyperlinks between existing pages in a Web site. When you've seen both of these options, you'll be in position to spin your Web pages together like a pro.

At this point, you might be wondering why you shouldn't just put all the information you have to offer on a single Web page. That's not a bad question, because you can do it if all the news fits on one page. Because you've learned to help visitors navigate with bookmarks, the sheer size of a page shouldn't be a problem. However, organizing your Web site into different pages is a big help in many situations. Sometimes a Web site is easier to maintain if the information is broken up into separate pages.

You might want to keep the information that you update frequently on a separate Web page. For example, you could link a price sheet that changes every day to a product list that stays the same for weeks. Another example is providing hyperlinks from your home page to late-breaking news. An organization could put a "latest meeting minutes" reference on one page, with hyperlinks to a page with the minutes of the meeting. In short, one important function of breaking up information onto separate Web pages is to make it easier for you to update and maintain the Web site.

Creating Hyperlinks to New Pages

FrontPage Explorer, working quietly in the background, keeps track of and maintains all the hyperlinks you define in your Web site—you only need to keep it open while you work.

NOTE Remember that the checklist of steps to ensure the integrity of your page still applies. Always open Explorer before you work on a page. Always open pages from Explorer or create new pages from within FrontPage Editor, and remember to save each page in Editor before you end an editing session.

You're using FrontPage Editor to create new pages and define hyperlinks between them. You're counting on the whole package to mesh when someone visits your site. Explorer is backing you up the whole way and making sure this will happen.

You can create a hyperlink to a page that doesn't exist yet. Sometimes the process of designing your Web site works that way. You're creating and adding text and graphics to your Web page, and you decide that some information should be placed in a separate, linked page. No problem. You can create a new page directly from the Create and Edit Hyperlinks dialog box. To create a hyperlink as you create a new page, follow these steps:

1. Select the text you want to hyperlink to a new page.
2. Click on the Create or Edit Hyperlink button in the FrontPage Editor toolbar.
3. In the Create Hyperlink dialog box, click on the Create a page and link to a new page icon, as shown in Figure 4.13.
4. In the New dialog box, select the first item, Normal Page, and click on the OK button, as shown in Figure 4.14.

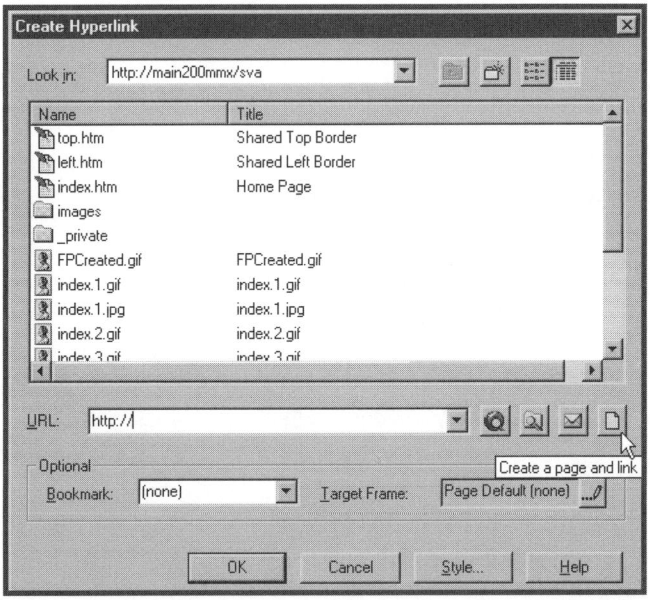

Figure 4.13

Creating and linking to a new page.

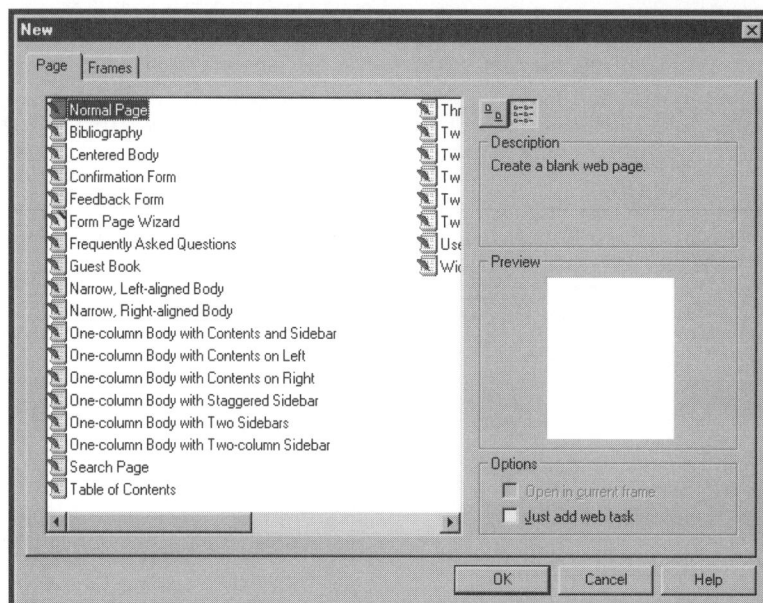

Figure 4.14

Creating a new page with a laundry list of possible page types.

NOTE

At this stage of the game, you're avoiding the more complex templates and wizards. You'll dive into them when you are more comfortable with creating pages from scratch.

5. FrontPage creates a new Web page for you. Because you don't want to edit the page right now, click on the Save icon and give your page a name, as shown in Figure 4.15.

6. Once the page has been saved, open the Window menu and click on your home page (your original page).

NOTE

A new page will always be the last item in the Window menu.

7. With your hypertext still selected, click on the Create or Edit Hyperlink icon. It's the same icon you clicked in step 2. Your new

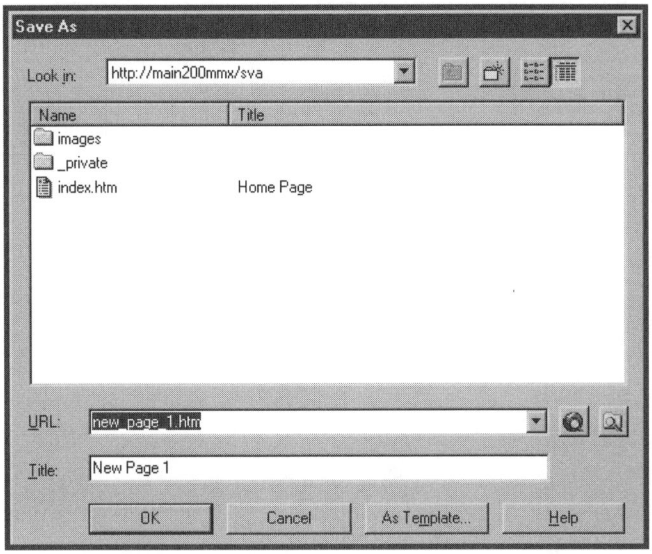

Figure 4.15

Saving your new Web page.

page should be listed in the URL edit field. If not, select your new page in the file list box.

8. Click on OK in the Create Hyperlink dialog box.

9. Finally, click on the Save icon to save your updated page.

TIP

■ ■

You can confirm the link between your home page and your new page in FrontPage Explorer, as shown in Figure 4.16.

■ ■

Creating Hyperlinks to Existing Pages

If you have already created and saved a page as part of your Web site, you can create hyperlinks to that page. You can also import existing pages into your Web site.

Say, for example, that you create a long document in a word processor that you want to use as a Web page. Most word processors have the capability

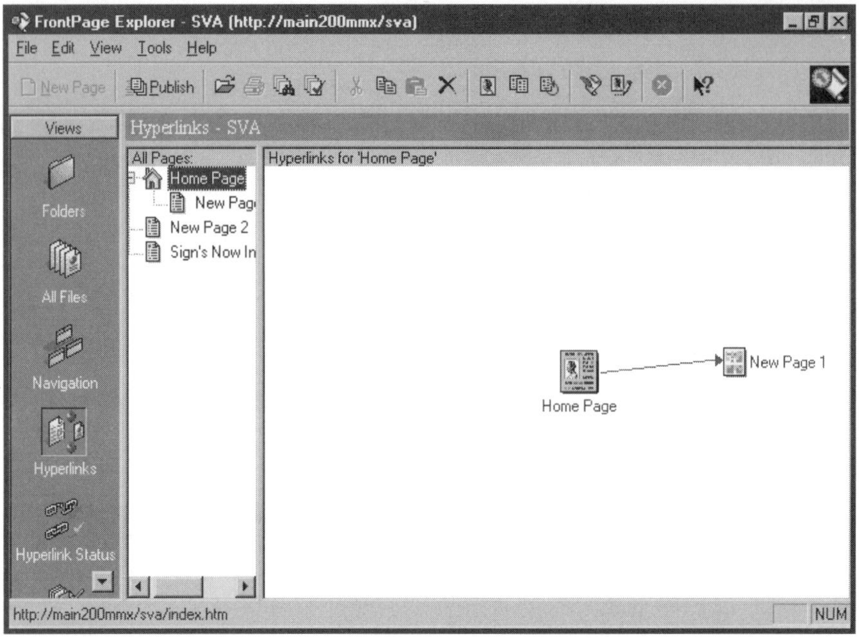

Figure 4.16

A new page is hyperlinked to your home page.

to save a page in HTML (Hypertext Markup Language), which is the format required to add text to your Web site. Also, many utilities are available that can do this for you. You can attach this file to your Web site using FrontPage Explorer and then use FrontPage Editor to create hyperlinks to it. You can use the following procedure to import an HTML file into a Web site:

1. Start by switching to FrontPage Explorer.
2. Select File, Import, and then click on the Add File button in the Import File to FrontPage Web dialog box.
3. From the Files Of Type list, select HTML pages.
4. Navigate to the folder on your drive or CD-ROM where the file is located and double-click on this file.
5. Click on the OK button in the Import File to Web dialog box.
6. Close the Import File to Web dialog box. Notice that the file appears in the Folder view of FrontPage Explorer.

●●

NOTE A look at the Hyperlinks view of FrontPage Explorer confirms that the new, imported page is not yet linked to the Index.htm page in the Web site.

●●

To create a hyperlink to an existing page, follow these steps:

1. Select the text that is to serve as the hyperlink to an existing Web page.
2. Click on the Create or Edit Hyperlink button in the FrontPage Editor toolbar.
3. Select the page from the list of files to which you want to link.
4. Click on OK to create the hyperlink.

Navigating Between Pages in FrontPage

Now that you've got more than one page to manage, you need to know how to get from one to the other. One page uses FrontPage Explorer and the other two use FrontPage Editor. To switch between pages using Front-Page Explorer, follow these steps:

1. Click on the Show FrontPage Explorer button, as shown in Figure 4.17.
2. Double-click on the page you want to switch to in the Hyperlink or Folders view.

To switch between open pages using FrontPage Editor, select <u>W</u>indow and then the page. You can also use the Back navigation button in the FrontPage Editor toolbar to go to the last page you worked on, or you can move forward by clicking on the Forward navigation button. The Back button is shown in Figure 4.18.

Figure 4.17

The Show FrontPage Explorer button.

Figure 4.18

The Back navigation button.

Creating Hyperlinks to Bookmarked Pages on the World Wide Web

Creating a hyperlink to another page is nice. However, to really send a visitor directly to where he or she wants to go, you can create hyperlinks that go to a specific bookmark on another page on the Web. To create hyperlinks to bookmarks on pages in the Web, follow these steps:

1. Select the text that is to serve as the hyperlink to a bookmark on an existing Web page.

2. Click on the Create or Edit Hyperlink button in the FrontPage Editor toolbar.

3. Select the Web page to which you want to link by clicking on its name in the file list box.

4. Select the desired bookmark in the Bookmark list box, as shown in Figure 4.19.

5. Click on OK to finalize the hyperlink and close the Create Hyperlink dialog box.

NOTE After you click on the file you want to use as your link and then click on the Bookmark list, your file is no longer highlighted. Don't be alarmed. FrontPage has stored the filename in the URL field.

TIP You can use Ctrl+click to test the hyperlink to a bookmark on another Web page.

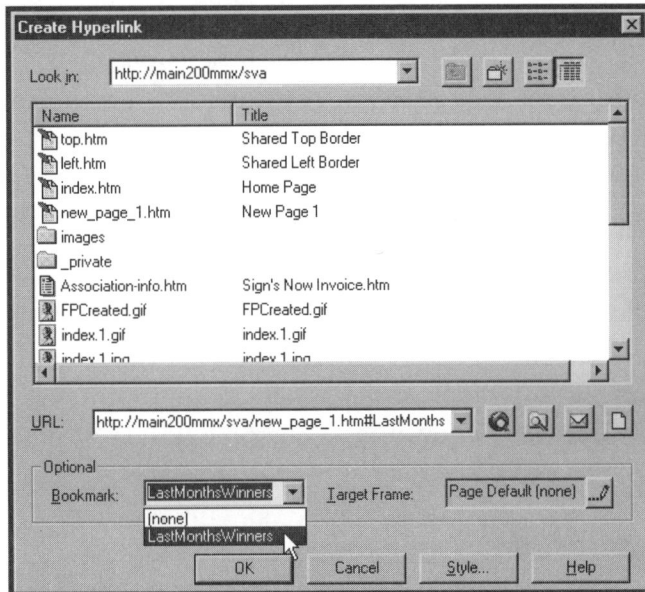

Figure 4.19

Selecting the page and bookmark to be hyperlinked.

6. As always, save your work on each page of FrontPage Editor before you exit your editing session.

Linking to the World Wide Web

One of my favorite ways to enhance a Web site is to hyperlink to a jazzy World Wide Web site. Hyperlinks can connect your site to other sites with similar information and can provide additional research resources or even support systems for your visitors.

Of course, it's great to get other sites to hyperlink to your Web site. Linking Web sites is a form of business and educational networking. How do you do that? One way is to ask. Occasionally, I'll visit a Web site and think that the people who visit this site might like to know about my Web site, and vice versa. I then just e-mail the Web sponsor and propose a trade: I'll let you put a link on my site if you let me put a link on yours. There are also businesses that arrange these trades. If your site stays on the World

Wide Web more than a month or two, you'll be approached by one of the commercial services that arranges these mutual links. Commercial services usually want you to host two hyperlinks to other sites in exchange for placing a link to your site on one other Web site. Somehow they parlay that uneven deal into a profit (don't ask me exactly how). You can make arrangements on your own to share links with compatible Web sites.

World Wide Web sites are identified by their address, which is technically called their URL (Uniform Resource Locator). You need to know the URL of a Web site to create a hyperlink to it. As you surf the Net, note the addresses that would make a good addition to your own site. To create a hyperlink to a World Wide Web site, follow these steps:

1. Select the text you want to use as hypertext, just as you did for other types of hyperlinks.

2. Click on the Create or Edit Hyperlink button in the FrontPage Editor toolbar.

3. If you know the address of the page you want to link to, type the address in the URL: edit box, directly after the default **http://** text, as shown in Figure 4.20.

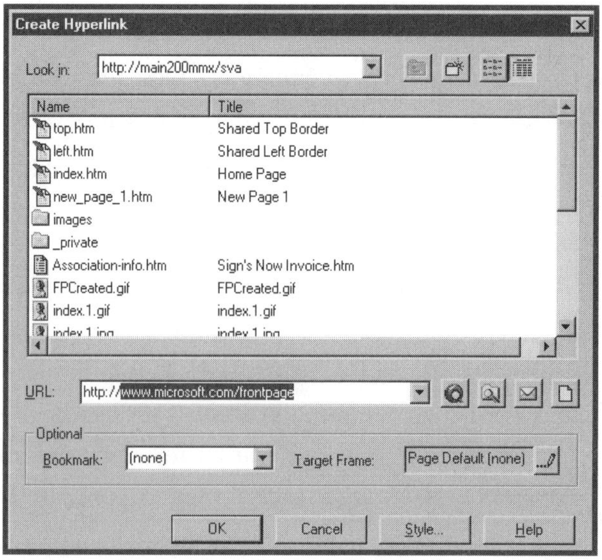

Figure 4.20

Linking to Microsoft's FrontPage site.

4. If you don't know the address of the page in step 3, that's OK. You can use your Web browser to find it by pressing the Use your Web Browser to select a page or file button, as shown in Figure 4.21.

5. Your browser will give you further instructions, as shown in Figure 4.22.

6. Once you've found the page you want for your link, copy the address to the Windows Clipboard (Ctrl+C), return to the Front-Page Create Hyperlink dialog box, and then paste (Ctrl+V) the address into the URL field.

7. Click on OK in the Create Hyperlink dialog box.

Figure 4.21

Use your browser to find a Web link.

Figure 4.22

The browser will tell you what to do!

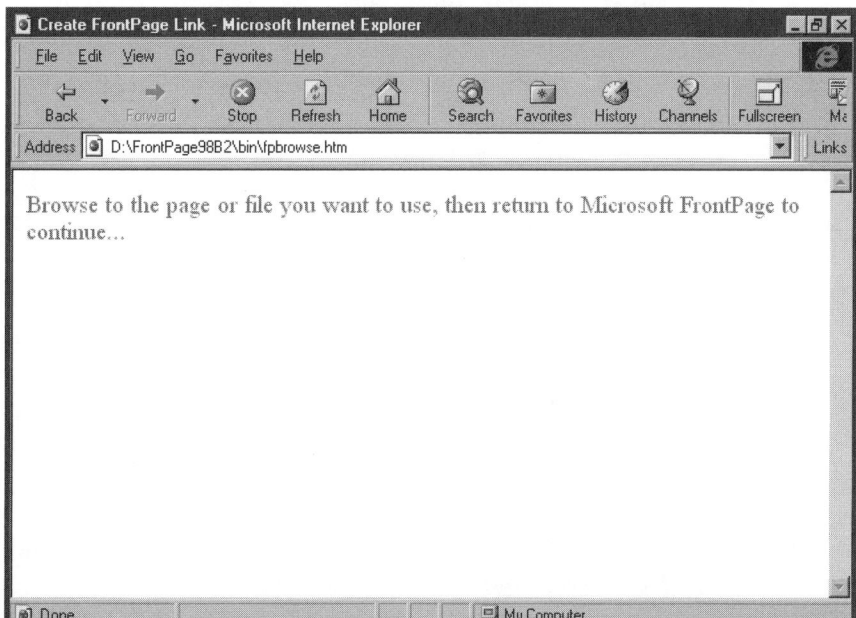

■■

TIP You cannot test hyperlinks to World Wide Web sites unless you are logged on to the Internet through your service provider and using an Internet server. However, Web hyperlinks display in the status bar when you place your cursor over the hypertext.

■■

Using Graphics As Hyperlinks

In the ever-escalating battle to create more intuitive and friendly Web sites, everything is going graphical. In the previous session, you saw how attractive images can add to the impact of a site.

Many designers are using graphical hyperlinks to enable visitors to visually and intuitively navigate around a Web site. A graphic of a big question mark can zip the visitor to help. A picture of a person can be a hyperlink to that person's biography. Click on a product and see a description of the product. You get the picture (excuse the pun).

Creating graphic hyperlinks involves concepts and procedures you have already learned. In the previous session, you imported graphics into a page. Earlier in this session, you created hyperlinks. Now you need to explore some design approaches, get the hang of assigning graphic hotspot hyperlinks, and then have some fun. One approach to using graphic hyperlinks is to create icon-type pictures or artistic text images at the top of a home page.

Assigning Graphic Hotspots

If you have created bookmarks on your page or you have other pages to which you will hyperlink a graphic, you're halfway to creating a linked image. Another option is to use a graphic hyperlinked to another World Wide Web site. If you have graphics on your page to use as hyperlink objects, you're ready to assign graphic hotspots that hyperlink all or part of a graphic to a bookmark or Web page. To make a graphic image a hyperlink, follow these steps:

1. Click on the graphic image that serves as a hyperlink.

2. Click on the Create or Edit Hyperlink button in the FrontPage toolbar.

3. Select or enter a hyperlink target, as shown in Figure 4.23.

4. Click on OK in the Create Hyperlink dialog box.

TIP

When you move your cursor over the hyperlinked graphic image, the hyperlink target address is displayed in the status bar (see Figure 4.24).

Many Web sites include *site maps*—graphic images with several hotspots, or hyperlinks, within them. A site map can be a button bar with several buttons, each with its own hyperlink. If you include graphic site maps and text hyperlinks, you can be sure that visitors to your site will find their way around—even if their browser has trouble with your site map graphic or they don't feel like waiting for it to materialize.

Figure 4.23

Defining a hyperlink target for an image.

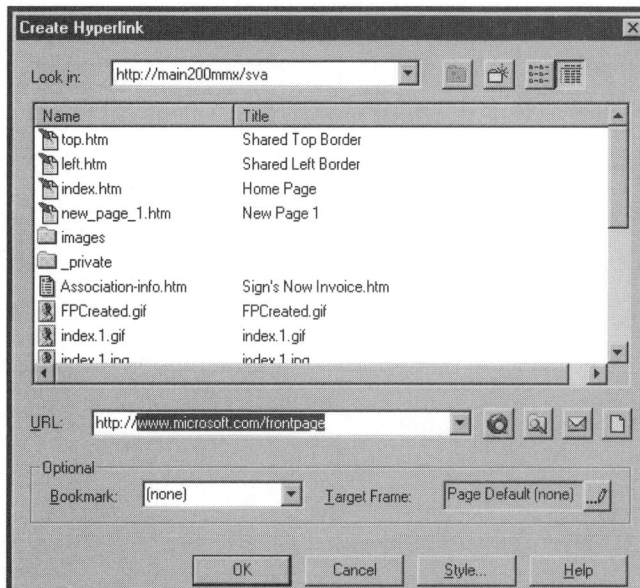

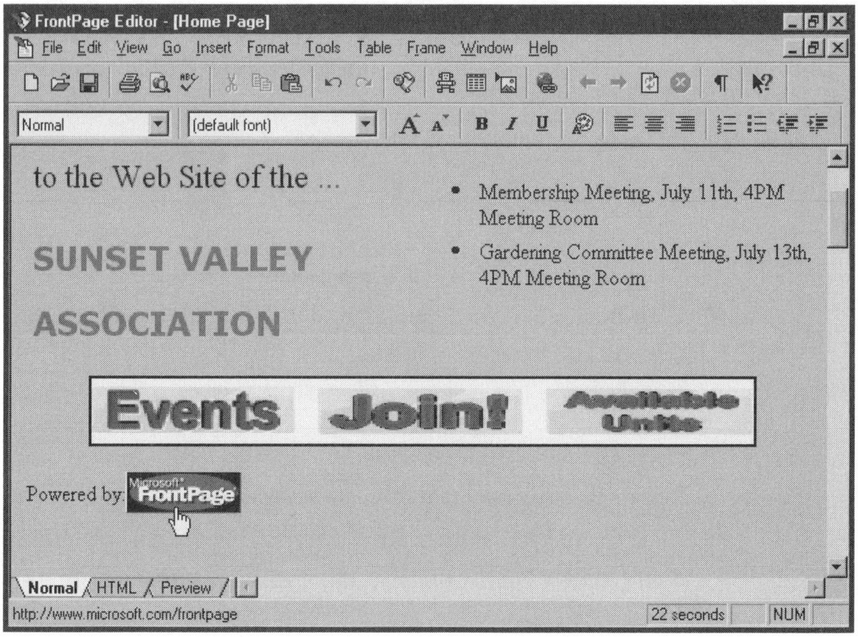

Figure 4.24

The image
hyperlink is
displayed in the
status bar.

If you've ever defined image maps before on your own—without Front-Page—you'll be pleasantly surprised that you don't need to deal with map files. FrontPage handles all files and links for you. It's as easy as drawing circles and rectangles, as you will see. When you select a graphic in Front-Page Editor, the Image toolbar becomes active, as shown in Figure 4.25.

The image toolbar includes 21 buttons described in Table 4.1.

Now you'll experiment with creating, editing, and testing graphic hotspots. To assign a rectangular graphic hotspot, follow these steps:

1. Click on the graphic image that contains the picture to launch the hyperlink, causing the Image toolbar to become active.

Figure 4.25

FrontPage Editor's
Image toolbar.

TABLE 4.1 FRONTPAGE EDITOR'S IMAGE TOOLBAR

Button	Function
Select	Allows you to select (and delete or edit) an already created hotspot
Rectangle	Allows you to draw a rectangular hotspot
Circle	Allows you to create a circular hotspot
Polygon	Allows you to create odd-shaped hotspots
Highlight	Highlights hotspots
Text	Creates new text messages
Make Transparent	Makes GIF images transparent
Crop	Crops the image to the size you want
Washout	Washes out or bleaches an image
Black and White	Removes the color from the image, leaving only black and white
Restore	Removes all the changes you've made and reloads the original
Rotate Left	Rotates the image 90 degrees to the left
Rotate Right	Rotates the image 90 degrees to the right
Reverse	Reverses the image
Flip	Flips the image upside down and back
More Contrast	Makes the image darker
Less Contrast	Makes the image lighter
More Brightness	Makes the image appear brighter
Less Brightness	Makes the image appear less bright
Bevel	Bevels (angles) the image border
Resample	Optimizes the resolution and file size of an image

NOTE A graphic hotspot can be the entire image or just part of the image.

2. Click on the Rectangle hotspot tool and draw a rectangle around the hotspot area, as shown in Figure 4.26. Don't worry if the rectangle isn't perfect—you can adjust the size of the hotspot later.

3. As soon as you release your mouse button, the Create Hyperlink dialog box appears. Select a Web page (and bookmark if you want) or Web address with which to hyperlink the graphic hotspot.

TIP When you move your cursor over an assigned hotspot, the filename of the hyperlink displays in the FrontPage Editor status bar.

4. Click on OK in the Create Hyperlink dialog box.

TIP You can test hotspot hyperlinks the same way you tested text hyperlinks—by holding down the Ctrl key while clicking on the hotspot.

To assign a circular graphic hotspot, follow these steps:

1. Click on the image that is to become a hyperlink; the Images toolbar then becomes active.

2. Click on the Circle hotspot tool and draw a circle starting from the middle of the hotspot area, as shown in Figure 4.27.

3. As soon as you release your mouse button, the Create Hyperlink dialog box appears. Select a Web page (and bookmark if you want) with which to hyperlink the circular hotspot.

4. Click on OK in the Create Hyperlink dialog box.

Figure 4.26

Defining a rectangular hotspot.

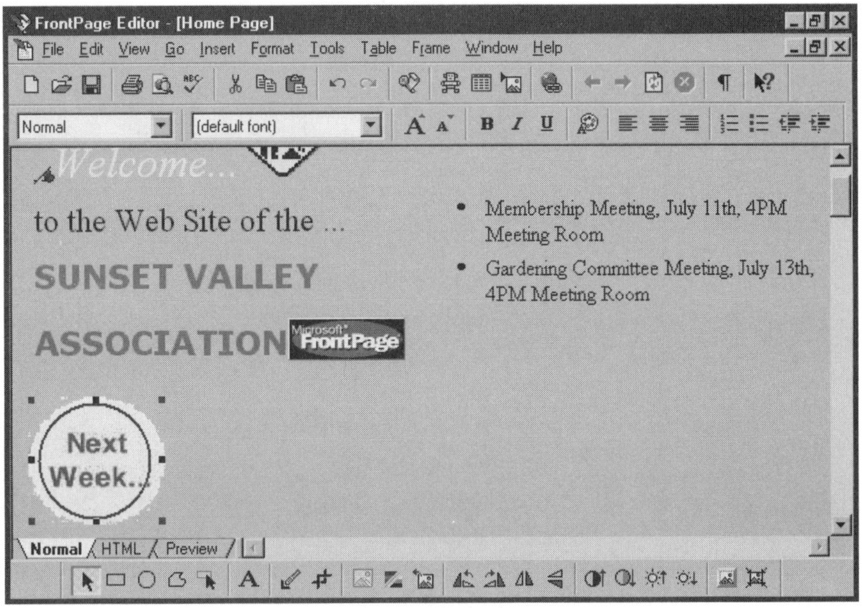

Figure 4.27

Defining a
circular hotspot.

The Polygon button in the Images toolbar enables you to outline odd-shaped objects. This feature allows you to create fun hotspots out of irregularly-shaped objects such as stars and icons. To assign an irregularly-shaped graphic hotspot, follow these steps:

1. Click on a graphic image to activate the Images toolbar and then click on the Polygon button, as shown in Figure 4.28.

2. Point the pencil-cursor at one corner of the hotspot and click.

3. Click again at the next nodal point in the polygon, as shown in Figure 4.29.

4. Continue to click at each nodal point until you have completed a polygon around the hotspot.

5. When you have completed the polygon, double-click.

6. As soon as you release your mouse button, the Create Hyperlink dialog box appears. Select a Web page (and bookmark if you want) with which to hyperlink the polygon hotspot.

7. Click on OK in the Create Hyperlink dialog box.

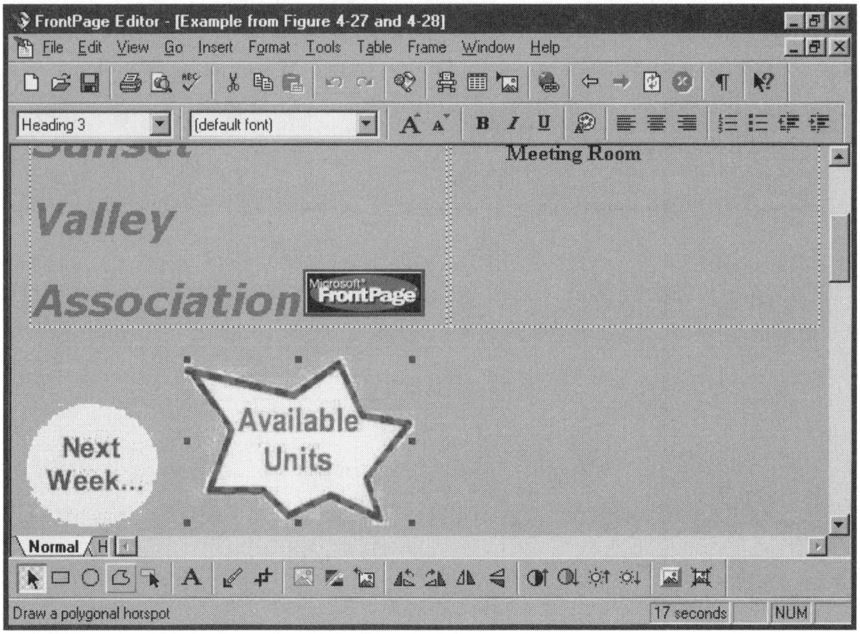

Figure 4.28

Selecting the polygon hotspot tool.

Figure 4.29

Outlining a polygon.

Editing a Graphic Hotspot

You can edit hotspot sizes and shapes. To edit hotspot properties, double-click on the hotspot. You edit a hotspot the same way you edit text hyperlinks. To edit a graphic hotspot, follow these steps:

1. Sometimes it's easier to identify hotspots if you can see them without the image in the background. You can view your hotspots by

clicking on the Highlight Hotspots button in the Images toolbar, as shown in Figure 4.30.

2. Deselect the Highlight Hotspots button to edit the hotspot size and shape.

3. Click on the Select button to select a hotspot to edit.

4. Click and drag on the small rectangular handles around the hotspot to resize it, as shown in Figure 4.31 with the "Events" hotspot.

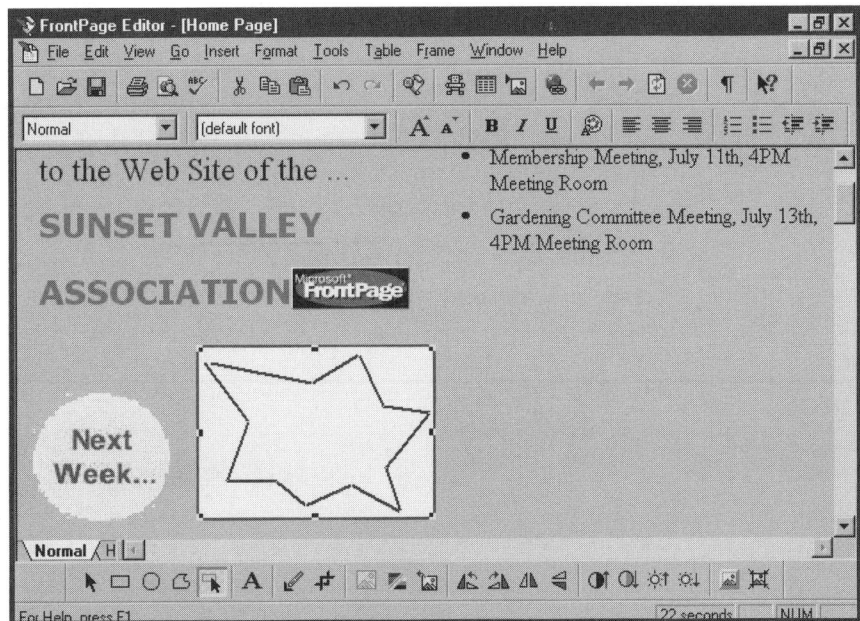

Figure 4.30

Highlighted hotspot.

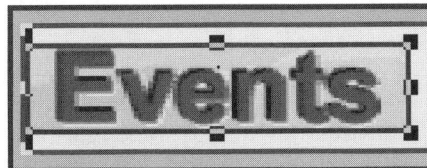

Figure 4.31

Resizing a hotspot.

Creating E-mail Hyperlinks

In this session, you have created hyperlinks to bookmarks within your Web page, to other pages in your Web site, and even to other sites within the World Wide Web. What a tangled web you weave! However, another very useful type of hyperlink exists that you haven't yet explored—e-mail hyperlinks.

In the Sunday sessions, you'll explore various ways to collect feedback from visitors to your Web site. One of the easiest ways is to provide a hyperlink to your e-mail address. The process is similar to the one you used to create Web hyperlinks. As long as your visitors' browsers have e-mail capability (such as Microsoft Internet Explorer and Netscape Navigator), they can click on a hyperlink (text or graphic) and send you e-mail. You could put your e-mail address on your site and let your visitors use their e-mail accounts to contact you, but using an e-mail hyperlink is much more convenient. If it's feedback you want, convenience is what you provide. To create an e-mail hyperlink, follow these steps:

1. Select the text (or graphic hotspot) you want to hyperlink to your e-mail address.

2. Click on the Create or Edit Hyperlink button in the toolbar.

NOTE If you're creating a hyperlink from a graphic hotspot, the Create Hyperlink dialog box opens automatically.

3. Click on the Make a hyperlink that sends e-mail button (the envelope), as shown in Figure 4.32.

4. Enter your e-mail address in the edit field, as shown in Figure 4.33 (This example uses my e-mail address).

5. Click on OK in the Create Hyperlink dialog box.

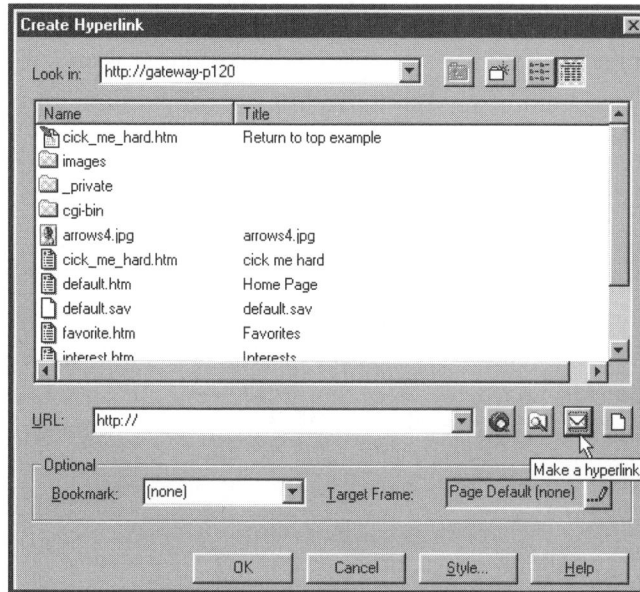

Figure 4.32

Creating an e-mail
hyperlink.

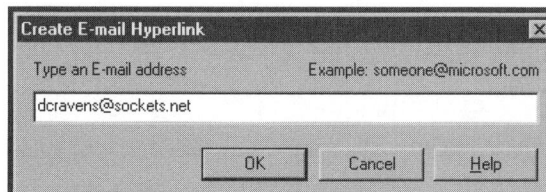

Figure 4.33

Defining an e-mail
hyperlink.

NOTE You need to have your Web site placed on the Internet to test this hyperlink. You'll cover that process in the Sunday sessions.

Examining Hyperlinks in FrontPage Explorer

Throughout this book, I emphasize that as long as you start FrontPage Explorer first and save new pages or changes to old ones on your Web site, you don't need to worry about the hyperlinks you create. FrontPage Explorer, working quietly in the background, makes sure that all the files you are linking are maintained in the proper directories.

To copy your Web site to an Internet Service Provider, use the Copy Web command in the FrontPage Explorer menu. Your entire site, with all its complex directories of files, is copied. FrontPage Explorer maintains proper directories and makes sure all the files needed to run your Web site are included on your provider. Still, you should visit FrontPage Explorer periodically and note the files and hyperlinks you've created. Files are viewed in Summary view. Site hyperlinks are best viewed in Hyperlinks view. To view files in Summary view in FrontPage Explorer, follow these steps:

1. In FrontPage Editor, click on the FrontPage Explorer button in the toolbar, as shown in Figure 4.34.

2. In FrontPage Explorer, click on the Folders view button in the View toolbar or pull down the View menu and select Folders, as shown in Figure 4.35.

NOTE The Folders view in FrontPage Explorer shows file sizes, file modification time and date, filename, and title.

To examine hyperlinks in FrontPage Explorer, follow these steps:

1. In FrontPage Editor, click on the FrontPage Explorer button on the toolbar.

2. Select the Hyperlinks button on the View toolbar.

Figure 4.34

Viewing FrontPage Explorer.

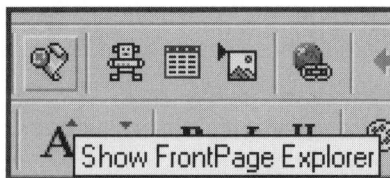

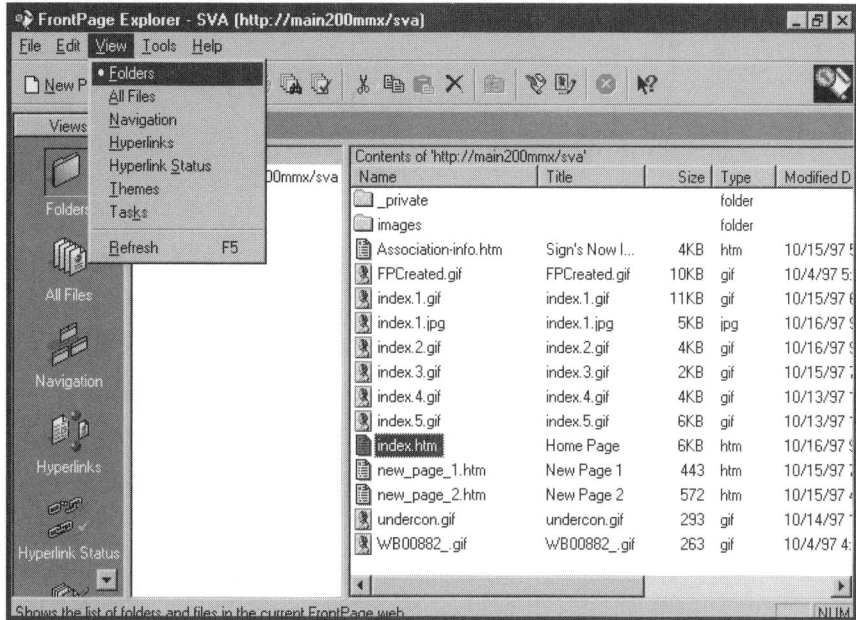

Figure 4.35

Switching to
Folders view
through the menu.

TIP You can drag the split bar between the three windows to see more of your hyperlinks, as shown in Figure 4.36.

---

3. Select Hyperlinks Inside Page in the View menu to see all the hyperlinks within a page (bookmarks). You can see details on a link by moving your cursor over it, as shown in Figure 4.37. Deselect Hyperlinks Inside Page if you want a less-cluttered view of your site.

TIP You can display (or hide) images by clicking on the Hyperlinks to Images button in the FrontPage Explorer toolbar, as shown in Figure 4.38.

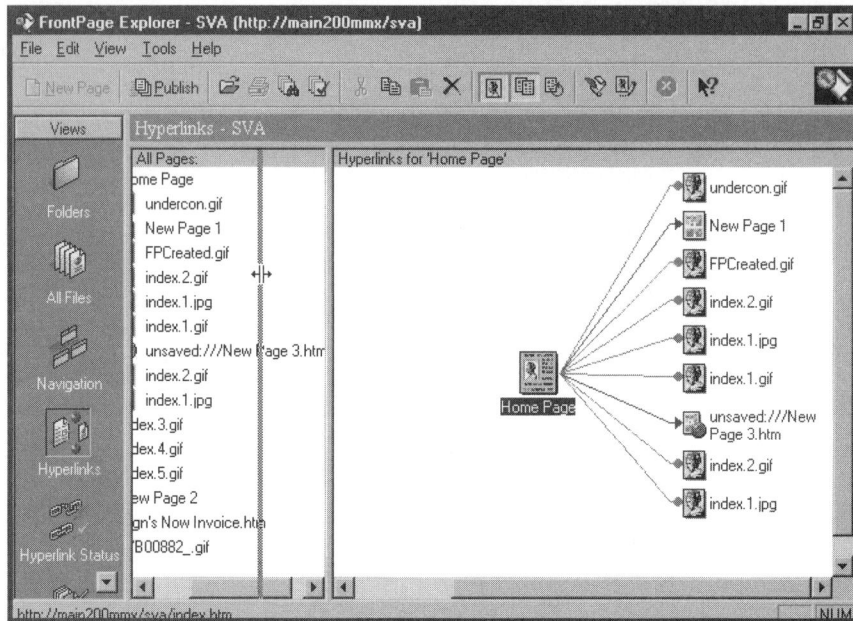

Figure 4.36

Show those hyperlinks.

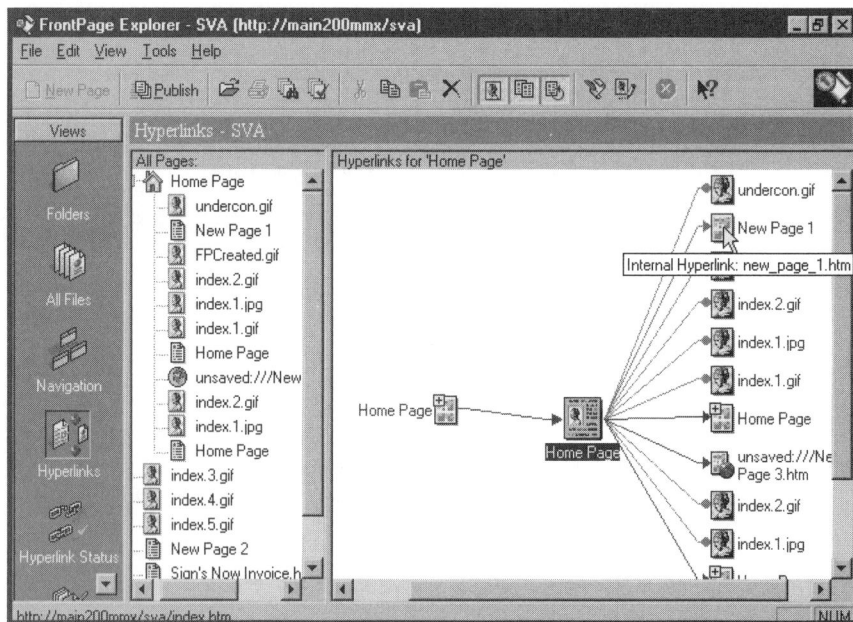

Figure 4.37

Viewing hyperlinks within a page.

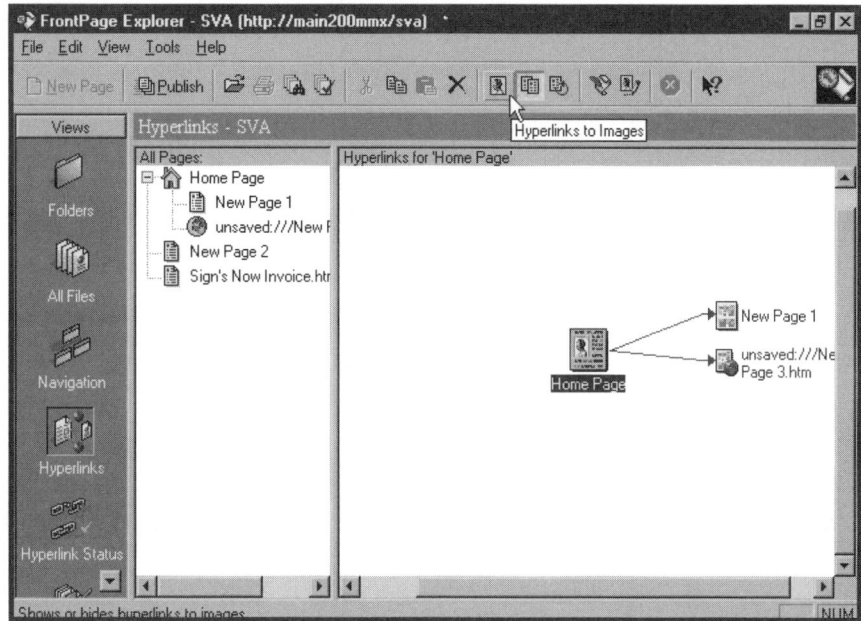

Figure 4.38

Viewing image hyperlinks.

Take a Break!

Your Web site is starting to hum. Not only does it look good, but you have explored the process of creating hyperlinks within, and from, your site. You could certainly skip ahead to the final session on Sunday, upload your Web site to a friendly Web site provider, and get online with a nice Web site.

However, you can still add more to your site in order to maximize its impact and functionality. For example, you still need to learn the whole process of creating forms and getting input. In this session, you began that process by allowing visitors to e-mail you directly from your site. Front-Page enables you to do much more—from creating forms to collecting user input to offering different formats for collecting that data. Start brainstorming about how you can use forms. Perhaps you can collect mailing lists and information from your visitors, sell your products, and even collect credit card information and take orders for products.

So give yourself a high-five, because you've accomplished quite a bit. Start thinking about how you'll take advantage of the features you'll be adding to your Web site on Sunday!

Letting Visitors Plug In with Forms

- Getting Information from Visitors with Forms
- Giving Visitors a Way to Submit Their Input
- Managing Form Results
- Saving Results As an HTML File
- Saving Results As a Text File

In earlier sessions, you created an attractive Web site. You formatted text, customized the site background, and inserted images. In the previous session, you created links that tied your site together and plugged it into the World Wide Web. Now you can create a site that is friendly and useful.

You next need to make your site a two-way street. Wouldn't you like to hear from your visitors? They can make suggestions as to how you can improve your Web site, place orders, tell you about themselves, or get on your mailing list—the possibilities are endless. The way to collect all this information from your visitors is to place input forms on your Web site. In designing an input form, you'll:

- Create the input forms that will enable you to collect information (You'll walk through the entire process later)

- Add Submit and Reset buttons so that visitors can send you their input (or bail out without sending the information)

- Define the input target (the file for storing the information collected from your Web site)

So, if you've had a healthy breakfast, a refreshing swim, and a quick jog—or maybe just a few cups of strong black coffee—you should be ready to start this session.

I know I keep reminding you about the routine for opening or creating a Web site, but if you remember the basic principles, you'll never experience the annoyance of losing pages or links in your Web site.

To review: Start in the Explorer and open your pages by double-clicking on them in the Folder or Hyperlink view. This way your Web site stays intact and will be ready to be copied to a Web site provider when the time comes (and it will come soon).

Getting Information from Visitors with Forms

Internet browsers that interpret HTML can handle a variety of input forms. Remember those tests that required filling in circles with a number 2 pencil? Those circles are available—only now they're called *radio buttons*, and a pencil isn't required. At the other extreme, you can also allow your visitors to write freestyle verse. In short, FrontPage offers so many ways to get information from your visitors that you should be able to find out just about anything you want to know, in any format you choose. When you collect information, you'll do so in one of these available formats:

- ✪ Check boxes
- ✪ Radio buttons
- ✪ Drop-down menus
- ✪ One-line text boxes
- ✪ Scrolling text boxes

You'll explore each of these formats for collecting visitor input. The input area in Figure 5.1 shows a Web site that uses each type of input format.

Using Check Boxes

A check box will always be either checked or unchecked. Room here for "maybe" or "sort of" doesn't exist. Sometimes this is a fine way to collect information from your visitors. Do they want to be on your mailing list?

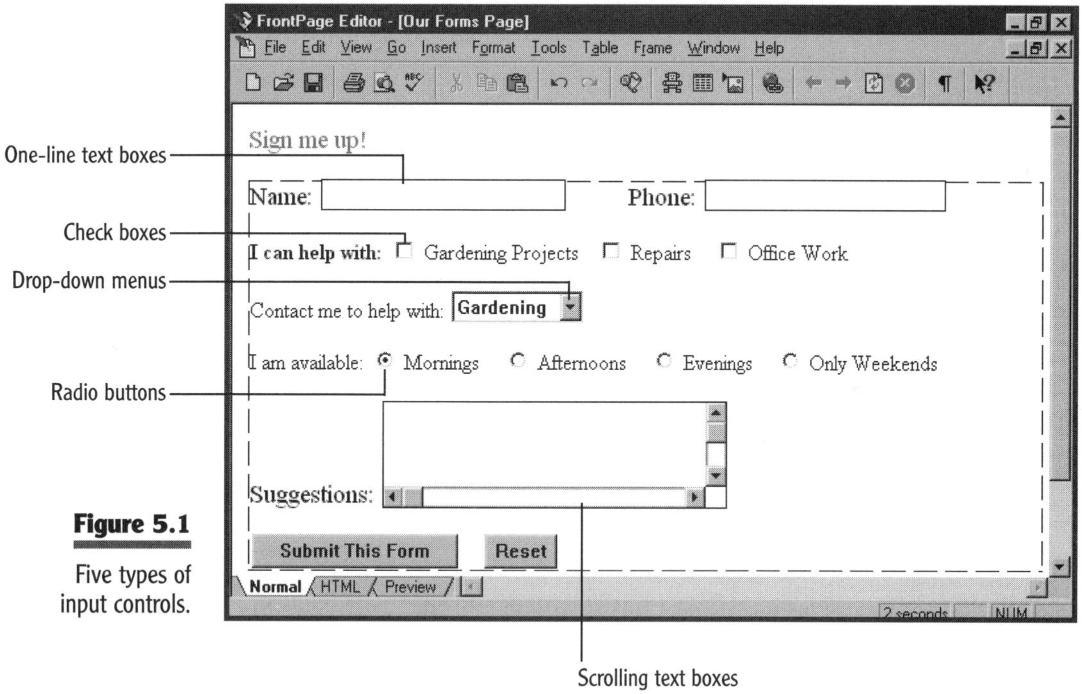

One-line text boxes —
Check boxes —
Drop-down menus —
Radio buttons —

Figure 5.1

Five types of
input controls.

Scrolling text boxes

Do they want to buy a product? Are they volunteering to work on the
construction project this weekend? Basic questions like these are appropriate for check box input. Can you have more than one check box on
your Web page? Sure. You can have as many as you want. However, each
check box gives your visitor only two options: to check it, or to leave it
unchecked.

If a check box is appropriate, placing one in a Web site is pretty simple.
You pose an option, decide whether the check box should appear checked
or empty (depending on which answer you want to suggest), and put the
check box on the page. For example, if you want to let your visitors select
from a list of products, check boxes enable them to select one, many, or
no items from the list. To place a check box, follow these steps:

1. Place your cursor on the spot in the page where you want the
   check box to appear.

2. Select <u>V</u>iew, Forms Toolbar to display the Forms toolbar if it's not already visible. The Forms toolbar is shown in Figure 5.2.

3. Click on the Check Box button in the Forms toolbar, as shown in Figure 5.3. If you are not inserting this check box into an already existing form, FrontPage creates the rest of the form, including the Clear and Submit buttons, for you.

4. Type a prompt to your visitor to the right of the check box, but before the Submit and Reset buttons. "Send me information" or "Sign me up!" should be fine. It can be frustrating to locate this spot with the mouse, so I suggest using the back arrow until the cursor is in place.

5. Right-click on the new check box and select Form Field Properties from the shortcut menu. In the Check Box Properties dialog box that appears, you must provide four elements of information: a name, the value (On or Off), the initial state of the check box (checked or unchecked), and the position in the Tab order.

TIP

The name and value fields define information that only you see. When you read the results of visitor input, a report displays the field name and value. For example, if a check box field name is "Send me a catalog" and the value is set to "On," your report states this: Send me a catalog—On.

You'll know that this person wants a catalog. What your visitor sees is simply the text you type on the page next to the check box.

Figure 5.2

The Forms toolbar.

Figure 5.3

The Check Box button.

6. Enter a name in the <u>N</u>ame area of the Check Box Properties dialog box. The name should be easy to interpret when input is posted to a file.

7. Enter a value in the <u>V</u>alue area that appears in the results file if the user selects the check box. "ON" is usually a nice choice.

8. Select an Initial State value of <u>C</u>hecked or N<u>o</u>t checked. This is where you get to suggest a response. You must set the default to either Checked or Not checked. The simple check box is not subtle in its method of collecting information.

9. The Tab order field specifies the order in which the controls on a page become the active control when the user presses the Tab key. For now, leave the Tab order field blank.

10. When you have entered a name and a value and have decided on an initial state for the check box, click on OK in the Check Box Properties dialog box, as shown in Figure 5.4.

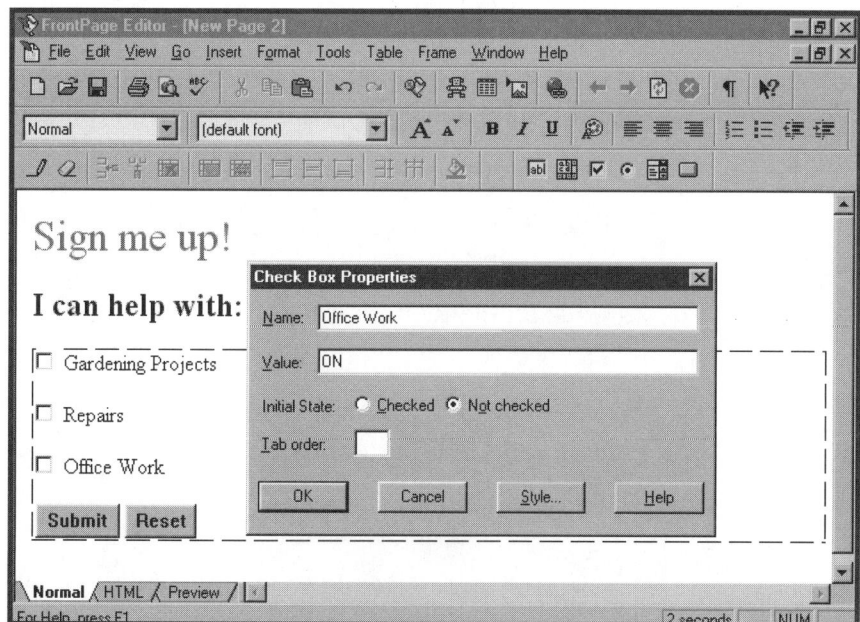

Figure 5.4

Defining
a check box.

NOTE
When you create a check box or any other input form, horizontal lines appear defining the form area. These lines are not visible to your visitors, but they identify the form. You'll examine how this works later in this session when you assign a target for the input and program the Submit and Reset buttons.

Using Radio Buttons—Shades of the Past

Very few of today's computer kids understand the history of radio buttons. You know, the type of buttons found on cars before the 1980s. In order to tune into a preset station, you had to press the radio button in, which pushed all the others out. Today's digital car stereos have changed the way radio buttons work, but the idea is still the same. When one radio button is on, all of the others are off.

Putting the car stereo history aside, radio buttons are a fine way to collect information if you're asking people to pick one item among multiple choices. You might be asking people to choose colors for a widget or having visitors decide whether to pay using Visa, MasterCard, or Discover. The concept to keep in mind is that only one button can be selected at a time. Therefore, radio buttons typically are put together in groups.

To collect information with radio buttons, follow these steps:

1. Click on the spot on your page where the first of your radio buttons is to appear.

2. Click on the Radio Button option in the toolbar, as shown in Figure 5.5.

3. Type a user prompt for the radio button. The final graphic result is shown in Figure 5.6.

Figure 5.5

Inserting a radio button.

Figure 5.6

The result of entering your user prompt.

I am available: ⊙ Mornings

4. Right-click on the radio button and select Form Field Properties. Then enter a group name in the Group Name area of the Radio Button Properties dialog box and a value in the Value area, as shown in Figure 5.7. Values for Radio Buttons work much the same as those for check boxes.

TIP

To remember the group name for radio buttons, just create one radio button, copy it as many times as needed, and then change the values, but not the group name.

5. Decide on an initial state for the radio button, but remember, only one button in the group can have an initial state of Selected.

6. Click on OK in the Radio Button Properties dialog box.

7. Add additional radio buttons with the same group name, but with different value names. You'll need to type new text prompts so that your visitors know what they're choosing. Copy and paste them and then change the values for the different radio buttons, as shown in Figure 5.8.

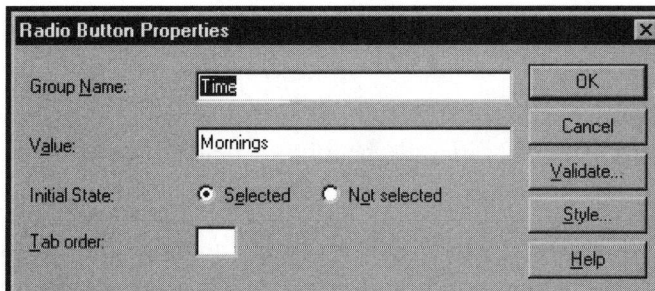

Figure 5.7

Defining a radio button.

Radio Button Properties

Group Name: Time
Value: Mornings
Initial State: ⊙ Selected ○ Not selected
Tab order:

OK | Cancel | Validate... | Style... | Help

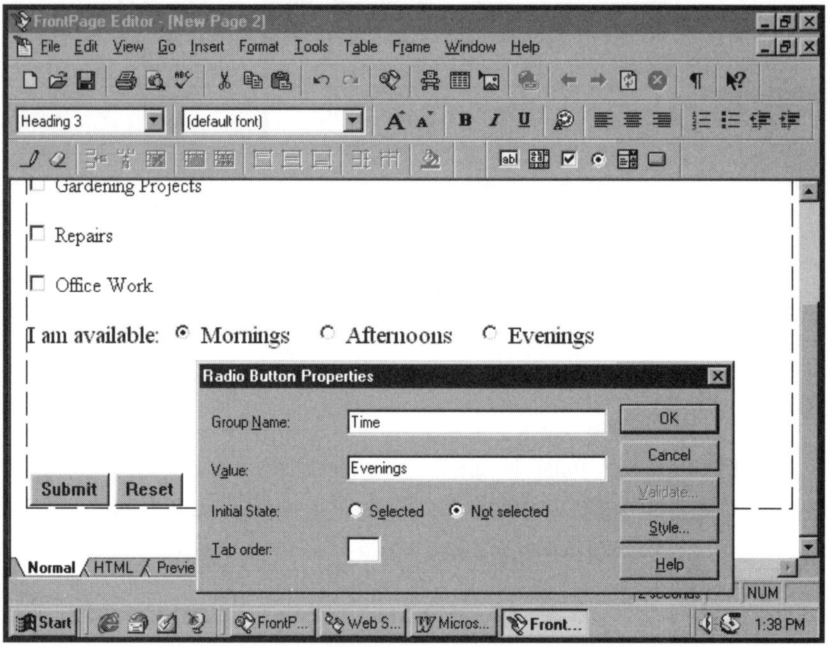

Figure 5.8

A group of
radio buttons.

Using One-Line Text Boxes

If the type of information you want to collect is a little too complex to fit into a check box or radio button (for example, your visitor's e-mail address), the one-line text box may be a better choice.

Examples of one-line input include phone numbers, names, addresses, etc. (Don't worry. If you want to give your visitors a lot of space to pontificate, scrolling text boxes are next.) Later, in the Saving Results as an HTML File section, you'll save one-line input to a file with the field name and the input, so you need to name the field something that will make sense when you try to sort through a file of collected responses. For example, you can call the phone field "Phone" and the address field "Address." To create a one-line text box, follow these steps:

1. Place your cursor on the page where the input form should appear. Click on the One-Line Text Box button in the Forms toolbar, as shown in Figure 5.9.

Figure 5.9

Creating a one-line
text box.

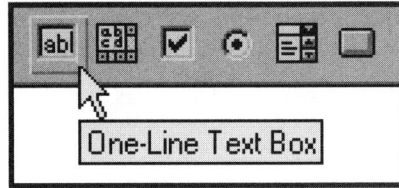

One-Line Text Box

2. Type a text prompt for your text box, as shown in Figure 5.10.

3. Right-click on the text box and select Form Field Properties from the shortcut menu. Enter a name for the field in the Name box of the Text Box Properties dialog box that appears. This field name does not display for visitors. The purpose is to help you remember the information you're collecting when you review it in the target file (see Figure 5.11).

4. Enter an initial value in the Initial value area only if you want to prompt your visitor to enter certain information. However, if you wanted to do that, wouldn't you be using a check box field? Not necessarily—you might want to suggest input, but not require it.

5. Define limits for the display of width in the Width in characters field.

Figure 5.10

Adding a prompt
for a text box.

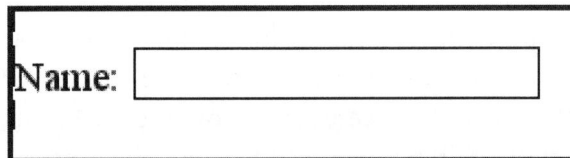

Name:

Figure 5.11

Naming the text
box field.

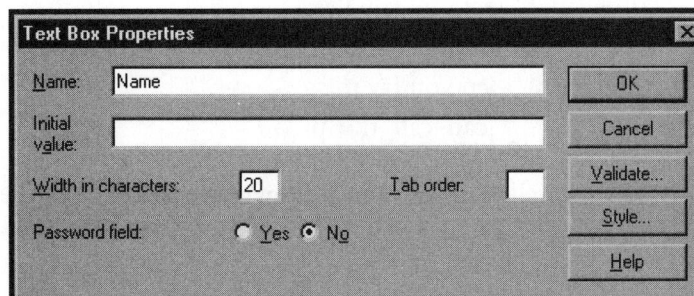

Text Box Properties

Name: Name

Initial
value:

Width in characters: 20   Tab order:

Password field: ○ Yes ● No

OK

Cancel

Validate...

Style...

Help

6. You can elect to make this field a *password field* (which means that the text the visitor enters will be treated as a password and displayed with asterisks). If this field is a password field, click on the Yes radio button.

TIP Defining passwords is beyond the scope of this session; however, selecting this feature even if you're not defining a password does have an advantage. Because password fields display as asterisks on the input screen, if you're asking a visitor to enter sensitive information, such as a credit card number, you can select the Yes radio button.

---

7. When you have defined at least the field name (and that is the only required element of a text box), click on OK in the Text Box Properties dialog box.

Using Drop-Down Menus

Your visitor can pick from a list of choices on a drop-down menu. Drop-down menus are more flexible than radio buttons because they allow the visitor to choose only one option, or if you wish, more than one option.

You can use Ctrl+click to choose more than one option when using a drop-down menu. If your visitors can choose more than one of the drop-down menu items, give them a hint with a helpful bit of text like "Use Ctrl while clicking to select more than one choice." Drop-down menus do not allow visitors to enter text—only to choose from a list you prepare. To create a drop-down menu, follow these steps:

1. Start creating a drop-down menu by clicking on your page at the spot where the form is to appear.

2. Click on the Drop-Down Menu button in the Forms toolbar, as shown in Figure 5.12.

3. Right-click on the Drop-Down Menu box and select Form Field Properties.

Figure 5.12

Inserting a drop-down menu.

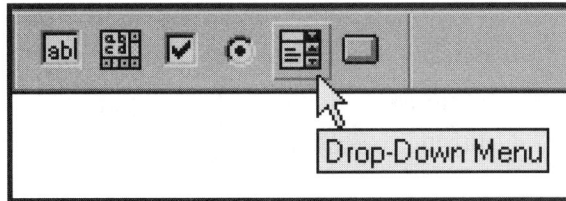

4. In the <u>N</u>ame area of the Drop-Down Menu Properties dialog box that appears, enter the field name to identify this input in the target file.

5. Click on the <u>A</u>dd button in the Drop-Down Menu Properties dialog box.

6. Enter a choice in the <u>C</u>hoice area of the Add Choice dialog box that appears.

7. In the Initial State area of the Add Choice dialog box, choose either <u>S</u>elected or <u>N</u>ot Selected to determine if the initial state of the choice will be selected when the visitor pulls down the list.

NOTE Remember, you can add more than one selected choice and define the initial state of more than one menu selection as Selected.

8. Use the Specify <u>V</u>alue area if you want different information to appear in your target file—for example, if the visitor chooses "I just want to bug you," from the menu, you can display that information as "bugging" in the results file.

9. When you have defined a menu choice, click on OK in the Add Choice dialog box.

10. Use the <u>A</u>dd button in the Drop-Down Menu Properties dialog box to add more choices to the menu, as shown in Figure 5.13.

11. When you've defined the drop-down menu, click on OK in the Drop-Down Menu Properties dialog box.

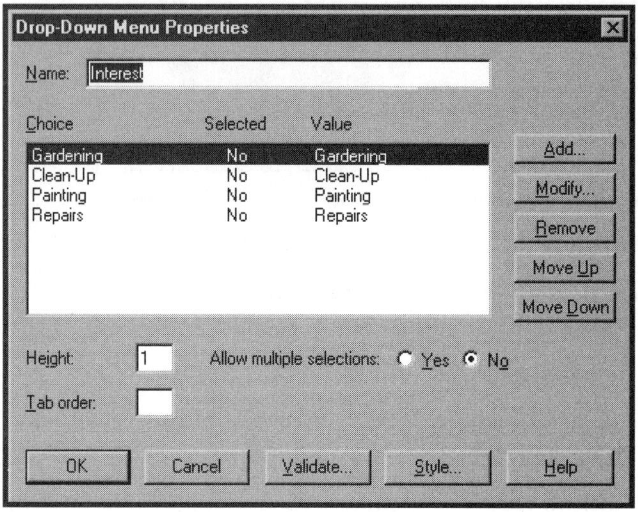

Drop-Down Menu Properties

Name: Interest

Choice	Selected	Value
Gardening	No	Gardening
Clean-Up	No	Clean-Up
Painting	No	Painting
Repairs	No	Repairs

Add...
Modify...
Remove
Move Up
Move Down

Height: 1   Allow multiple selections: ○ Yes ● No

Tab order:

OK   Cancel   Validate...   Style...   Help

Figure 5.13

Four choices
added to the
drop-down menu.

TIP You can change drop-down menu properties by double-clicking on the menu in FrontPage Editor.

Using Scrolling Text Boxes—Freeform Input

If you're soliciting poetry or general comments, the scrolling text box is the best choice. This box scrolls from left to right, up and down, or both, just like a little window on the page with its own vertical and horizontal scroll bars. Scrolling text box input is also attached to a field name, so when you read it in the target file, you can tell what it's about. To gather input in a scrolling text box, follow these steps:

1. Place your cursor where the text box is to appear (perhaps beneath a heading like "Comments?") and then click on the Scrolling Text Box button in the Forms toolbar, as shown in Figure 5.14.

2. Right-click in the scrolling text box and select Form Field Properties from the shortcut menu.

3. Enter a field name in the Name area of the Scrolling Text Box Prop-

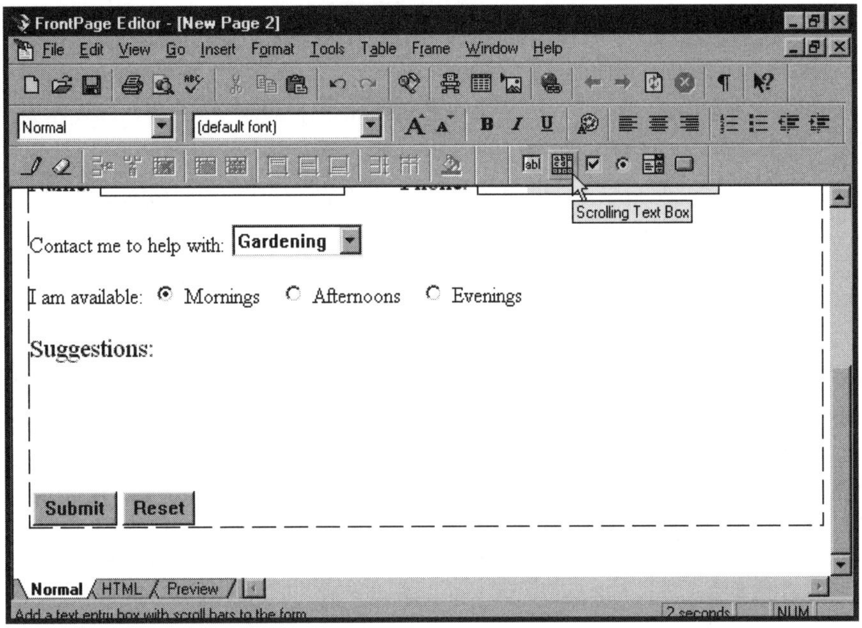

Figure 5.14

Inserting a
scrolling text box.

erties dialog box, as shown in Figure 5.15. You need to enter something in the Initial value area only if you want to prompt your visitor with some suggested text.

NOTE The Width in characters and Number of lines fields do not constrain the amount of text
that can be entered—they only define the form size. You'll learn a better way to adjust
this in a minute.

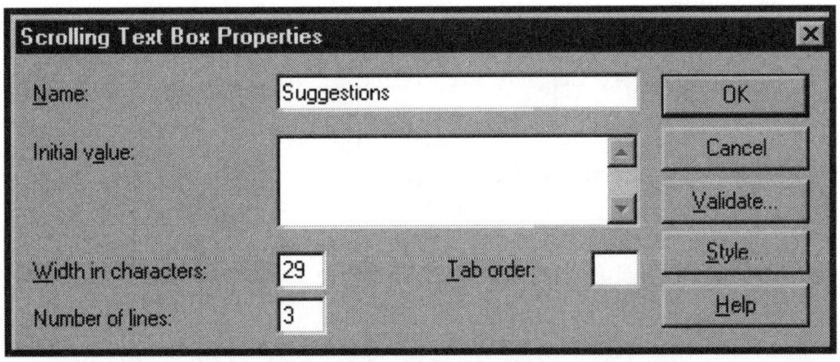

Figure 5.15

Naming a
scrolling text box.

4. Click on OK in the Scrolling Text Box Properties dialog box when you've defined a name for the field.

Adjusting the Form Size

You can change the size of scrolling text boxes, one-line text boxes, and drop-down menus. You didn't pay too much attention to the options for assigning form size in the dialog boxes because it's easier to do this right on the FrontPage Editor page. To resize a form, follow these steps:

1. Click anywhere in the form. Handles (small rectangles on the top, bottom, and corners of the form) appear.

2. Click and drag on a handle to resize the form, as shown in Figure 5.16.

NOTE   You will not be able to resize list boxes until there are items in the list.

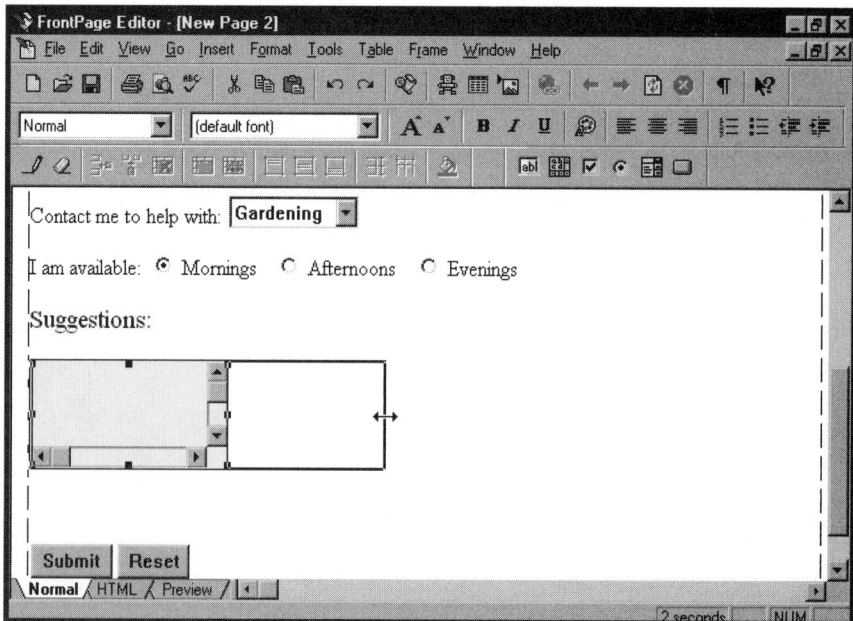

Figure 5.16

Resizing a scrolling text box.

Take a Break!

So far, you've designed some very nice, if eclectic, input forms. You can allow a visitor to enter any pertinent information. The next step is to assign properties to your forms so that this valuable information gets shuttled down the information highway to a file where you can collect and use it.

Before you move on and do that, though, it's time for a stretch. Take some time to create and modify your input forms, and then be sure to save the page you're working on in FrontPage Editor. Assuming you started the page from FrontPage Explorer, saving your work in Editor ensures the integrity of your Web site. If FrontPage Explorer detects Web pages that are not linked to the site, it prompts you to link them when the pages are saved in Editor.

After you create some input forms, relax for a bit. Think about how you would like to get the information being collected. In a text file? Or perhaps in an HTML file that can be viewed using FrontPage Editor or your Web browser.

Giving Visitors a Way to Submit Their Input

At this point, you're all dressed up with nowhere to go. You've created five different types of input forms: check boxes, radio buttons, drop-down menus, one-line text boxes, and scrolling text boxes. What happens, however, when your visitors interact with your form? So far, nothing. They can see their input on their own screens, but as soon as they leave your Web site, the input is gone forever.

The Submit and Reset Buttons

The next step in the process of actually collecting data is to look at the push button that allows your visitors to submit the information they typed into the form. This Submit button is accompanied by a Reset button that allows the user to say, "Oh, never mind," and either enter new information or just give up. The Submit and Reset buttons are placed automatically by FrontPage when you insert the first control on your form.

Omitting a Reset button can be annoying to your visitors—but omitting a Submit button means you'll never see the information your visitors enter in your form. In short, every form needs a Submit button.

If you've actually been creating a Web site and following along even loosely with this book, you've got some input forms on a Web page in FrontPage Editor. As you work with the forms, you need to know the following points:

- Input forms are bounded by dashed lines—one above and one below the form.

- A form can include just one input object (such as a one-line text box) or a bunch of objects (such as several radio buttons). All the input objects bounded by the dashed lines are part of the same form. Only one Submit button is required per form.

- When you right-click within a form (between the dashed lines), a shortcut menu appears containing Form Properties as one of its options, as shown in Figure 5.17. If you right-click elsewhere in a page, you won't see the Form Properties option. Try it and see.

Each form should have one Submit button and one Reset button. The Reset button is normally on the same line as, and to the right of, the Submit button. In order to learn about buttons, go ahead and delete the Submit button by clicking on it and pressing the Delete key.

After you re-create Submit and Reset buttons in your form, you'll finish the process by defining the destination and format of the information you're collecting. To place a Submit button, follow these steps:

1. Place your cursor after the end of your last input object—a check box, a group of radio buttons, a text box, and so on.

2. If you want to place your Submit button on a separate line (and most folks do), press Enter to create a new line for the Submit button.

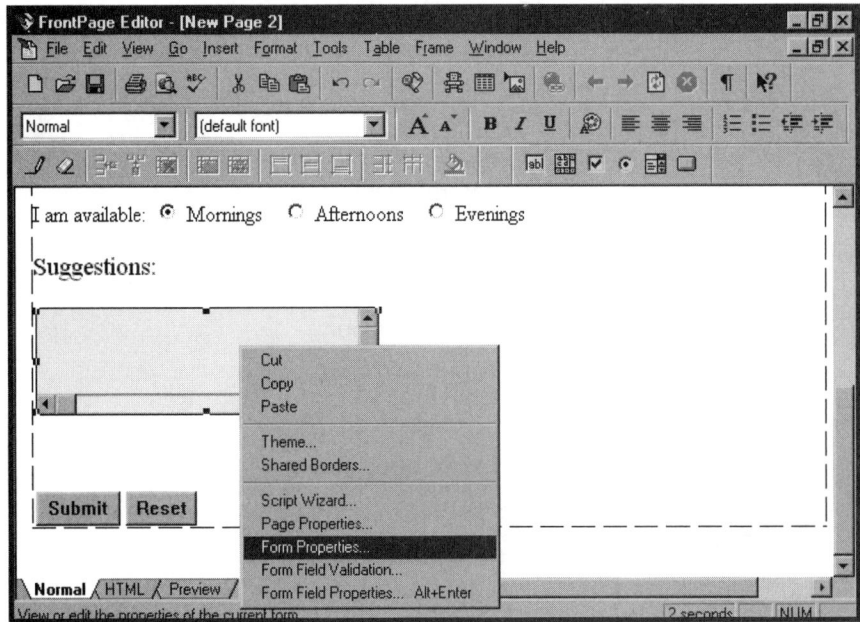

Figure 5.17

Opening the
Form Properties
dialog box.

3. Click on the Push Button option on the Forms toolbar, as shown
in Figure 5.18.

Right-click on the new Submit button and select Form Field Properties.
Because all you are doing is creating a button to submit the contents of a
form, a button name isn't necessary.

4. Enter additional text in the Value/Label box in the Push Button
Properties dialog box if you want to edit the label that appears on
the screen, as shown in Figure 5.19.

TIP

Many Net cruisers are used to seeing the word "Submit" on Submit buttons, but you can
place any text you want on the Submit button. Even if you want to get creative, you
should keep the word "Submit" somewhere on the button. You can even embellish it with
"Submit Response Now," or something similar.

Figure 5.18

Inserting a
push button.

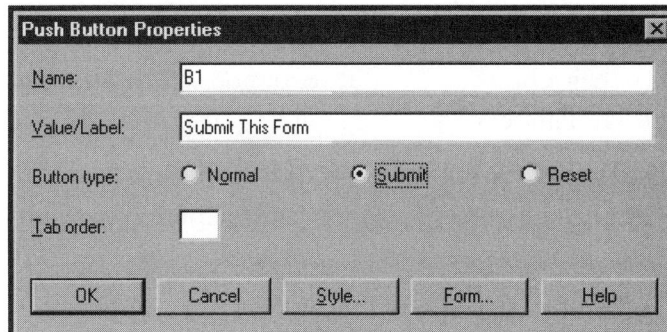

Figure 5.19

Editing the Submit
button label.

5. When you have edited the text that you want to appear on your
Submit button, make sure the Submit radio button is selected and
then click on OK in the Push Button Properties dialog box. A Submit button appears in your form, as shown in Figure 5.20.

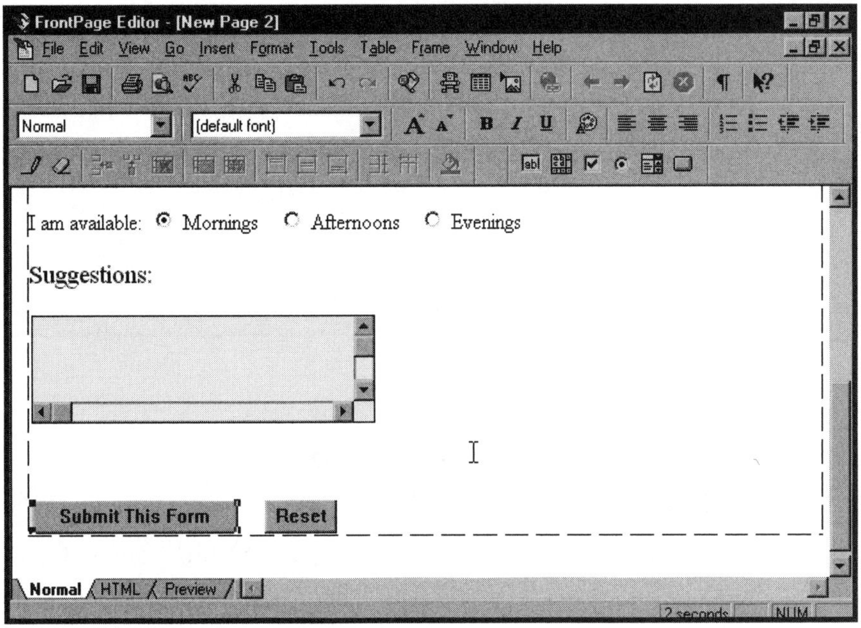

Figure 5.20

Submit this!

> **NOTE**
>
> Should you ever need to replace the Reset button, the procedure is the same as the one outlined for the Submit button, with one exception: Instead of selecting the Submit radio button, you would select the Reset radio button.

You might want to change the label on a button (but not the Submit or Reset button) after you have placed it. Editing the Value/Label field on a button is easy. To edit Push Button Properties, follow these steps:

1. Double-click on the push button whose properties you want to edit.

2. Make changes in the properties assigned to the push button (see Figure 5.21).

3. Click on OK in the Push Button Properties dialog box.

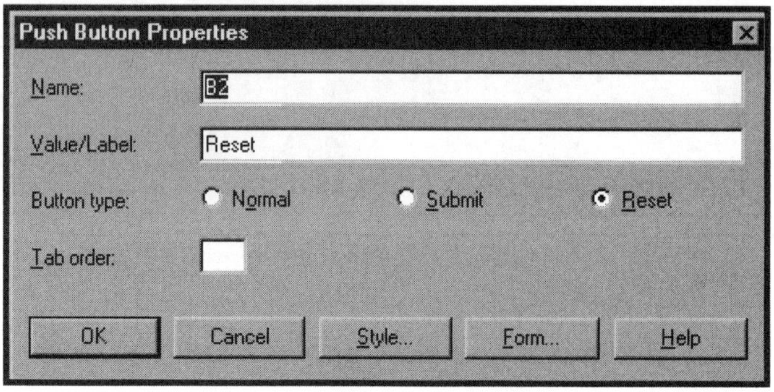

Figure 5.21

Editing the Reset
button label.

Using More Than One Form Within a Form Outline

You can have many form objects within a single form outline. An input form that has radio buttons, check boxes, a drop-down menu, and text boxes is shown in Figure 5.22.

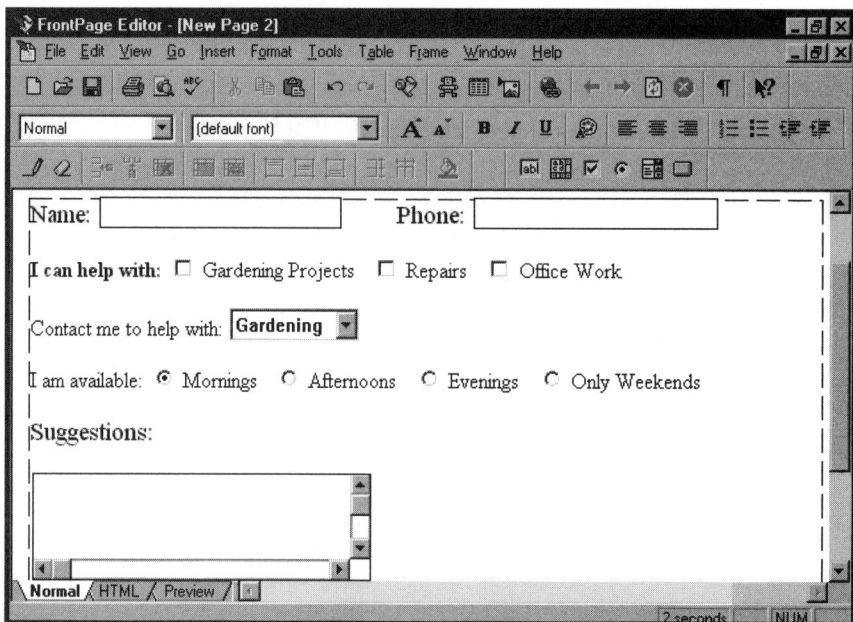

Figure 5.22

So many questions
in just one form!

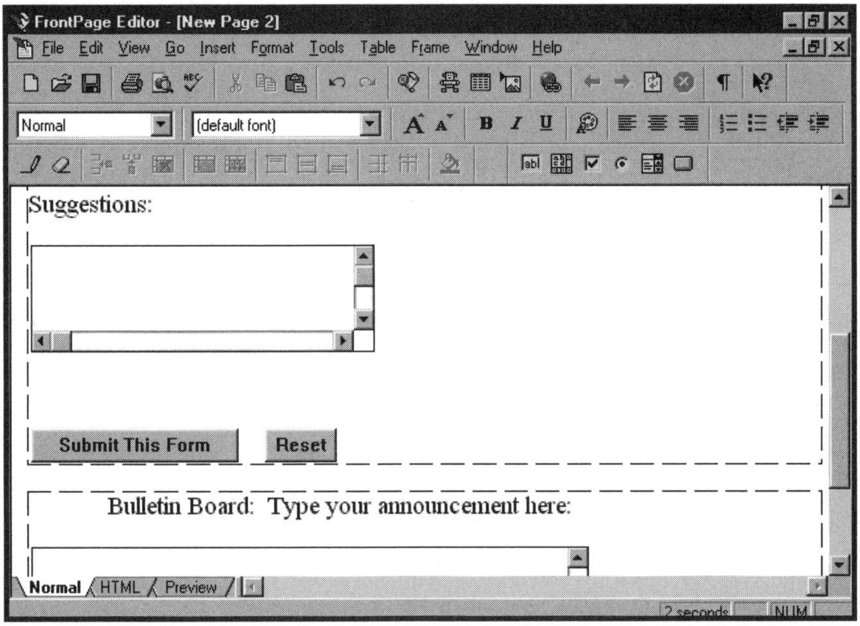

Figure 5.23

Two forms—you can tell by the dotted lines around each.

You can organize your input form objects into more than one form. For example, you might want to collect information about your visitors and then access that information yourself in a form that enables you to tally the information, generate form letters, or just keep the information out of view from your visitors. At the same time, you might want to collect information on the same page that is accessible to visitors. You can do this by organizing your form objects into more than one form, as shown in Figure 5.23. All of this will make more sense when you actually explore the different forms for collecting input.

Managing Form Results

After you've defined and refined your form, you need to decide what should happen when a visitor clicks on the Submit button. In the old days, HTML coders who wanted to collect input in forms had to either create or borrow executable programs written in programming languages such as Visual Basic and Perl. These batches of programming code were called CGI (Common Gateway Interface) scripts. In fact, what most folks did to create a form was to find prefab CGI scripts at Web sites and plug them into their HTML code. Thank goodness FrontPage lets you move past having to deal with CGI's.

In FrontPage, you can use the Form Handler to determine what happens when a visitor submits input. Although the Form Handler is one of the most important components of FrontPage, it's not the most intuitive. The Form Handler offers five options for handling input:

○ Custom ISAPI, NSAPI, or CGI Scripts

○ The Internet Database Connector

○ The Discussion Component

○ The Registration Component

○ The Save Results Component

The Custom ISAPI, NSAPI, or CGI Scripts option enables you to plug into an existing, custom-coded, data-collection programming module. The Internet Database Connector option is used with programmed queries for Internet databases. You can use the Internet Database Connector with programs such as Microsoft Access 97 to let users work with online databases through your Web site. This process is beyond the scope of this book, but you can check out a good reference book, such as Prima's *Hands On Access 97*, if this is a feature you need. The other three Form Handler options are different kinds of FrontPage Components. FrontPage Components are automated features that perform functions in Web sites. In the next session, you'll explore many of these handy little tools and witness the dynamic things they do in your Web site.

Selecting one of the form options in the Form Handler is easy. The first trick to making sure that the option works is to ignore all the options except for the Save Results Component. Before you make that choice, take a quick look at the other options.

Custom ISAPI, NSAPI, or CGI Scripts

As a concession to those who would want to do some of their own coding, FrontPage allows form input to be handled by custom ISAPI, NSAPI, or CGI scripts, which you can write or copy from someone.

ISAPI and NSAPI are both similar to CGI. ISAPI stands for Internet Server Application Programming Interface, and NSAPI stands for Netscape Server Application Programming Interface. While these two competing programming languages battle it out for supremacy in the Form Handler coding universe, you can ignore them both and simply use the powerful, convenient, and easy-to-use Save Results Component that comes with FrontPage.

If you've written a custom script (and you most likely have not), you can choose this option. If, for some reason, you feel you need to find a custom CGI script, here is one source:

FIND IT ON ▶ THE WEB

http://www.nlc-bnc.ca/pubs/netnotes/notes19.htm

If you don't have a custom CGI script, just be thankful that you don't need to write or copy CGI scripts anymore, and move on.

NOTE Some ISP's do not allow user-written CGI scripts because of a perceived security risk to their servers.

Using the Internet Database Connector

The Internet Database Connector option enables you to create a file that stores queries using the Microsoft Internet Information Server. These queries work with online databases compatible with a universal database format called *Open Database Connectivity* (ODBC). ODBC and Internet database queries are used in customized, sophisticated database applications that are well beyond the scope of this book.

Using the Discussion Component

You can use the Discussion Component to create input forms that interact with a page where other input is posted so that a visitor can read other contributions and then add comments. However, a discussion page can be created in an easier and better way, and I advise staying away from the Discussion Component in the Form Handler. Use the Discussion Web Wizard if you want a full-fledged, interactive forum with a generated table of contents so that visitors can find discussion areas of interest. You'll explore this when you investigate some of FrontPage's wizards and templates at the end of the weekend.

- -

NOTE

You may have noticed that you've been avoiding wizards and templates. The problem with jumping into wizards and templates right away is that the moment you want to modify them, you'll need skills and tools you're unprepared to utilize. I'll hold off with the wizards and templates until you master the skills you learn here. This way, when you do enter the world of wizards, you'll be prepared.

- -

Using the Registration Component

Another option for handling a form is to create a Registration Component. This allows you to restrict your Web site to users who have been assigned a passcode. If you want to do this, use the FrontPage Registration Page Template. This process is explored in Appendix B, "Taking a Shortcut with Templates."

Using the Save Results Component

The Save Results Component in the Form Handler gives you the option of collecting input in eight different formats.

I'll show you all of them, but they boil down to variations on two possibilities:

✿ Saving the results to an HTML page

✪ Saving the results to a text file

If you save your results as an HTML file, your visitors can see the input with a Web browser. This is handy for creating bulletin boards and other information that should be shared by all visitors. The bulletin board in Figure 5.24 is a result of input being sent to an HTML page that can be accessed by any visitor to the Web site.

You can restrict visitors to the results page by not publicizing the URL address of the page where the input was saved. You can still view the input because you know the page where it was stored.

FrontPage gives you some variety in formatting HTML target files. Figure 5.25 shows an example of a target page using an HTML definition list with fields formatted as terms, and input formatted as definitions.

Directing input to HTML files opens up many possibilities for sharing input. Not only are your visitors getting information from your page and

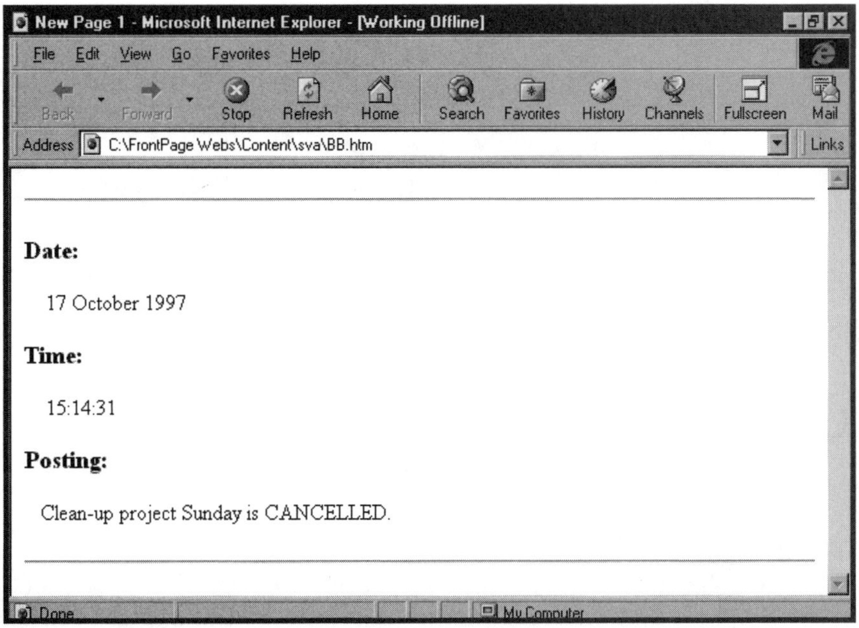

Date:

  17 October 1997

Time:

  15:14:31

Posting:

  Clean-up project Sunday is CANCELLED.

Figure 5.24

Input form results displayed on an HTML page.

sending responses, but they are contributing to the Web site itself. Which, in an endless loop, contributes to a dynamic Web site.

On the other hand, saving input as text files is loaded with just as much potential as using HTML pages as targets for input. Imagine collecting the names and fax numbers of everyone who visits your site and following up with a fax the next day. You can also sort visitors by the product or topic they have indicated they want information about. The possibilities are as endless as the number of readers of this book, which undoubtedly is a large number.

FrontPage does not come with a text processor or spreadsheet. Windows 95 provides a crude text processor to view text-formatted input. The real fun, in my opinion, comes from dumping that input into a program such as Word or Excel and manipulating it. Results opened as a Word document can easily be used as data files for mailing lists. When a results document is opened in Excel, it can be edited, organized, and even sorted,

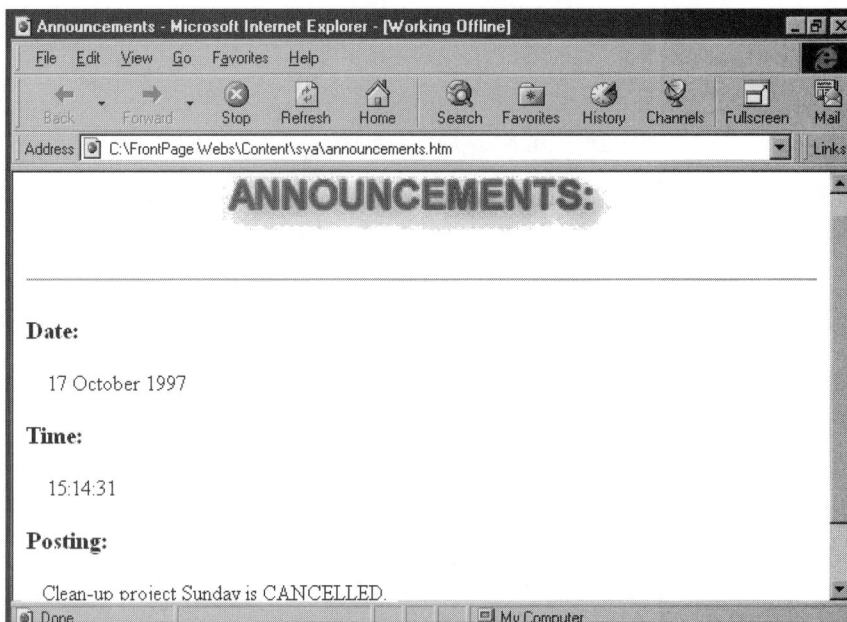

Figure 5.25

Displaying input results using HTML styles.

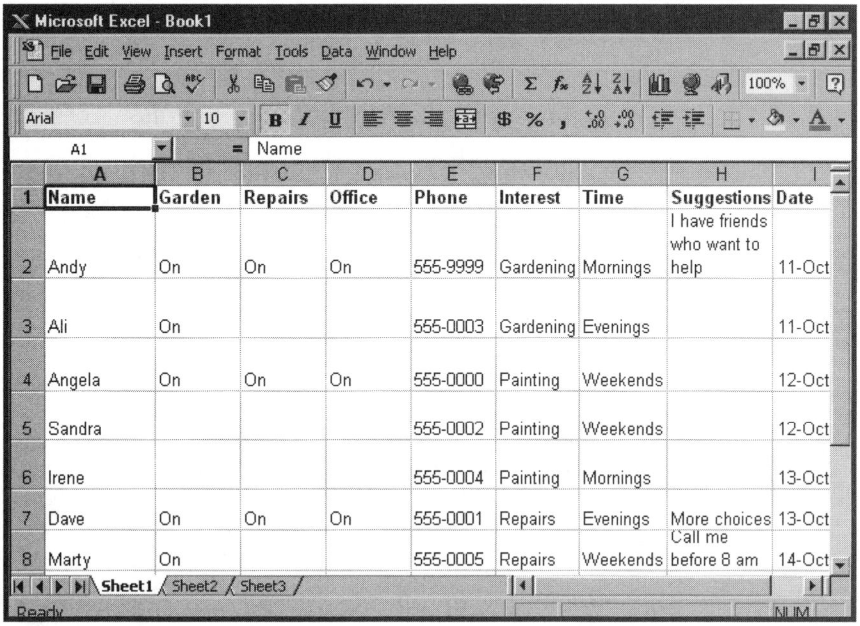

	A	B	C	D	E	F	G	H	I
1	Name	Garden	Repairs	Office	Phone	Interest	Time	Suggestions	Date
2	Andy	On	On	On	555-9999	Gardening	Mornings	I have friends who want to help	11-Oct
3	Ali	On			555-0003	Gardening	Evenings		11-Oct
4	Angela	On	On	On	555-0000	Painting	Weekends		12-Oct
5	Sandra				555-0002	Painting	Weekends		12-Oct
6	Irene				555-0004	Painting	Mornings		13-Oct
7	Dave	On	On	On	555-0001	Repairs	Evenings	More choices	13-Oct
8	Marty	On			555-0005	Repairs	Weekends	Call me before 8 am	14-Oct

Figure 5.26

Input form data sent to Microsoft Excel.

as shown in Figure 5.26. First, save your form input as an HTML page; then save the input as a text file.

Saving Results As an HTML File

I've touched on some of the useful aspects of being able to take input off the Internet and stash it in a file that visitors can view. The most expedient way to do this is to store your data in one of the HTML formats available in the Form Handler. These formats are listed in Table 5.1.

In each of the four HTML file options, your visitors' input is placed in an HTML file. You, or your visitors, can go to the URL you assign to this page and see the results. FrontPage places a handy bookmark at the top and bottom (a Go to Top hyperlink at the bottom and a Go to Bottom hyperlink at the top). The Go to Bottom hyperlink is handy—you can use it to zip right to the bottom of the list and see if anyone has contributed new input through your form. Table 5.1 provides five choices for formatting input in an HTML Web page.

To save form input as an HTML page, follow these steps:

1. Open a page that has a form on it. An ideal form for saving to HTML pages is something like a "Guest Book" or comments form, where visitors can share comments on a topic of discussion or leave you messages. You can then make the results HTML page accessible via a link, or you can keep it a secret.

2. Right-click within the form to which you are assigning Form Handler properties.

3. Select Form Properties from the same shortcut menu you've seen before.

TABLE 5.1 FORMATS AVAILABLE IN THE FORM HANDLER

Format	Results
HTML	The results are stored in an HTML page with a horizontal line separating each new entry.
HTML definition list	The results are saved in definition list format, with a defined term and an indented definition. This is handy for input forms with two fields, such as Name and Suggestion, where you want to indent the contents of the second field (see Figure 5.25).
HTML bulleted list	The results display as a bulleted list. This works best with single-field input forms.
Formatted text within HTML	The results go into an HTML Web page, but some formatting features display, such as extra spacing between fields that are not normally available in HTML.
Text database	The results will be stored in a text file with the values separated by either a comma, tab, or space.

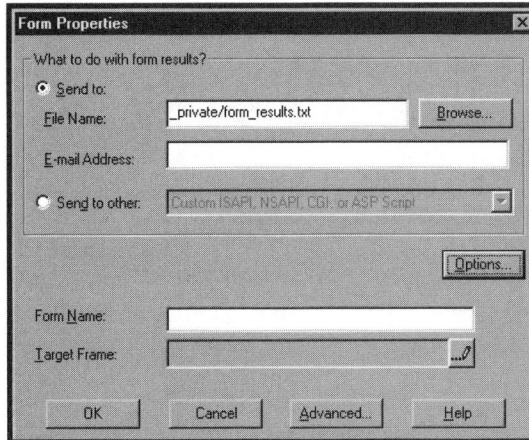

Figure 5.27

The Form
Properties
dialog box.

> **TIP**
> If Form Properties is not an option on the shortcut menu, your cursor is not inside the form.

4. Press the Options button in the Form Properties dialog box, as shown in Figure 5.27.

5. With the File Results tab selected, pull down the File Format drop-down list. Next, select HTML, as shown in Figure 5.28.

> **TIP**
> The File Results tab allows you to define a second file to save input results, which can be in a different format (and must utilize a different filename).

6. Select OK to close the Options for Saving Results of Form window.

7. To write the HTML to a file, select the Send To radio button and enter a meaningful filename (such as form_results). To have the HTML results sent to you as an e-mail message, enter the target e-mail address.

8. Click on OK to complete the file format selection.

9. Save the Web page with the form in FrontPage Editor.

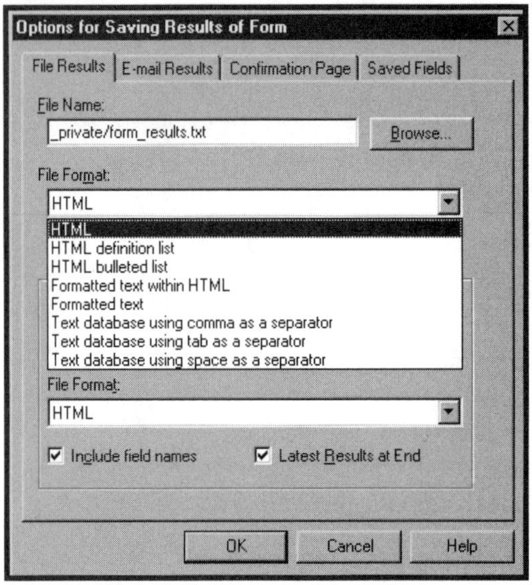

Figure 5.28

Selecting the
results file format.

Creating Links to Input Form Results

Because you defined an HTML (also known as HTM) file as the target
for your results, you can visit the results file from your Internet browser
and see the results right on the Web.

If your results file is something you want to share with your visitors, you'll
want to add a convenient link so that visitors can review all the input.
Create a link to your results page and then test the form. To create a link
to a results page, follow these steps:

1. Save your page in FrontPage Editor, with the results for the form
   defined.

2. Right-click in the form area and select Form Properties from the
   shortcut menu.

3. In the Form Properties dialog box, click on the Options button.

4. Click and drag to select the filename in the File Name area. Do not
   highlight the directory path, just the filename.

5. Press Ctrl+C to copy the filename to the Clipboard.

6. Cancel the Options for Saving Results of Form and Form Properties dialog boxes.

7. Type text below the form that is to become a link to the bulletin board, as shown in Figure 5.29.

TIP You could also use a graphic hotlink here.

8. Select the text and click on the Create or Edit Hyperlink button in the FrontPage Editor toolbar.

9. Double-click on the private directory.

10. In the URL area, position the cursor at the end of the text and paste the copied filename from the Windows Clipboard (using Ctrl+V), as shown in Figure 5.30.

11. Click on OK in the Edit Link dialog box.

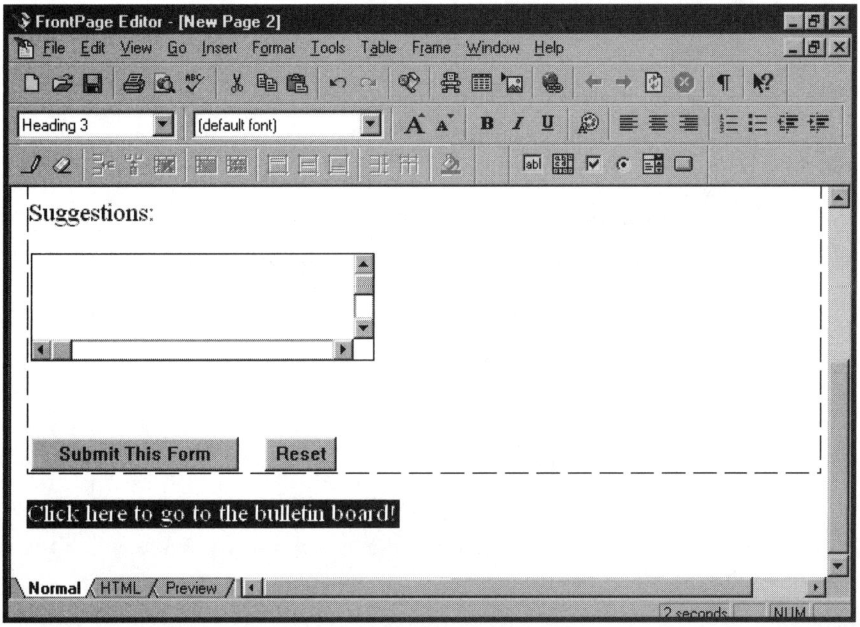

Figure 5.29

Letting visitors view a results page.

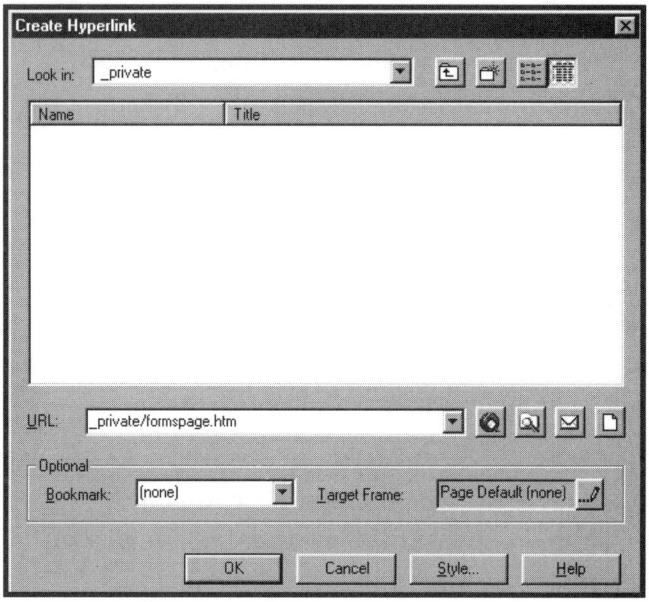

Figure 5.30

Defining a link to your results page.

Preparing an HTML Page to Receive Form Results

The page that you designate to receive input is just like any other HTML page that you create or edit in FrontPage Editor. You can place headings and links as well as edit the background on that page. And perhaps you should, especially if you want to make the page accessible to others. To edit an HTML results page, follow these steps:

1. Press Ctrl while clicking to follow the link you defined to your results page.

TIP If your results file does not show up as a file in your site in FrontPage Editor, switch to FrontPage Explorer and select View, Refresh from the menu.

2. Place your cursor before the text "Form Results Inserted Here" and press Enter to create a line for a heading.

3. Type a heading for the page. You may also choose to insert a graphic, as shown in Figure 5.31.

4. Place your cursor at the end of the text "Form Results Inserted Here" and press Enter to create a new line.

5. Place an appropriate link back to the home page for your Web site, as shown in Figure 5.32.

TIP

Don't forget to send your visitors back to an appropriate bookmark on the home page.

6. Save changes to your results file.

Did you save changes to all the Web pages you've worked on in FrontPage Editor? Just checking.

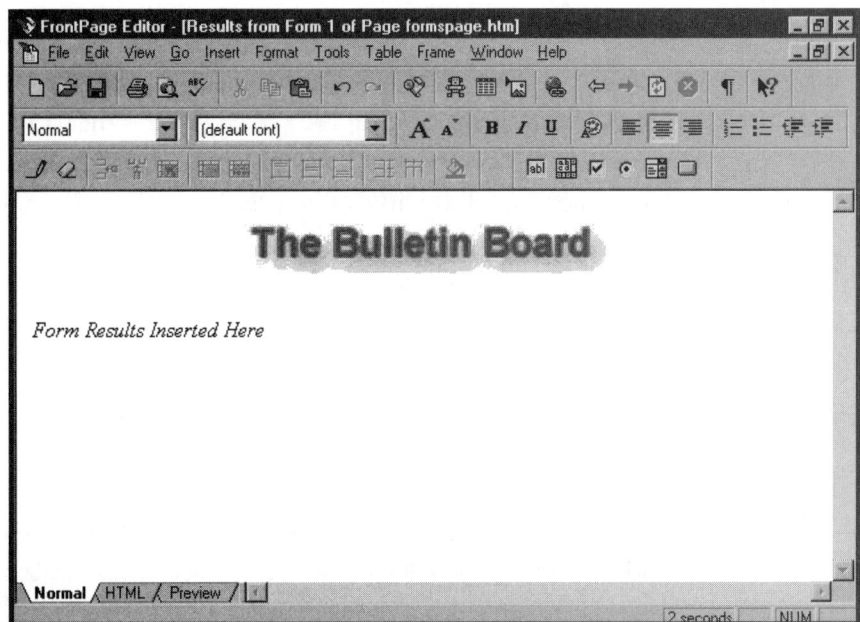

Figure 5.31

Making the results page a friendly place to visit.

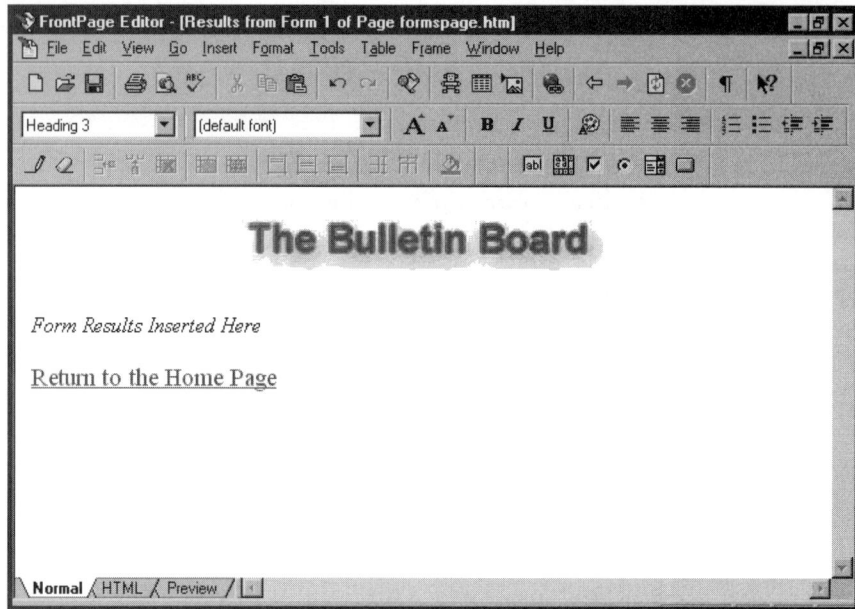

Figure 5.32

Don't leave your
visitors stranded!

Testing Your Input Form

Now that you have defined a results file, you have completed the most
complex part of creating a Web site up to this point. To test your form,
use a Web browser. Testing your form ensures that it works and gives you
a visitor's perspective so that you can add adjustments, if necessary, to
make the form clear and easy to use. To test your form, follow these steps:

1. Open the page with your input form in FrontPage Explorer. Save it.

2. Use the Preview in Browser menu item located on the FrontPage
   Editor File menu to open your Web page with an input form using
   your Web browser.

3. Enter and submit several messages in your form, as shown in
   Figure 5.33.

NOTE   Each time you submit a form, FrontPage provides a confirmation message and a link
back to the form, as shown in Figure 5.34.

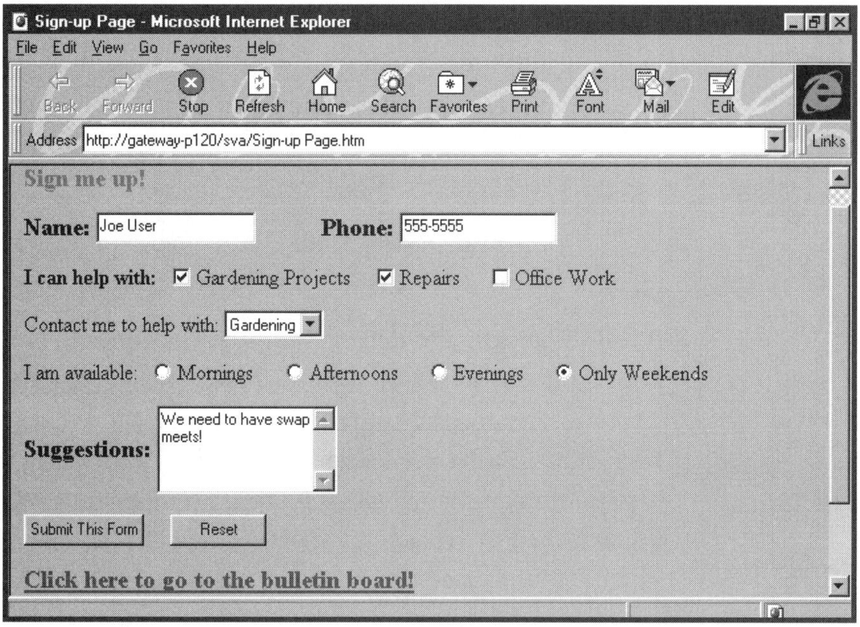

Figure 5.33

Hello? Hello? Can anybody read this?

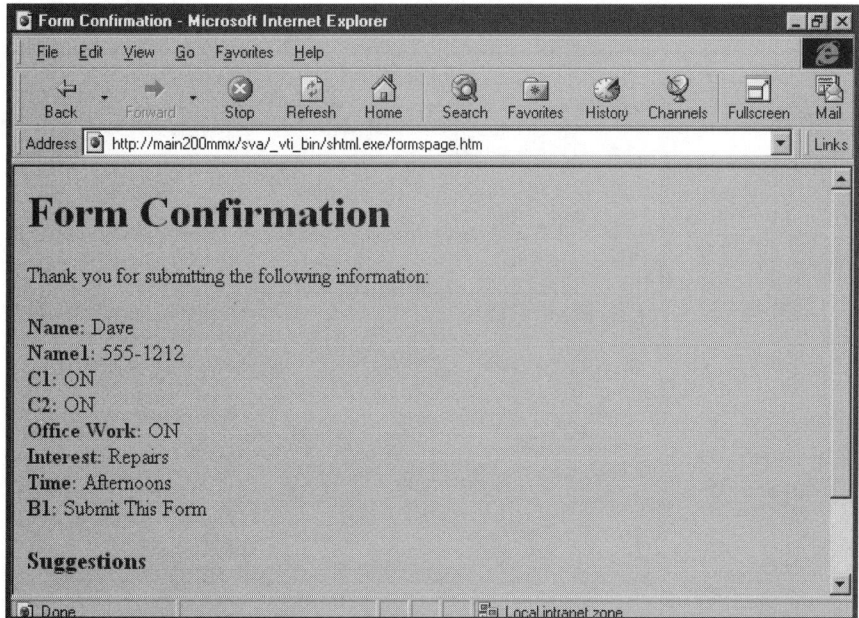

Figure 5.34

Confirmed!

4. When you have submitted a few messages to your form, follow your link to the results page or type the address of your results page in the URL area of your browser, as shown in Figure 5.35.

Maintaining a Bulletin Board

You (or others) may decide that, as a Web administrator, your responsibility is to edit the contents of a visitor-accessible page.

A full discussion and debate of ethics, freedom of speech, and good taste is beyond the scope of my job here. However, somebody has to take responsibility for the contents of an accessible Web site and touch it up from time to time. One approach used by many Web site administrators is to delete comments when necessary, but to acknowledge that the page was censored by replacing the offending comment with a message such as

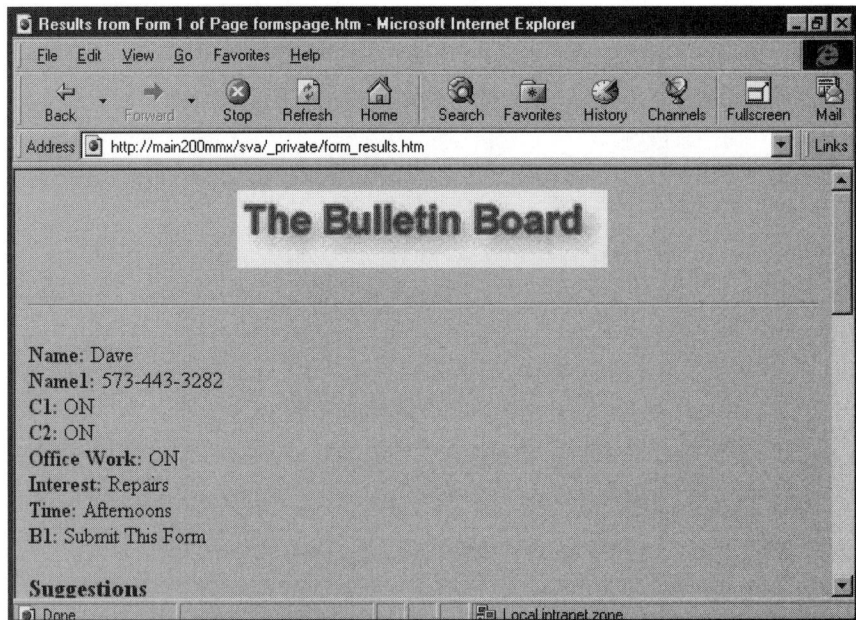

Figure 5.35

Results posted on a Web page.

"A comment was deleted here for violating the Web site rule against bad grammar," or something similar. To edit visitor input in a results page, follow these steps:

1. There is no need to exit your Web browser, for you can edit a page as it is being accessed by visitors.

2. Open the results page in FrontPage Editor.

3. Edit the results file just as you would any other FrontPage HTML file, by cutting, pasting, or editing text. Site administrators will be tempted to become power mad, as shown in Figure 5.36.

4. After you've edited the results page, save your changes and reload the page in your Internet browser. Edited changes to the page are reflected when you visit your page with your browser, as shown in Figure 5.37.

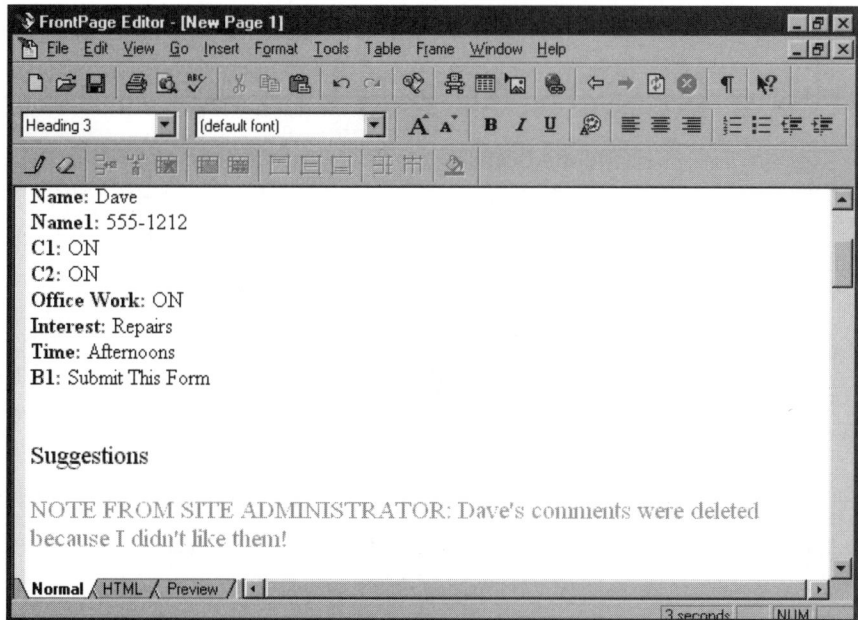

Figure 5.36

Censoring on the fly in the FrontPage Editor.

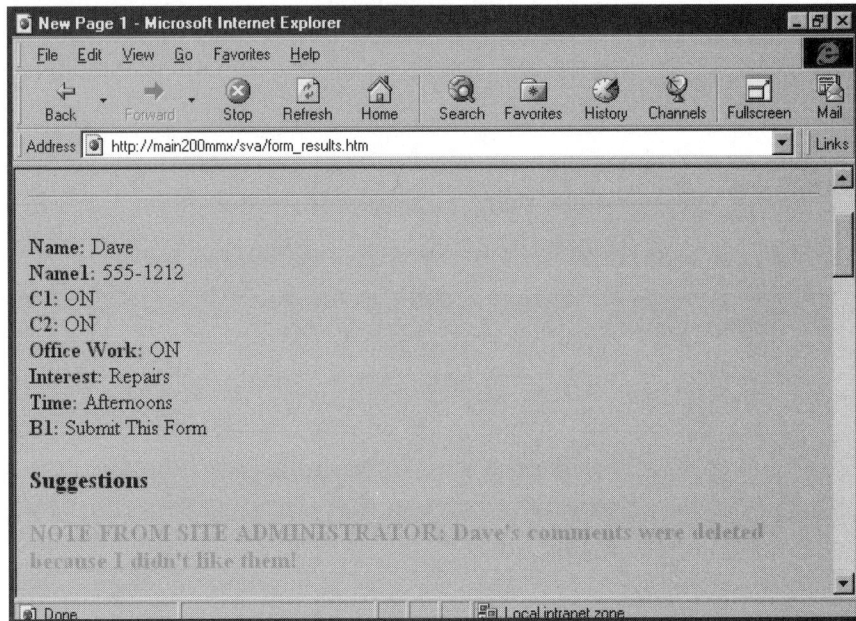

```
New Page 1 - Microsoft Internet Explorer                          _ | 8 | X
 File   Edit   View   Go   Favorites   Help                            e

  ←  .    →  .     ⊗       ↻       ⌂        ⊕        ⊞       ⊕       ♀       ⊡      ⊠
 Back   Forward   Stop   Refresh   Home    Search   Favorites History  Channels Fullscreen  Mail

 Address  http://main200mmx/sva/form_results.htm                    ▼  | Links


   Name: Dave
   Name1: 555-1212
   C1: ON
   C2: ON
   Office Work: ON
   Interest: Repairs
   Time: Afternoons
   B1: Submit This Form

   Suggestions

   NOTE FROM SITE ADMINISTRATOR: Dave's comments were deleted
   because I didn't like them!

  Done                                      Local intranet zone
```

Figure 5.37

Dave's comments
have been
censored!

Saving Results As a Text File

I've touched on some of the useful aspects of being able to take input off the Internet and stash it in a file that can be used to tabulate a poll, generate form letters, or just print a report. The most expedient way to do this is to store your data to one of the four text formats available in the Form Handler (see Table 5.2).

These four text output options are of two main types: formatted text and delimited text. Formatted text is easier to handle if you want free-form word processing. Delimited text is necessary if you'll be dumping the input results into a spreadsheet database or a Microsoft Word file in which you organize the data in a table.

Using a Formatted Text File As a Target for Input

The main difference between sending input data to an HTML file (as you did earlier) and sending it to a text file is that a text file cannot be edited

TABLE 5.2 THE FORM HANDLER	
Format	**Results**
Formatted text	This is the way to save text that you want to read in your word processor.
Text database using a comma as a separator	This format saves input and places a comma between fields. If you're using a database or spreadsheet that supports comma-delimited text (and many do), try this format.
Text database using a tab as a separator	This format works like comma-delimited text (preceding), but it places a tab between fields. It works nicely for importing data into Microsoft Word or Excel.
Text database using space as a separator	Chances are that your database, spreadsheet, or word processor prefers tab- or comma-delimited fields over space-delimited fields. Those space-delimited fields can be unreliable, given that your input will probably also have spaces. It's an option, but you don't have to use it.

on the Web with your Internet browser. You can probably open an HTML file with any of today's hi-tech word processors, but that's not going to be the most convenient form in which to edit your input data.

When you save input to a formatted text file, you can open the text file from FrontPage Explorer, which automatically launches your default word processor. You can set the file to launch a word processing program such as Word by using an appropriate extension when you assign a target filename. To send input data to a formatted text file, follow these steps:

1. Right-click on the form with the data that is to be sent to a formatted text file.

2. Select Form Properties from the shortcut menu.

3. Click on the Options button.

4. In the File Format drop-down list, select Formatted Text, as shown in Figure 5.38.

5. If you've already defined one results file and want to add an optional second one, enter the name of the new file in the Optional Second File group box. If you don't know the name of the file, press the Browse button and browse for it.

NOTE You have the option of saving results to a visitor-accessible Web Page in HTML format, a formatted text page, or both.

TIP Here's one of my favorite tricks: If you attach the filename extension *.doc to your filename, you can open the file in Word directly from FrontPage Explorer by double-clicking on the file.

6. Click on OK in the Options for Saving Results of Form dialog box as well as the Form Properties dialog box.

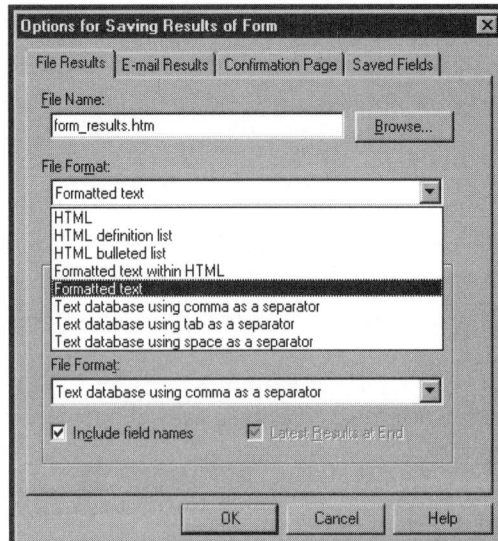

Figure 5.38

Saving form results as formatted text.

You can then test a form that sends results to a formatted text file using your Internet browser, just as you tested the form that sends results to an HTML page. One difference is that you won't be able to edit your results with your browser—you'll need to open the results file from within FrontPage Explorer. To test a form sending input to a formatted text file, follow these steps:

1. Save your page with the defined form in FrontPage Editor.

2. Open the Web page with the input form using your Internet browser.

3. Enter data in the form, just as you did earlier with a form that saved input to an HTML page. Fill out and submit several test input forms so that you can give your system a real workout.

4. Switch to FrontPage Explorer.

NOTE If you haven't sent input to your formatted text file, the file is not yet showing in the Folder view.

5. Select View, Refresh from the FrontPage Explorer menu to update the file list in Folder view.

6. When the FrontPage Explorer Folder view is refreshed, the new text format results file is listed in Folder view. Double-click on the file, or right-click and select Open from the submenu.

7. If you open your results file in your favorite word processor, you can format the text any way you like. Input results can become part of a report, a table, or a memo—the possibilities are endless. One use of input form results is shown in Figure 5.39.

TIP If you want to define or change the default word processor that opens filenames with a set extension, you can use the Configure Editors tab in the Options dialog box, which is accessed from the tools menu.

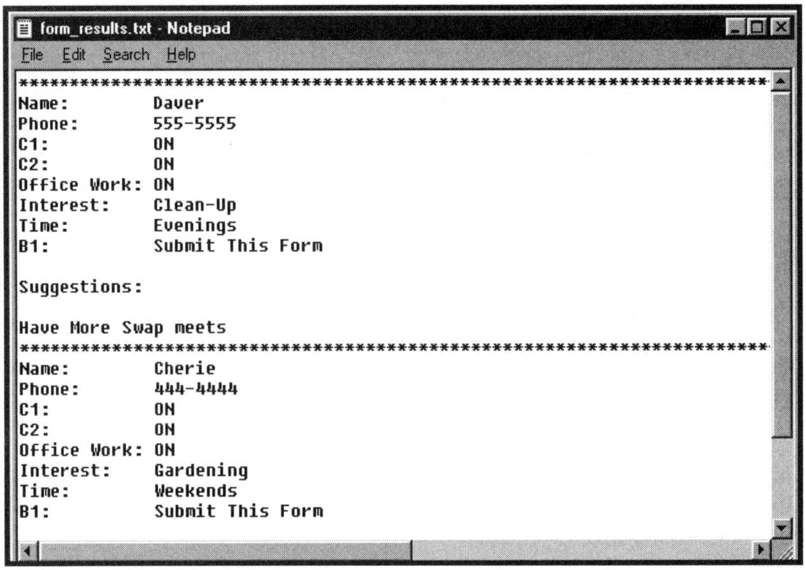

```
form_results.txt - Notepad
File Edit Search Help
**********************************************************************
Name:         Daver
Phone:        555-5555
C1:           ON
C2:           ON
Office Work:  ON
Interest:     Clean-Up
Time:         Evenings
B1:           Submit This Form

Suggestions:

Have More Swap meets
**********************************************************************
Name:         Cherie
Phone:        444-4444
C1:           ON
C2:           ON
Office Work:  ON
Interest:     Gardening
Time:         Weekends
B1:           Submit This Form
```

Figure 5.39

Here are the results pumped to a formatted text file.

Using a Delimited Text File as a Target for Input

Nothing stands between working with formatted text and delimited text—they both stash input in a text file that's accessible with a text editor. Delimited files do, however, fit nicely into spreadsheets and database files, so they have some unique advantages that are worth exploring.

Again, you can launch the editing application from FrontPage Explorer if your filename extension is registered in Windows 95. For example, you can use an *.xls filename extension with a delimited text file and jump right into viewing your input in spreadsheet format.

NOTE Each time you get input from visitors, your results file changes. New data gets appended to your results file. If the results are being saved as text, more text gets stuck on at the end. To refresh the text file, don't open the file from your word processor. This will be an old file that doesn't include new results. Instead, launch your word processor by opening your text file from FrontPage Explorer.

To use delimited text results with a spreadsheet, follow these steps:

1. Right-click on a form with fields that work well in a spreadsheet format, and then select Form Properties.

2. Click on the Options button.

3. Select Text database using tab as a separator from the File Format list.

The tab-delimited text format also works smoothly with Excel.

4. Enter a filename with an *.xls filename extension in the File Name area, as shown in Figure 5.40.

5. Click on OK in the Options for Saving Results of Form and Form Properties dialog boxes.

6. Save your page with the form in FrontPage Editor.

7. Open the Web page using your Internet browser.

8. Enter data in the form, just as you did earlier with a form that saved input to an HTML page.

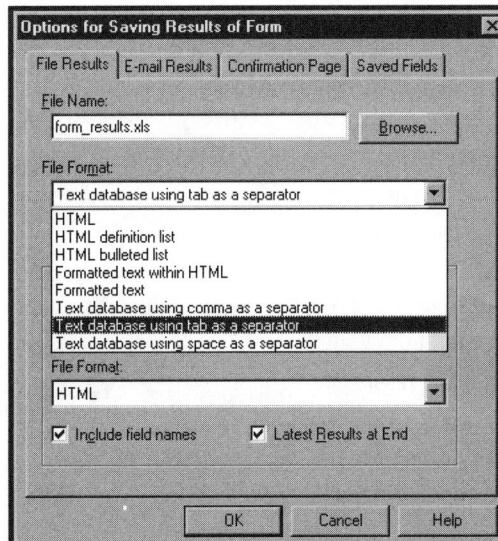

Figure 5.40

Defining a results file with an *.xls file extension.

Use the Submit button and the confirmation form to take you back to the form.

9. You don't need to exit your browser to view or edit the Form results. Switch to FrontPage Explorer and use View, Refresh to update the file list in Folders view.

10. Double-click on the new results file in the Summary view of Front-Page Explorer to launch an associated application for your new file.

If you added an *.xls extension to the filename and you have Excel on your computer, you'll see (and be able to format or edit) the results in Excel (see Figure 5.41).

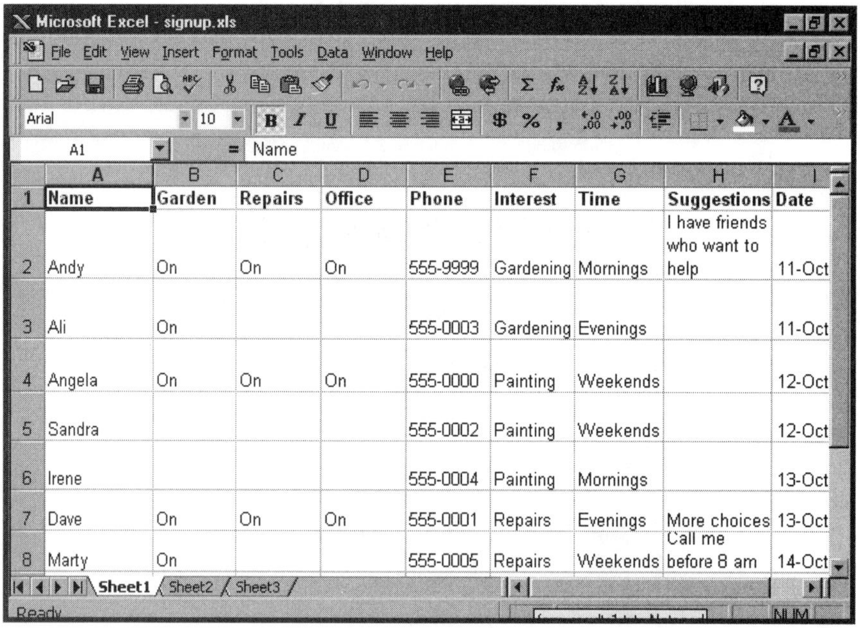

Figure 5.41

Web input results in an Excel spreadsheet.

	Name	Garden	Repairs	Office	Phone	Interest	Time	Suggestions	Date
2	Andy	On	On	On	555-9999	Gardening	Mornings	I have friends who want to help	11-Oct
3	Ali	On			555-0003	Gardening	Evenings		11-Oct
4	Angela	On	On	On	555-0000	Painting	Weekends		12-Oct
5	Sandra				555-0002	Painting	Weekends		12-Oct
6	Irene				555-0004	Painting	Mornings		13-Oct
7	Dave	On	On	On	555-0001	Repairs	Evenings	More choices	13-Oct
8	Marty	On			555-0005	Repairs	Weekends	Call me before 8 am	14-Oct

Take a Break!

At this point in the process, you've constructed a powerful Web site. The site looks good; you accomplished that early in the game using formatting, graphic images, backgrounds, and tables. It's hyperlinked with easy-to-follow links to bookmarks, other Web pages on your site, and the Internet.

In this session, you added a whole new dimension to your Web site—the ability to interact with your visitors. You explored methods to collect and save input accessible to visitors on the Web, and you diverted that input to forms where you'll organize it off the Web and use it any way you choose.

You might conclude that you've got enough tools now to create a really functional Web site—and you do. If you're itching to put the site up on the World Wide Web right now, I can't blame you.

You will, however, find some features in the next session that give your site a more polished look and feel—things such as header and footer files that provide continuity between all the pages in your site, annotations that can only be read by you (not your visitors), images or text that go away at a set date, search engines to help visitors find just what they're looking for, generated tables of contents, and more. Finally, at the end of the weekend, you'll walk through the process of copying your site to an Internet Service Provider that can host your page for you. I'll help you find a friendly one.

So take a break, a real one this time. You have accomplished quite a bit. A truly professional Web site is within your grasp!

Activating FrontPage's Handy Components

- ✿ What Are FrontPage Components?
- ✿ Keeping a Task List
- ✿ Placing Properties on a Page

As Web cruisers become more sophisticated, the excitement of simply finding information on a Web site begins to wane. Your visitors have seen many Web sites, so you should make your site as pleasant and convenient a place to visit as possible.

Your site has tastefully formatted text and headings, and it includes graphic images and plenty of convenient links that allow your visitors to jump here and there (and back). In the last session, you created input forms that allow visitors to interact with the site in a number of ways—from posting an opinion to placing an order. Still, folks have come to expect in professional Web sites various features that you don't have yet. These features may include the following:

❖ A table of contents
❖ A search box so that visitors can find items of interest in your site
❖ Footers and headers that are uniform from page to page
❖ Objects that appear (and disappear) on your site according to a set schedule

Your site may not have these features yet, but it will. With forms under your belt, you'll find the features you create in this session to be fun and easy, and after you've explored them all, you'll probably use several to enhance your Web site.

What Are FrontPage Components?

Previous versions of FrontPage offered built-in components called Web-Bots (or simply bots, which is short for robots). FrontPage's robot metaphor comes from the capability of these components to interact dynamically with your site. For example, a Timestamp component changes whenever your site is updated. A Table of Contents component regenerates a table of contents every time a new page is added to the site. A Replace component inserts information from FrontPage Explorer on a page and changes that information when the data in FrontPage Explorer changes.

Unfortunately, Microsoft found that most people just didn't get the Web-Bot concept. So what did Microsoft do? It kept the WebBot functionality, but changed the WebBot name. For FrontPage 98, WebBots are called FrontPage components.

In short, FrontPage components are a set of handy, automated functions that plug into your Web site. Together, they give you the ability to create a site that interacts with itself, constantly updating, changing, and facilitating visitors' needs.

Types of FrontPage Components

The FrontPage Component menu item is located in the Editor's Insert menu (shown in Figure 6.1) and lists nine components. FrontPage has more—in fact, you've stumbled on at least one already. You used the Save Results component to send form input to files. Here, you'll focus on the nine components found on the FrontPage Component menu list, as shown in Figure 6.2. The FrontPage components are listed in Table 6.1 with a short description of each.

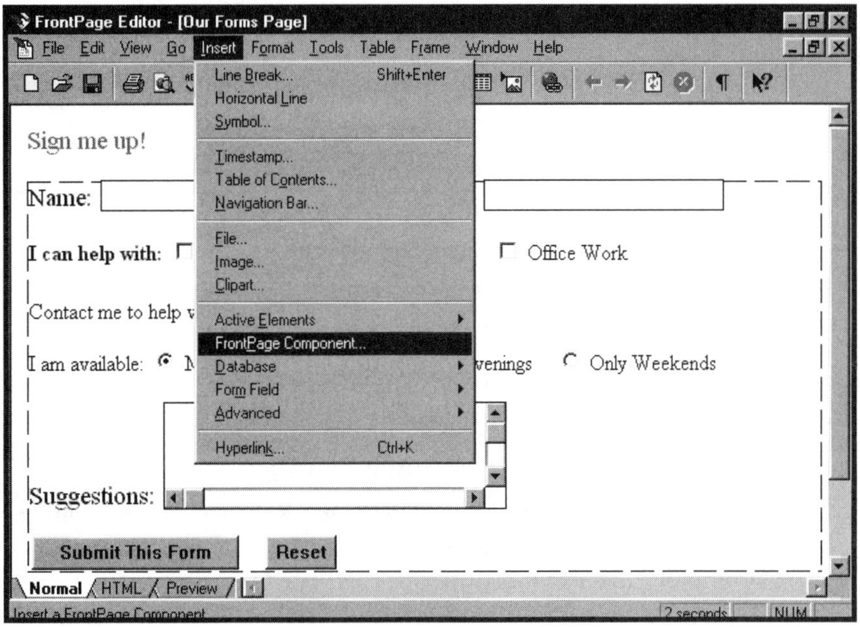

Figure 6.1

The FrontPage
Component
menu item.

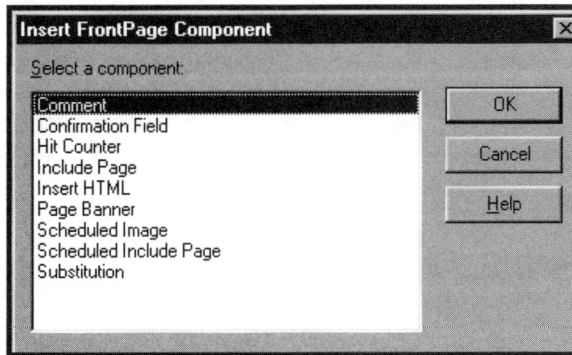

Figure 6.2

FrontPage
components.

TABLE 6.1 FRONTPAGE COMPONENTS

Type of FrontPage Component	Description
Comment	Adds text that can be viewed in FrontPage Editor but is not seen by visitors to the Web site
Confirmation Field	Part of creating a registration page that forces visitors to your Web site to sign a registration form before entering
Hit Counter	A counter that automatically increments every time someone visits your site
Include Page	Allows you to place one Web page inside another—ideal for headers and footers
Insert HTML	Allows you to paste HTML directly into a page without including that page in your site
Page Banner	Uses the same text or image as a banner on your pages
Scheduled Image	An image that appears only during an assigned time period
Scheduled Include Page	A file that appears only during an assigned time period
Substitution	Plugs in information from FrontPage Explorer

Leaving Yourself Messages with Comment Text

Comments can be viewed in FrontPage Editor, but the text is invisible to visitors to your Web site. One reason to leave these "secret messages" on your site is to remind yourself of tasks that need to be accomplished, as illustrated with the "Don't forget" text in Figure 6.3.

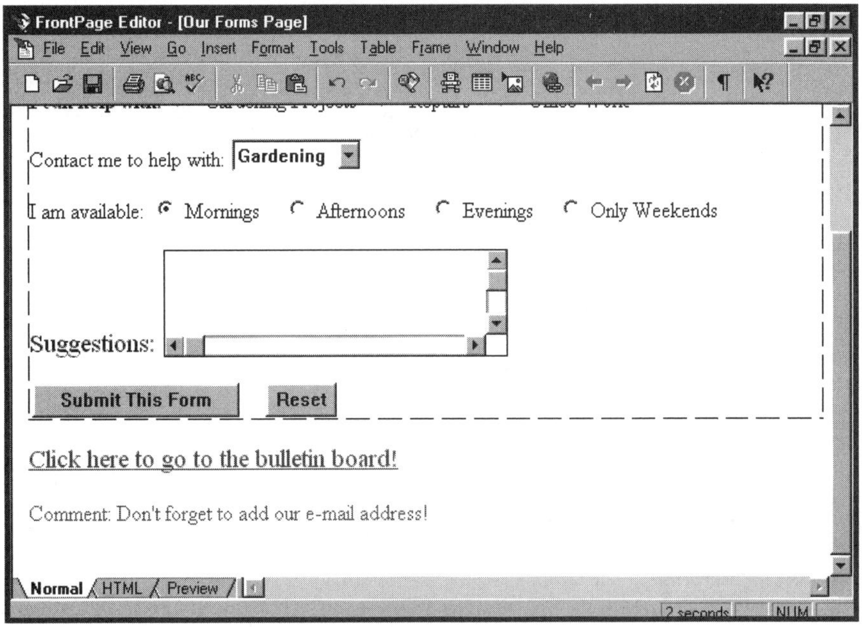

Figure 6.3

Adding a comment.

If you're collaborating with other developers on a Web site, comment text can be a form of communication with the other Web site authors (see Figure 6.4).

To place a comment, follow these steps:

1. Place your insertion point at the spot in the page where you want to display the comment.

TIP

Because visitors do not see the comment, your only consideration is to pick a location that is convenient to you and the other developers who will read the comment text.

2. In the Insert menu, select FrontPage Component, or click on the Insert FrontPage Component icon on the toolbar, as shown in Figure 6.5.

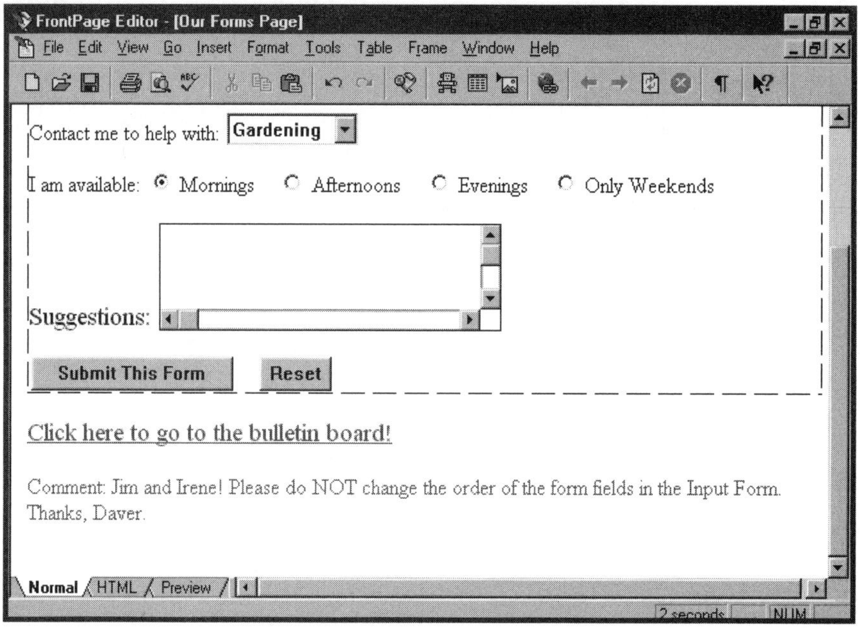

Figure 6.4

Using a comment when working with co-developers.

Figure 6.5

Wonder why it looks like a robot?

3. Select Comment in the Insert FrontPage Component dialog box and then click on OK.

4. The Comment dialog box appears, as shown in Figure 6.6.

5. Type the comment text in the Comment area of the Comment dialog box, as shown in Figure 6.7.

6. After you enter (and edit, if necessary) your comment, click on OK in the Comment dialog box.

To edit annotation text, follow these steps:

1. Move your cursor to the comment. The cursor becomes a cute little robot, as shown in Figure 6.8.

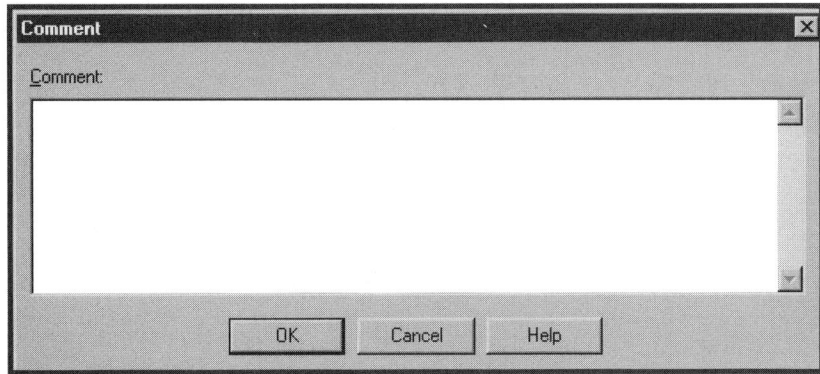

Figure 6.6

Ready for
comment text.

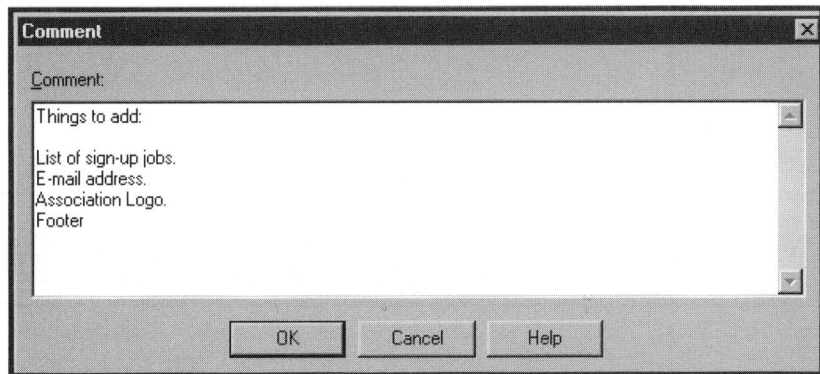

Figure 6.7

Inserting comment
text in a Web page.

2. Double-click on the comment text with the special robot cursor.

3. The Comment dialog box appears, and you can edit the text, as shown in Figure 6.9.

TIP   You can also open the Comment dialog box by right-clicking on the comment and selecting Properties from the shortcut menu.

4. When you finish editing the comment text, click on OK in the Comment dialog box.

Figure 6.8

High-tech program, but not a high-tech robot icon!

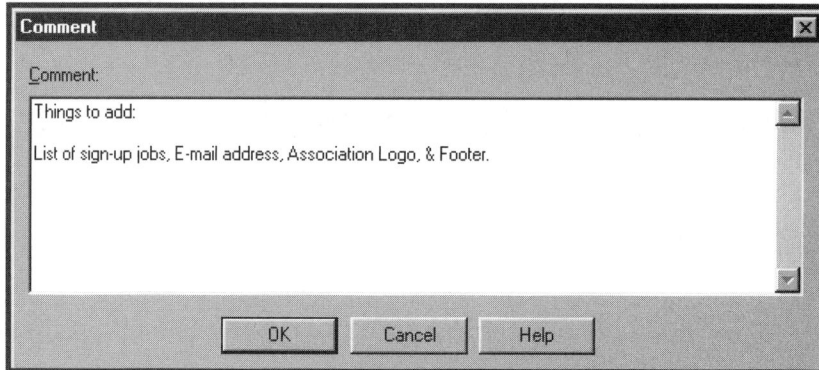

Figure 6.9

Editing a comment.

To delete a comment, follow these steps:

1. Right-click on the comment.

2. Select Cut from the shortcut menu, as shown in Figure 6.10. You may also press the Delete key.

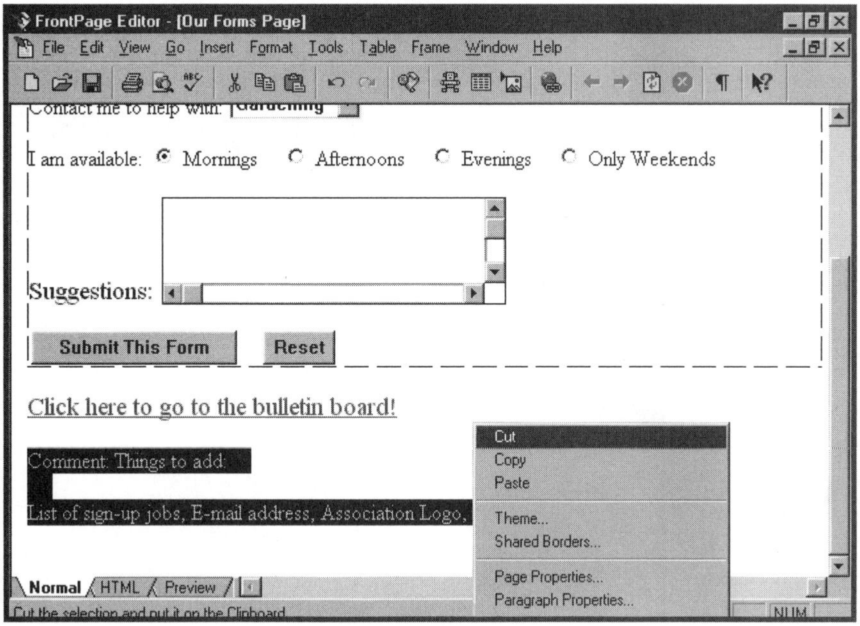

Figure 6.10

The comment
disappears!

Keeping a Task List

FrontPage has another way to keep notes on needed changes to a Web site. Annotation text is fine for leaving a note on a single page, but it has its limitations and can be an awkward way to keep track of tasks if you have a long list of things to be done—including creating new pages.

FrontPage Explorer's Tasks view enables you to keep track of tasks as you work. It can mark completed tasks and save a list of the work you have done on a site (a handy feature if you're lucky enough to be billing for your work). The Tasks view can be selected from the FrontPage Explorer's Views list, as shown in Figure 6.11. You can keep the Tasks view window open while you work in FrontPage Explorer or FrontPage Editor and refer to it to remind you of required work.

If your Tasks window gets lengthy, you can sort it by clicking on any of the column headings. For example, if several developers are working on a

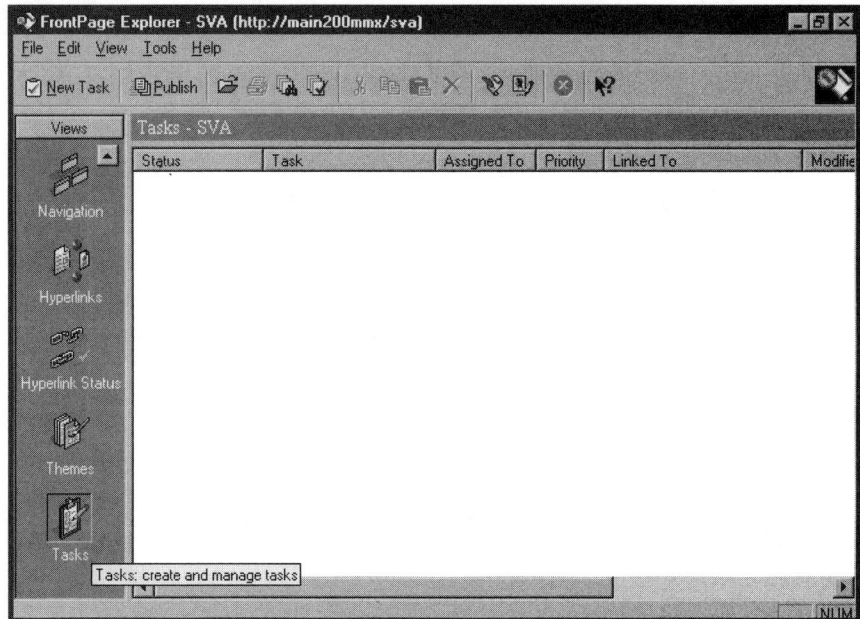

Figure 6.11

The FrontPage
Explorer's Tasks
view.

project, you can click on the Assigned To column heading to sort the
tasks by developer, as shown in Figure 6.12.

To create a new task, follow these steps:

1. Click on Tasks in the Views toolbar. You may need to scroll to the
   bottom to see it.

2. Right-click in the Tasks view and select New Task from the pop-up
   menu.

3. Enter a short description in the Task Name area of the New Task
   dialog box, as shown in Figure 6.13.

TIP To display the tasks by status, you can click on the Status heading or select Show History in the View menu.

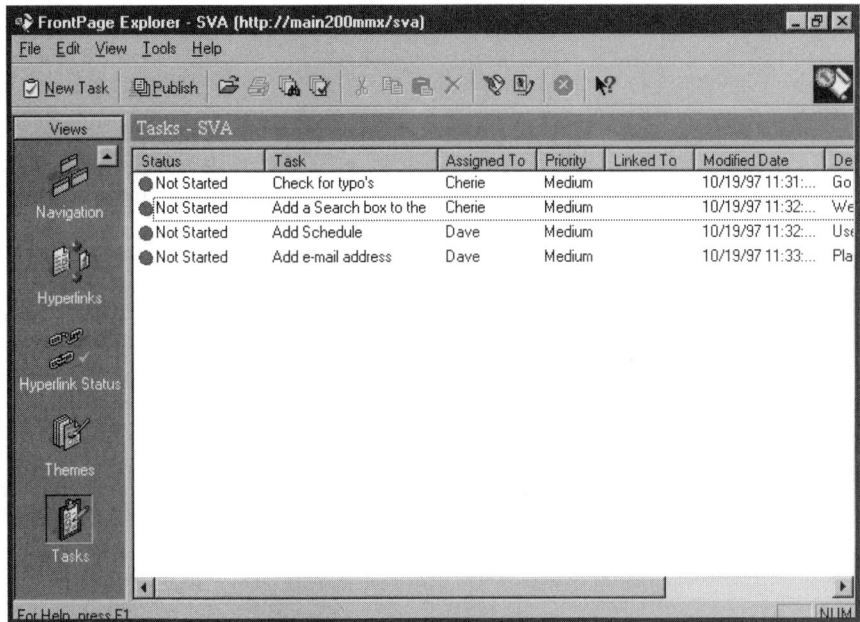

Figure 6.12

Work to do—
sorted by
"Assigned To."

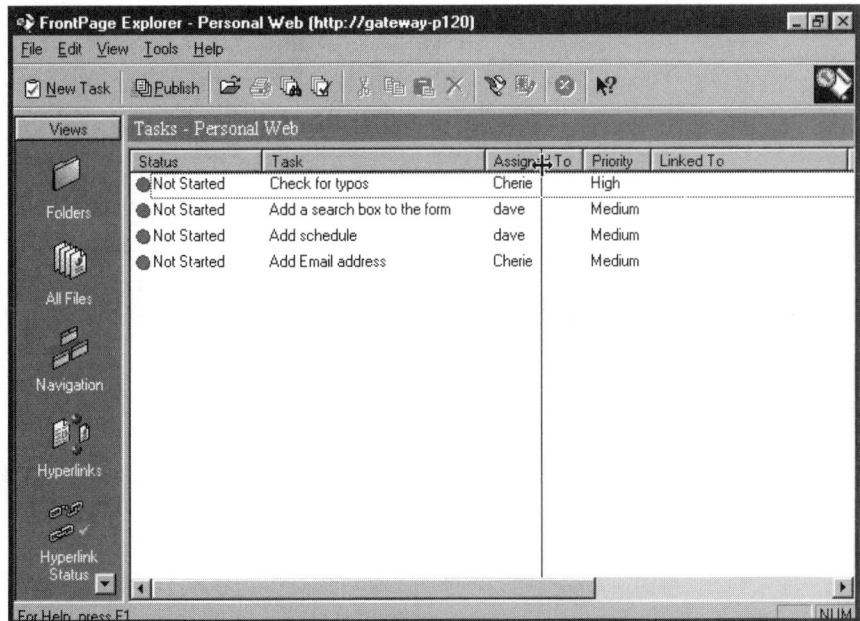

Figure 6.13

Adding a task to
the Tasks view.

4. Enter the name of the person responsible for the task in the Assign To area of the New Task dialog box.

5. Select a priority by using the High, Medium, and Low radio buttons.

6. Type a longer explanation of the task in the Description area, if necessary.

7. When you have completed the New Task dialog box, click on OK.

To edit a task in the Tasks window, follow these steps:

1. Right-click on the task in the Tasks list.

2. Select Edit Task from the pop-up menu.

3. Make any changes to the task details and click on OK in the Task Details dialog box.

FrontPage has two ways to remove a task from the Tasks list. You can mark the task as completed, but leave it as part of the list (helpful if you're keeping track of your work on a project), or you can delete the task. To mark a task as completed in the Tasks list, follow these steps:

1. Right-click on the task in the Tasks list.

2. Select Mark Complete from the pop-up menu.

The status of the task will change to "Completed," and the status color will change to green. To delete a task from the Tasks list, follow these steps:

1. Right-click on the task in the Tasks list.

2. Select Delete from the pop-up menu or click on the Delete icon (the black X) on the toolbar.

TIP

If you can't see an element in the dialog box, you can adjust column widths in the Tasks window by clicking on and dragging the lines between column names, as shown in Figure 6.13.

> **NOTE** The Linked Page element of the Tasks list is designed to work only when you create a site using FrontPage templates and wizards and is not available for individually created lists.

Attaching Headers and Footers with the Include Page Component

As your Web site expands, you'll find it handy to create headers and footers. Headers and footers can be separate files that appear on the top and bottom, respectively, of any Web page. They can also include images and links. One user-friendly approach is to have links to pages in the footers so that when your visitors scroll to the end of a page, they can easily jump directly to any page.

With your copy and paste skills, you *could* just create some text (or even an image to go at the top of each page) and copy it everywhere in your site. However, the advantage of creating a separate header or footer page is that when you edit it, FrontPage automatically updates the headers and/or footers on each page where the file has been inserted. All this is possible through the Include Page component. To create a footer, follow these steps:

1. Using the FrontPage Editor, create a new Web page that will become your footer, as shown in the example in Figure 6.14.

> **NOTE** Don't worry about a background for this page—it will adopt the background of the pages in which it is inserted.

2. Add the text for your footer and format it as Heading 6. As you noticed when you first started formatting, this style isn't really a heading at all, but it's great for fine print.

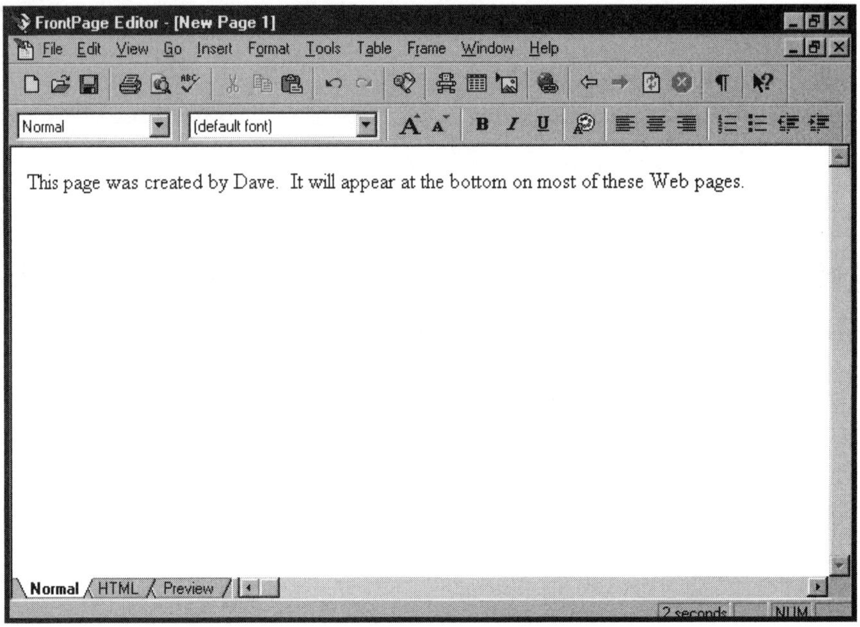

Figure 6.14

Creating a
footer page.

3. Insert any graphics or links that you want included in your footer.

4. Traditionally, footers are saved with the filename Footer.htm. Try
   this.

If you have created and saved a Footer.htm page, it's time to insert it into
other pages on your Web site. To include a page, follow these steps:

1. Open or go to the page where you want to include the footer (or
   header).

TIP You can move to any open page by pulling down the Window menu, as shown in Figure 6.15, and then selecting that page.

2. Place your cursor at the bottom of the page if you're inserting a
   footer (the top of the page for a header).

3. Select the Insert, FrontPage Component menu item.

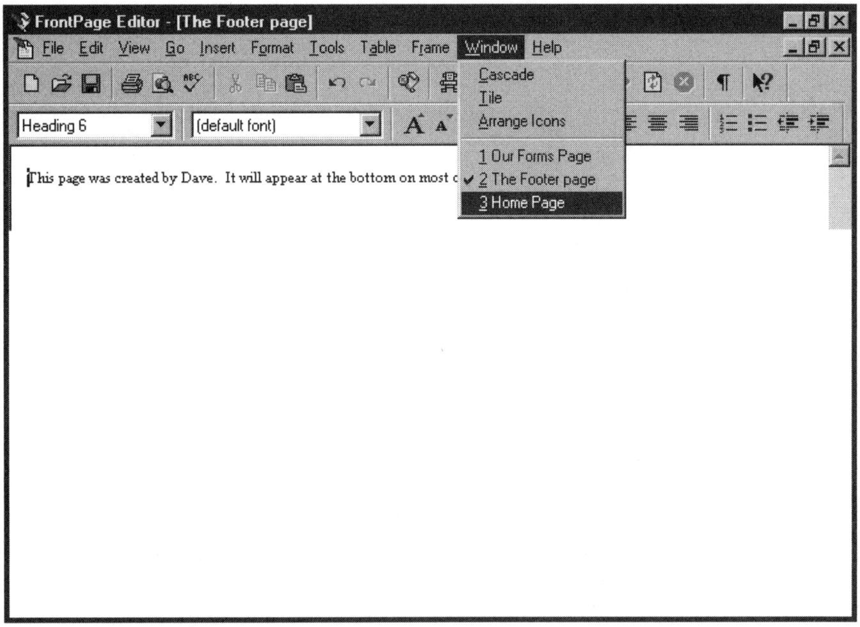

Figure 6.15

Switching windows.

4. Double-click on Include Page.

5. In the Include Page Component Properties dialog box, click on Browse to see a list of saved pages in the Web site (see Figure 6.16).

6. Click on the page you want to insert from the list in the Current Web dialog box, as shown in Figure 6.17.

7. Click on OK in the Current Web dialog box.

8. Click on OK in the Include Page Component Properties dialog box.

The footer will appear on the page, as shown in Figure 6.18.

Figure 6.16

Defining an included page.

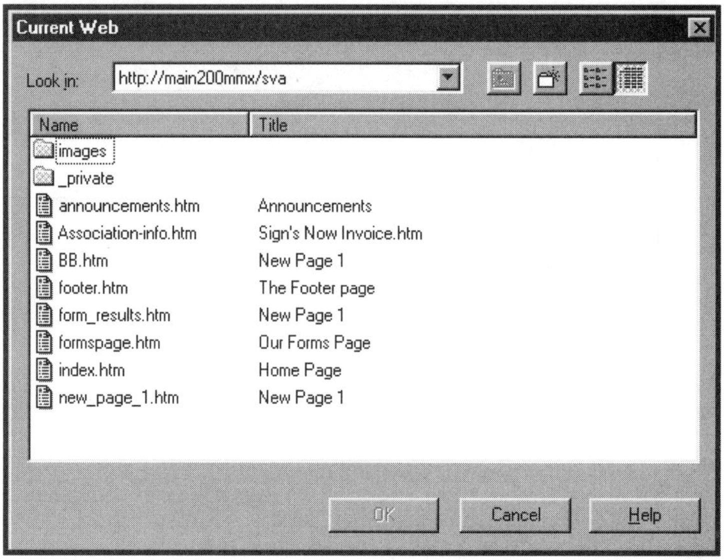

Figure 6.17

Selecting an
included page.

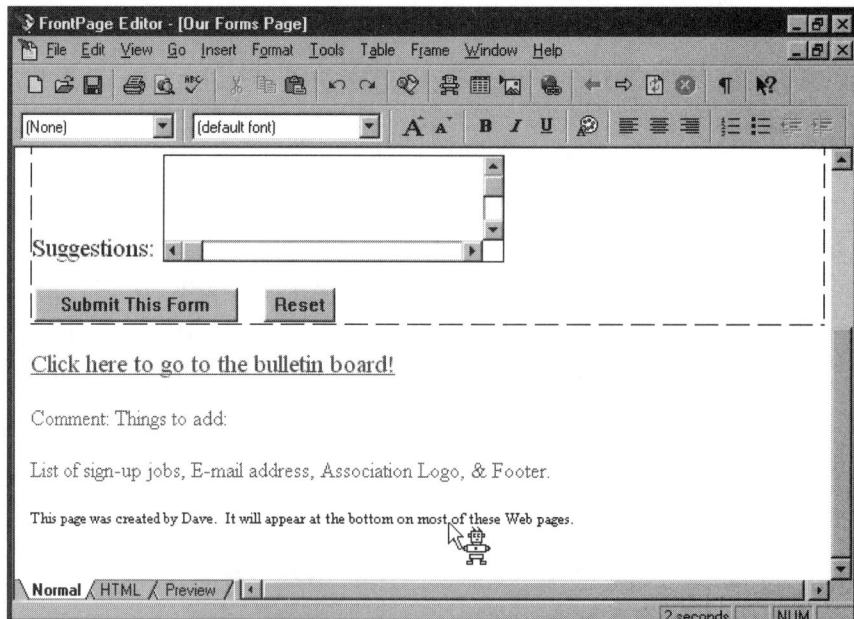

Figure 6.18

Like magic, the
footer appears!

To edit an included file, follow these steps:

1. Move your cursor over the included file. The cursor becomes the robot.

2. Right-click on the inserted file.

3. Select Open filename from the shortcut menu, as shown in Figure 6.19.

4. Make any editing changes to the included file.

5. Save the included file.

6. Return to the page where the file was inserted. You can use the Window menu to do this.

7. Select View, Refresh. This refreshes all links and inserted file updates on the page.

Figure 6.19

About to edit an included page.

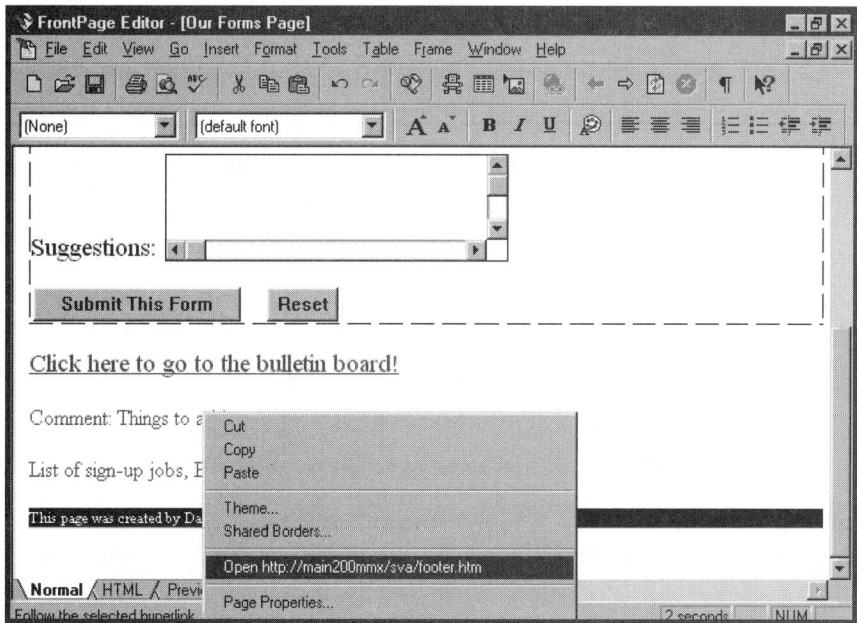

TIP Try including your footer file on several pages, updating it, and examining the changes on each page where the footer is included.

Scheduling Images

You know those late-night infomercials that end their pitch with, "If you call within the next 24 hours, you get the vegi-slicer included at no extra charge"? How about print ads with offers like "expires 12/31/97" that come in a box of cereal you purchased in 1998? The purpose of these challenging philosophical questions is not simply to vent against annoying sales pitches. There are times when you want a time-sensitive message to display on your Web site. One of the valuable things about the format of a Web site is that it instantly updates. Yesterday's message is not today's message. This is true even if you're gone during the time that your message should be changing. Outdated information can be useless or even disruptive for you or your company.

FrontPage enables you to schedule images that will appear and disappear on cue. A picture of a skier racing down the slopes can be replaced by a diver in the swimming pool when summer rolls around. Your "24th Anniversary" logo can switch to the "25th Anniversary" at the appointed time and date, and all this can be preprogrammed.

The process of placing scheduled images involves assigning them to appear and disappear on set dates. The Scheduled Image component includes an option to assign an alternate image to appear the rest of the time. To place a scheduled image, follow these steps:

1. Before you place a Scheduled Image component, the image (as well as any replacement images) should be imported into your Web site in FrontPage Explorer.

NOTE
You explored the process of importing graphics into FrontPage Explorer in the Saturday Afternoon session of this book. A quick reminder: Switch to FrontPage Explorer, select File, Import, click on the Add button, and navigate to the file you want to import.

2. Place your cursor at the point where the scheduled image should appear.

3. Select Insert, FrontPage Component.

4. Click on Scheduled Image and then click on OK in the dialog box, as shown in Figure 6.20.

5. Click on the Browse button in the Scheduled Image Properties dialog box and then double-click on the filename of the image to display during the dates you define. The scheduled image filename appears in the Image to include area of the Scheduled Image Properties dialog box, as shown in Figure 6.21.

6. If you want to define an alternate image that will appear when the scheduled image isn't scheduled, click on the Optional Image to include before or after the given dates area of the Scheduled Image Properties dialog box and then click on the Browse button.

7. Double-click on the filename of the image to appear when the

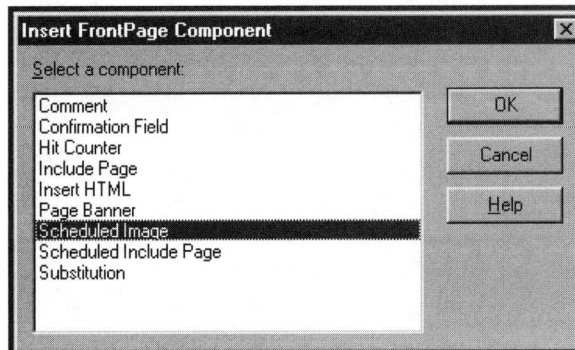

Figure 6.20

Inserting a scheduled image.

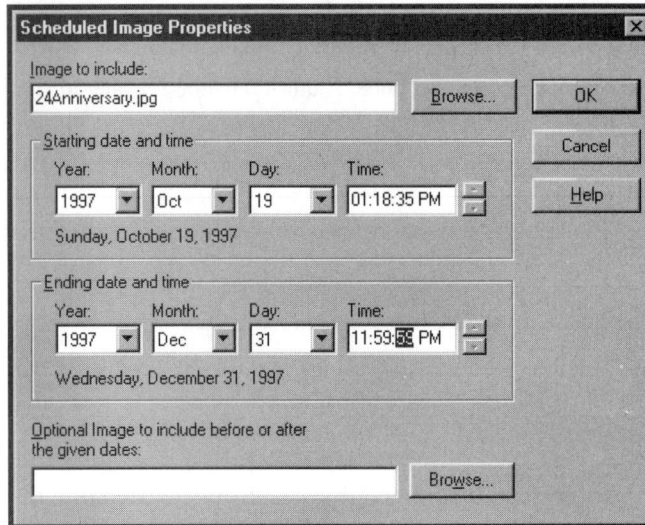

Figure 6.21

Scheduling an image—easier than programming your VCR.

scheduled image does not display. The alternate image filename appears in the Optional Image area of the Scheduled Image Properties dialog box, as shown in Figure 6.22.

8. Type the date to start the display of the scheduled image in the

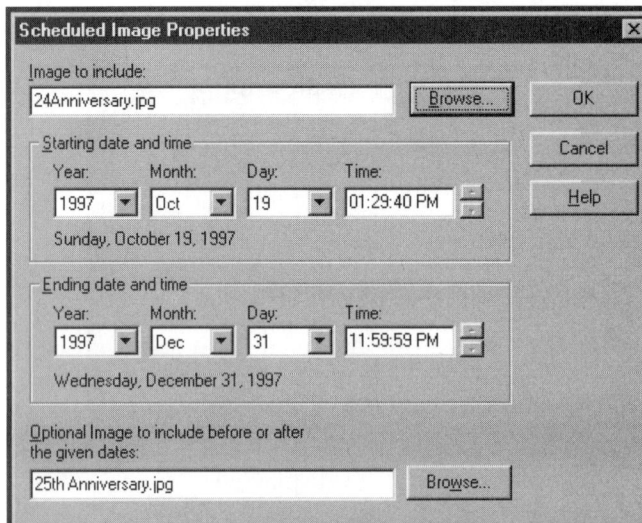

Figure 6.22

Selecting an alternate image to appear.

Starting date and time area of the Scheduled Image Properties dialog box.

9. Enter the time and date the scheduled image should "turn off" in the Ending date and time area; then click on OK in the Scheduled Image Properties dialog box.

10. Save the page with the included scheduled image.

NOTE If you defined an optional image, one of your two images will display.

Scheduling Pages

Including a page within a page is not a new concept. You already inserted an included footer page. However, the Scheduled Include Page component allows you to do this with a twist—you can restrict the included page to a defined schedule.

To insert a scheduled include page, you need two, maybe three, pages: a page that will host the include page, a page to insert, and an alternate page to include. The process goes much more smoothly if both (or all three) pages are ready to go before you start working with the Scheduled Include Page component. Two different pages that could be used as scheduled include pages are shown in Figure 6.23.

TIP You can view all open pages by selecting Window, Tile.

If your creative juices are stimulated sufficiently by this example (or you have a better idea of a scheduled include page), then try creating one of your own. To place a scheduled include page, follow these steps:

1. Create a page to include (two pages if you'll be assigning an alternate included page to display when the scheduled include page is "not scheduled").

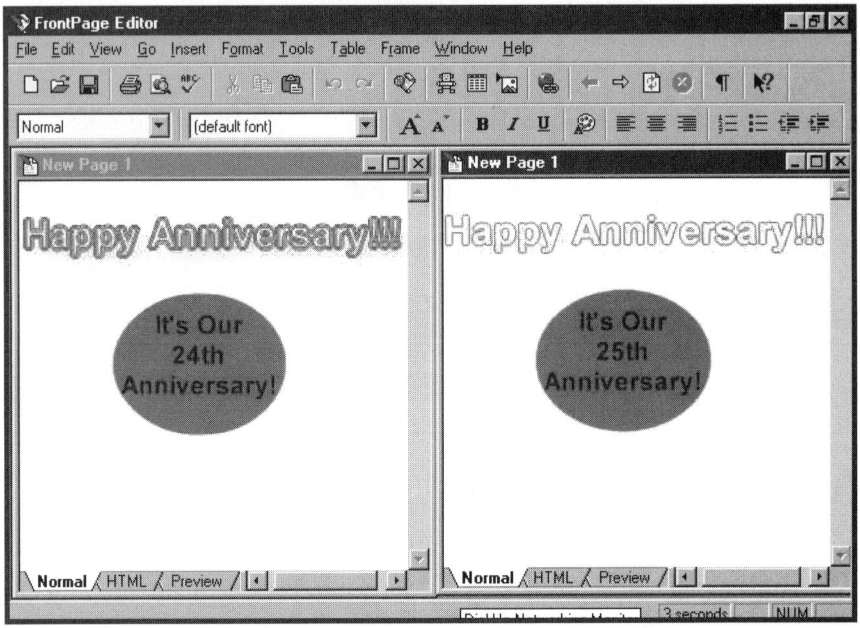

Figure 6.23

Alternate
scheduled pages.

> **NOTE** When you created a footer, you used an included page. The difference here is that the included page displays only on schedule.

2. Make sure that you have saved the page to include as well as the alternate page, if you're creating one.

3. Place your cursor at the spot in your page where the scheduled include page is to appear.

4. Select Insert, FrontPage Component and click on Scheduled Include Page.

5. Use the Browse buttons to select a scheduled page file and an alternate page file.

6. Enter dates to turn the scheduled include file on and off.

TIP

This part of the process is identical to defining parameters for a scheduled image. Your Scheduled Include Page Component Properties dialog box should look something like the one shown in Figure 6.24.

7. When you have defined the scheduled include file (and, optionally, an alternate file), click on OK in the Scheduled Include Page Component Properties dialog box. If you scheduled your included file to appear today, it should display on the page, as shown in Figure 6.25.

To edit a Scheduled Include Page component, follow these steps:

1. Move your cursor over the Scheduled Include Page component object. The cursor becomes a robot.

2. Double-click on the Scheduled Include Page component object and make changes in the Scheduled Include Page Component Properties dialog box.

NOTE

You can change scheduled include dates as well as the included page(s).

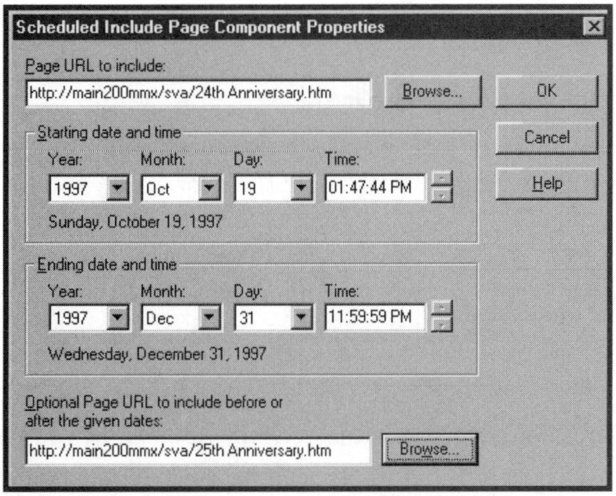

Figure 6.24

Getting ready for the 25th anniversary.

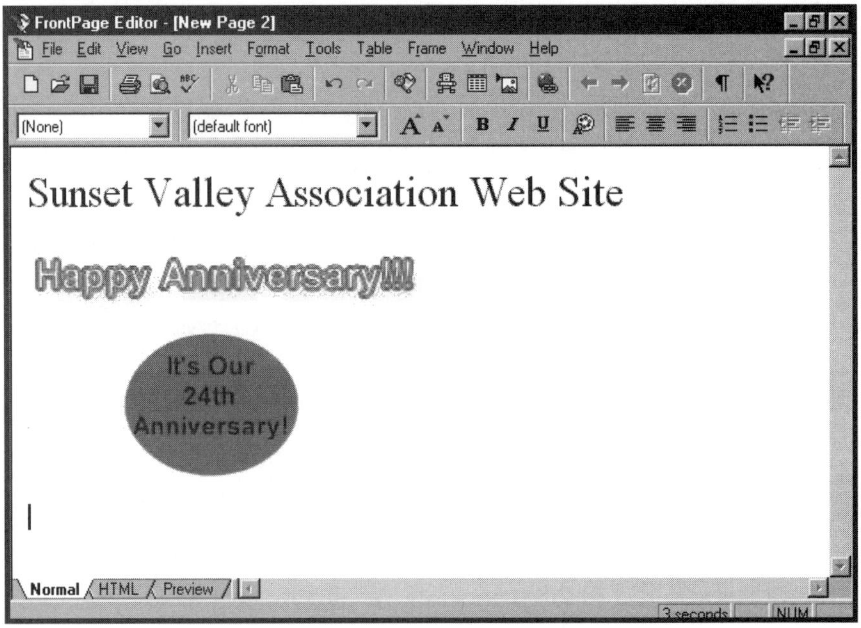

Figure 6.25

The scheduled
page will change
when the clock
strikes 1998.

3. Click on OK in the Scheduled Include Page Component Properties
dialog box when you've finished editing your Include parameters.

Substituting Pages

In order to appreciate what the Substitute component can contribute to
your site, check FrontPage Explorer to see some of the Web properties it
has been quietly storing. To edit file properties, follow these steps:

1. Switch to FrontPage Explorer.
2. Right-click on a file in Folders view and select Properties from the
pop-up menu. The resulting dialog box is shown in Figure 6.26.
3. Click on the Summary tab of the Properties dialog box.
4. Enter a comment that describes the page in the Comments area of
the Properties dialog box, as shown in Figure 6.27.

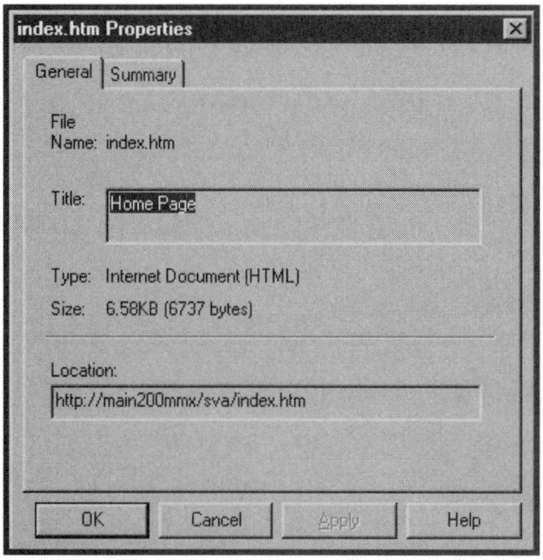

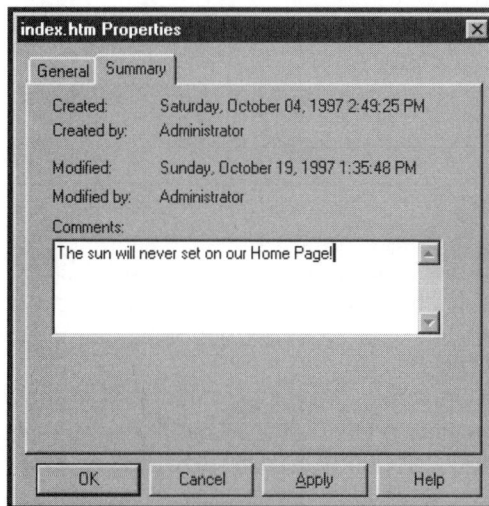

Figure 6.26

Page properties.

Figure 6.27

Defining page comments.

TIP

You cannot edit the Created date, Created By field, or any modification information, but you can edit the Comments area of the Properties dialog box.

5. Click on OK in the Properties dialog box.

Placing Properties on a Page

Now that you've examined and created some page properties, you can plug this information into the Web page using the FrontPage Substitution component. A Substitution component is an object within the Web page that can display any information found in the Page Properties dialog box (see Table 6.2).

To place a Substitution component on a page, follow these steps:

1. With the page you're editing open in the FrontPage Editor, place your cursor in the spot where the Substitution component should go.

2. Select Insert, FrontPage Component, and then click on Substitution.

TABLE 6.2 THE SUBSTITUTION COMPONENTS	
Substitution Component	**What It Does**
Author	This is the person who created the page; the name is listed in the Created By field of the page's Properties dialog box in FrontPage Explorer.
Modified By	This denotes the person who last modified the page; the name is listed in the Modified By field of the page's Properties dialog box in FrontPage Explorer.
Description	The Description component is replaced by whatever you type in the Comments field in the Properties dialog box in FrontPage Explorer.
Page URL	If you select this Substitution component, the URL of the page will display.

3. Click on OK in the Insert Component dialog box.

4. Pull down the <u>S</u>ubstitute with list in the Substitution Component Properties dialog box.

5. Select one of the Substitution options. In Figure 6.28, the Author option is selected.

6. Save the page with the Substitution component.

You can also edit a Substitution component. First, select a different one by double-clicking on the Substitution component, as shown in Figure 6.29.

Figure 6.28

Inserting the page's author.

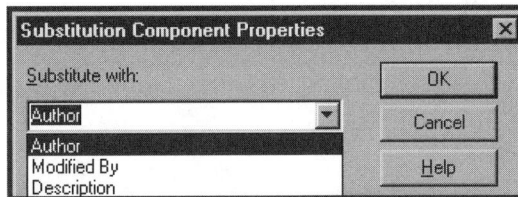

Figure 6.29

Editing a Substitution component.

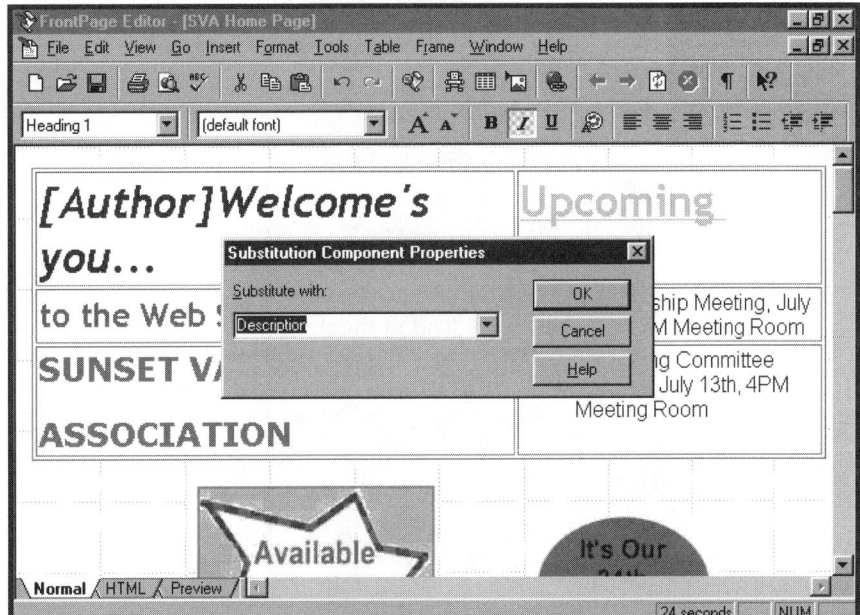

Recording the Number of Page Hits

Even if you're an infrequent Web traveler, you've probably noticed sites that count the number of people who have visited. These sites either have odometer-like counters or messages that say "You're the 1,000,000th person to visit this site," even if you're the first person to visit it.

FrontPage makes it very easy to add one of these hit counters by using the Hit Counter component. In no time, you'll know exactly how active your site is. To place a Hit Counter component, follow these steps:

1. From within FrontPage Editor, place your cursor in the spot where you want the hit counter to go.

2. Select Insert, FrontPage Component, and then double-click on Hit Counter. You'll see the Hit Counter Properties dialog box, as shown in Figure 6.30.

3. Select which counter style you want by choosing the appropriate

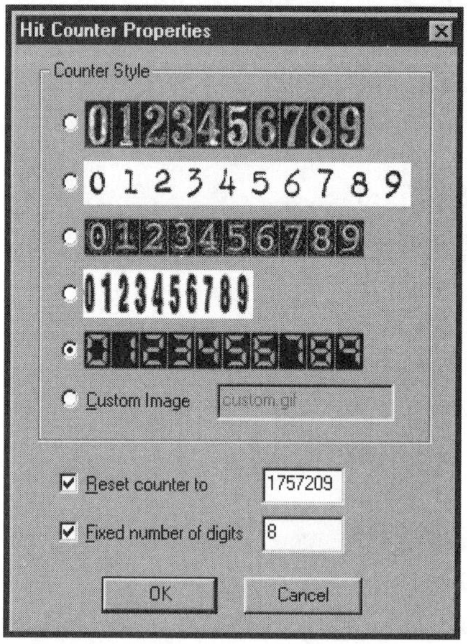

Figure 6.30

The Hit Counter Properties dialog box.

radio button in the Counter Style area. If you want to use your own graphic, select Custom Image and supply the graphic name.

4. The Reset counter to check box gives you license to embellish. By checking this box, you can set the starting value for your counter. So if you're like everyone else on the Web, you'll start with at least 1000! By not checking this box, your count will start at zero.

5. The Fixed number of digits check box lets you specify how many digits the counter will have. If you want it to be similar to a car's odometer, then check the box and specify 5. If you don't want any leading zeros in the number, leave the box unchecked.

6. Click on OK to close the Hit Counter Properties dialog box.

A rather optimistic example of what the Hit Counter component might exhibit is shown in Figure 6.31.

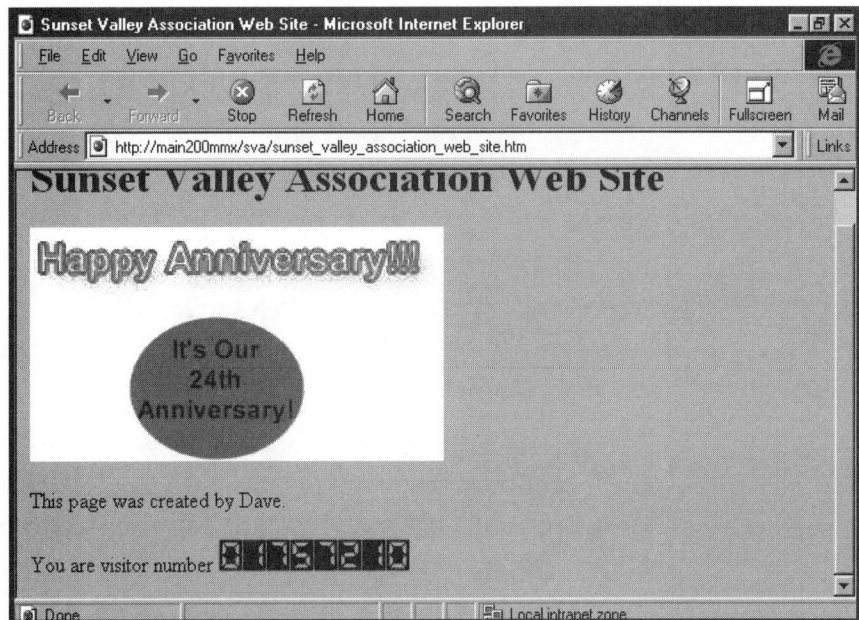

Figure 6.31

Really, this page has had almost two million hits!

The Standout FrontPage Components

By now you're used to going to the Insert menu and selecting FrontPage Components. These are not as scary as they were when you started this afternoon. Three other components exist that are worth mentioning: Search, Table of Contents, and Timestamp. In previous versions of Front-Page, these powerful components were grouped along with the rest of the FrontPage components. But for reasons unknown to yours truly, they have been moved. That's OK, because these are three components worth learning about.

Helping Visitors Search Your Site

If your Web site is a short, single page, your visitors don't need a search box to find exactly what they're looking for. However, if you have many pages, long pages, or both, providing a search component is great help for your visitors.

The search component that FrontPage creates isn't intuitive—it just searches for text. For example, if you have information in your site on "pricing," don't expect a visitor to get there by searching for "cost." The visitor must use the same wording that you use; therefore, you must either include some explanation with the search component you create or try to include text within your page that searchers are likely to look for.

Placing a search box in your Web site is really easy. After you place the search box, you can touch it up with a little explanation, some helpful tips, and a heading.

The final step in creating a search component is to test it. Testing your search component helps you to refine the relationship between anticipated search terms and your text. If you try out your search box and don't find what you hoped to find, the solution is to add text to your pages. To create a search box, follow these steps:

1. Place your cursor where you want to insert the search component.

> ┌─────┐
> │ **TIP** │ ■
> └─────┘
> You might want to place the search box (or a link to it) at the top of your home page.
>
> ■

2. Select Insert, Active Elements, Search Form, as shown in Figure 6.32.

3. The Search Form Properties tab of the Search Form Properties dialog box should feel familiar because you are defining a one-line input form with options to rename the Submit and Reset buttons. The defaults of calling the Start Search button "Start Search" and the Clear button "Reset" should work fine (see Figure 6.33).

4. Now select the Search Results tab (see Figure 6.34). If you think a calculated percentage ratio of matched characters, the file creation date, and the file size are going to be of real interest to your visitors, then select the check boxes for Score (Closeness of Match), File Date, and File Size (in K bytes). You can try them and then change the search form properties if you end up deciding that

Figure 6.32

Active Elements can give your Web site even more power.

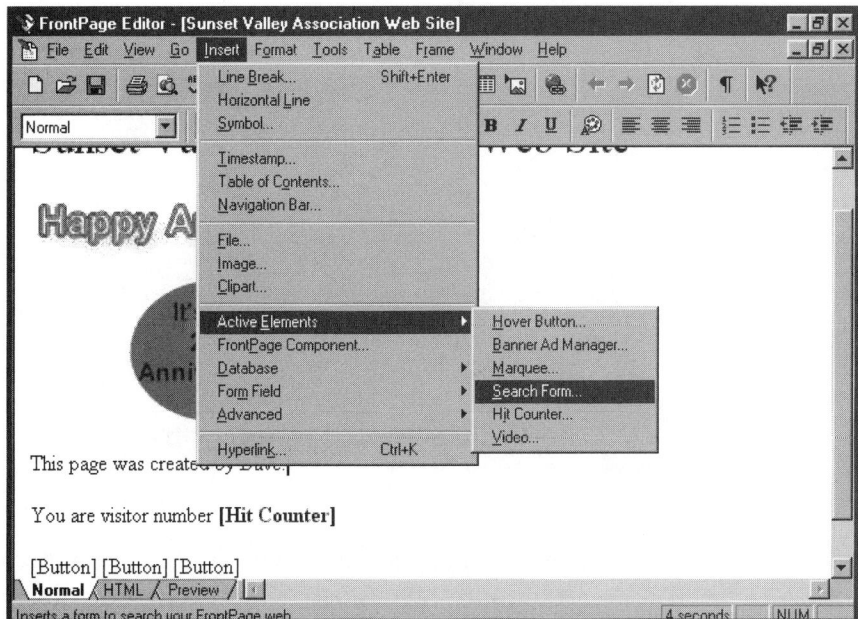

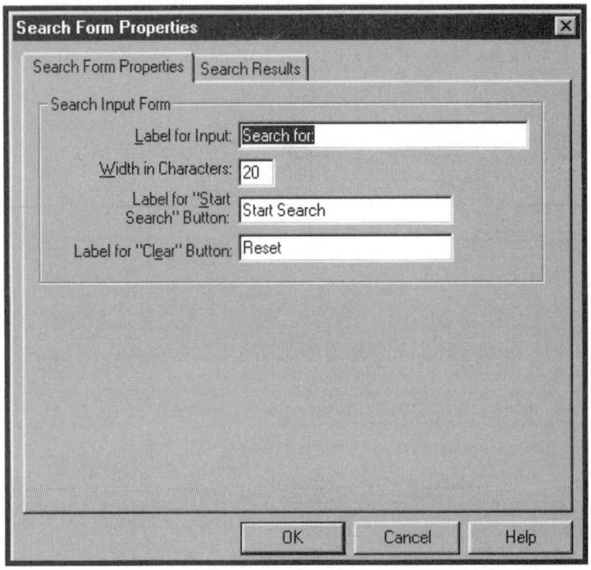

Figure 6.33

The Search Form
Properties
dialog box.

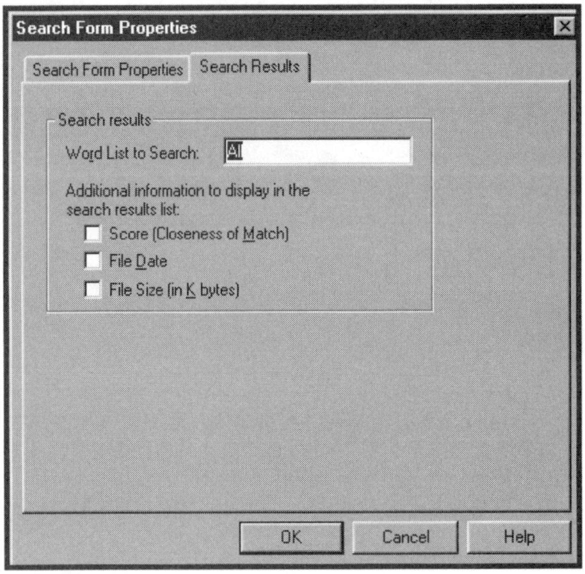

Figure 6.34

The Search Results
tab of the Search
Form Properties
dialog box.

they're not that helpful. You don't need to tamper with the default
suggestion of "All" for the Word List to Search option.

5. When you've looked at and edited the Search Results properties, click on OK in the Search Form Properties dialog box.

6. You might want to add some helpful text above the search component, as shown in Figure 6.35.

7. Save your page to update your site.

To edit the Search component properties, follow these steps:

1. Double-click on the Search component object.

2. Edit the properties and click on OK in the Search Form Properties dialog box.

3. Remember to resave your page.

To test your search component, follow these steps:

1. Launch your Web browser and go to the page with the search component.

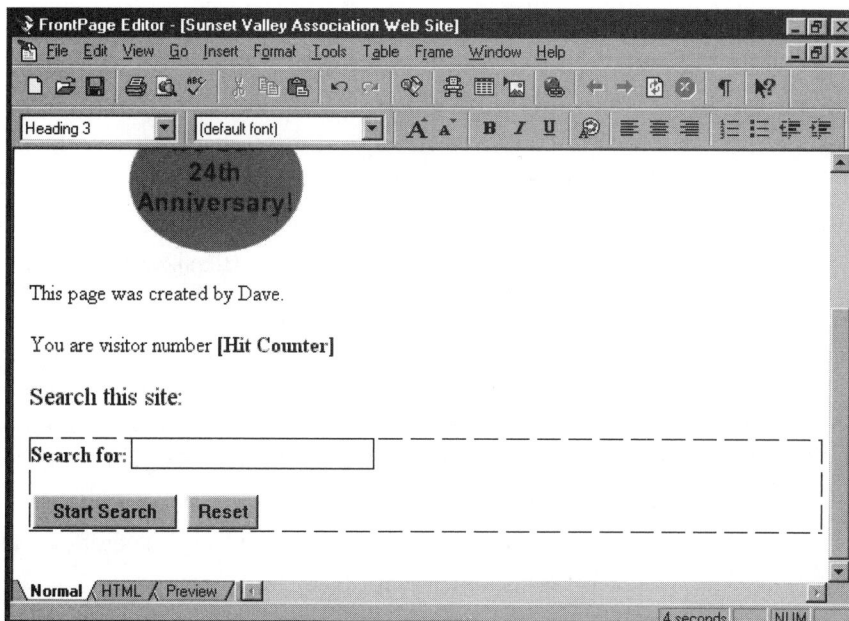

Figure 6.35

Visitors can now search your site.

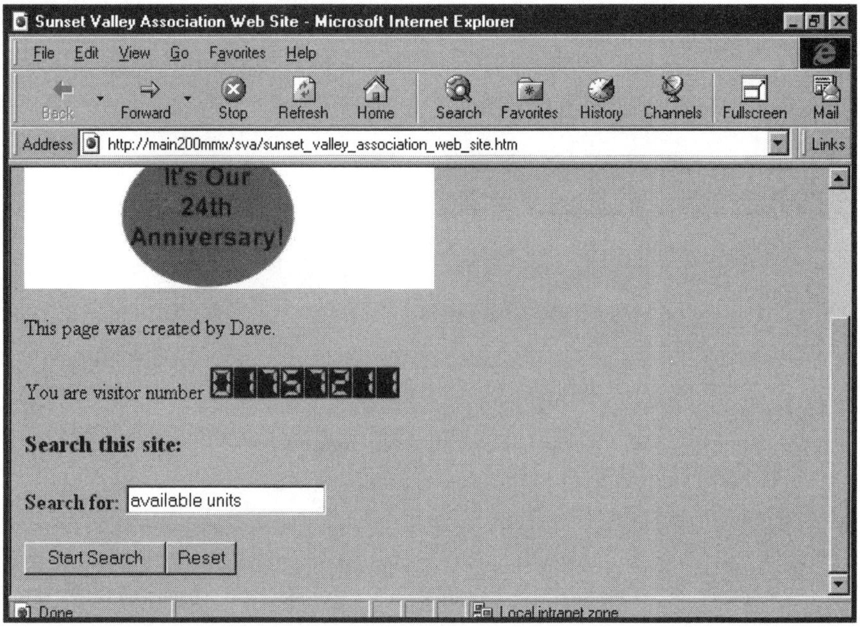

Figure 6.36

Try searching for available units.

2. Try entering some text in your search component and then click on the Start Search button, as shown in Figure 6.36.

3. Examine the results of the search. A table with files that contain matching text will display with the filenames linked to the pages with matching text, as shown in Figure 6.37. If you selected the relevant check boxes, then the file size, date, and closeness of match will also appear.

4. Try following the links from the list created by the search.

TIP

After testing your search component, you can add text to pages back in FrontPage Editor so that they are linked to search text. You can save changes in FrontPage Editor and retest your search using your Web browser—all in a nearly endless quest to provide a functional search component.

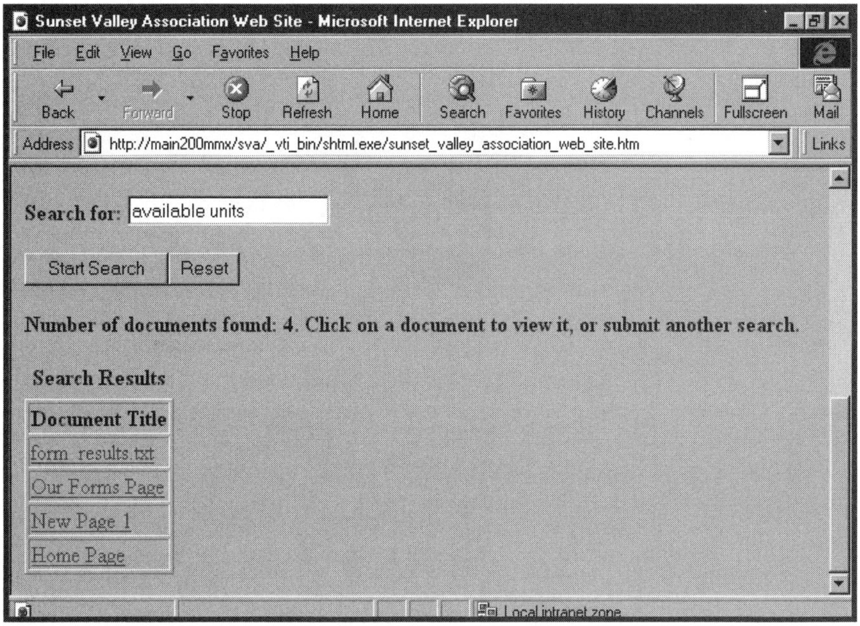

Figure 6.37

Search results.

Creating a Dynamic Table of Contents

You've already explored at least two ways to help visitors find their way around your site from your home page. You can place useful linked text and images at the top of the page, and you can provide a search box. A list or collection of images or text hyperlinks is what most visitors expect to find as a functioning table of contents.

A generated table of contents is most useful in a running discussion Web site. This is a topic you'll explore when working with the Discussion component in Appendix C of this book.

Another function of a generated table of contents is to provide a type of index of all the pages in your Web site for your visitors. Because you're about to generate that list, you should rename any Web pages that have default names that are not descriptive. Your visitors can then go to a page called "Bulletin Board" instead of one called "Results of Index 1," for example. To change a page title, follow these steps:

1. In FrontPage Editor, right-click and select Page Properties from the shortcut menu.

2. The page title is located in the <u>T</u>itle area of the General tab on the Page Properties dialog box. A title that won't be very helpful to visitors when they see it in a table of contents (Results from Form 3 of Page Index2.htm) is shown in Figure 6.38.

3. Edit the page title in the <u>T</u>itle area, as shown in Figure 6.39.

4. Click on OK in the Page Properties dialog box and save the page. Now, when you generate a table of contents, the page title will be useful and descriptive.

To generate a table of contents, follow these steps:

1. Place your cursor on the page in which the table of contents is to appear. You can type a heading such as "Site Contents" if you think this might help your visitors.

2. Select the <u>I</u>nsert, Table of C<u>o</u>ntents menu item.

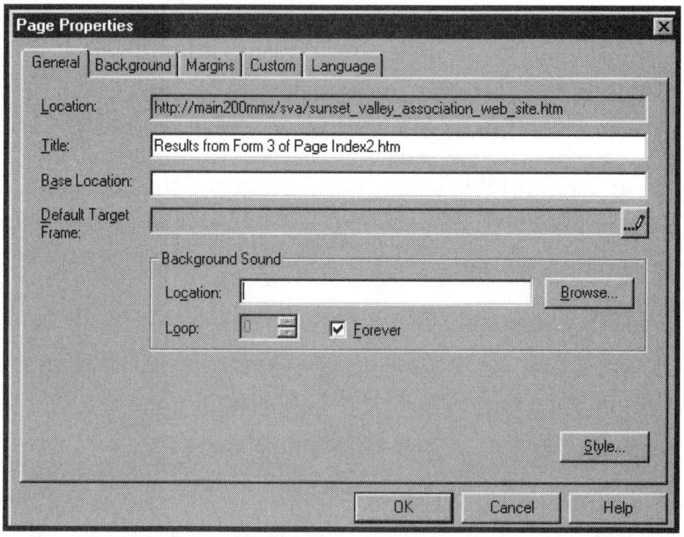

Figure 6.38

This page title doesn't tell visitors much.

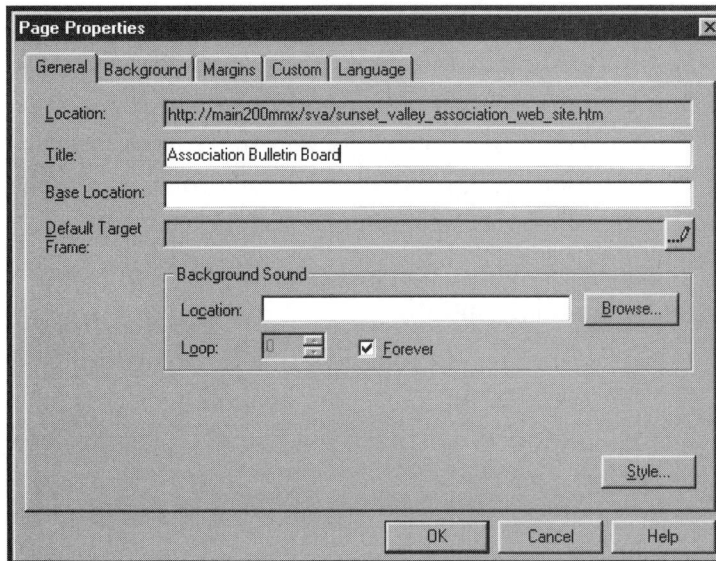

Page Properties

General | Background | Margins | Custom | Language |

Location: http://main200mmx/sva/sunset_valley_association_web_site.htm

Title: Association Bulletin Board

Base Location:

Default Target Frame:

Background Sound

Location: _____ Browse...

Loop: 0 ☑ Forever

Style...

OK | Cancel | Help

Figure 6.39

A more informative page title.

3. In the Table of Contents Properties dialog box in the area labeled Page URL for the Starting Point of Table, enter index.htm. This ensures that all pages are listed in the table of contents.

4. The Heading Size area of the Table of Contents Properties dialog box (shown in Figure 6.40) allows you to make one basic decision. Do you want the Home Page displayed as a title? If you want to create your own title, select "none" from the drop-down menu. If you do want to display the home page as a title, select a heading size for the text.

5. Click on the Show each page only once check box to ensure that pages with multiple links don't end up in the table of contents multiple times.

6. Click on the Show pages with no incoming hyperlinks check box if you want to display pages that are a part of your Web site but don't have defined links to them. One example might be results files from user input forms. If you want those files to be accessible from the table of contents (which will create a link), select this check box.

7. Click on the Recompute table of contents when any other page is edited check box if you want your table of contents updated each time you edit your site and create (or delete, or rename) Web pages. This is one of the best things about letting FrontPage generate a table of contents. Normally you'll want to enable this option, as shown in Figure 6.40.

8. When you've completed the Table of Contents Properties dialog box, click on OK.

9. Feel free to add your own title to the table of contents—especially if you selected "none" as your heading style in the Table of Contents Properties dialog box. One example of a title is shown in Figure 6.41.

To test your Table of Contents component, follow these steps:

1. Save the page with the Table of Contents component.

2. Use the Preview in Browser menu item on your Web browser and go to the page in your Web site with the generated table of contents.

3. Test the links in the generated table, as shown in Figure 6.42.

You can modify your generated table of contents by:

○ Adding new pages and saving them

○ Deleting pages

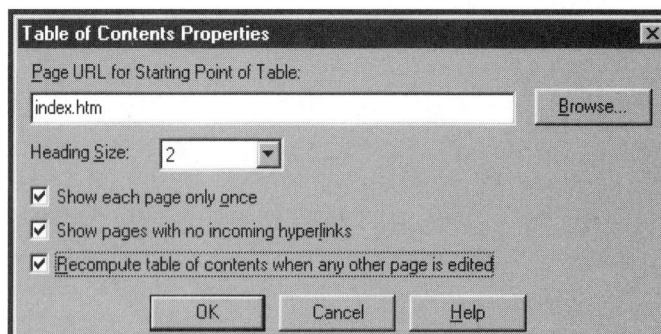

Figure 6.40

Defining a table of contents.

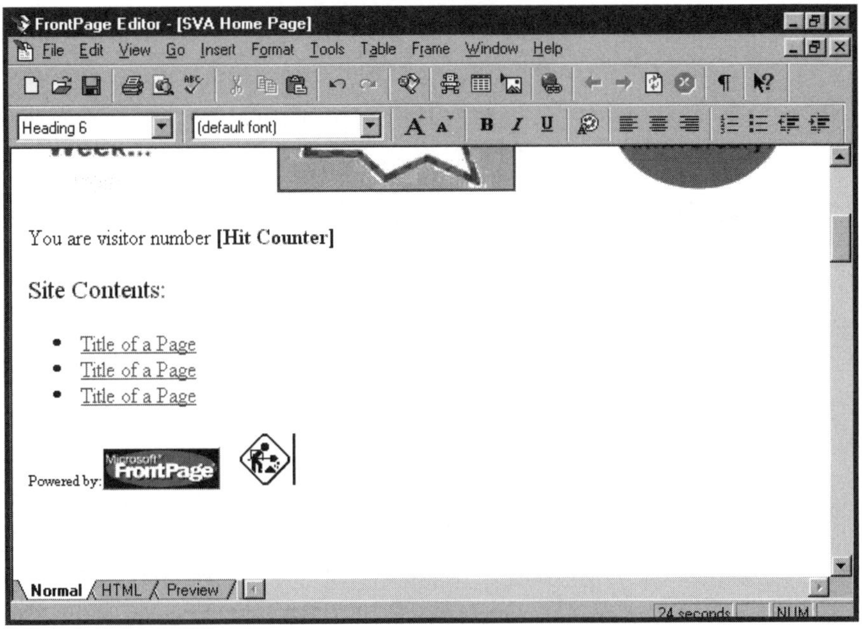

Figure 6.41

The table of contents doesn't tell you much in FrontPage Editor.

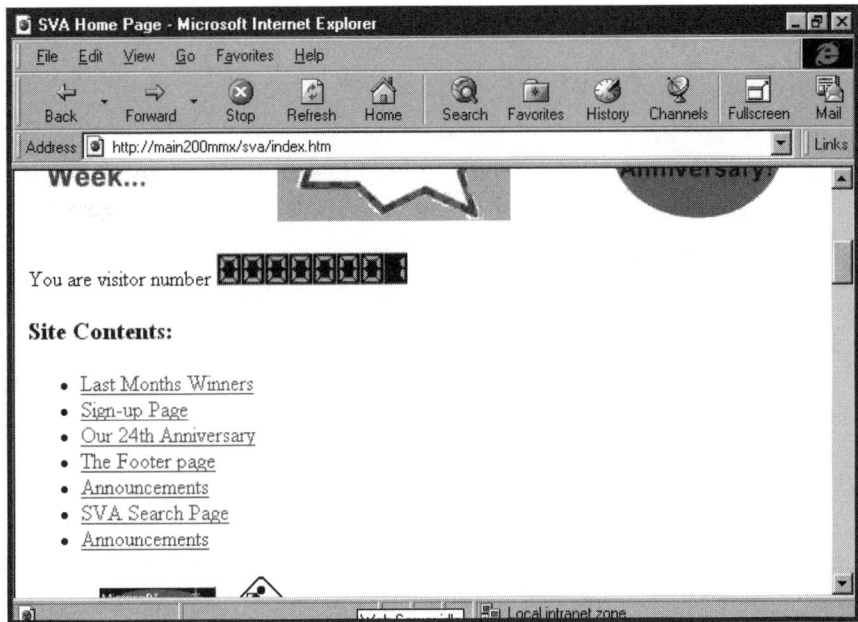

Figure 6.42

Table of contents—viewed with a browser.

- Editing page titles and saving the edited pages
- Reloading the page with the table of contents in your browser, causing it to update

Timestamping Your Page

The finishing touch on your Web site is to place a timestamp on a page. Timestamping is like those freshness dates you find on Twinkies at the grocery store—the ones that say "Best Used By December, 2043." Many people tend to throw out items with obsolete dates stamped on them. The same goes for Web site visitors. They're looking for fresh stuff, and one way to show them you've got it is to timestamp your page.

A message indicating that your page was updated as of yesterday lets visitors know there's something new to see. Of course, you need to actually update the page, but FrontPage allows you to inform visitors that the page was changed even if the only change was something automatic, such as a visitor adding a comment to the site or a scheduled image changing. To place a timestamp, follow these steps:

1. Enter into the page the text to precede the timestamp. You can use text such as, "This page was last updated."

2. Place your cursor in the position you want the timestamp to appear.

3. Select the Insert, Timestamp menu item.

4. Pull down the Date Format list and select a format to display the date, as shown in Figure 6.43.

5. Click on the Date this page was last edited radio button to display the date you last made changes to a page and saved them.

6. Click on the Date this page was last automatically updated radio button to display the date the page was last changed—by your personal updates or by any other change made to the page.

7. You can select a Time Format from the list. Select (none) to display only the date.

Figure 6.43

Selecting a timestamp format.

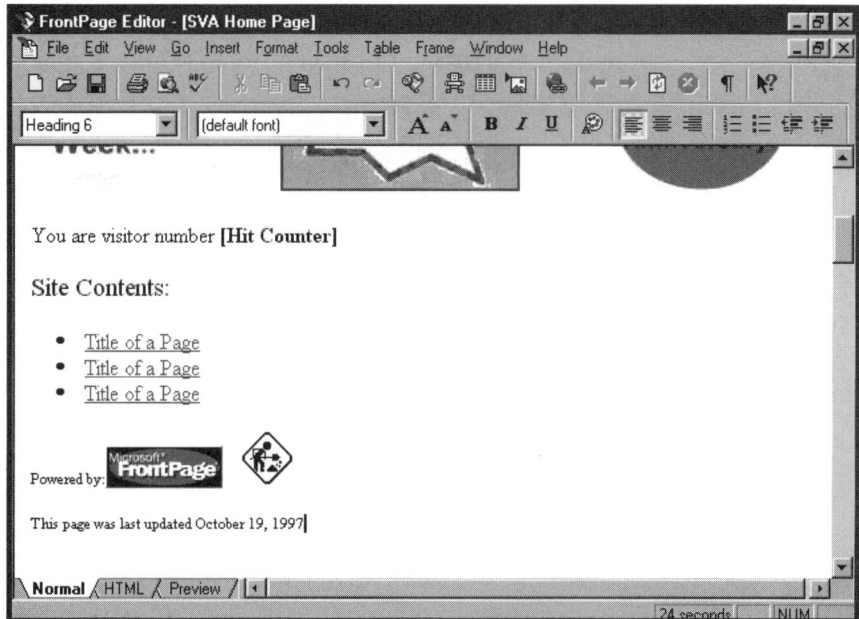

Figure 6.44

This page is fresh as of October 19.

8. Click on OK in the Timestamp Properties dialog box and note the date displayed on your page (see Figure 6.44).

Take a Break!

By now you've explored all the main features of FrontPage and have digested enough to create a sophisticated Web site. What remains is to actually post your Web site. You may feel that you're ready to do that now, or you might want to deviate from the plan and experiment a bit before you finalize your site for posting. If you've been working along with me through this book, you've had a chance to find out which features you like and which ones you won't need in your Web site.

One possibility, now that you've mastered the fundamental elements of creating Web sites in FrontPage, is to use the wizards and templates. They can save you some of the grunt work of manufacturing a site and allow you to edit a site to your taste and needs. Because the wizards and templates you're interested in will vary depending on the type of site you're creating, I address these approaches to Web site building in the appendixes. Another "scenic route" detour at this point is to browse through the appendixes to see if the wizards, templates, and the Registration component covered in them are things you might want to use in building your site.

After your site is created, it's time to publish it from the default site you created on your computer. I've mainly aimed this book at readers who are creating a Web site on their own PCs, and who will be copying that site to a Web space they rent from a provider. A growing number of Web site providers have configured their Web sites to work very smoothly with FrontPage. I've used many of them, and I share some advice in the Sunday Evening session of this book on how to find a good one.

If you have been working with a site on the Internet and have posted it, you can skip through the beginning of the next session and pick up where I discuss maintaining an existing site. If your Web site is part of an intranet, you'll need to find out from your network administrator how to copy your FrontPage Web site to the local intranet server.

Of course, after you copy your Web site to the Internet, the process of improving, monitoring, and maintaining that site is ongoing, and I discuss that, too. The light is shining at the end of the tunnel—you're about to get on the Net!

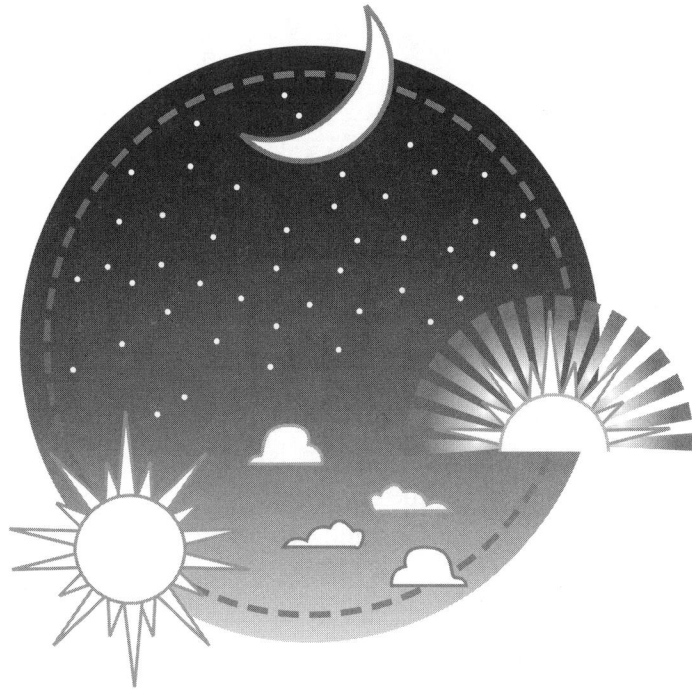

Publishing Your Site on the World Wide Web

So far, you've covered techniques to create a sophisticated, powerful, and attractive Web site. However, you can do more than that. You'll find that the possibilities are endless. Also, you'll continually refine your Web design skills as you get feedback from your site. Now it's time to publish your site on the World Wide Web.

You may decide to explore some of the FrontPage templates and wizards in the appendixes of this book before you make your Web site available. These appendixes address features that some people don't want or need in their Web site. If you do want to include any of the features covered, take a detour to the appropriate appendix and then come back to this page when your site is finished.

How do you get your Web page from your computer's practice Web site to the World Wide Web? You need the following:

- A FrontPage Web site. You have this—you've been working on one all weekend.

- An Internet service provider (ISP), such as The Microsoft Network, that enables you to access the Internet from your computer's modem.

- A Web site provider that will rent you space to put your FrontPage site on the Web. This may be the same as your ISP.

Dozens of companies can provide you with easy-to-access space on the World Wide Web. Publishing your site to the space you rent is pretty simple. The hard part is doing comparison shopping to figure out the best deal.

I'll give you some information to help you shop for a Web site provider. Web site providers offer a range of pricing options, from stripped-down models to sites with some extras. I'll show you how to contact and bargain with these providers through e-mail, and I'll give you some tips on what to look for in your site provider.

After you make a deal with a site provider, FrontPage makes it easy to publish your site on the Web. Most of the providers I recommend can sign you up via e-mail and get you started immediately. Finally, I'll also discuss strategies for attracting visitors to your site.

Selecting an Internet Service Provider

In order for you to copy your FrontPage site from the Personal Web Server on your own computer to the World Wide Web, you must be connected to the Internet. Up until now, it was possible to test your site on your own computer. Not anymore. That breathtaking Web site of yours is ready to publish on the Web, and to do that, you'll need an Internet connection.

The folks who provide access to the Internet are called Internet service providers (or ISPs, for short). ISPs handle the process of physically connecting your computer to the Internet. They purchase Internet connections and sell you access to those connections.

You might already have an ISP. Gee, who doesn't these days? How could you live without e-mail? But will your current Internet service provider be sufficient to publish your site on the Web? Not necessarily.

Not every Internet service provider handles transmitting FrontPage Web sites to site providers on the Web. For example, an America Online connection does not handle this process. If you're using America Online as

your Internet service provider or you encounter snags in publishing your site, you're going to need to contract with another ISP to send your FrontPage site to the Web. Many ISP's now offer Web hosting services, so if you already have an ISP, check with it.

Shopping for a Web Site Provider

Contracting for space for your Web site is a little like renting a post office box from the U.S. Postal Service. Just as the cost for renting a postal box is determined by its size, the cost for publishing your Web site is usually linked in some way to the amount of space you need for your site. The point is not to keep your Web site so small that it isn't useful. But, if you know how much space you need for your Web site, you can shop around and get a good deal.

The main factors are deciding whether you want a domain name, figuring out the size of your Web site, and connecting to The Microsoft Network (or another provider) so that you can copy your site without any problems. First, I'll discuss the factors involved in selecting a Web site provider to host your site.

Features You Should Look for in a Web Site Provider

Don't be intimidated by the prospect of selecting a Web site provider. Use this list to decide which features you need:

- ✿ Reliability. In my experience, every Web site provider I've worked with has been pretty reliable. When I have had difficulties, I've been able to get quick responses to my questions via e-mail.

- ✿ Free trial usage. Testing how well a Web site provider handles your site before you buy can save you a lot of grief.

- ✿ Technical support. Nearly every provider offers some type of technical support. Often, a quick way to judge the support an ISP provides is to send it a question before you commit yourself to renting a Web site. See how quick, useful, and friendly the response is. In general, I think you'll be happy. It isn't like shopping for a used car—the folks who provide Web site space tend to be people who really enjoy seeing your site get on the Web, and they want to help.

○ Speed of service. Some Web site providers provide faster service than others, but it's difficult to determine this without testing them. Many sites provide demo pages or other ways to test your site before you purchase space. This will tell you more than the claims they make about their bandwidth capabilities. Bandwidth is the amount of data a site provider can transfer per second, and it depends on a number of factors. For instance, a busy site with a faster bandwidth might end up being slower than a less busy site with a slower bandwidth—hence the need to test them out.

○ Acceptance of passcodes. If you plan to use a passcode (see Appendix D), you'll want to make sure your provider can handle it—not all of them want to.

○ Acceptance of e-mail. If you plan to use an e-mail address in a form handler, a feature you explored when you learned to create forms, you might want to verify it with the site provider.

Some Web site providers have options for free Web sites. Usually, the amount of space a host provides is too small to support a site created in FrontPage. Free space that's provided as part of other packages (for instance, by your Internet service provider) usually doesn't support Front-Page extensions, so important features of your site, such as forms, won't work. America Online, for example, provides 10MB of free space to AOL subscribers, but it doesn't support FrontPage extensions.

After you've selected a provider, it should give you the following information:

○ The URL for your Web site

○ The name of your domain or directory on the site

○ A password and account username that gives you access to your directory

Domain Names

No matter how low budget your Web site provider is, it's going to give you a URL (Uniform Resource Locator) address for your Web site. This address might not be pretty. For example, the address could contain numerous slashes, such as

http://Infonow.ifn.com/commerce/users/yourname

Like I said, it's not pretty, but it works. What if you want an address that's really flashy? For example:

http://topdog.com

To get one, you need to contract with your Web site provider for a domain name. Domain names are the "vanity plates" of Web sites. Is having "Hot Lips" on your car's license plate a top priority? An easy-to-remember site name can make it easier for people to remember your URL (site address), thus increasing traffic to your site.

How much more traffic? If you'll be attracting visitors with a freeway billboard listing your URL, having a site name that is easy to remember is a big plus. Is it worth it to get a domain name? You be the judge. If you're running a business, it probably is. If you're just making a political statement, it may not be. Here are two points to consider in deciding the importance of a domain name:

✿ When people visit your site and like it, you can encourage them to add your site to their list of favorite sites (stored by their Web browsers). After they do this, they never need to remember your site address again.

✿ If visitors will be coming to your site via links with other sites (more on this later), it really doesn't matter what your site name is.

One intriguing feature that many site providers offer is a fake domain name site. Basically, the fake domain site allows you to rent space from a Web site provider without purchasing an expensive domain name, and your site gives out something that looks like a domain name to your visitors. Usually these fake domain names are cheaper than a real domain name, but more expensive than a long, difficult URL. One advantage of having a real domain name is that if you switch your Web site provider, you can take the domain name with you.

Many providers arrange for a custom domain name at "cost," for a fee, or both. "Cost" is usually between $100 and $200 to register a name for two years. Most sites might charge you more to let you use the domain name when you rent space from them. Why? Because it's a pain to change the domain name.

Web Size and Cost

When you do comparison shopping for a Web site, you should know how much space you need to rent. Most Web site providers have different pricing, depending primarily on how big your site is.

Unfortunately, FrontPage doesn't yet have a quick, easy way to determine the size of your site. If that feature shows up next year, give me some credit; I've suggested it to Microsoft many times.

You might be wondering why you can't just get out your calculator and total the size of the files listed in Summary view in FrontPage Explorer. Many files associated with your Web site are not listed in the Summary view, such as files that help handle forms.

Your "workaround" solution is to find the size of the directory holding all your files in Windows Explorer (not FrontPage Explorer, but the one that comes with Windows). Finding the directory with your Web site in FrontPage Explorer isn't easy. To estimate the size of your Web site, follow these steps:

1. Right-click on the Start button in the Windows 95 Taskbar and select Find, as shown in Figure 7.1.

2. In the Find: All Files dialog box, enter the name of your Web site. Then, in the Look in list, select the drive to search, as shown in Figure 7.2.

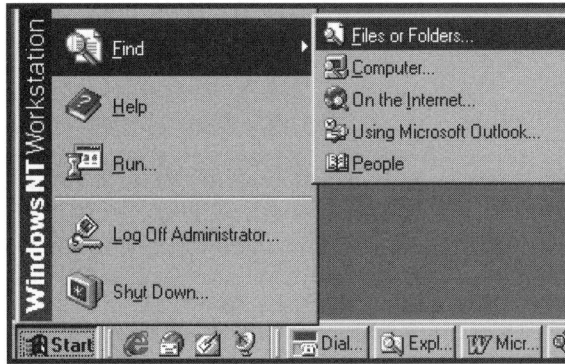

Figure 7.1

Finding your Web site on your computer.

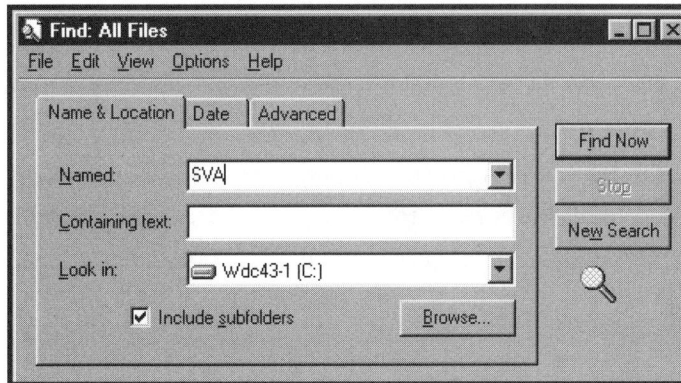

Figure 7.2

I know that Web site is here somewhere!

TIP

If you're not sure as to which drive contains FrontPage, select My Computer from the Look in drop-down list.

3. Click on the Find Now button in the Find: All Files dialog box.

NOTE

When the results appear, you can maximize the Find window to see the filenames more easily.

4. Scroll through the long list of files that match your search criteria until you come to a folder with the name of your Web site, as shown in Figure 7.3.

5. Right-click on the file folder that has the name of your Web site in the Find dialog box and then select Properties from the shortcut menu.

6. Note the number of files in the folder, the number of directories, and the total file size, as shown in Figure 7.4.

This information may be helpful as you shop for a Web site provider. Being able to tell potential providers, "I'm shopping for 439K of space for a site with 108 files and 13 folders (or directories)" will:

○ really impress them

○ help them give you accurate estimates of your monthly cost to rent a site

○ let you brag to your friends about the size of your Web site—if that's important to them

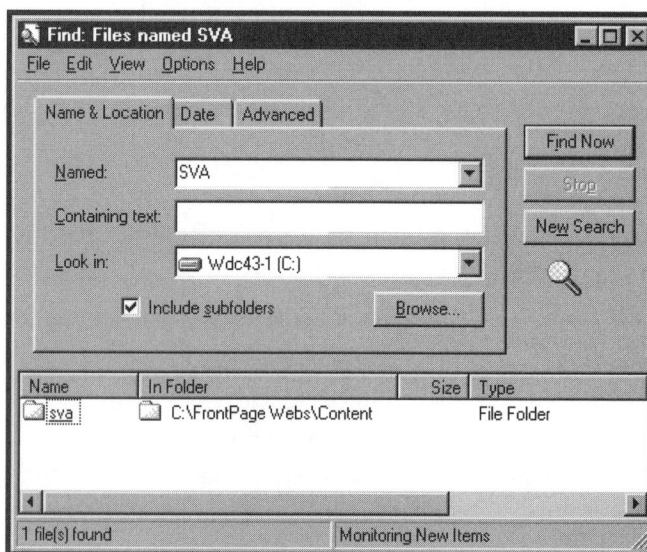

Figure 7.3

Found it!

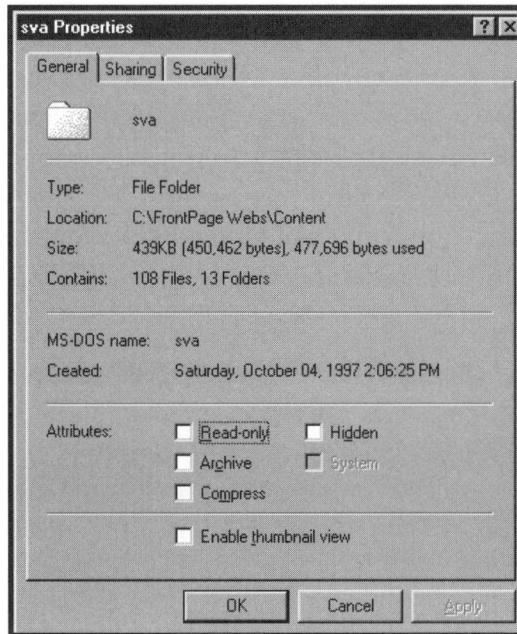

Figure 7.4

Estimating Web site size.

If your Web site provider is friendly, it will factor in additional space for discussion postings, new pages you might want to add, and so on. But knowing the current size of your Web site should be enough information for a Web site provider to give you a price.

7. Exit the Find dialog box when you copy the folder size and contents onto a large scrap of paper and stick it on your wall for future reference.

TIP

When looking for computer space to rent, always rent more than you need. In this example, you would need 439K of space, but in reality, you would want to rent at least 4MB of space. That gives your site room to expand. Besides, at today's prices, 4MB is probably less than the minimum amount some vendors offer.

Shopping at Dave's Web Site Provider: CyberMall

You can compare pricing, select a Web site provider, and in many cases publish your Web site to the World Wide Web—all in an evening. That's because you can do your shopping from your computer. Many Web site providers allow you to upload your site on a "try now, pay later" basis, or they take credit cards. After you know the size of your site and whether you have the need for priority types of technical support, it's time to go shopping.

Not so long ago, however, finding a Web site provider tuned into Microsoft FrontPage was a real hassle. You're lucky that those days are gone! Table 7.1 lists some providers that now support FrontPage-created Web sites. I've surveyed and/or tested most of the Web site providers registered with Microsoft as supporting FrontPage. If you stick with a provider on this list, you shouldn't have a problem publishing your site to the World Wide Web. However, you'll need to check to verify current pricing.

You should be aware of the following when contacting Web site providers:

- ✪ Free test period. The site providers give you a period to try the site out before billing you. Some providers don't advertise this feature, but they may let you try them out for a week if you ask. I would. In one week, you'll know for sure if you like the service you're getting.
- ✪ Password-restricted pages. All the sites listed say they allow you to create password-restricted pages, as described in Appendix D, "Creating a Password-Protected Site."
- ✪ Domain names. Domain name registration is the cost to register your domain name (usually for two years) with InterNIC, the company that administers Internet domain names. InterNIC charges $100 to register your domain name for two years. Be aware of companies that want to charge you more than this.

TABLE 7.1 DAVE'S CYBERMALL	
Web Site Provider	**Contact**
Akorn	www.akorn.net
AIS	www.aisnetwork.net
BitShop	www.bitshop.com
ComCity	www.comcity.com
Coron	www.coron.com
CrWeb	www.crweb.com
CSD Internetworks	www.kenton.com
Digiserve	www.digiserve.com
Digital Publishing Resources	www.digipub.com
FrontPage Now	www.frontpagenow.com
Instant Technologies	www.instantech.com
Internet Web Service Corp.	www.iwsc.com
Internet Presence Providers	www.ipp.com
Shore.net	www.shore.net
Superb Internet	www.superb.net
Vivid Net	www.vivid.net

✪ Web hosting. New service providers are popping up every day. The back of any of the popular computer magazines has a section devoted to Web hosting.

TIP Double-check all information with your provider before you make a final commitment!

Publishing Your Site on the Web

When you've shopped around and found a good deal, you're ready to publish your FrontPage site on the World Wide Web. Remember, the site provider should have given you the following items:

✪ A URL

✪ A login name

✪ A password

If you don't have these three things, contact your site provider again and get this information. To publish your site to the Web, follow these steps:

1. You must log on to the Internet through your Internet service provider.

2. Open the site to be published in FrontPage Explorer.

3. Select File, Publish FrontPage Web from the FrontPage Explorer menu.

4. Enter the URL your Web site host gave you in the combo box, as shown in Figure 7.5.

TIP In case you still need an Internet service provider, you can click on the icon in the Click here to find an Internet service provider to host your FrontPage Web dialog box.

Figure 7.5

Where is your Web site going to be published?

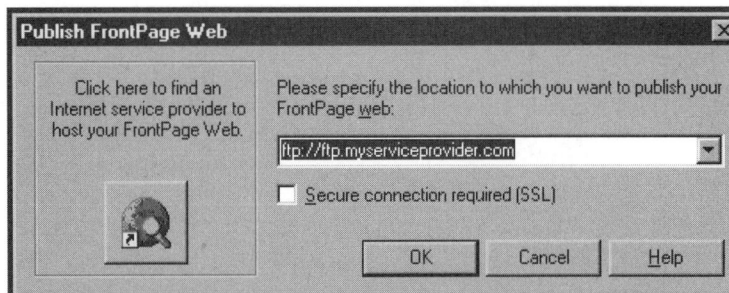

Figure 7.6

Specify a location or get help.

5. Enter your FTP server name and directory path in their appropriate fields in the Microsoft Web Publishing Wizard and click Next, as shown in Figure 7.7.

TIP

If http://fp.dev-com/sva is your site, then the server is http://fp.dev-com and your directory is sva.

6. Enter the login name you received from your Web site provider in the User Name area of the Microsoft Web Publishing Wizard dialog box, as shown in Figure 7.8.

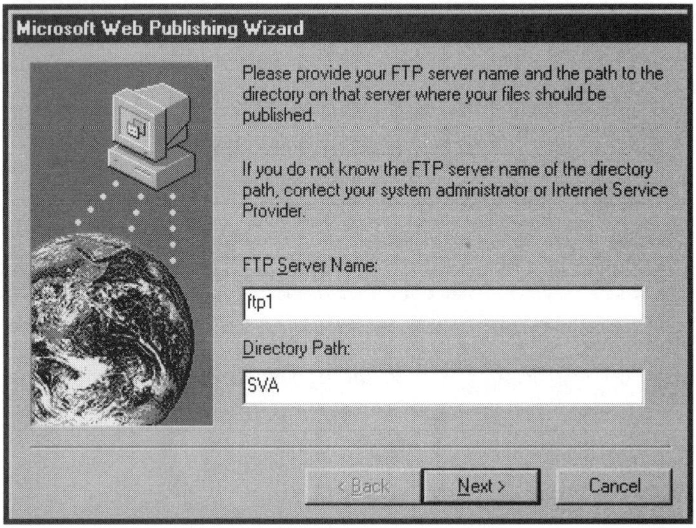

Figure 7.7

The Publishing Wizard needs to know the server name and directory path.

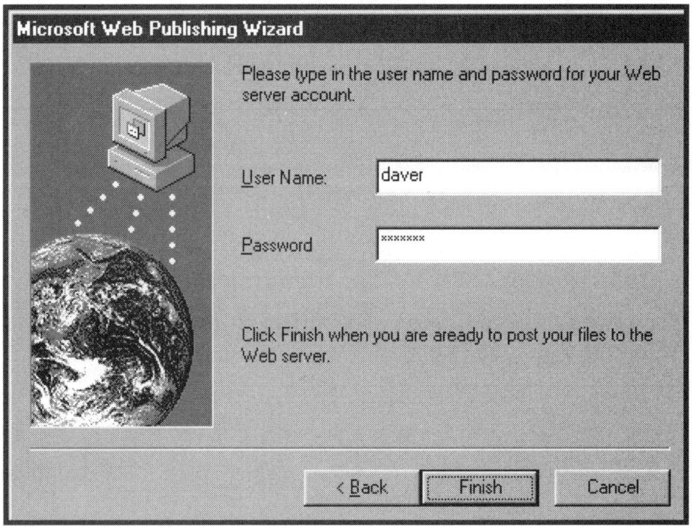

Figure 7.8

All that's left is your user name and password.

7. Enter the password provided by your Web site provider in the Password area of the Microsoft Web Publishing Wizard dialog box.

> **TIP** Passwords are case-sensitive! If your password is "secret," you cannot type "Secret." If the name and password are rejected, contact your service provider to make certain you were given the correct login name and password.

Take a Break!

Publishing your Web site to the World Wide Web takes awhile. Go wash the dishes and come back in five minutes. The status bar in FrontPage Explorer updates you as to the percentage of your Web site that has been published.

Maintaining Your Web Site

You've uploaded your Web site to your contracted Web site provider, but your work isn't over. All the dynamic features you added will come to life. If you created input forms, visitors to your site will be leaving messages that you'll want to pick up. Also, as you visit your site and get feedback from other visitors, you'll want to edit the site contents.

Each time you edit your site or open results files created by form input, you need to log on to your site using the password provided by your Web site provider. After you log on to your site, you can read input files and also edit the site online.

Editing Your Site

As soon as you copy your Web site to your new home on the World Wide Web, you have two copies of that site. One copy is on your hard drive, and the other copy resides on a server somewhere in New Jersey, Seoul, Minneapolis, or wherever. Editing your site online requires that you spend a lot of time logged on to the Internet. Depending on the deal you have with your Internet service provider, you might be paying for that time, and you may be tying up your phone line while you edit online. Another consideration is that editing a site online is slower than editing using the FrontPage Personal Web Server.

One option is to do all your editing using the copy of your site that remains assigned to the Personal Web Server. You can make changes to your site before you log on to the Internet, and then recopy your site to your Web site provider using the same steps you just walked through.

The limitations of recopying your site are that pages that have been changed by visitors, such as pages created by input forms, get replaced when you copy the entire site to your site provider. If your site has input forms that are linked to other pages on the site, recopying is not a good option for editing your site.

My technique is to go to my site using my Internet browser, make careful notes on what needs to be changed, and then crank up FrontPage and make those changes. To edit your site on the Net, follow these steps:

1. Log on to the Internet using Microsoft Internet Explorer or another Internet browser.
2. Select File, Open FrontPage Web from the FrontPage Explorer menu.
3. Click on the More Webs button in the Getting Started dialog box.
4. Click on the Select a Web Server or Disk Location drop-down list and select your Web site. If it's not listed, type in the Web address.
5. Click on OK in the dialog box.

TIP

You'll be prompted for an access name and password. You need to be sure the access name is the correct one for your Web site.

6. Enter the domain name and password for your site, as shown in Figure 7.9, and then click on OK in the Name and Password Required dialog box.

7. Sit and wait awhile. Almost there. Opening a site on the Web is slower than opening one on your own computer.

8. Edit any of your pages, just as you have been doing throughout this book.

9. When you have finished editing a page, remember to save it.

TIP ■ Saving pages on the Web takes longer than when you're just saving to the Personal Web Server.

---

10. When you've finished making changes to your site (or reading pages that were created or edited by form results), remember to exit your Internet service provider so you don't increase your monthly charge too much.

Getting Listed

You're now on the Net. You'll be tempted to visit your site each hour, looking to see if anyone has responded to your input forms. Hmm. Where is everybody?

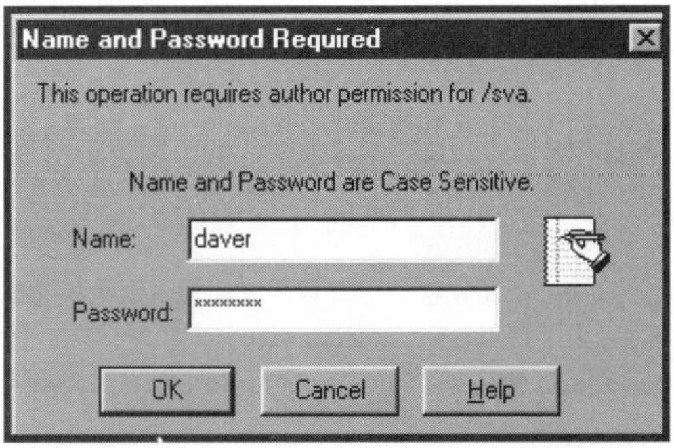

Figure 7.9

Remember, passwords are case sensitive.

> **Name and Password Required** ⊠
>
> This operation requires author permission for /sva.
>
> Name and Password are Case Sensitive.
>
> Name: daver
>
> Password: ********
>
> OK   Cancel   Help

Well, so far, nobody but you, your kids, your parents, your cat, and your significant other knows about your Web site. How do you attract visitors? One element of attracting visitors is to tell everyone about your site by putting it on your business card, including it in your ads, and so on. A good reference is Prima Publishing's *Increase Your Web Traffic In a Weekend*, by William Stanek.

Much of your target audience is to be found on the Web. After all, people already surfing the Net have to have Internet access. How do they find you? Here are some options:

- Your Web site provider may have programs set up that register you with search engines. If not, or if you want to supplement those efforts, register yourself when you use a search engine.
- Exchange links with others.
- Get listed in site directories.

Explore these gateways to attract visitors. To get listed on a search engine, follow these steps:

1. Access a search engine. Your Internet service provider will give you access to one.
2. Enter a search topic where you should be listed, as shown in Figure 7.10.
3. Click on the Search button, or whatever button begins the search in your Web browser.
4. When your site doesn't show up as one of the 11,994 sites that match the search criteria you entered, scroll to the bottom of the page. There, you can normally find a link to a page that allows you to add a new URL to the search engine, such as the one shown in Figure 7.11.

Each search engine is different, but they all allow the addition of your site to their list somewhere, as shown in Figure 7.12.

Figure 7.10

Searching for your site.

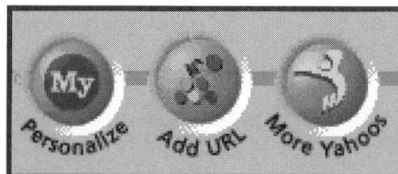

Figure 7.11

Adding your site to the search engine.

Make a habit of adding your URL to every search engine you come across, even though most search engines warn you that it takes weeks to get listed.

After a few months of adding your URL to search engines, your site will start to pop up when folks go looking for what you have to offer. It took me a year or so to get my site to come up when people looked for unauthorized FrontPage support listings, even though I had the advantage of not having much competition.

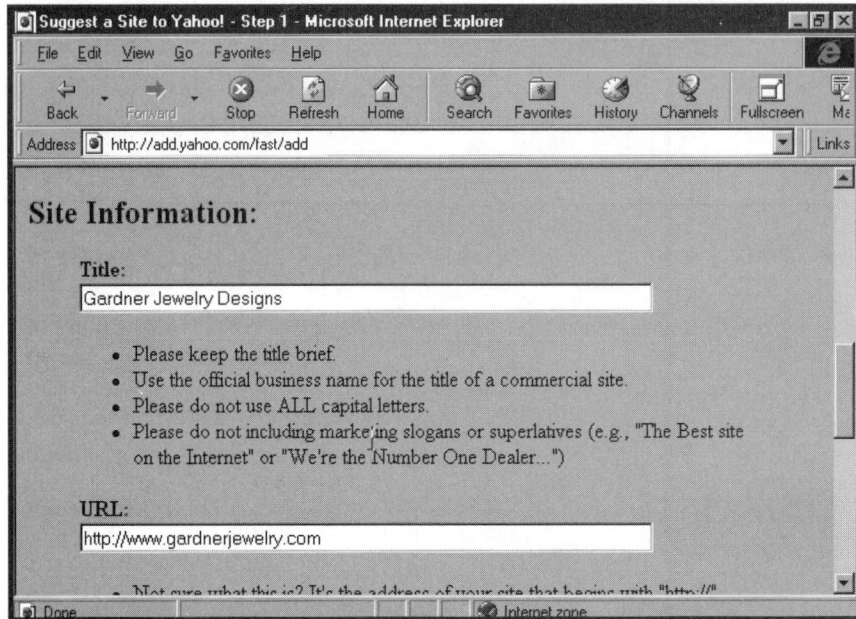

Figure 7.12

Put my site in your list!

Services exist that will submit your Web site to search engines for you. One such service is called Submit-it. Its address is

FIND IT ON ▶
THE WEB

http://www.submit-it.com/

One of the most common ways visitors find your site is via links from pages they've already visited. For this reason, you should exchange links with other sites. Is there a home page for a professional association you belong to? A client who likes your work? Ask if a link to your site can be included on their site, and, in return, you should offer to provide a link from your site to theirs.

You should also get your site listed in site directories. Many Internet service providers have directories of all the sites on their Web. This gives you exposure to everyone visiting the Web site provider, which is quite a few people. This is generated automatically by the server, and you do not have to do anything other than own Web space to appear on this list.

Ongoing Support

You made it! You started with pretty much nothing and ended up creating and posting a sophisticated Web site. If you got detoured along the way, you can stretch the weekend out a bit.

As you continue to develop and maintain your Web site, you'll want to share your experiences, joys, frustrations, and tips. Here are a few resources:

FIND IT ON ▶
THE WEB

- Microsoft's FrontPage Support Web site can be found at **www.microsoft.com/FrontPageSupport/**

- You can get live phone support from Microsoft by calling 206-882-8080 between 7:00 A.M. and 5:30 P.M. Pacific Time, Monday through Friday. If you're having trouble installing FrontPage 98 or getting it started, these are the people to call. Have the serial number on your disk handy when you call Microsoft.

Most of all, have a good time using Microsoft FrontPage 98!

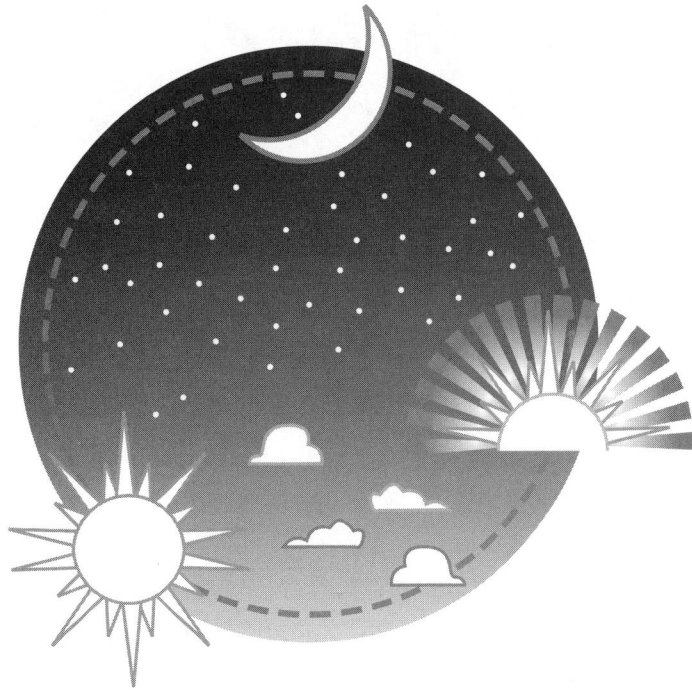

Installing FrontPage

Hardware and Software Needed to Use Microsoft FrontPage 98

The FrontPage packaging itemizes the system requirements needed to install the program, which are also outlined below.

○ A PC with a 486 processor or higher (You'll be much happier with something like a 166MHZ Pentium or faster)

○ Windows 95 or Windows NT version 4.0 (FrontPage does not run under Windows 3.1)

○ Microsoft Office 97 for Windows (While the packaging says this software is required, you can get along without it if you don't have it)

○ 16MB of memory (You'll really want 32MB using either Windows 95 or Windows NT)

○ 30MB of available hard disk space . . . you'll fill that up in a hurry! FrontPage Web pages aren't petite. If you don't have a few hundred MB's free, you might want to expand your hard drive capacity before embarking on this weekend experience. Prima's *Upgrade Your PC In a Weekend* is a good place to start.

○ CD-ROM drive—this drive is necessary to Install FrontPage, unless you're purchasing the downloaded version from Microsoft's Web site.

○ VGA or higher resolution video adapter (SVGA with at least 256 colors)

○ A mouse or compatible pointing device

You also need to have access to the Internet via an Internet Service Provider (ISP), and you'll need an Internet browser that allows you to visit World Wide Web sites. Microsoft Internet Explorer is bundled inside FrontPage 98 and it works fine. The installation procedure for Internet Explorer assists you in finding and signing up with an ISP. Netscape Navigator 3.0 or higher also works well with FrontPage sites, although FrontPage places videos on Web sites in a way that is more easily viewed using Internet Explorer.

FIND IT ON ▶
THE WEB If you are using an older version of Internet Explorer or Netscape, you should download the latest version. The latest version of Microsoft Internet Explorer can be found at **www.microsoft.com/ie**. If you use Netscape, the latest version can be found at **www.netscape.com**.

How to Get FrontPage Up and Running

Follow the instructions to install Microsoft FrontPage. The installation program that comes with FrontPage has simplified the process, and the following provides some background, advice, and step-by-step help. Microsoft FrontPage is a suite of four programs: The Personal Web Server, FrontPage itself, the Microsoft Image Composer, and Microsoft Internet Explorer.

When you insert the FrontPage CD into the drive, it will autorun, and you will most likely be presented with a dialog box like that of Figure A.1. You will see this dialog box unless you already have Microsoft's Personal Web Server installed (odds are you don't). It allows you to test your Web site on your own computer before you contract with a site provider to place your site on the World Wide Web. Even after you post your site on the Web, the Personal Server comes in handy for editing your site offline on a server. Although the Personal Web Server can enable your computer to function as a World Wide Web site on the Internet, its most practical use is to test your Web site on your computer before you copy or upload it to a site provider.

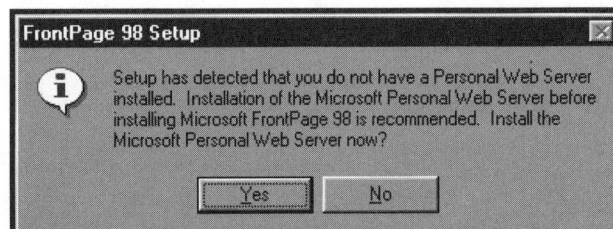

Figure A.1

You'll need to install the Personal Web Server first.

FrontPage 98 Setup

Setup has detected that you do not have a Personal Web Server installed. Installation of the Microsoft Personal Web Server before installing Microsoft FrontPage 98 is recommended. Install the Microsoft Personal Web Server now?

Yes   No

Installation of the Personal Web Server is very straightforward. You'll read through the License Agreement and will probably have to insert your Win95 CD when needed. After doing so, several files will be copied, and you'll be prompted to restart your computer. Do so!

Upon rebooting, you'll know the Personal Web Server has been installed if you see its icon located on the Taskbar (see Figure A.2). You'll also see the FrontPage 98 Installation Options, as shown in Figure A.3.

To install FrontPage itself, click on the Install FrontPage 98 graphic. This will launch the install program and you'll see the ever-familiar Welcome dialog, as shown in Figure A.4.

The Setup program is mostly automated, requiring very little input from you to install FrontPage. The Typical Setup option works very well and is highly recommended (see Figure A.5). If you absolutely know what you're doing and have specific reasons for doing so, you may elect to choose the Custom Setup.

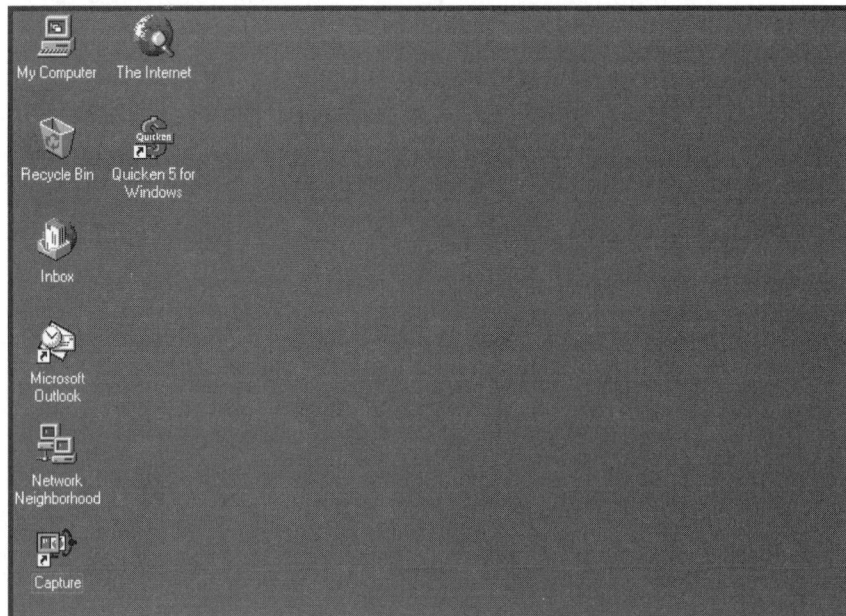

Figure A.2

The Personal Web Server is up and running.

Figure A.3

The FrontPage 98 Installation Options.

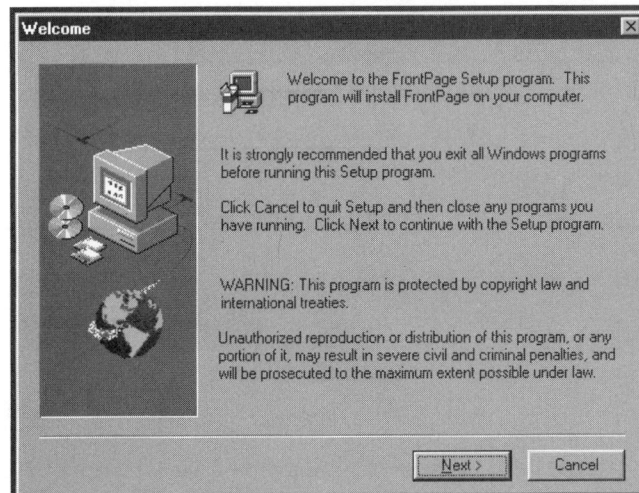

Figure A.4

Welcome to the FrontPage Setup Program.

NOTE

If you would like FrontPage installed to a particular drive or directory, you may specify it in the Setup Type dialog.

At this point, the CD-ROM will blink and the FrontPage files will be copied to your system. This may take a few minutes depending on the speed of your computer. When it is finished, don't be alarmed upon see-

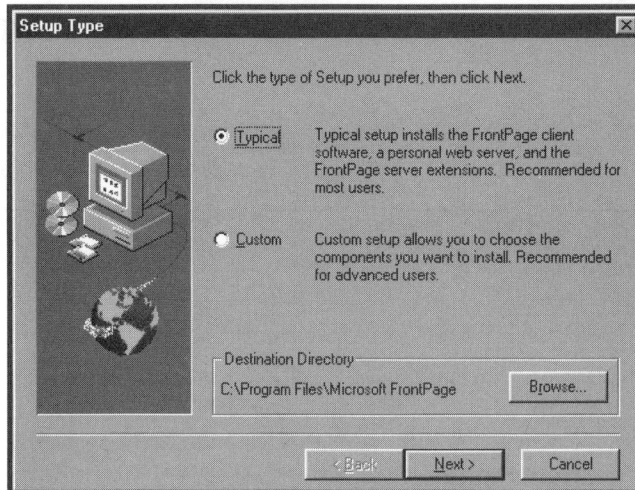

Figure A.5

Selecting a Typical installation.

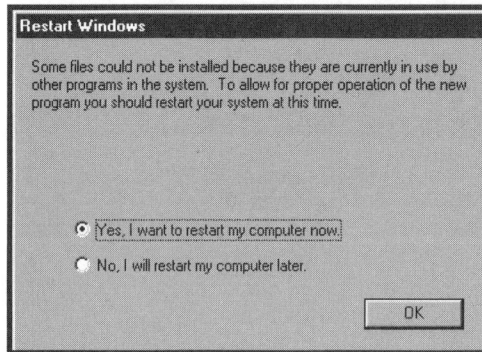

Figure A.6

Nothing is wrong—it's just time to restart!

ing the Restart Windows dialog box (see Figure A.6). Although it indicates that some files could not be copied because they were in use, this is quite normal, and the files will be copied as Windows 95 starts up.

Upon restart, I also recommend installing Microsoft Image Composer. It's optional, but it's a powerful graphics package that lets you design all kinds of images that enhance your Web site. To install it, you may either run Setup.exe from the FrontPage 98 CD-ROM, or just press the Open button on your CD-ROM drive, and press it again to close the drive. This will cause the FrontPage 98 Setup program to auto-start. Now you're ready for your weekend adventure to begin!

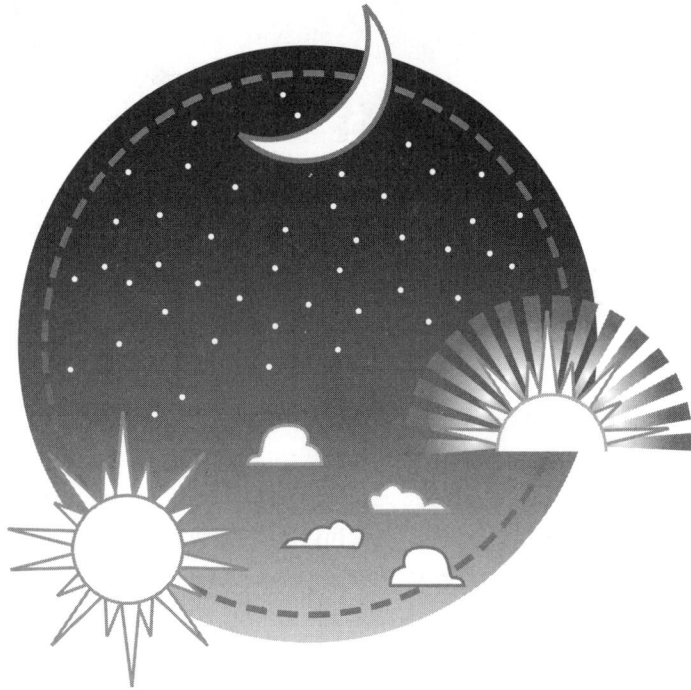

Taking a Shortcut with Templates

The FrontPage prefabricated templates simplify the process of creating Web pages or entire Web sites. As you add pages to your site or even develop an entire site from templates, you'll create pages with features you already know how to use.

The Customer Support template, for example, creates a site with a Welcome page and hyperlinks to the kinds of information visitors would want in a customer support site. The creators of this page template used a Heading 1 title at the top of the page, so they must have known how to assign styles to text. They created horizontal lines. They created hyperlinks between hypertext at the top of the page and bookmarks lower on the page, and they inserted graphic images. These features are incredibly difficult to manipulate. With the Customer Service template, you can create a Web site like the one shown in Figure B.1.

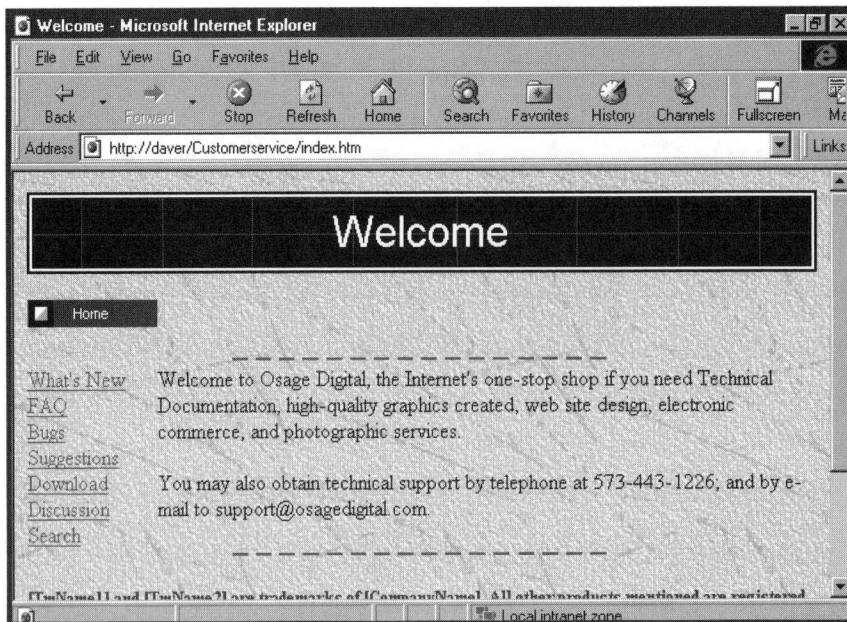

Figure B.1

A Web site from a template—haven't you done this?

Wait a minute, you know how to do all this stuff. This means that by using templates, you can let FrontPage do some of the grunt work if you want.

Why didn't you skip over most of this book and begin with templates? You could have, but as soon as you start to edit a template-generated page, you need to know what you're working with and how to change it. Using templates is a good way to save time, but it doesn't replace the knowledge of the basic skills you've acquired. In fact, you'll need those skills to use the templates.

FrontPage has two basic types of templates—templates that create an entire Web site, and ones which create a page in a Web site. Templates that create an entire Web site are opened from FrontPage Explorer. Templates that create a single page are initiated from FrontPage Editor. I'll start with templates for single pages.

FrontPage comes with templates for over 25 specific types of pages. The New Page dialog box, which you'll explore, lists many other things in addition to these templates. Several wizards are also available from this dialog box, and you'll look at them in Appendix C, Making Frames with a Wizard.

Using a Template

Creating new pages using templates can save you quite a bit of time. However, some template pages require more editing than others, and some of that editing is more intuitive than the changes that need to be made to template-generated forms.

After you create and edit a Web page using a template, you need to link it to your site via hyperlinks to and from other pages. Remember, without a link to your new page, nobody will get there from your home page. You'll probably also want to link the page back to your home page.

You can further integrate this page into your Web site by inserting the same footers and/or headers that you use throughout your site. You can blend the whole site aesthetically by using the same page background for your new page that you use on your home page. To create a new page with a template, follow these steps:

1. Open an existing Web site or start a new one in FrontPage Explorer.

2. Switch to FrontPage Editor and select File, New.

3. Click on the template you want to use. In Figure B.2, the Frequently Asked Questions template is selected. A miniature preview of this page's layout appears in the lower right corner of the dialog window.

4. Click on OK in the New dialog box.

5. Read the advice in the Comment area at the top of the new page. The Comment text is shaded, and when you move your cursor over it, the Robot icon appears, as shown in Figure B.3.

6. Many templates come with generic graphic images, but you may

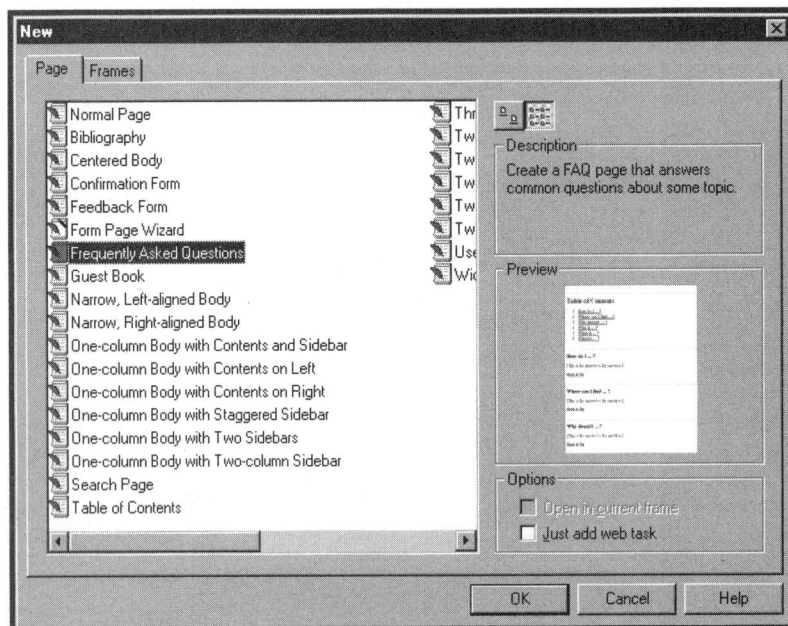

Figure B.2

Choosing a template.

insert your own image. First, delete the undesired images by selecting them, right clicking, and choosing Cut from the popup menu.

7. Examine hyperlinks and bookmarks in the page before you start
   editing. Those are your clues as to how the template-generated page
   is organized. In this case, listings at the top of the page are linked
   to bookmarks later in the page. Placing your cursor over the bookmark reveals the name of the bookmark on the status bar, as shown
   in Figure B.4.

8. Press Ctrl+left click to follow hyperlinks from hypertext. Templates
   link generic items to other generic items. If the template links work
   for the page you're designing, they can save you time. Also, sometimes the hyperlinks provide good models for how to organize your
   site. By following the existing links in the template, you'll eventually
   be able to figure out how the template page is organized. In the
   case of the Frequently Asked Questions template, no external
   hyperlinks exist.

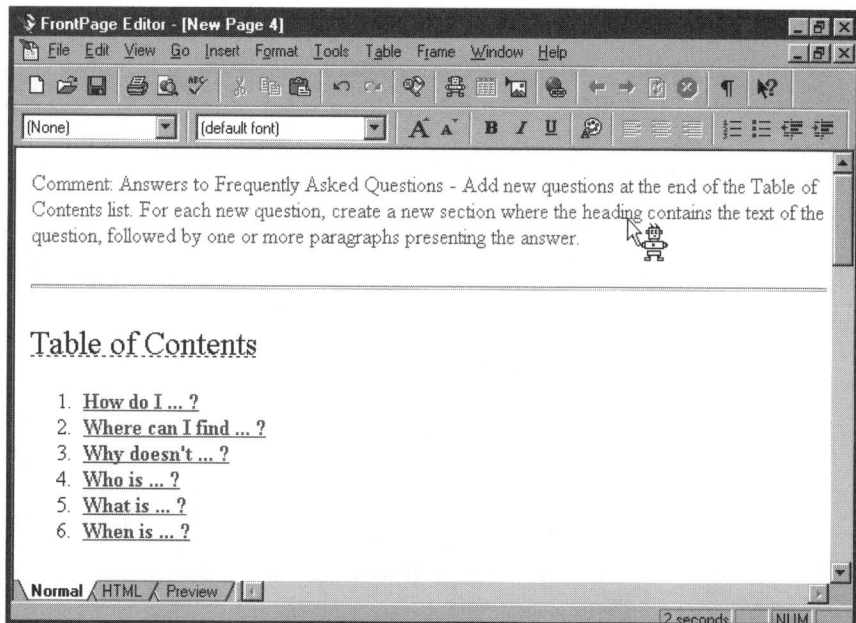

Figure B.3

The robot cursor
appears.

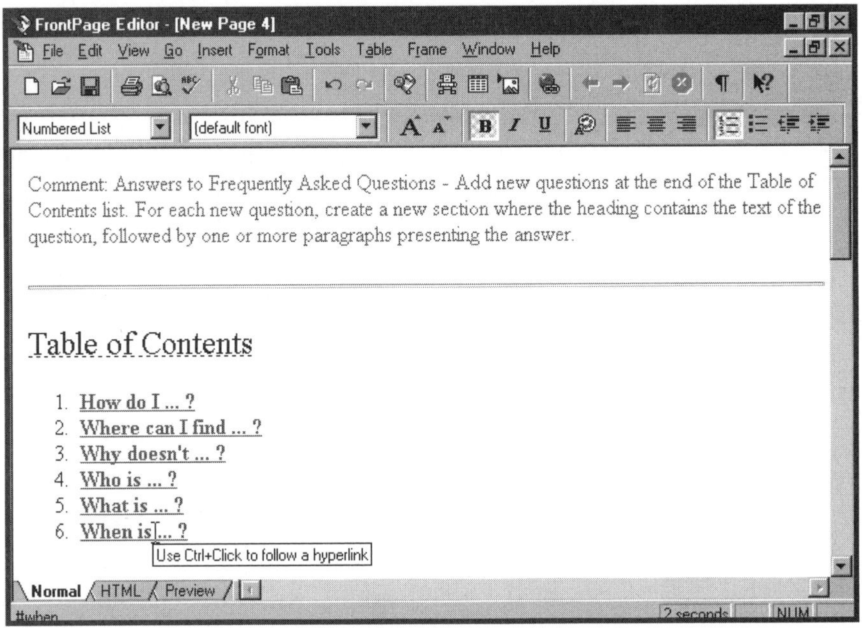

Figure B.4

Checking out template hyperlinks.

9. Continue to delete and replace the generic images on the page.

10. Change the generic bookmark and link text, but be careful not to delete the bookmark or link properties. If you simply delete the existing text and type new information, you'll likely erase the defined hyperlinks. Type the new information inside the existing text, as shown in Figure B.5.

11. After you've entered new bookmark text, you can delete the old text.

12. You'll probably want to create new bookmarks as you enter new questions and topics, as shown in Figure B.6.

13. You must change the link properties, or create new links. To do this, just right-click and drag. To highlight the potential hyperlink, select Properties from the shortcut menu and enter the correct link information, as shown in Figure B.7.

Figure B.5

Inserting text in the middle of a hyperlink.

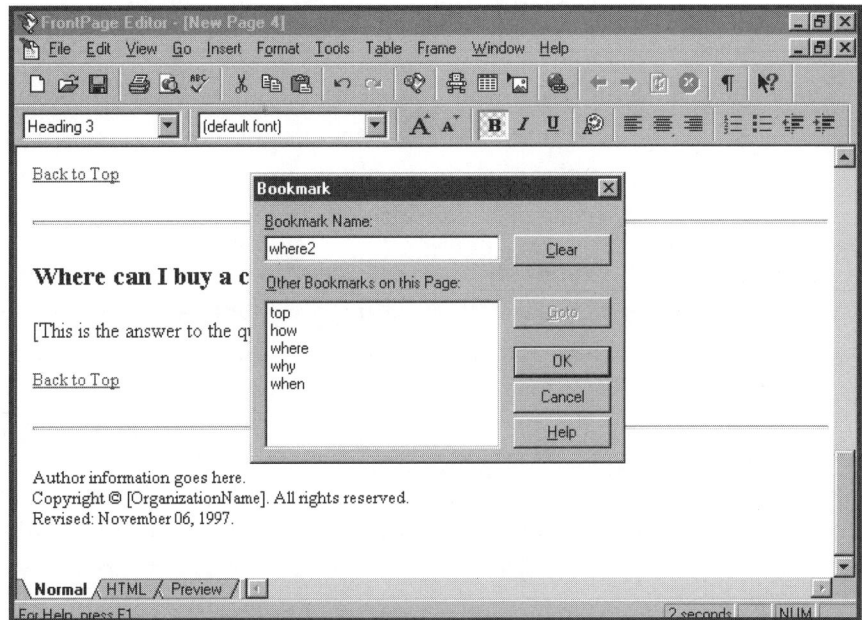

Figure B.6

Creating new bookmarks.

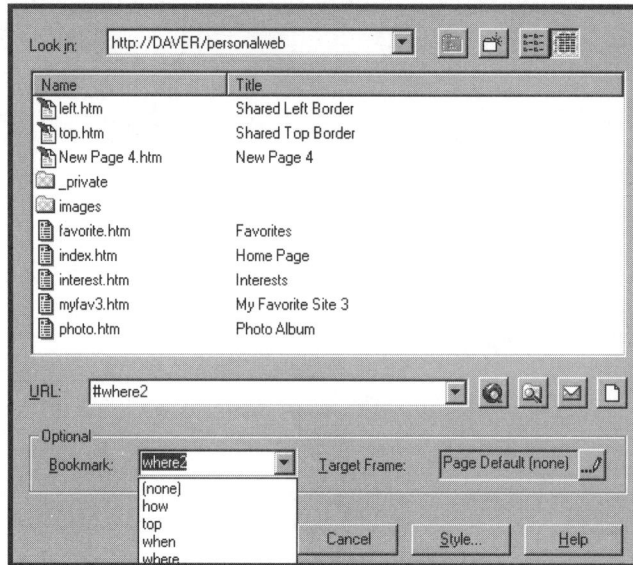

Figure B.7

Changing hyperlinks.

14. Check the page carefully to make sure that you have changed all the generic text and images and corrected all hyperlinks.

At this point, you may be asking yourself just how much time was saved by using a template to generate the page. This varies depending on the complexity of the page. Of course, you'll have to spend some time carefully going over your page before you can use it.

Don't forget that you still need to make the new page match your existing Web pages. Integrating your new Web page into your site involves inserting footers and/or headers, matching page backgrounds, and creating hyperlinks to and from the home page. You must then save your new page and give it a title and filename. To match your new page to your Web site, follow these steps:

1. Use the Include Page component to include header and/or footer pages in your newly generated page, as shown in Figure B.8.

2. Match the background to that of the index (home) page by

Figure B.8

Making your pages mesh by adding an included footer.

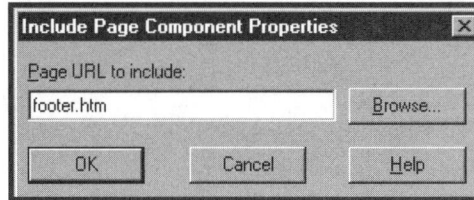

Include Page Component Properties

Page URL to include:

footer.htm   Browse...

OK   Cancel   Help

Figure B.9

Matching backgrounds for a color-coordinated Web site.

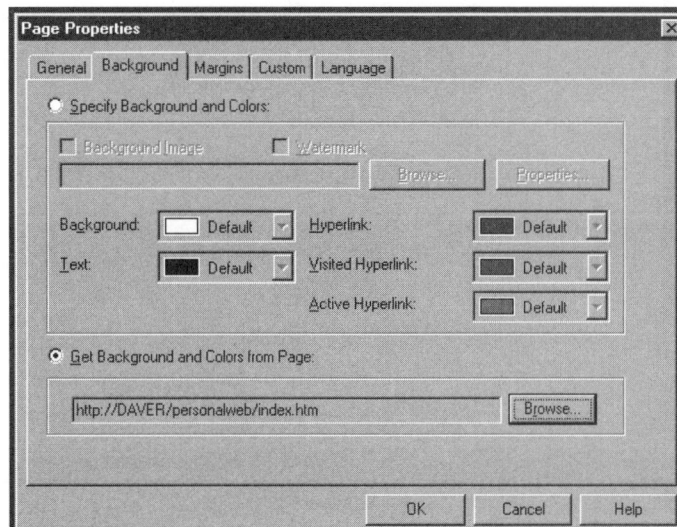

Page Properties

General | Background | Margins | Custom | Language

○ Specify Background and Colors:

☐ Background Image   ☐ Watermark

Browse...   Properties...

Background: Default   Hyperlink: Default

Text: Default   Visited Hyperlink: Default

Active Hyperlink: Default

● Get Background and Colors from Page:

http://DAVER/personalweb/index.htm   Browse...

OK   Cancel   Help

right-clicking on the page, selecting Page Properties from the shortcut menu, and linking the page background to the index page, as shown in Figure B.9.

3. Create a convenient hyperlink to the home page, as shown in Figure B.10.

4. Save the new page with an appropriate title (you can let FrontPage figure out the URL), as shown in Figure B.11.

5. Create a graphic and/or text hyperlink from your home page to the new page.

6. Save your home page with the newly defined link.

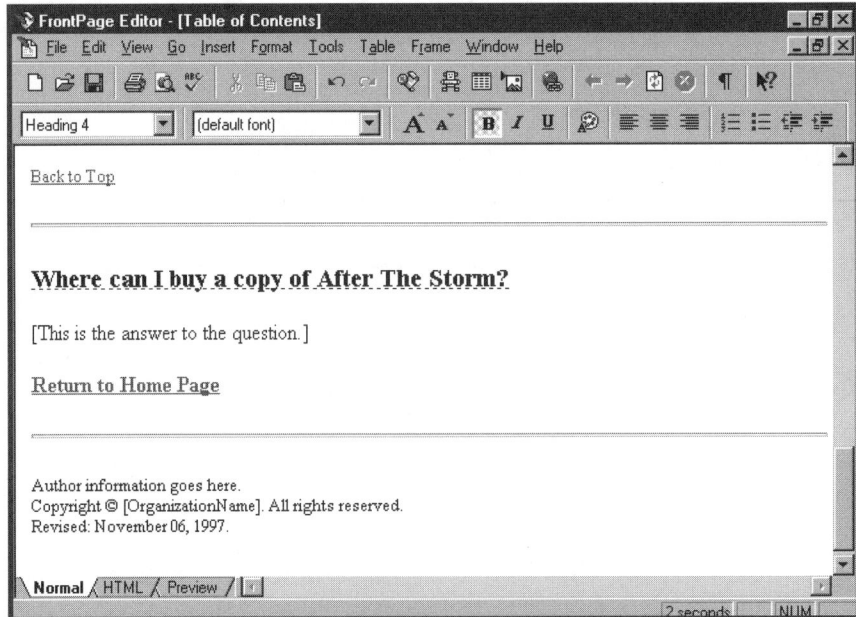

Figure B.10

Give visitors a way to go home.

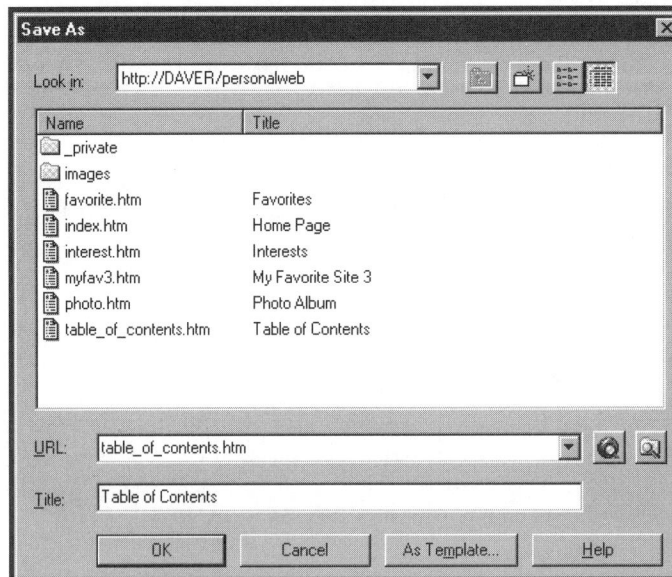

Figure B.11

FrontPage attempts to give your page a name.

Using Templates to Create Forms

Because forms take time to create, templates are especially helpful in generating pages with lots of forms. For example, using the Feedback Form template, you can easily create a form to receive feedback from your visitors. By default, this form has more than 10 input objects, all neatly lined up. You can delete any of the objects if you choose. It's fine to use the page which the template generates if you do not need highly customized feedback.

You will, however, have to define certain form properties. For example, where will the form output go? Of course, you'll want to edit the specific questions being asked by the form. You can explore this process by creating a feedback form. To create a form by using a template, follow these steps:

1. Open an existing Web site or start a new one in FrontPage Explorer.
2. Switch to FrontPage Editor and select File, New.
3. Click on the template you want to use. In Figure B.12, the Feedback Form template is selected.
4. Click on OK in the New dialog box.
5. Edit the text that goes with the form objects as needed. For example, in Figure B.13, "Praise" is changed to "Thank Us."
6. Double-click on a form object to edit its properties. In the example in Figure B.14, the field name of the old "Praise" field is changed to "Thanks."

TIP Changing the field name makes it easier to interpret the data in the results file. The field name need not match the text label adjacent to it, but it's more convenient if it does.

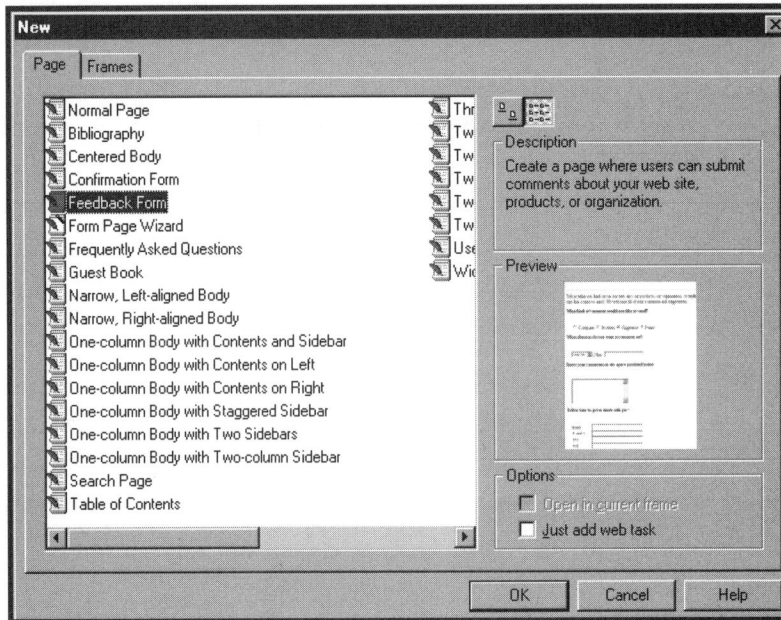

Figure B.12

Selecting the
Feedback Form
template

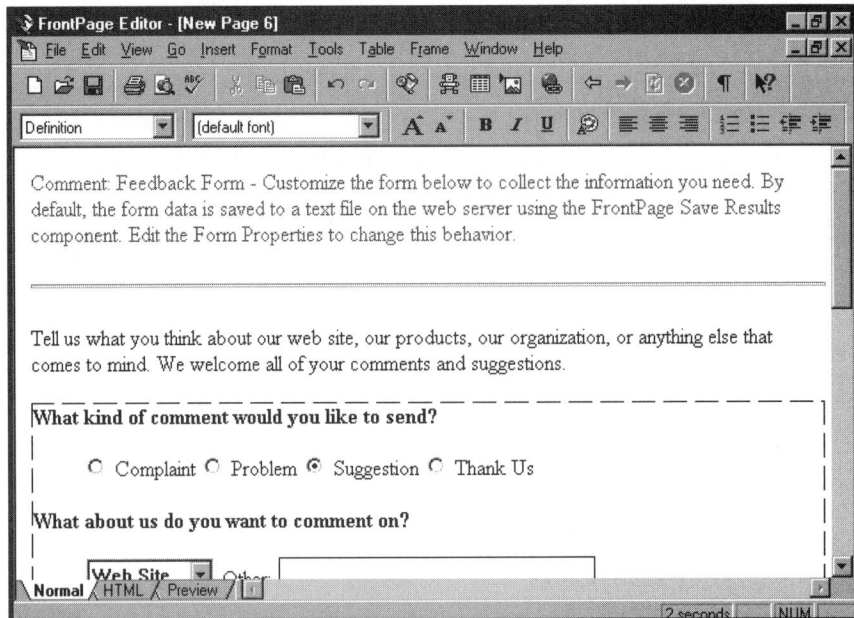

Figure B.13

Changing the
default text
in the form.

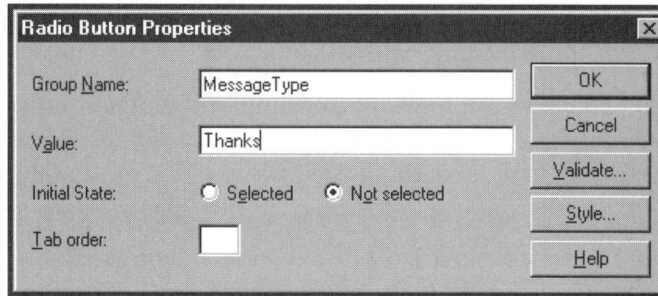

Figure B.14

Changing the radio button's properties.

7. You can edit the labels or contents of any form object. For example, in Figure B.15, the drop-down menu is changed to allow for different options.

TIP You can always delete large chunks of input objects if you don't want them.

8. After you have edited the contents of the form, right-click within the form and select Form Properties from the shortcut menu.

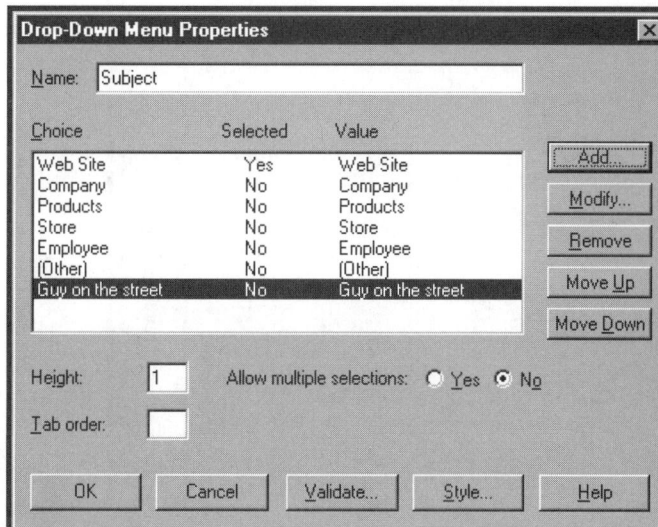

Figure B.15

Changing the default values for the drop-down list.

9. Select the Send To radio button and select a filename where you want the results of the form saved.

10. Click on the Options button and then choose a results filename and format.

Make a note of the filename to which you assign the results.

11. Click on the Saved Fields tab and deselect any of the fields you do not want to include in your results file, as shown in Figure B.16.

12. Click on OK in the Options for Saving Results of Form dialog box and then click on OK in the Form Properties dialog box.

13. Save the new page with a title and filename.

14. Use the steps discussed earlier in this session to link and integrate this new page into your Web site.

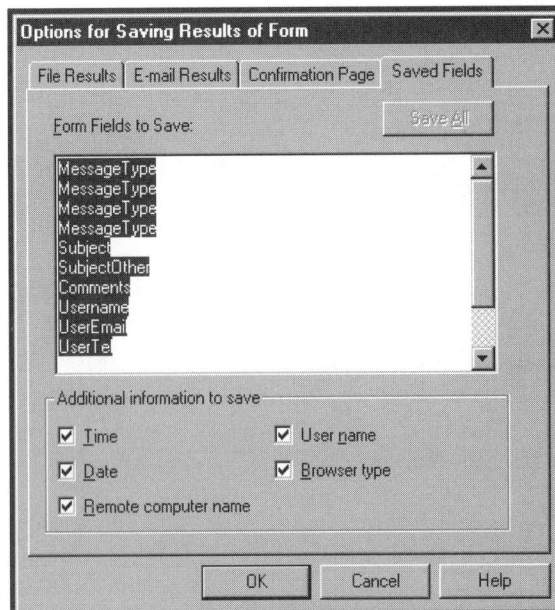

Figure B.16

Selecting the fields you want in the results file.

Using Templates to Create Web Sites

Up to now, you've investigated two typical templates for creating Web pages from FrontPage Editor. However, if you really want to save time, you can quickly create an entire "proto" Web site using the templates in FrontPage Explorer. You can use the New Web templates in Explorer to add a Web page to an existing site, but you're more likely to use one of these templates to create a new Web site from scratch.

Surveying Web Site Templates

Go to the FrontPage Explorer. Click on the New menu item and select the FrontPage Web option. The New Web dialog box includes a couple of wizards (which is a topic for Appendix C). Table B.1 is a list of the templates and wizards.

TABLE B.1 WEB SITE TEMPLATES AND WIZARDS	
Template/Wizard	**Description**
Corporate Presence Wizard	This wizard creates a ready-to-roll Web site for your corporation or business.
Customer Support Web	This template has all the pages you need to provide instant, online support for your clients.
Discussion Web Wizard	This wizard creates a site with a full table of contents, making it perfect for a discussion site.
Empty Web	This template creates a completely empty web.
Personal Web	This template generates a simple, four-page site with sections for interests, a photo album, and favorite links.
Project Web	A little more esoteric, this template helps you organize a project as well as assign and keep track of tasks.

The Project Web template is pretty specialized. If you're into project management, this web template is the perfect match for your Gantt tables in Microsoft Project. One of the pages that comes with this web is a Schedule page, as shown in Figure B.17.

Project management is really a topic for another book. However, if you're interested in this template, feel free to dive into it on your own. The Personal Web and Customer Support Web templates are both handy. You can experiment with the Personal Web template on your own—you're already familiar with most of the things in it. The page generated by the Personal Web template is shown in Figure B.18.

All you need to do here is modify the text on the home page and create hyperlinks to the other pages that FrontPage has created for you. You need to edit those pages, too, but FrontPage gives you a great head-start. In less than one hour, you could have your own personal Web site on the Net.

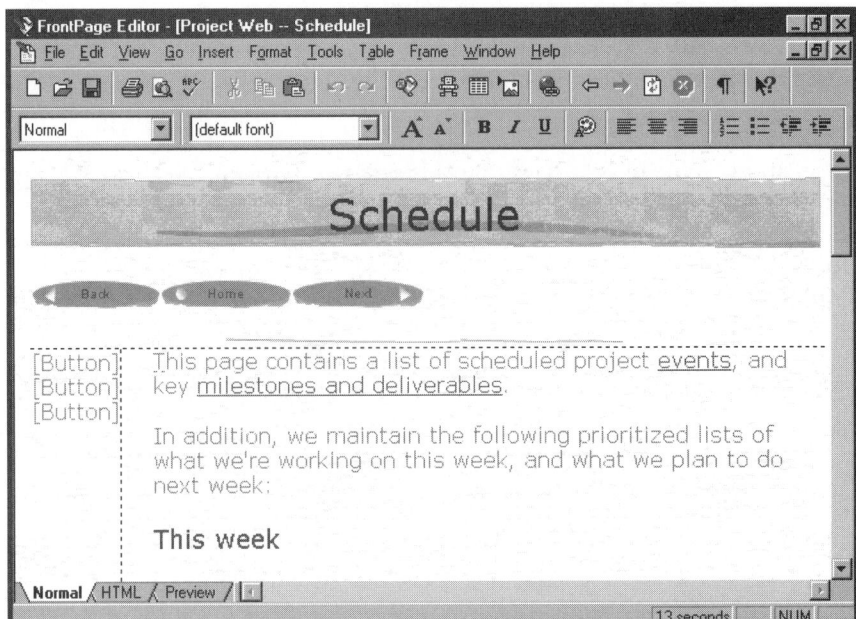

Figure B.17

The Schedule page in the Project Web template.

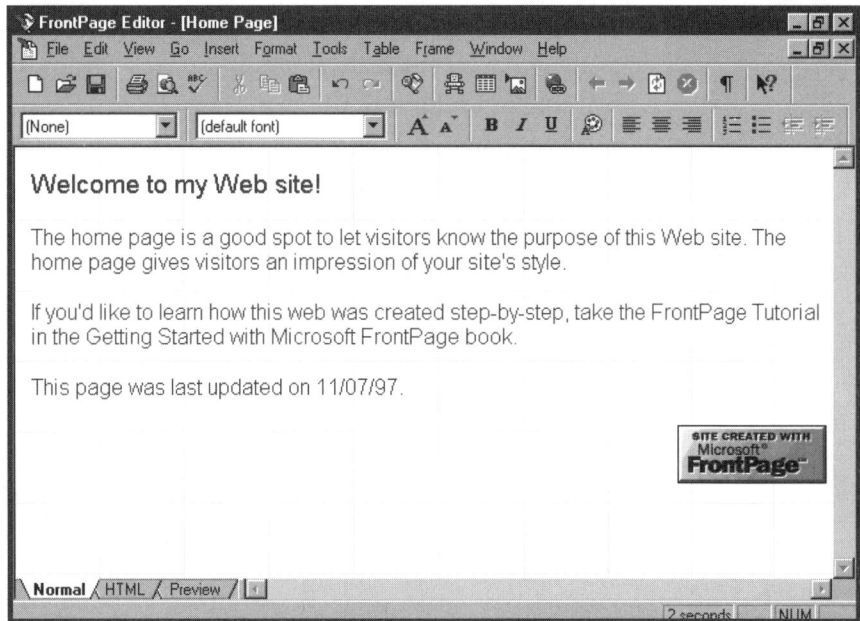

Figure B.18

Results of using the
Personal Web
template.

The Customer Support Web

The Customer Support web template makes using web templates worthwhile. If you're looking for a way to make your clients, friends, creditors, or customers feel wanted and cared for, this could be the solution.

The Customer Support web template generates a Web site with pages for welcoming visitors (a home page), finding out what's new, getting answers to Frequently Asked Questions (FAQs), reporting bugs, making suggestions, joining discussion groups (similar to the bulletin board you created), and searching for needed information. To create a Customer Support web with a template, follow these steps:

1. Open FrontPage Explorer. If any Web sites are open, close them.

TIP You might want to attach this site to an existing web. In that case, ignore Step 1. I think you'll be happier, however, with creating this as a single Web site.

2. From the FrontPage Explorer, select File, New, FrontPage Web, and click on the Customer Support Web option in the Wizard list, as shown in Figure B.19.

TIP You can create the site using the Personal Web Server (default) and then copy it to a Web site provider, as you learned in the Sunday Evening session.

3. Enter a name for your new site in the Web name area of the New FrontPage Web dialog box.

4. Click on OK in the New FrontPage Web dialog box. Examine the new Web site in the Hyperlink view of FrontPage Explorer. The "Customer Support—Web Template" page is the home page. You can see that footer and header files have been created, as

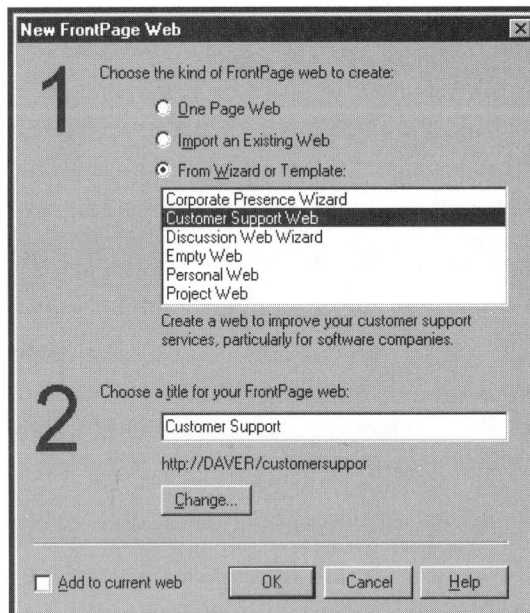

Figure B.19

Creating a Customer Support web.

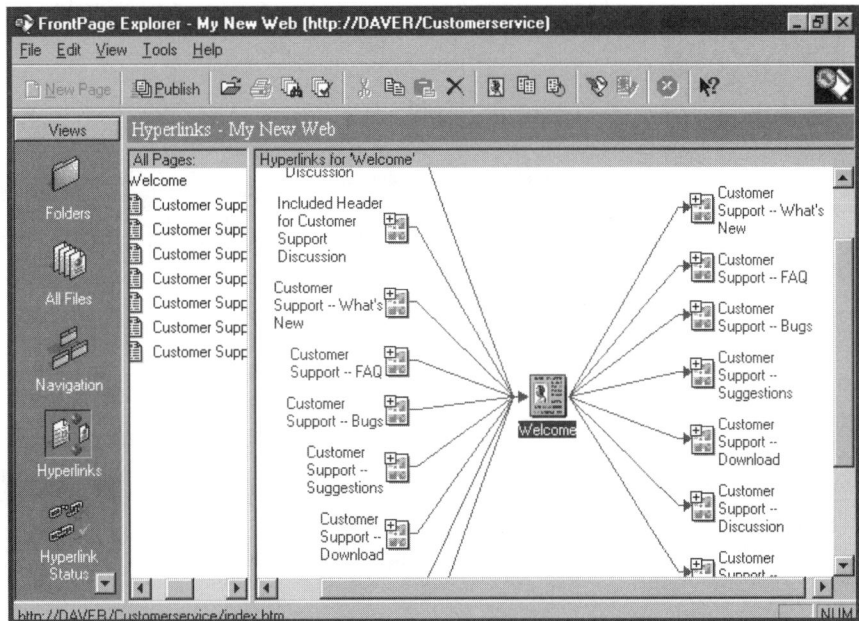

Figure B.20

A Hyperlink view of the Customer Support site.

well as Bug Reports and Suggestions from Customers pages (see Figure B.20).

5. Double-click on the Welcome page in the Hyperlink view of Front-Page Explorer to launch FrontPage Editor to view this page.

6. Edit the home page as needed and then save the changes.

7. Follow the link to the What's New page and edit it, as shown in Figure B.21.

8. Save changes to each page as you edit them.

9. You can edit the page banner by right-clicking on the banner graphic and selecting FrontPage component properties from the shortcut menu, as shown in Figure B.22.

10. Follow the hyperlinks to the Bugs, Suggestions, Discussion, FAQs, and Search pages. You're familiar with everything there.

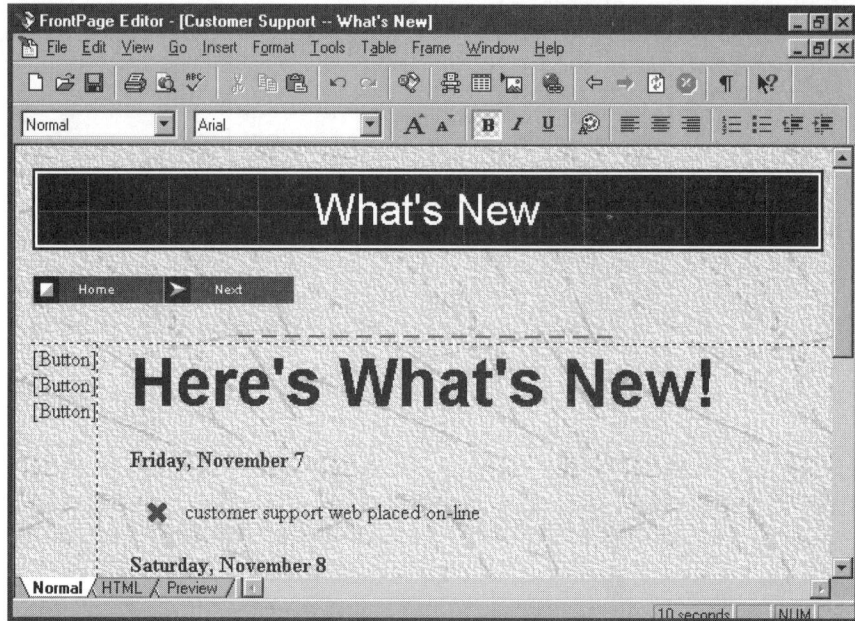

Figure B.21

Editing the What's New page.

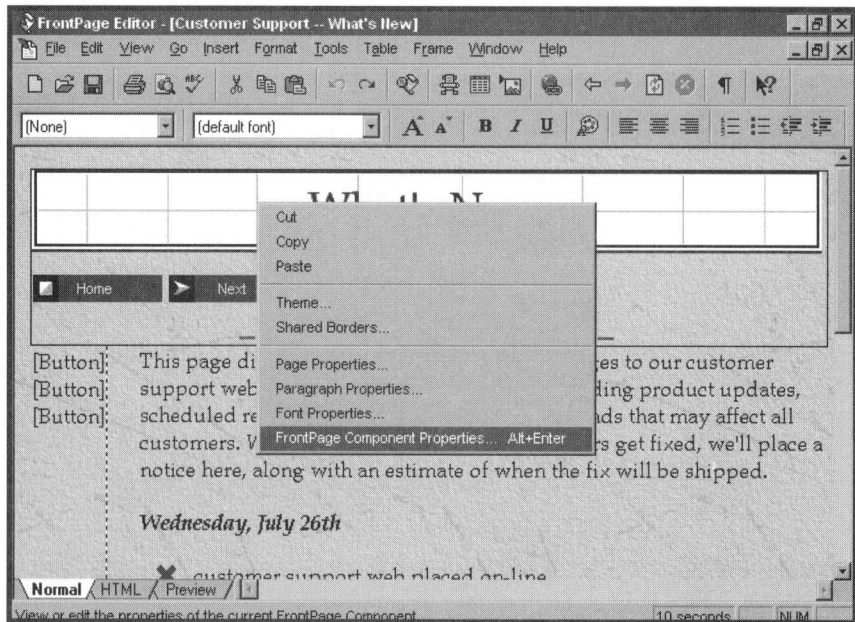

Figure B.22

About to edit the page banner.

TIP The Download page is discussed after you finish these steps. You might decide you don't want it. If this is the case, you can delete the hyperlinks to that page and then delete the page itself from your web in FrontPage Explorer.

11. When you've finished editing your site, save all the pages in Front-Page Editor.

12. Test your new site using your Web browser and then make any needed changes.

Downloadable FTP Pages

Once upon a time, and it was not a very long time ago, there was an Internet (but not what is now called the *World Wide Web*). Folks visited each other from high atop university libraries and from deep within corporate research departments. They transferred files to and from each other in a very crude way. Their files could not be read on sight, and they didn't have formatted text, images, and hyperlinks. In short, they weren't HTML files, and they definitely weren't created using FrontPage. These files used a different file protocol, called File Transfer Protocol (or FTP). FTP files were not recognized or interpreted by Web browsers.

The Download page generated by the Customer Support Web template comes with hyperlinks to FTP files. If you have some good reason to provide such a link, edit the hyperlinks on that page so they point to your FTP files. These files are not created with FrontPage.

Today, the terms "World Wide Web," "Web," and "Internet" are often synonymous. Technically, however, FTP files are on the Internet, but not on the Web. Will this file format continue to be used, or will it wither away like the dinosaurs? Only time will tell.

Templates, Reconsidered

There is a time and place for using a template. For instance, if you're creating a form to register people for a conference, you might save time by borrowing some ideas from the folks who designed FrontPage. On the other hand, if creativity is essential, you have to remember that 20 million other FrontPage users all have the same templates as you.

The skills you have honed over the course of working through this book enable you to examine, use, reject, and/or edit any of the templates FrontPage provides. In short, if you're designing a page where you can use a template, use it. However, if you're designing the Web site for an online abstract art gallery, for example, you should probably start from scratch.

Making Frames
with a Wizard

rames enable visitors to view your Web site in "windows." You can let your visitors view and scroll through more than one page at a time by placing each page in a frame. In this appendix, you'll explore the Frame Wizard in FrontPage Editor, which allows you to create Web sites with frames.

Wizards — Ones You Already Know, Plus a Special One

As you travel through FrontPage, you may notice that, occasionally, menu options include wizards. Wizards are different from templates—they're automated programs within FrontPage that walk you through a particular task. FrontPage Explorer, for example, has two wizards in the Explorer's New FrontPage Web dialog box. One creates a Discussion web, and one creates a Corporate Presence web. These wizards prompt you to select items you want in your Web site, as shown in Figure C.1.

Based on selections you make using radio buttons and filling in the blanks, these wizards create an entire Web site for you. You still need to

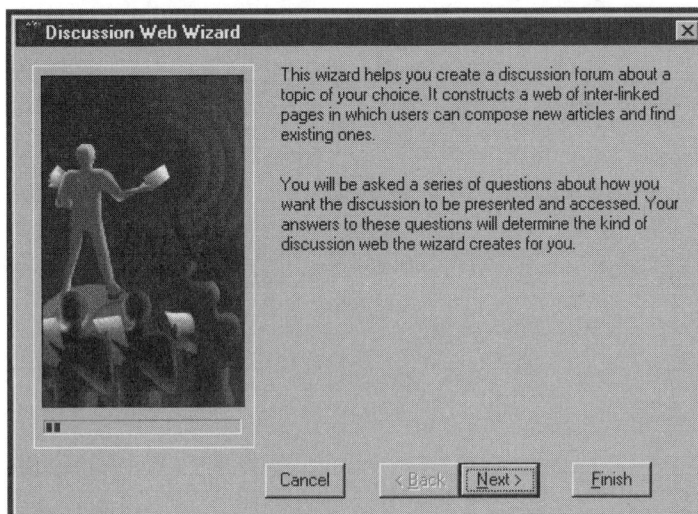

Figure C.1

The Discussion Web Wizard.

edit the pages that the wizard generates; therefore, you still need to know the mechanics of FrontPage.

In the File, New menu, FrontPage Editor has wizards that also lead you, step by step, through the process of creating a Web page. Feel free to experiment. You can use these wizards to create and edit pages quickly. In this way, wizards are similar to templates, because they give you a head start creating pages. FrontPage also has one special wizard—the Frames Wizard.

What Are Frames?

If you're familiar with Microsoft Windows, think of each frame as a window. The Web site shown in Figure C.2 has two frames.

If a frame has more information than will fit in the viewer's frame, a frame-friendly browser displays the frame in a window with scroll bars so

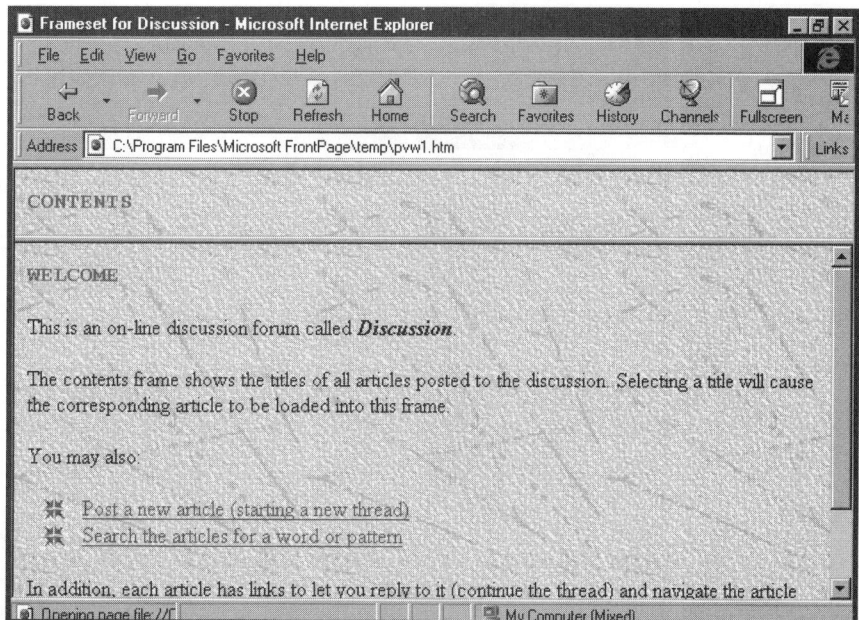

Figure C.2

A Web site with top and bottom frames.

that the viewer can move through each frame independently. In the example shown in Figure C.3, a user scrolls down the right frame while the left frame stays put.

Creating a frame involves at least four pages. Here are the basic elements of a page with frames:

○ A page to "hold" the embedded pages. The Frames Wizard creates it. Think of this as the wooden part of a window frame. It holds the separate panes of glass in place.

○ At least two embedded pages. These are created in FrontPage Editor, the old-fashioned way. These are like the individual panes of glass within a window. The whole window is what you see in your Web browser. As with a real window, the frame will hold as many panes of glass as you want, but to begin a frames Web site, you need at least two pages to act as panes.

○ That mysterious fourth element is a backup page. This alternate page is created so that visitors who are using a browser that doesn't

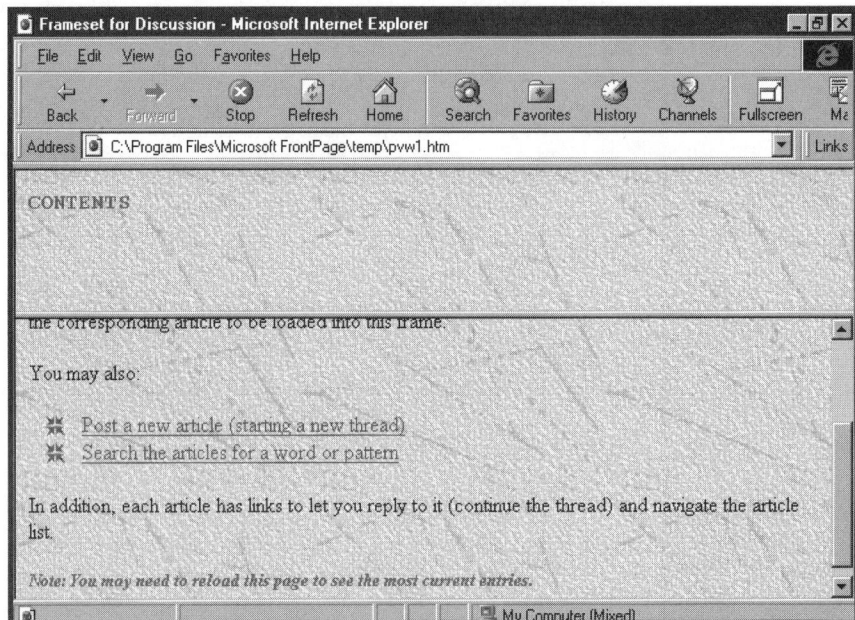

Figure C.3

Scrolling frames.

recognize frames can view your site. The frame feature is supported by many Web browsers, but Microsoft Internet Explorer 2.0 isn't one of them. Because not all browsers recognize frames, you need to have a backup page so that some of your visitors won't get a message telling them the page cannot be loaded into their browser. (Internet Explorer 3.0 and later versions as well as Netscape Navigator 2.0 and later versions do support frames.)

Before you use FrontPage's Frames Wizard, you need to create, beforehand, each of the pages that will go into a frame, and a backup page for those people who visit your site with a browser that doesn't support frame viewing.

Getting Ready to Frame

You should get your three pages done before you run the Frames Wizard. Many approaches exist for designing frames, but the approach most often used is to create a two-column page with one frame on the left and one on the right. That way, users can scroll down one side of the page while leaving the other side in place.

The approach I walk you through here involves one frame on the left side of a page that takes up about a quarter of the user's screen, and one frame on the right side of the frame page that takes about three quarters of the screen. The user can scroll down either side. If you don't have a browser that supports frames, you'll create a page that puts the same information on one page.

All this has to be thought through before initiating the Frames Wizard. Then, if things don't fall into place, you can go back into the Frames Wizard and make adjustments. To create pages for a frame page, follow these steps:

1. Create a new Web page in FrontPage Explorer and give the page a name such as contents.htm (or some other fitting title).

2. Edit the page by double-clicking on it. This opens the page in the FrontPage Editor.

3. Select Frame, New Frames Page in the menu. This opens the New dialog box, as shown in Figure C.4.

4. For a Contents frame on the left and a Main frame on the right, select the Contents Frame option.

5. Click on the OK button in the New dialog box to create the frame page, as shown in Figure C.5.

You'll now concentrate on the left side of the page, which will be your Contents frame. In this frame, you'll put the various topics that the user can select. If the topic in the left frame is selected, the hyperlinked text will appear in the right frame.

6. For the Contents frame, if you already have a page you would like to use, click on the Set Initial Page button and specify the page. If you need to create a Web page that holds the Contents choices, click on the New Page button and create your page, as shown in Figure C.6.

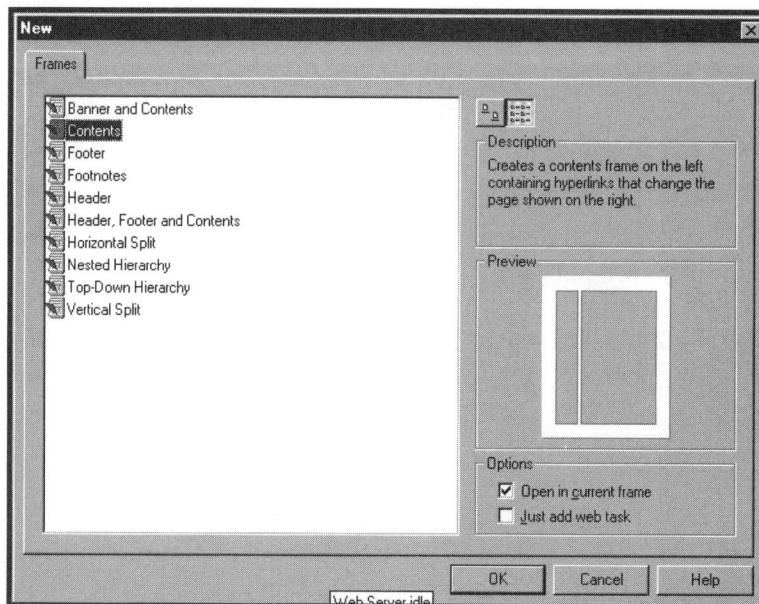

Figure C.4

Choosing the type of frame you want

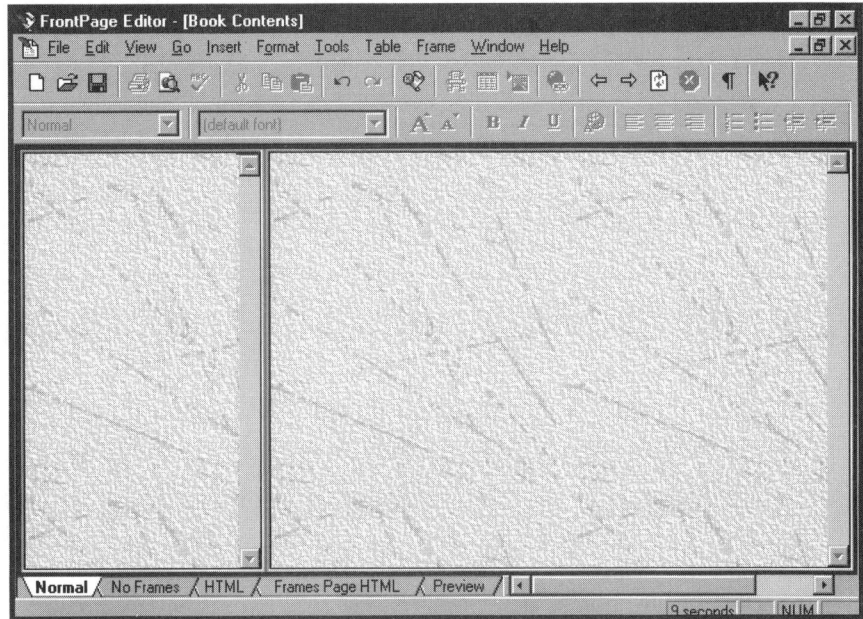

Figure C.5

Presto! Your
frames page has
been built.

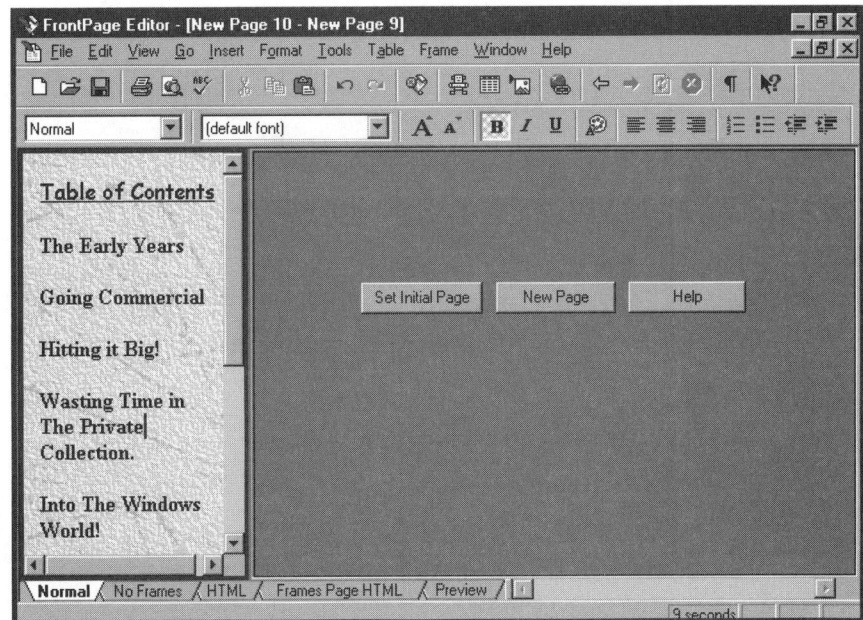

Figure C.6

Creating your
Contents frame
on the fly.

TIP You can include on a contents page all the fun things you learned to place on any Web page, such as images, included files, page backgrounds, font colors, themes, and so on.

---

7. With the Contents frame taken care of, you can turn your attention to the Main frame. Because the Main frame reflects what the user selects in the Contents frame, the Main frame should have a consistent background. You can do this by using the same theme you used in the Contents frame.

What you must do next is create a page for each of the items in the Contents frame. An example of this is shown in Figure C.7. Once the target pages are built, each item in the Contents frame will become a hyperlink. To finish off the frames page, follow these steps:

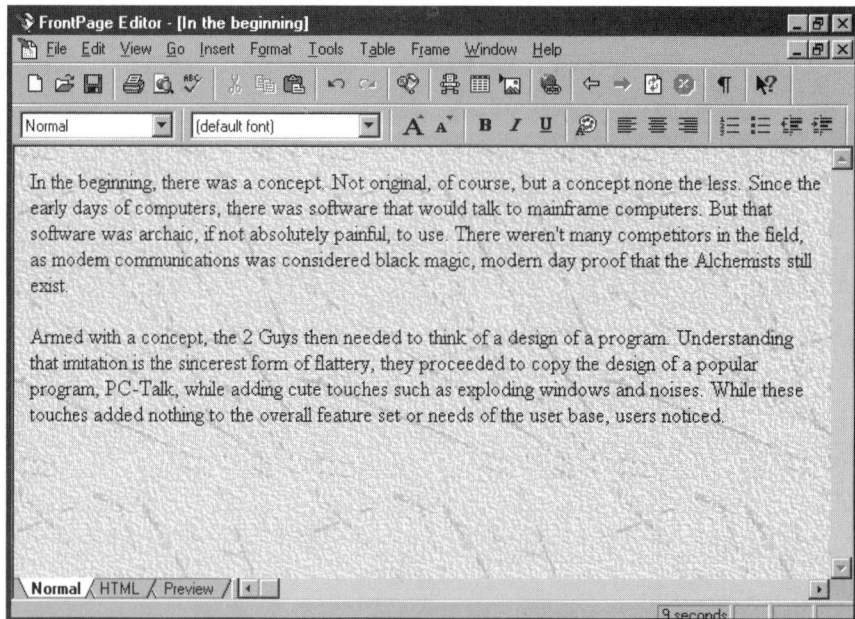

Figure C.7

The page that will be linked to The Early Years text.

8. In the Contents frame, highlight an object (text or graphic) that will be displayed in the Main frame.

9. Press the Create or Edit Hyperlink button on the toolbar to create the hyperlink in the Create Hyperlink dialog box, as shown in Figure C.8.

10. Highlight the page that will be hyperlinked to the text or graphic you previously highlighted.

11. Click on the Change Target Frame button, as shown in Figure C.9.

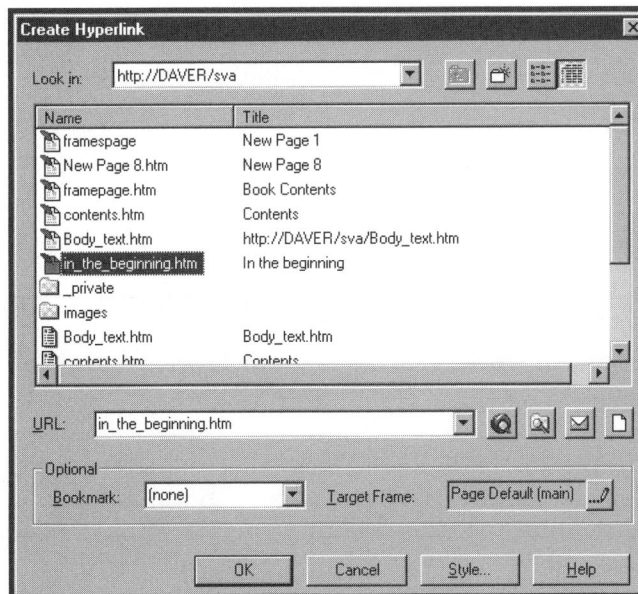

Figure C.8

Assigning the hyperlink.

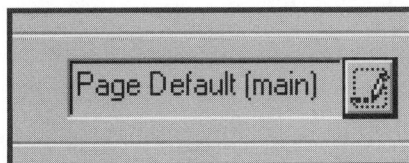

Figure C.9

The Change Target Frame button.

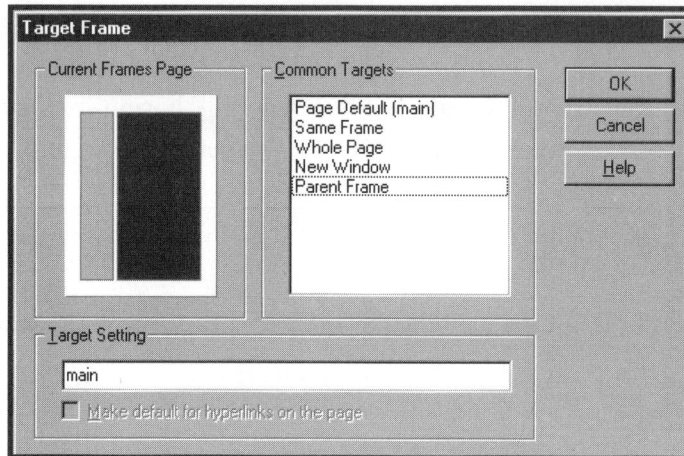

Figure C.10

Selecting the
target frame

12. In the Current Frames Page of the Target Frame dialog box, click on the frame where you would like the hyperlinked page to display, as shown in Figure C.10.

13. Click on OK to close the Target Frame dialog box.

14. Click on OK to close the Create Hyperlink dialog box.

You should repeat steps 8–14 for each item in the Contents frame. That's all there is to it.

To test your frame page, click on the Preview tab on the tab bar. Your result should look similar to what is shown in Figure C.11.

Supporting Browsers That Don't Support Frames

As mentioned earlier, not every browser supports frames. All current browsers (Netscape 2.0 and later, Internet Explorer 3.0 and later) support frames, but older browsers from Spyglass or Quarterdeck might not. These older browsers become less used and more obsolete as the months roll by, so should you be concerned with supporting them with nonframe

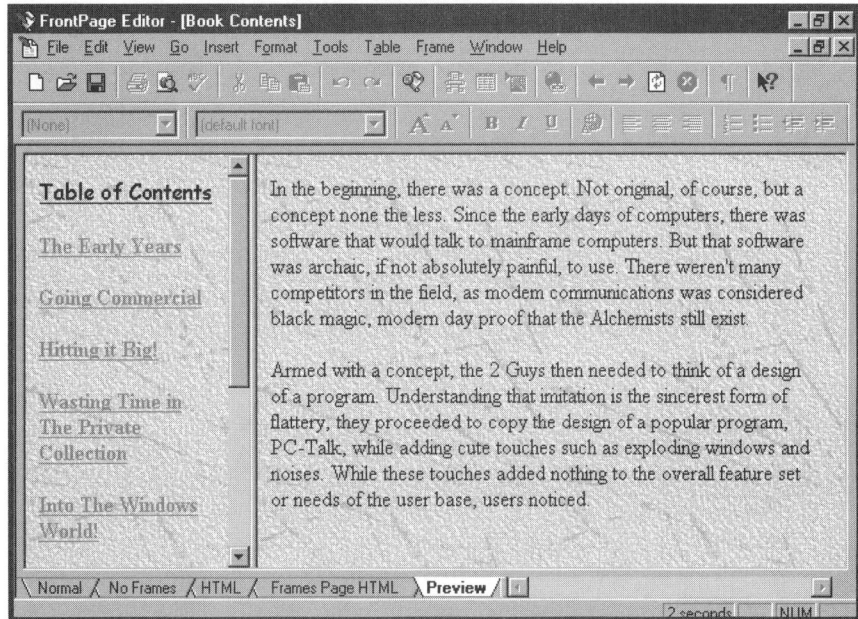

Figure C.11

The finished frame page. What a story!

pages? That question is better answered with another question: How easy (or difficult) is it for you to offer the same level of content and not use frames?

In other words, some Web sites naturally lend themselves to the use of frames. Any kind of catalog or showroom, for example, is a natural for frames. These kinds of sites, in particular, should not be concerned with the older browsers because these browsers do not support SSL (Secure Sockets Layer), which is mandatory for electronic commerce and credit card transactions.

If you choose to provide alternate page support for the older browsers, I recommend the following:

1. Highlight your hyperlinks in the Content frame.
2. Copy them to the Windows Clipboard by selecting Edit, Copy.
3. Click on the No Frames tab on the tab bar.

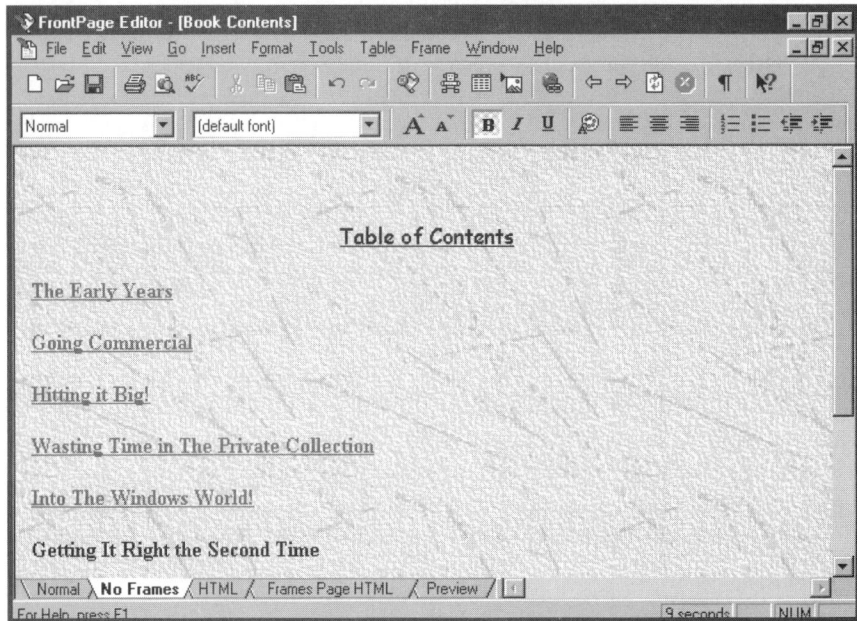

Figure C.12

Supporting browsers that don't display frames.

4. Paste your hyperlinks into the page by selecting Edit, Paste.

5. Give your page the same background, theme, or graphics used in the other pages, as shown in Figure C.12.

6. Be sure that all open pages are saved.

Viewing Your Frame Page

When you visit your frame page using a Web browser, one of two things will happen. You'll either see your frame page with frames, or you'll see the alternate Web page—it depends on whether your browser supports frames. To visit a site with frames, follow these steps:

1. Launch your Web browser.

2. In the URL address line in your Web browser, enter the site address exactly as it appears in the FrontPage Explorer title bar.

TIP

■ ■

If you created your frame page somewhere besides the index page, navigate to that page in your browser.

■ ■

If your browser doesn't support frames, you'll see the alternate page. If you haven't designated an alternate page, you'll see the unpleasant message shown in Figure C.13. If your browser does support frames, you'll see the frame page, as shown in Figure C.14.

TIP

■ ■

You should test your frame page with a browser that supports frames as well as with one that does not. Try navigating around both frames in the frame page.

■ ■

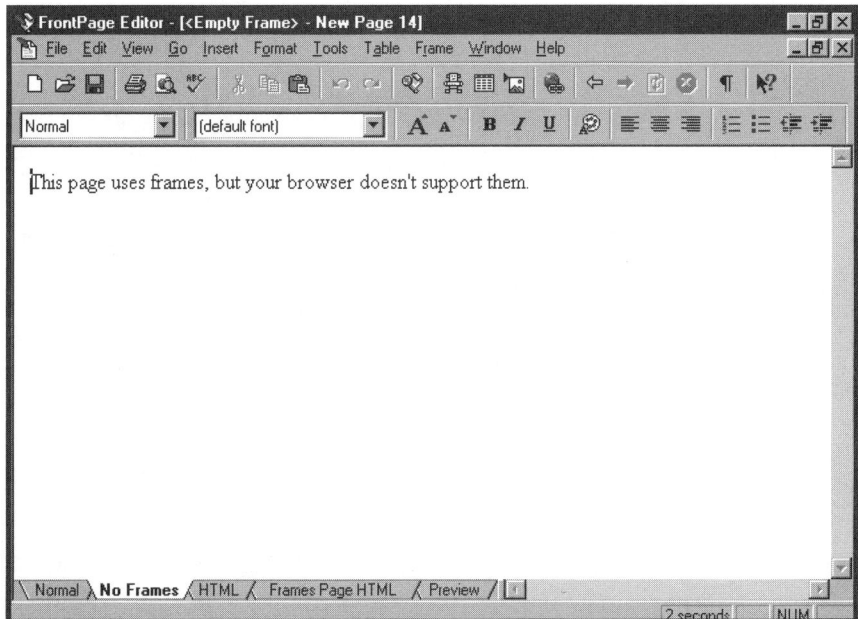

Figure C.13

Some browsers don't support frames.

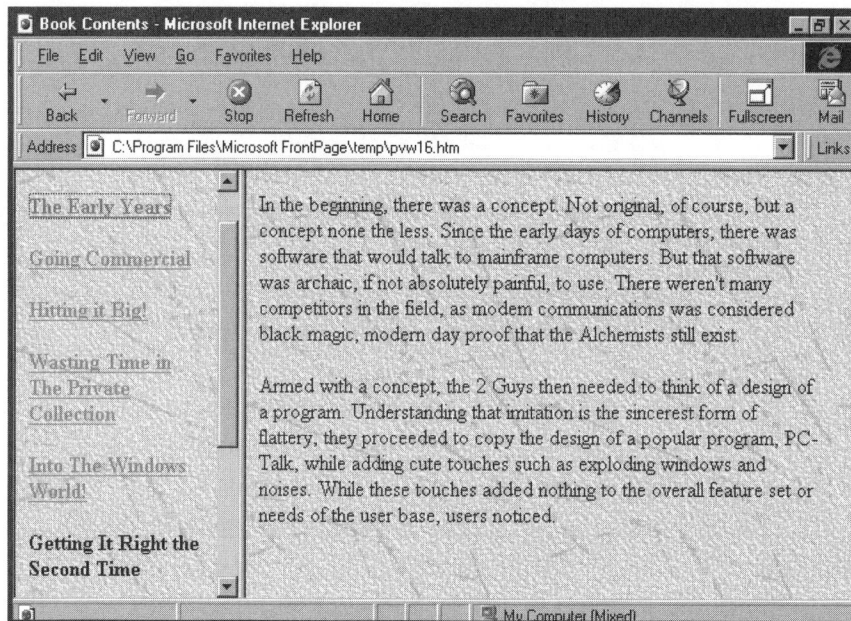

Figure C.14

Viewing frames.

Editing Frame Configuration

As you'll soon come to appreciate, FrontPage supports WYSIWYG (What-You-See-Is-What-You-Get) editing of frame pages. This is a vast improvement over the previous versions of this product, which lacked this important feature. However, you might still need to tweak some settings. For example, you might need to adjust the relative sizes of the frames or make the frames resizable.

To edit a frame, follow these steps:

1. Right-click on the frame page you want to edit in FrontPage Editor and select Frame Properties.

2. In the Frame Properties dialog box, which is shown in Figure C.15, you can specify how the frame will appear in the user's browser.

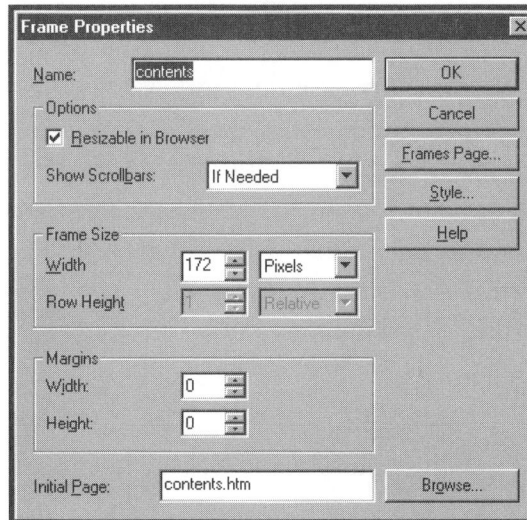

Figure C.15

Tweaking the frames

3. To change the title of the frame page, highlight the contents of the Name field and type in the new title.

4. Most of the time, your frames will be resizable. However, if your page is designed in such a way that resizing frames produces unacceptable results, uncheck the Resizable in Browser check box.

5. If the frames are resizable, do you want scrollbars visible? Most of the time, the default value of If Needed makes the most sense; however, you can also choose Always or Never.

6. You can specify the initial size of the frame by typing a value into the Width field. This width can be set in pixels, or it can be set as a percentage of the page.

7. If your frame uses margins, you can enter the Width and Height of the frame's margins.

8. To change the page used in the frame, type a valid HTML filename in the Initial Page field, or click on the Browse button to locate the page.

To Frame or Not to Frame?

As millions of browsers—including users of America Online and other Internet access providers—assist their users in downloading Internet Explorer 4.0, the critical mass will shift. More and more people will be surfing the Web with browsers that do interpret frames. Some day you won't need to have an alternate page for those browsers not capable of using frames. For now, though, if you want to be sure your page is accessible to everyone, you should use one.

A nice, neat, two-frame page can pack twice as much information and can make users feel even more in control of what they're seeing. In short, when used carefully, frames generally enhance a site. The choice, of course, is yours.

Creating a Password-Protected Site

Front Page enables you to assign password protection to your site so that only those individuals to whom you have assigned user names and passwords can enter.

You might want to restrict visitors to a page on your Web site for many reasons. Access can be restricted to paying clients, members of your organization, selected employees, or just people you like. The New York Times Web site, for example, currently requires visitors to first contact the paper to get a password before they can read all the news that's fit to print via the Web. Even though The New York Times doesn't charge you to browse its pages on the Web, it does have an accurate count of how many people are registered, which it can present to advertisers when selling space. When a visitor attempts to visit a password-protected site, an imposing dialog box appears, as shown in Figure D.1.

If an uninvited user enters an invalid password, he will not be able to get beyond the Enter Network Password dialog box. If he cancels the Password dialog box, he will end up at a dead end, as shown in Figure D.2.

One limitation of the password protection in FrontPage is that it must be applied to an entire Web site. You cannot, for example, protect only one page in your site. The workaround is to arrange with your FrontPage-friendly Web site provider to use two different Web sites—one that's open to the public at large, and one that's restricted to registered visitors. You can discuss this when you shop for a site.

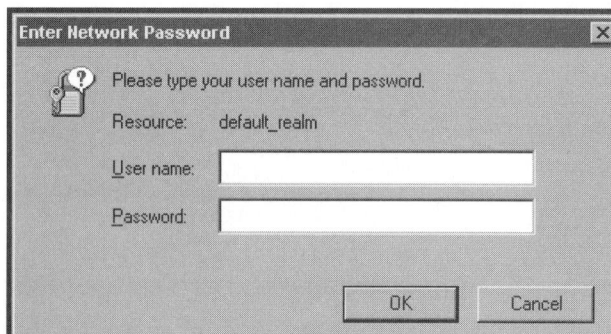

Figure D.1

Halt! Who goes there?

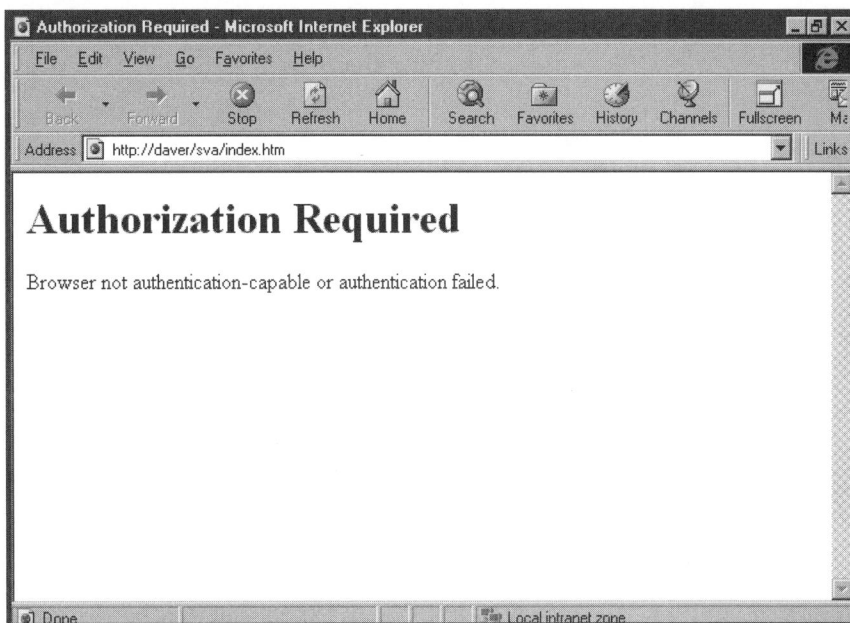

Figure D.2

Oops! Wrong password.

Not all Web site providers allow you to password-protect your site. The distinction is that the Web site provider must assign you administrator, rather than author, rights to your web. Check with your Web site provider before you rent space if password protection is going to be necessary for your site.

Defining Unique Permissions for Your Site

Although you cannot define different permission rules for the various pages within your Web site, you can assign password-protection rules to your entire Web site. Again, this is dependent on your Web site provider giving you administrator rights to your own site—something you need to check first. If you need to assign password protection to your site, first ask a prospective site provider, "Do I have administrator or author rights to edit my site?" If the answer is "author rights only," you'll need to negotiate an arrangement for administrator rights or else shop for a Web site provider that offers them. To assign unique permissions, follow these steps:

1. Open your Web site in FrontPage Explorer.

TIP

You can test this process using the Personal Web Server, but you'll need to redo it when you have copied your site to a Web site provider, as discussed in the Sunday Evening session, "Publishing Your Site on the World Wide Web." Copying a site from your default or local host site (using the Personal Web Server) to an Internet Web site provider will not copy password protection.

2. Select Tools, Permissions from the FrontPage Explorer menu.
3. In the Settings tab, select the Use unique permissions for this web radio button, as shown in Figure D.3.

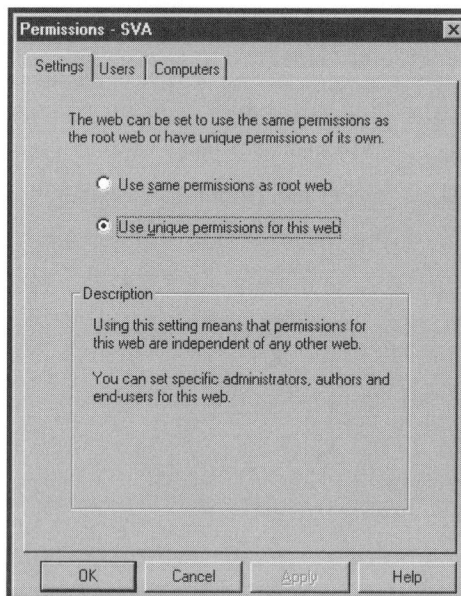

Figure D.3

Choosing unique permissions for your Web site.

> **TIP**
>
> If you have your own server, you don't need to define unique settings. However, if the Settings tab appears in your Permissions dialog box, you do.

4. Click on OK in the Permissions dialog box.

Restricting Your Site to Registered Users Only

Restricting access to registered users only is as simple as clicking on a radio button. After you assign password protection, you need to define registered users and assign them passwords. First, though, you need to protect the site. To restrict access, follow these steps:

1. Open in FrontPage Explorer the site to which you are assigning password protection.

2. Select Tools, Permissions from the FrontPage Explorer menu. You should have previously defined unique permissions for this site in the Settings tab of the Permissions dialog box.

> **NOTE**
>
> If you did select unique permissions in the Settings tab of the Permissions dialog box but the radio buttons in the End Users tab are grayed out, you must contact your Web site provider to arrange for authorization to assign permissions.

3. Click on the Users tab in the Permissions dialog box. Notice the current Permissions setting. The Everyone has browse access radio button should be selected.

4. In the Users tab of the Permissions dialog box, click on the Only registered users have browse access radio button, as shown in Figure D.4.

5. Click on OK in the Permissions dialog box.

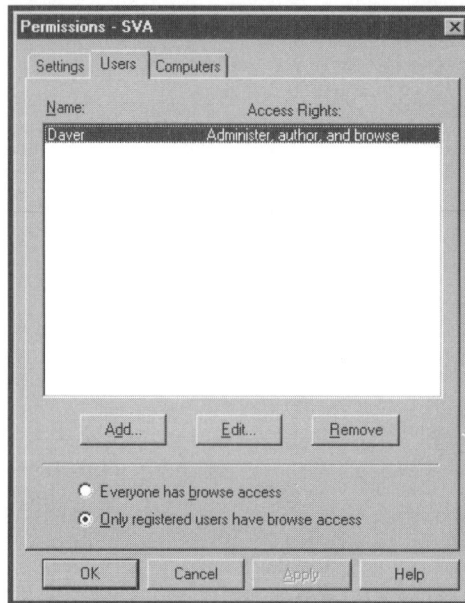

Figure D.4

Only registered users will see your Web site.

You can now test your site for access using your Web browser. Your own user name and password are the same as the name and password you use each time you open or edit the site in FrontPage Explorer.

Creating Lists of Authorized Users in the Root Web

Access to a password-protected Web site is granted by creating a list of approved visitors and assigning them passwords. Normally, if you define password protection, you have a plan to select and inform registered users of their passwords. Of course, you'll always be able to access the site because you're the administrator (or author). You can use the same password that you use to open and edit the site. To assign registered users, follow these steps:

1. Open in FrontPage Explorer the site to which you are assigning registered users.

2. Select <u>T</u>ools, <u>P</u>ermissions from the FrontPage Explorer menu.

TIP You must have previously defined unique permissions for this site in the Settings tab of the Permissions dialog box.

---

3. On the Users tab in the Permissions dialog box, click on the Add button.

4. Enter the registered user's access name in the Name area of the Add Users dialog box, as shown in Figure D.5. Make sure you tell this visitor exactly how his access name is spelled, including uppercase and lowercase characters.

5. Enter the registered user's password in the Password area of the Add Users dialog box.

6. Reenter the registered user's password in the Confirm Password area of the Add Users dialog box.

TIP Carefully note the user's password, including uppercase or lowercase notation.

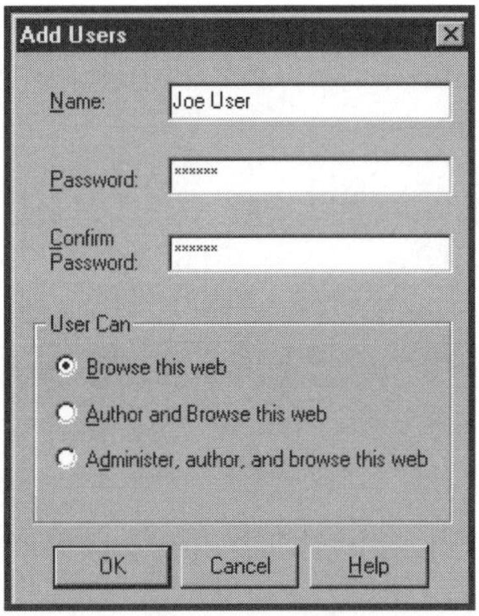

Figure D.5

Assigning a password to Joe User.

7. Click on OK in the Add Users dialog box.

8. Repeat the process as necessary to enter more registered users. Make sure you carefully inform all registered users of their user names and passwords.

9. When you have entered all the registered users and their passwords, click on OK in the Permissions dialog box.

You can assign more registered user passwords later by repeating these steps.

TIP

Unless you want registered users to be able to create new Web pages or modify your site, be sure to select the Browse This Web radio button in the User Can group box. Otherwise, the user will have full access to your site, including the ability to delete it!

Password-Protection Issues

You may see more flexible password protection in future versions of FrontPage. The current requirement that an entire site must be protected does not make it easy for you to enable visitors to enter your site, register, and get a password before they can access other pages.

As emphasized earlier, not many Web site providers are set up to let you take advantage of this feature. If password protection is important to you, shop carefully and make sure that you can test the site before committing yourself to a long-term contract.

Finally, there's nothing magic about password protection. I'm no expert on cracking codes, but I wouldn't put my personal diary on a Web site and rely on a password to keep out unwanted visitors. In spite of these limitations, however, FrontPage does let you restrict a site to registered users in a straightforward way.

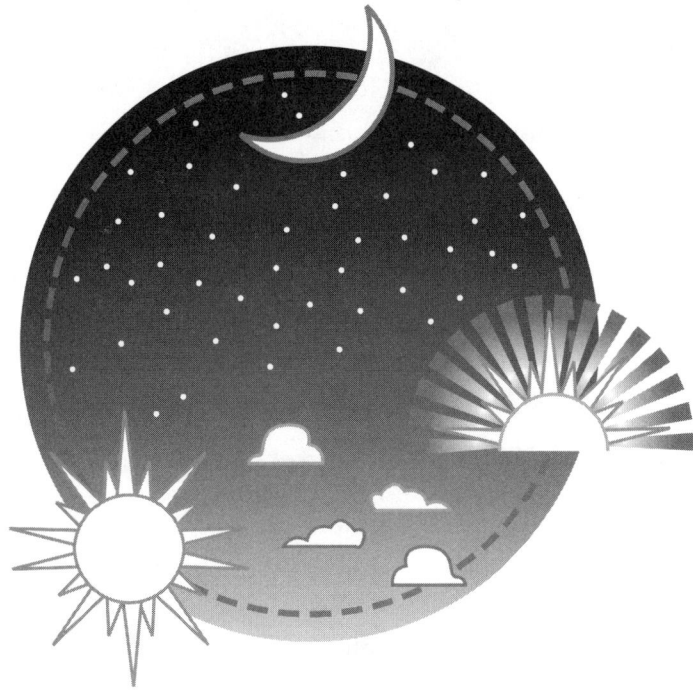

Video! Sound!

FrontPage enables you to place video or sound files on your Web pages. Background sounds can be attached to any page in your Web site. You have the option of playing your sound file once, many times, or endlessly.

When to Use Sound and Video

Like all good things, sounds can be abused, overdone, or done badly. In this way, sounds are analogous to page backgrounds. If they're too noisy, they distract from the Web site. I personally find those insanely loud disco beats that run endlessly on some sites a little distracting. Maybe that ambiance works at the BeeGees' retro site, but not when I'm shopping for a scanner on the Web. Using the right sounds can add a whole new dimension to your site.

Videos can be placed in your FrontPage Web pages as easily as you placed graphic images. FrontPage lets you display a video player on the page so that visitors can play videos when they drop by.

CAUTION

◆◆

Sounds and videos can be protected by copyrights. Violating those copyrights is easy if you're not careful. If you copy a sound or video from a disk or a Web site, make sure that no publisher or creator rights are attached to it. Just because it's on the Web doesn't mean it's freely available to use. A video player is shown in Figure E.1.

◆◆

Will Your Visitors Hear the Noise? See the Light?

Before you think about the nuts and bolts of placing audio and video files in your Web site, let's talk accessibility. Microsoft Internet Explorer version 3.0 introduced the first Web browser that could interpret sound and video files without any additional software. Additional software packages

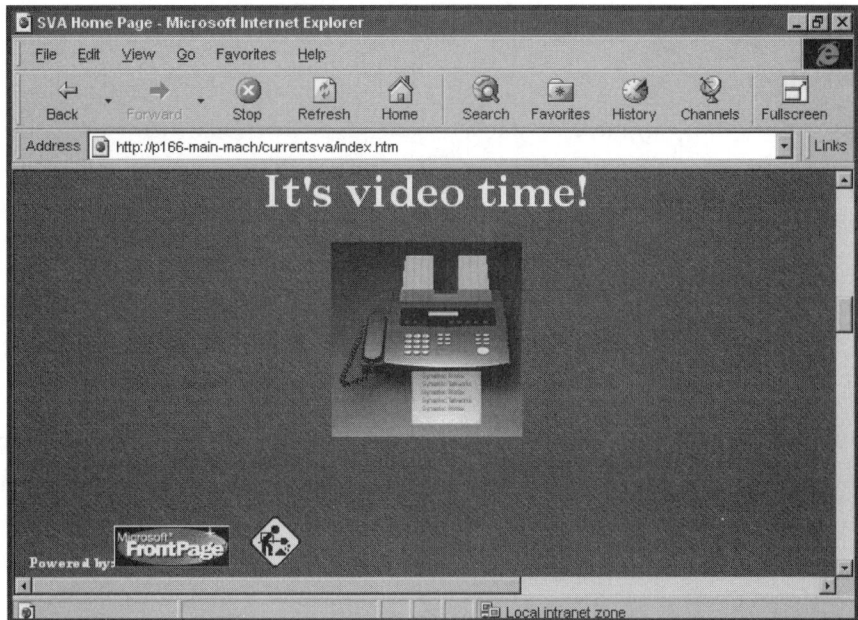

Figure E.1

Video at a Web site.

(called *plug-ins*) are necessary to watch videos and hear attached sound files using Netscape Navigator 3.0. Therefore, some Netscape visitors probably won't be able to hear or see your sound or video, unless they're using version 4.0 or later.

Of course, visitors who don't hear your background sounds won't know what they're missing. (That is, unless you place a big message on your screen saying, "If you can't hear this, you're missing out!")

Your video player, however, takes up a nice chunk of the page, and visitors who can't watch will definitely know they're missing something. One option is to provide an alternative graphic image for them.

TIP

You can also put a message on your Web site suggesting that your visitors download Internet Explorer so that next time they can hear and see everything you have to offer.

Assigning Background Sounds

You need two things to attach a sound file to your Web page: a sound file and a Web page. If you just came back from the computer store with a CD-ROM titled "One Billion Noises," then you've got a lot of choices. Just find some files in the *.wav file format and get set to plug them into your Web site.

If you aren't the owner of a large collection of background sound files, I'll bet you can find a few on your hard drive. For example, you can use one that came with other programs you've installed.

Use Windows Explorer (not FrontPage Explorer) to locate *.wav files on your hard drive. To find sound files on your hard drive, follow these steps:

1. Right-click on the Start button or use your favorite method to open the Windows Explorer.

2. Select Tools, Find, Files or Folders from the Windows Explorer menu.

3. In the Find Files dialog box, enter *.wav in the Named field and navigate to the folder with Windows in the Look In box.

4. Click on the Include Subfolders check box and then click on OK in the Find Files dialog box.

5. In a minute or two, you'll see a list of files you can use as background sounds in your FrontPage web, as shown in Figure E.2.

6. Leave this Find File window open because you'll refer to it later when you add a sound file to your site.

This part is almost too easy. It's just like adding a background image to your site, only easier. To add sound files to a page, follow these steps:

1. Open the Web page in the FrontPage Editor to which you want to assign a background sound.

2. Right-click on the page and select Page Properties from the shortcut menu.

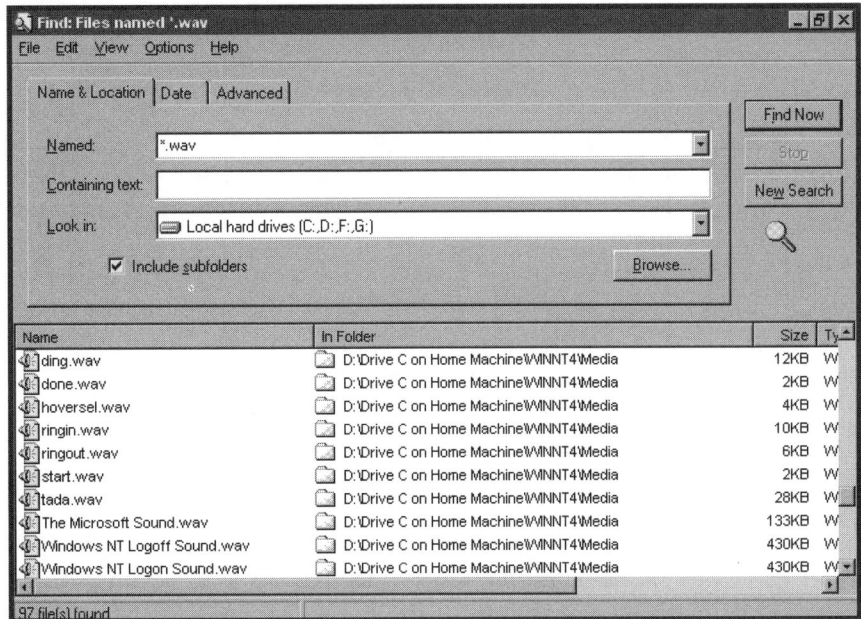

Figure E.2

Browsing through the sounds.

3. Select the General tab if not already selected.

4. In the Background Sound group box in the Page Properties dialog box, click on the <u>B</u>rowse button.

━━━

TIP Now is the time to switch back to your Find Files window and note the name and location of an interesting sound file.

━━━

5. Click on Select File on your computer icon.

6. Use the Select File dialog box to navigate to the sound file you located using the Find File window, as shown in Figure E.3.

7. Click on OK in the Select File dialog box.

8. You can click on OK in the Page Properties dialog box now or make some decisions as to how many times to repeat your sound.

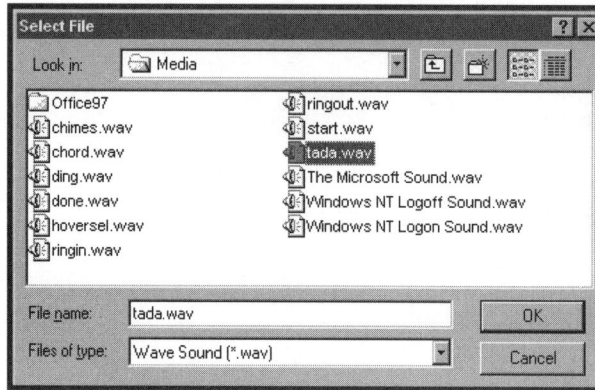

Navigating to a
sound file.

Here are your choices: Play the sound as many times as you want or play it forever. Once is nice. More? Depends on the message. A pleasant tune might work well over and over. A loud chainsaw noise works best as a one-time attention grabber. To loop your sound, follow these steps:

1. Right-click on your page and select Page Properties from the short-cut menu (if the Page Properties dialog box is not already open).

2. Click on the General tab. Uncheck the Forever check box in the Background Sound group if you want to specify how many times the sound file will play.

3. In the Loop spin box, choose the number of times to repeat your sound. In Figure E.4, the song is set to play four times.

4. Click on OK in the Page Properties dialog box.

5. Preview your page in your Web browser and decide if you want to change the sound file or the number of times it repeats.

TIP You'll note in the status bar that adding a sound file greatly increases your page-loading time. Fortunately, visitors will still see your page while they wait for the sound file to load. You can decrease loading time by selecting a shorter sound file. A short sound file that repeats itself takes less time to load than a long sound file that plays once.

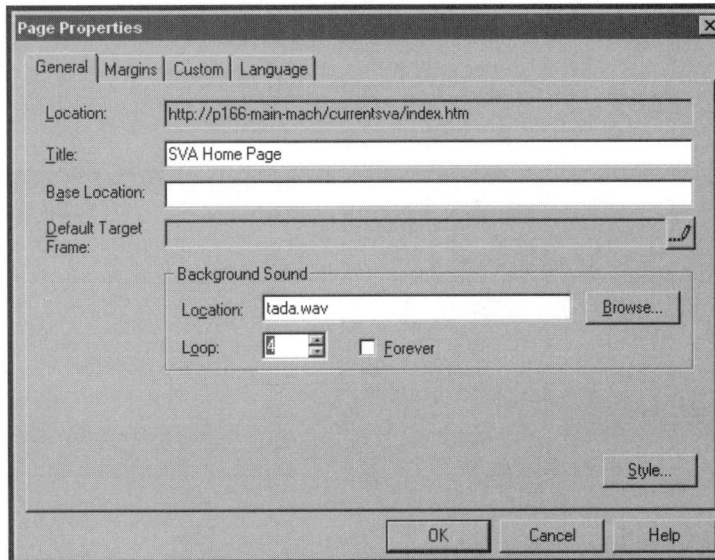

Figure E.4

Repeating a sound four times.

Taking Your Visitors to the Movies

To add video to your site, you need an *.avi file. Although I could almost promise that you have some sound files on your hard drive, I can't make that same commitment when it comes to video files. If you have no AVI files, take a look on the Web. Go to any of the popular search engines and search for AVI. You'll find no shortage of files available.

Checking Out Videos

Once you find a video file you like, right-click on the hyperlink to that video and select Save Video As from the shortcut menu. Make sure you're not violating anyone's copyright when you copy the video file. Select a file folder and filename and then click on OK in the dialog box to save the *.avi file to your hard drive, as shown in Figure E.5.

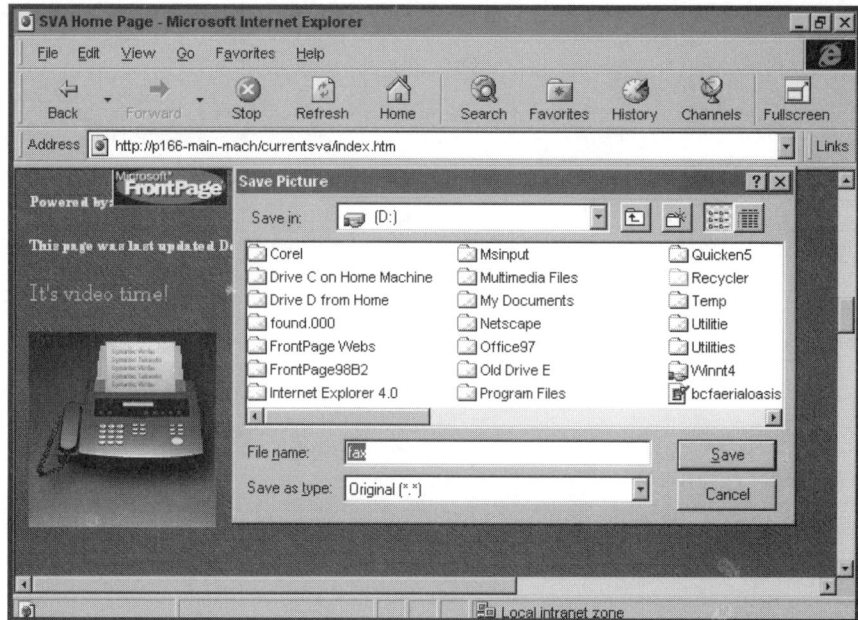

Figure E.5

Copying an AVI
video file.

NOTE These files take a long time to download. They're big!

Inserting a Video in Your FrontPage Web

This part's easy. You need a Web page (and you've got one if you've made it this far in the book). You need an *.avi format video file. If you don't have one, search the Web for AVI video files using your favorite search engine.

Your main decision is whether you want to include a video viewer with your video. I think you do, because it's much easier for your visitors to watch your video as often as they like. To place a video on a page, follow these steps:

1. Use FrontPage Editor to open the page on which the video will be placed.

2. You might want to enter some text to alert your visitors that it's show time, as shown in Figure E.6.

3. Select Insert, Active Elements, Video.

4. In the Video dialog box, navigate to a folder with a video file and then double-click on the file, as shown in Figure E.7.

The video is inserted into your Web page! To add controls to an online video, follow these steps:

1. Right-click on the inserted video file in FrontPage Editor.

2. Select Image Properties from the shortcut menu.

3. In the Image Properties dialog box, the Video tab will be selected because you opened this dialog box by right-clicking on a video.

4. Click on the Show Controls in Browser check box to give your visitors a little on-screen video player when they visit. This is highly recommended.

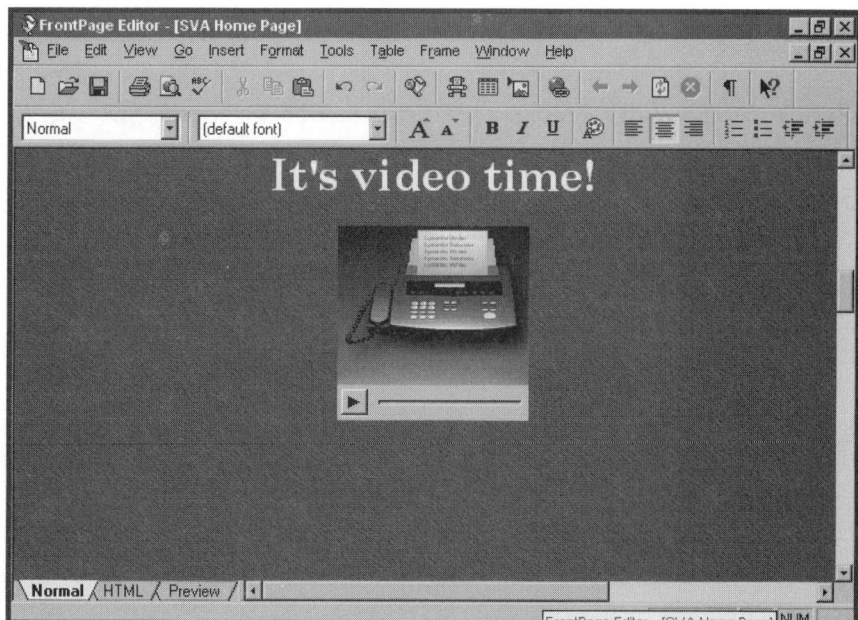

Figure E.6

Making a title for a video

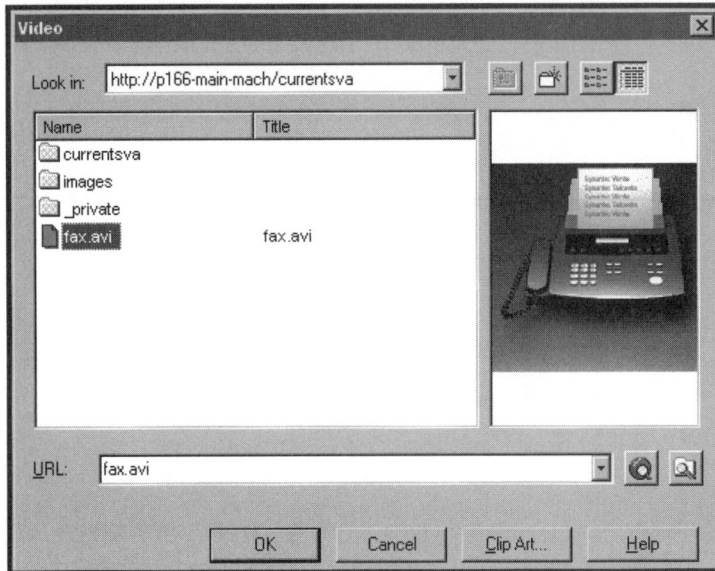

Figure E.7

Selecting an AVI
video file for
a Web page.

5. You can select from a variety of options for how to activate the video and how often it will run. If you chose the Show Controls in Browser option, your visitors can make these decisions. If you want to decide for them, use the check box options.

6. Click on the General tab and use the Text edit box to enter alternative text that displays for visitors who do not have a video-playing browser, as shown in Figure E.8.

TIP You can also assign an alternative GIF or JPEG image to display in browsers that cannot interpret video files.

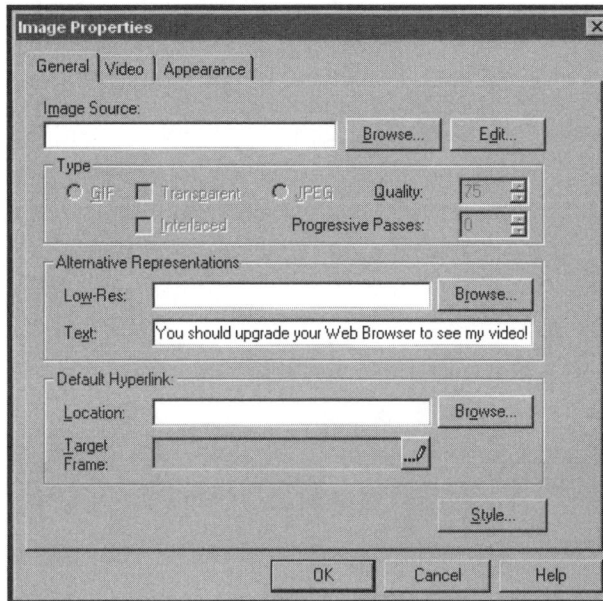

Figure E.8

Alternative text for those without video-playing browsers.

7. When you've defined how the video will be presented, click on OK in the Image Properties dialog box.

8. Save your page and use the Preview in Browser menu item to test out your video.

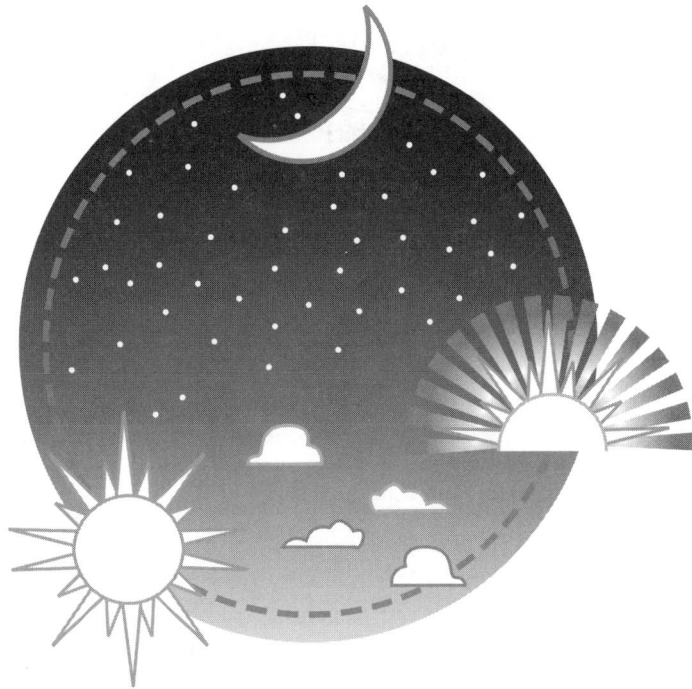

What's on the
CD-ROM

The CD-ROM that accompanies this book contains numerous tools, examples, and utilities to assist you in your Web publishing endeavors. For example, animation tools, Web tools, HTML editors, Windows utilities, and numerous source pages used for the screen shots in this book are some of the items included.

Running the CD-ROM

To make the CD-ROM more user friendly by taking up less of your disk space, no installation is required. This means that the only files transferred to your hard drive are the ones you choose to copy or install.

CAUTION Significant differences between the various Windows operating systems (Windows 95 and Windows NT) sometimes render files that work in one Windows environment inoperable in another. Prima has made every effort to ensure that this problem is minimized. However, it's not possible to eliminate it entirely. Therefore, you may find that some files or directories appear to be missing from the CD-ROM. These files are, in reality, on the CD-ROM, but remain hidden from the operating system. To confirm this, view the CD-ROM using a different Windows operating system.

Windows 95

Because no installation routine exists, running the CD-ROM in Windows 95 is a breeze, especially if you have the autorun feature enabled. Simply insert the CD-ROM in the CD-ROM drive, close the tray, and wait for it to load. If you have disabled the autorun feature, place the CD-ROM in the drive and follow these steps:

1. From the Start menu, select Run.
2. Type D:\primaCD-ROM.exe (If D is the CD-ROM drive).
3. Select OK.

The Prima User Interface

Prima's user interface is designed to make viewing and using the CD-ROM's contents quick and easy. It contains four Category buttons, six Option buttons, a title list, a description text box, a URL box, and Next and Previous buttons. Select a Category button to display a list of available titles. Choose a title to see a description and the associated URL. At the title screen, select an Option button to perform the desired action.

Category Buttons

The four Category buttons are as follows:

- *Book Examples*. Example files and source code from *Create Front-Page 98 Web Pages In a Weekend*.
- *HTML Tools*. An assortment of HTML editors and tools.
- *Multimedia*. Clip art, sound files, multimedia tools, and more.
- *Web Tools*. Custom controls, Java applets, and animation tools, to name a few.

Option Buttons

Once you've selected a category, you'll want to perform an action. This is accomplished by clicking on one of the following buttons:

- *Explore*. Clicking on this option in Windows 95 and NT allows you to view the folder containing the program files using Windows Explorer. Right-clicking on this option in Windows 95 and NT brings up the Windows File Manager from which you can easily explore the CD-ROM.
- *Install*. If the selected title contains an installation routine, selecting this option begins the installation process. If no installation is available, an appropriate message is displayed.

> **NOTE** You can install some of the shareware programs that do not have installation routines by copying the program files from the CD-ROM to your hard drive and running the executable (*.exe) file.

- *Information.* Click on this button to open the Readme file associated with the highlighted title. If no Readme file is present, the Help file is opened.

- *Exit.* When you're finished and ready to move on, select Exit.

- *Prev.* This button takes you to the previous screen. Please note that this is not the last screen you viewed, but the screen that actually precedes the current one.

- *Next.* This button takes you to the next screen.

The Software

This section gives you a brief description of some of the software you'll find on the CD-ROM. This is just a sampling. As you browse the CD-ROM, you'll find much more.

- *1-4-All HTML Editor.* A 32-bit, tag based, shareware HTML editor for Windows 95 and NT.

- *Animagic GIF.* A powerful animation tool that outputs GIF files that are 10 to 80 percent smaller than non-optimized GIFs.

- *Banner*Show.* A tool that lets you create slide show-like presentations of images and text on Web pages.

- *GoldWave.* A sound editor, player, recorder, and converter for Windows 95 and NT.

- *HTML PowerTools.* A collection of powerful HTML utilities, including a spell checker, syntax analyzer, rulebase editor, and more.
- *RiadaCartel.* With RiadaCartel, you can insert moving LED signs into your Web pages to provide advertising, information, instruction, or even user interaction.
- *WebPainter.* An easy-to-use tool for creating eye-catching animated graphics for Web pages.
- *WinZip.* One of the leading file compression utilities for Windows 95 and NT.

Index

A

AIS, 271

Akorn, 271

alignment

    Image Composer sprites, 93-95, 105

    of paragraphs, 41

    of tables, 60

All Files view, 9

alternative text, 120-122

America Online, 262-263

    free Web sites on, 264

    Internet Explorer 4.0, downloading, 326

Animagic GIF, 350

Arial font, 42-43

Arrange tool, Image Composer, 82

audio. *See* sounds

authorized users lists, creating, 332-334

.avi files, 341

B

background colors, 68-69

background images, 70-71

backup page, 314

Banner*Show, 350

bevel in hotspot, 155

BitShop, 271

black and white hotspot, 155

blinking text, 44-45

boldfacing characters, 42, 43-44

book examples on CD-ROM, 349

bookmarks, 131-132

    assigning bookmarks, 133-136

    bookmarked pages, hyperlinks to, 148-150

    checking out, 140-141

    clearing bookmarks, 139

    defining hyperlinks to, 136-139

    properties, changing, 135-136

    renaming, 136

    with templates, 293, 295

    using bookmarks, 132-133

borders

    alternative text, setting off, 121-122

    for tables, 59, 62

breaking up page, 57-58

brightness of hotspot, 155

browsers

    alternate page support for older browsers, 321-322

    frames, support for, 320-322

    older browsers, use of, 43, 321-322

    previewing Web page, 24-25

Browse This Web radio button, 334

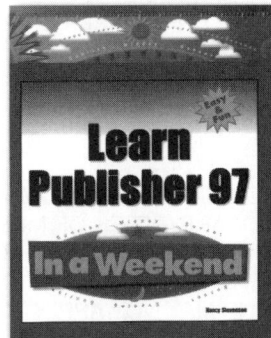

License Agreement/Notice of Limited Warranty